PHILIP'S

MODERN
SCHOOL
ATLAS

92ND EDITION

CONTENTS

Note: Each section is colour-coded on this contents page and on the heading of each page for ease of reference.

Published in Great Britain in 1998
by George Philip Limited,
an imprint of Reed Consumer Books Limited,
Michelin House, 81 Fulham Road,
London SW3 6RB,
and Auckland and Melbourne

Ninety-second edition
© 1998 George Philip Limited
Cartography by Philip's

ISBN 0–540–07555–8 Paperback edition
ISBN 0–540–07556–6 Hardback edition

BRITISH ISLES MAPS

A separate map key is provided on the first page of the World Maps section.

SETTLEMENTS

■ **LONDON**   ■ **GLASGOW**   ▣ **BRADFORD**   ▣ **Brighton**   ◉ Gateshead

◉ Aylesbury   ◎ Sligo   ⊙ *Selkirk*   ○ *Burford*   ○ *Lampeter*

Settlement symbols and type styles vary according to the population and importance of towns

⬢ Built up areas   □ London Boroughs

ADMINISTRATION

▬▬▬ International boundaries   **W A L E S**   Country names

▬▬ National boundaries   KENT   Administrative area names

▬▬▬ Administrative boundaries   *EXMOOR*   National park names

COMMUNICATIONS

═══ Motorways
═══ *under construction*

▬▬ Major roads
▬▬▬ *under construction*
⌐----⌐ *in tunnels*

▬▬ Other important roads
▬▬▬ *under construction*
⌐----⌐ *in tunnels*

▬▬ Main passenger railways
▬▬▬ *under construction*
⌐----⌐ *in tunnels*

▬▬ Other passenger railways
▬▬▬ *under construction*
⌐----⌐ *in tunnels*

▬┼▬ Canals
▬┼┼▬ *in tunnels*

⊕ Major airports   ⊕ Other airports

PHYSICAL FEATURES

⌒ Perennial rivers   ▲444 Elevations in metres

⬭ Tidal flats   ▼38 Depths below sea level in metres

⬬ Lakes or reservoirs

⌐-⌐ Reservoirs under construction

ELEVATION AND DEPTH TINTS

	Height of Land above Sea Level	Land below Sea Level	Depth of Sea

in metres   1000 750 500 400 200 100 0   150 300 600 1500 3000 6000   in feet

in feet   3000 2250 1500 1200 600 300   0 20 50 100 200 500 1000 2000   in metres

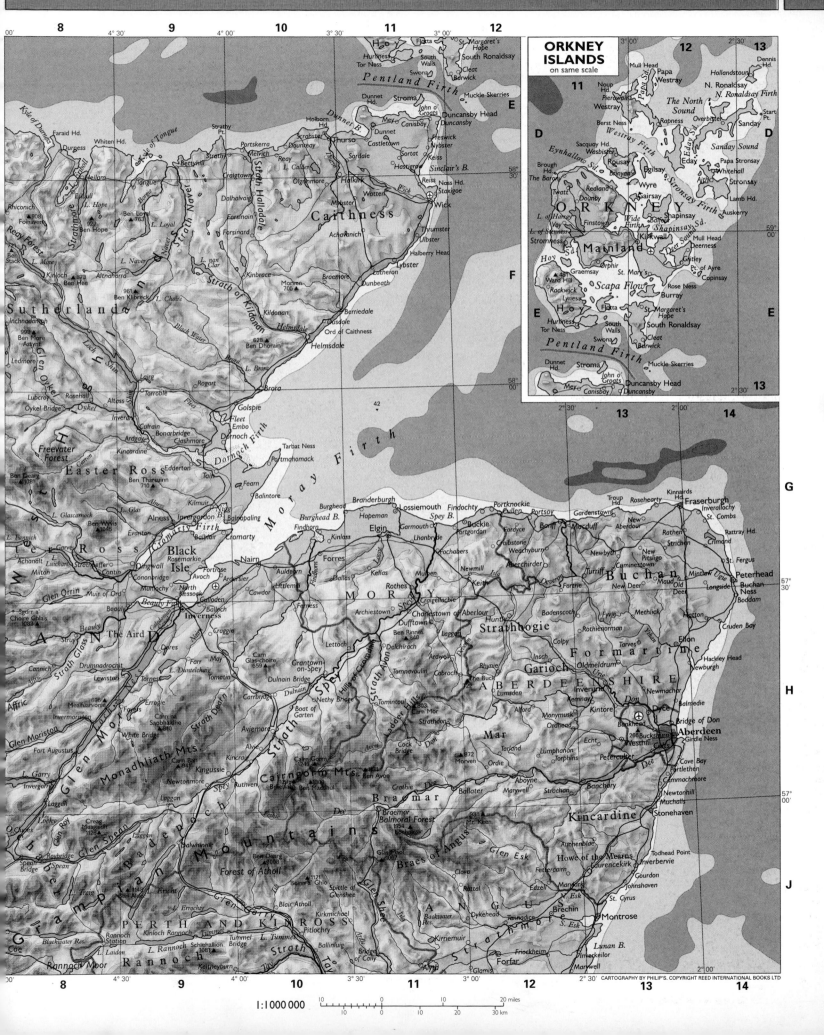

ORKNEY
ISLANDS
on same scale

CARTOGRAPHY BY PHILIP'S. COPYRIGHT REED INTERNATIONAL BOOKS LTD

1:1 000 000

10   0   10   20 miles
10   0   10   20   30 km

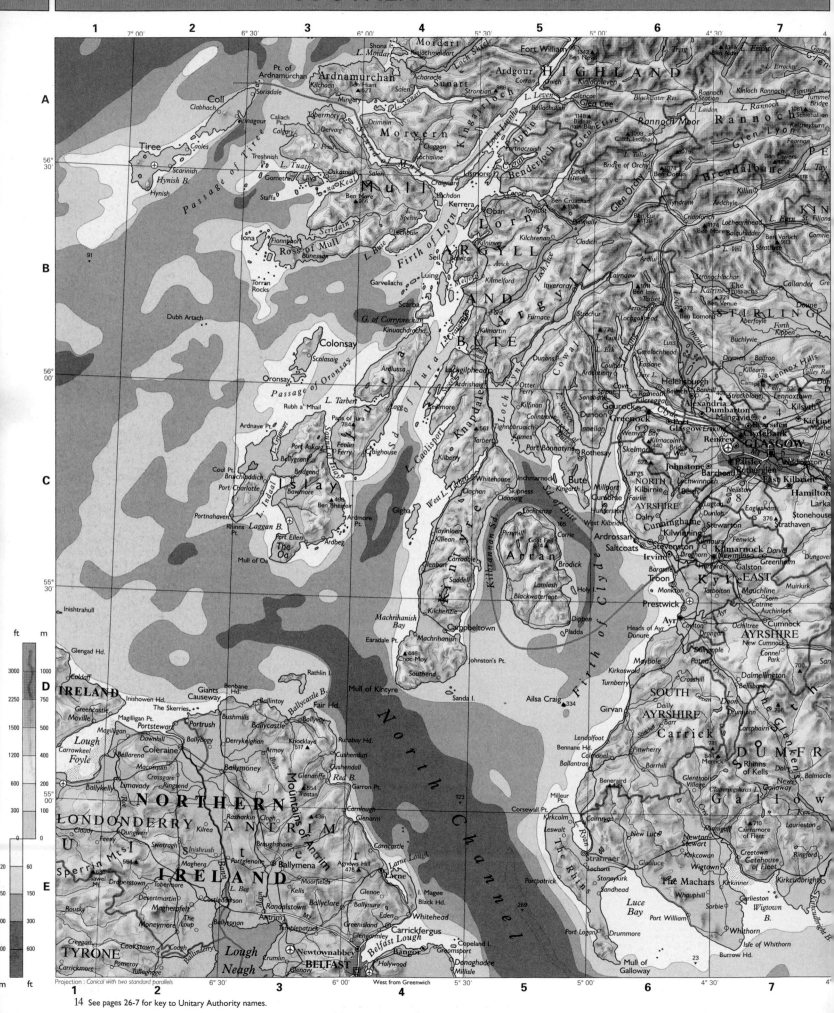

See pages 26-7 for key to Unitary Authority names.

Projection : Conical with two standard parallels

1:1 000 000

20 miles

30 km

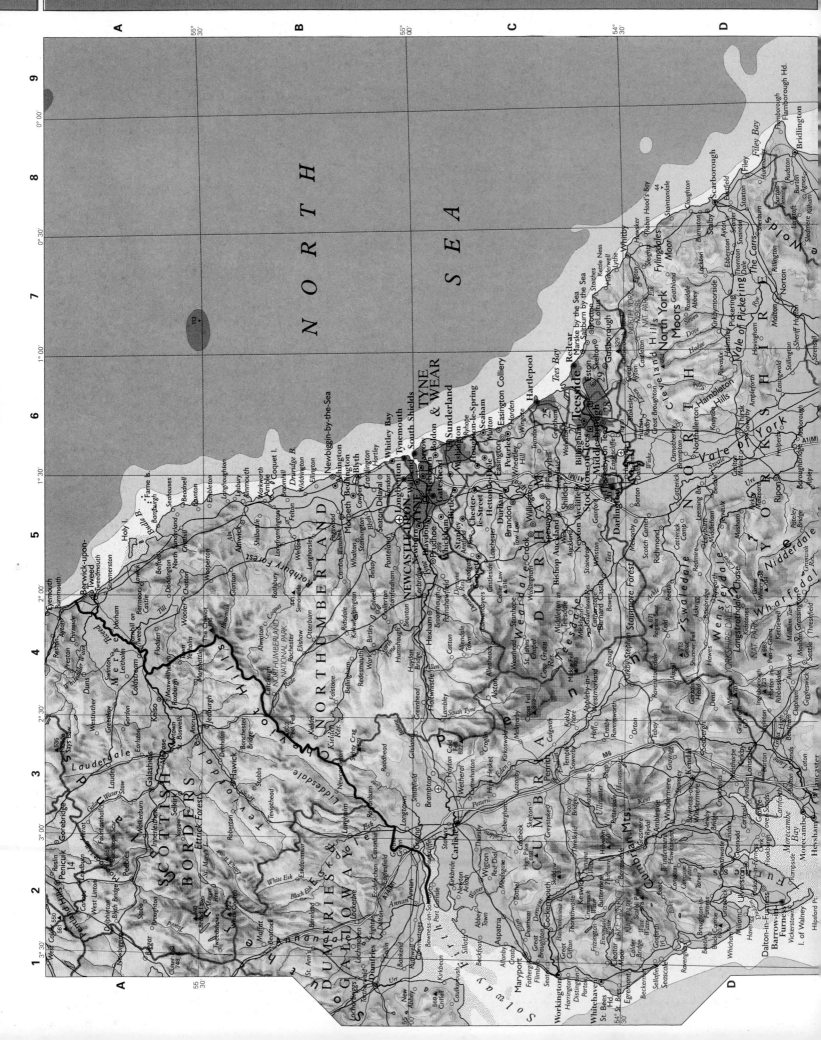

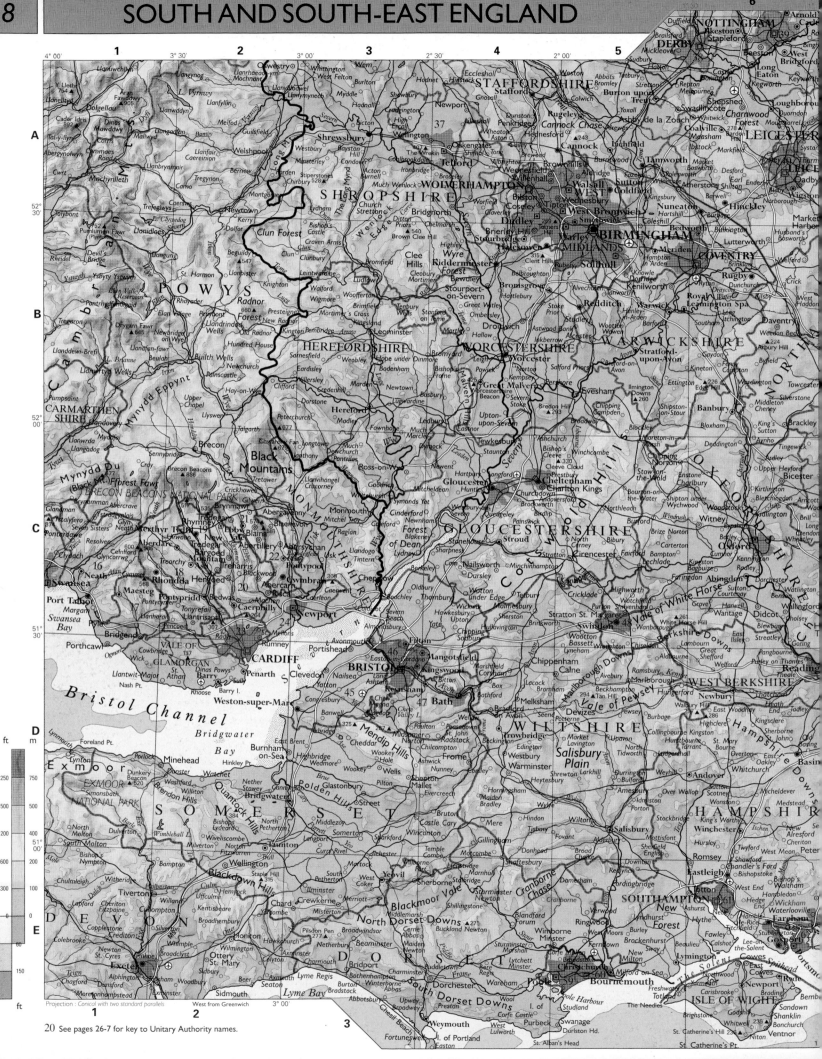

Projection : Conical with two standard parallels   West from Greenwich

LINCOLNSHIRE

NORFOLK

CAMBRIDGESHIRE

SUFFOLK

BEDFORDSHIRE

HERTFORDSHIRE

ESSEX

BUCKINGHAMSHIRE

GREATER LONDON

SURREY

KENT

WEST SUSSEX   EAST SUSSEX

The Wash

The Fens

Breckland

Thames Estuary

Strait of Dover

FRANCE

Peterborough   Cambridge   Bedford   Northampton   Milton Keynes   Luton   Stevenage   St. Albans   Watford   Harlow   Chelmsford   Colchester   Ipswich   Norwich   Great Yarmouth   Lowestoft   King's Lynn   Grantham   Stamford   Kettering   Wellingborough   Bury St. Edmunds   Newmarket   Ely   Thetford   Diss   Dereham   Cromer   Sheringham   Felixstowe   Harwich   Clacton-on-Sea   Southend-on-Sea   Basildon   Brentwood   Romford   Enfield   Harrow   LONDON   Windsor   Slough   Maidenhead   Bracknell   Woking   Guildford   Dorking   Reigate   Redhill   Crawley   Horsham   Tunbridge Wells   Tonbridge   Sevenoaks   Maidstone   Rochester   Gillingham   Chatham   Gravesend   Dartford   Bromley   Croydon   Epsom   Sutton   Kingston upon Thames   Ashford   Canterbury   Whitstable   Herne Bay   Margate   Broadstairs   Ramsgate   Sandwich   Deal   Dover   Folkestone   Hythe   New Romney   Rye   Hastings   Bexhill   Eastbourne   Brighton   Hove   Worthing   Littlehampton   Bognor Regis   Chichester   Haywards Heath   Burgess Hill   Lewes   Newhaven   Seaford

Romney Marsh   The Weald   South Downs   North Downs   Ashdown Forest

Calais   Boulogne-sur-Mer   C. Gris-Nez   Wimereux   Guînes   Marquise   Rinxent

CARTOGRAPHY BY PHILIP'S. COPYRIGHT REED INTERNATIONAL BOOKS LTD

East from Greenwich

1:1 000 000

52°30'   52°00'   51°30'   51°00'
1°00'   1°30'
0°00'   0°30'   1°00'

IRISH SEA

St. George's Channel

Cardigan Bay

Caernarfon Bay

Tremadog Bay

Liverpool Bay

CHESHIRE

STAFFS.

SHROPSHIRE

HEREFORDSHIRE

GLOUCESTERSHIRE

MONMOUTHSHIRE

POWYS

GWYNEDD

CLWYD

FLINTSHIRE

DENBIGHSHIRE

WREXHAM

ISLE OF ANGLESEY

CONWY

CEREDIGION

CARMARTHENSHIRE

PEMBROKESHIRE

Liverpool, St. Helens, Widnes, Runcorn, Wallasey, Birkenhead, Hoylake, West Kirby, Heswall, Chester, Crewe, Nantwich, Sandbach, Knutsford, Whitchurch, Market Drayton, Newport, Telford, Wellington, Bridgnorth, Shrewsbury, Ludlow, Leominster, Bromyard, Worcester, Kidderminster, Stourport-on-Severn, Stourbridge, Bewdley, Great Malvern, Malvern Hills, Ledbury, Ross-on-Wye, Hereford, Gloucester, Forest of Dean, Tewkesbury, Newent, Chepstow, Monmouth, Tintern, Raglan, Abergavenny, Blaenavon, Ebbw Vale, Tredegar, Merthyr Tydfil, Brecon, Brecon Beacons National Park, Black Mountains

Holyhead, Holyhead B., The Skerries, Carmel Hd., Amlwch, Llanfairpwllgwyngyll, Bangor, Menai Bridge, Beaumaris, Caernarfon, Snowdonia National Park, Porthmadog, Pwllheli, Abersoch, Bardsey I., Criccieth, Harlech, Barmouth, Fairbourne, Tywyn, Aberdyfi, Machynlleth, Dolgellau, Cader Idris, Bala, L. Bala, Corwen, Llangollen, Ruthin, Denbigh, St. Asaph, Rhyl, Prestatyn, Abergele, Colwyn Bay, Rhos-on-Sea, Llandudno, Great Ormes Hd., Conwy, Betws-y-Coed, Blaenau Ffestiniog

Aberystwyth, Borth, Aberaeron, New Quay, Cardigan, Fishguard, Strumble Hd., St. David's, St. David's Hd., Ramsey I., St. Bride's Bay, Skomer I., Skokholm I., Grassholm I., Milford Haven, Haverfordwest, Pembroke, Tenby, Saundersfoot, Narberth, Whitland, Carmarthen, St. Clears, Laugharne, Kidwelly, Llanelli, Llandovery, Llandeilo, Ammanford, Lampeter, Llandysul, Newcastle Emlyn, Tregaron, Rhayader, Llandrindod Wells, Builth Wells, Llanwrtyd Wells, Knighton, Presteigne, New Radnor, Mynydd Preseli, Pembrokeshire Coast National Park

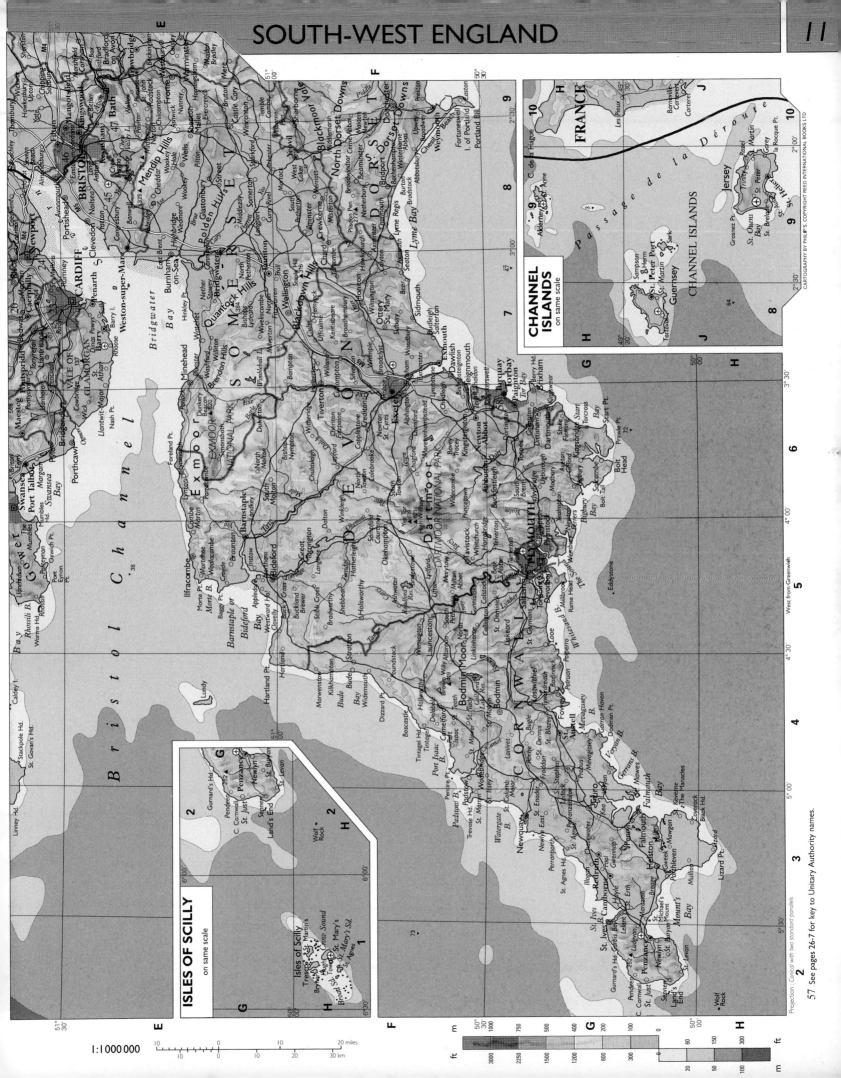

ISLES OF SCILLY
on same scale

CHANNEL ISLANDS
on same scale

FRANCE

CARTOGRAPHY BY PHILIP'S. COPYRIGHT REED INTERNATIONAL BOOKS LTD

Projection: Conical with two standard parallels

57 See pages 26-7 for key to Unitary Authority names.

1:1 000 000

West from Greenwich

Projection : Conical with two standard parallels

West from Greenwich

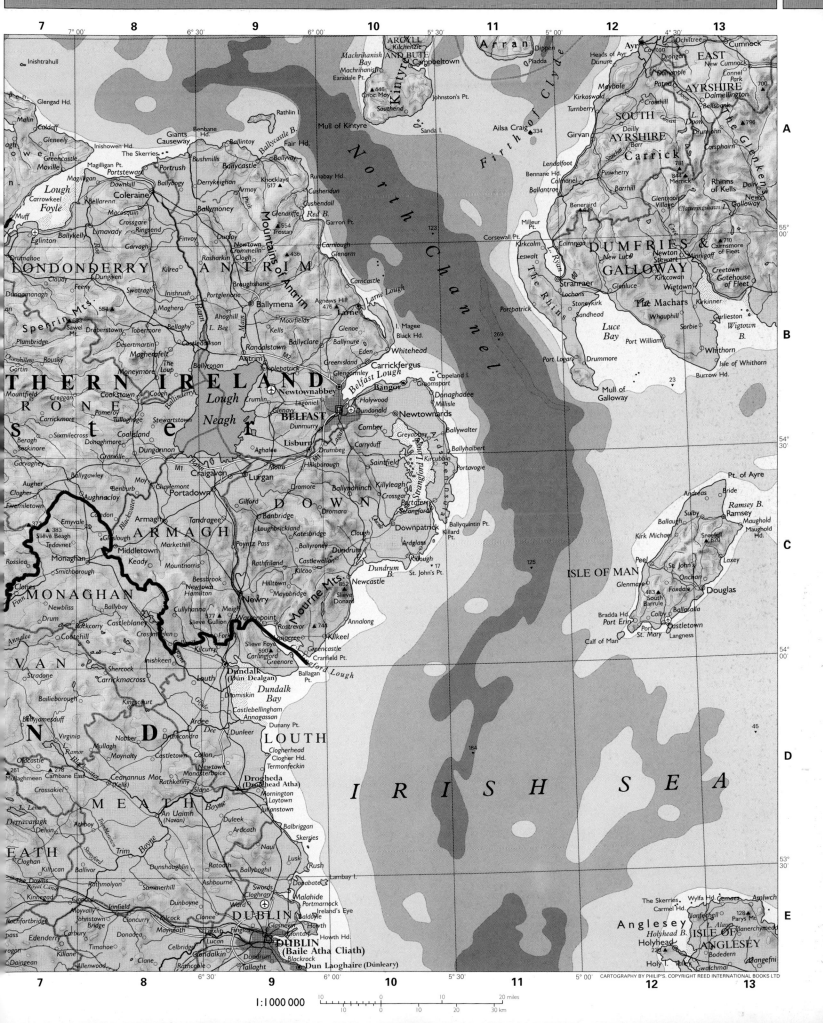

1:1 000 000

CARTOGRAPHY BY PHILIP'S. COPYRIGHT REED INTERNATIONAL BOOKS LTD

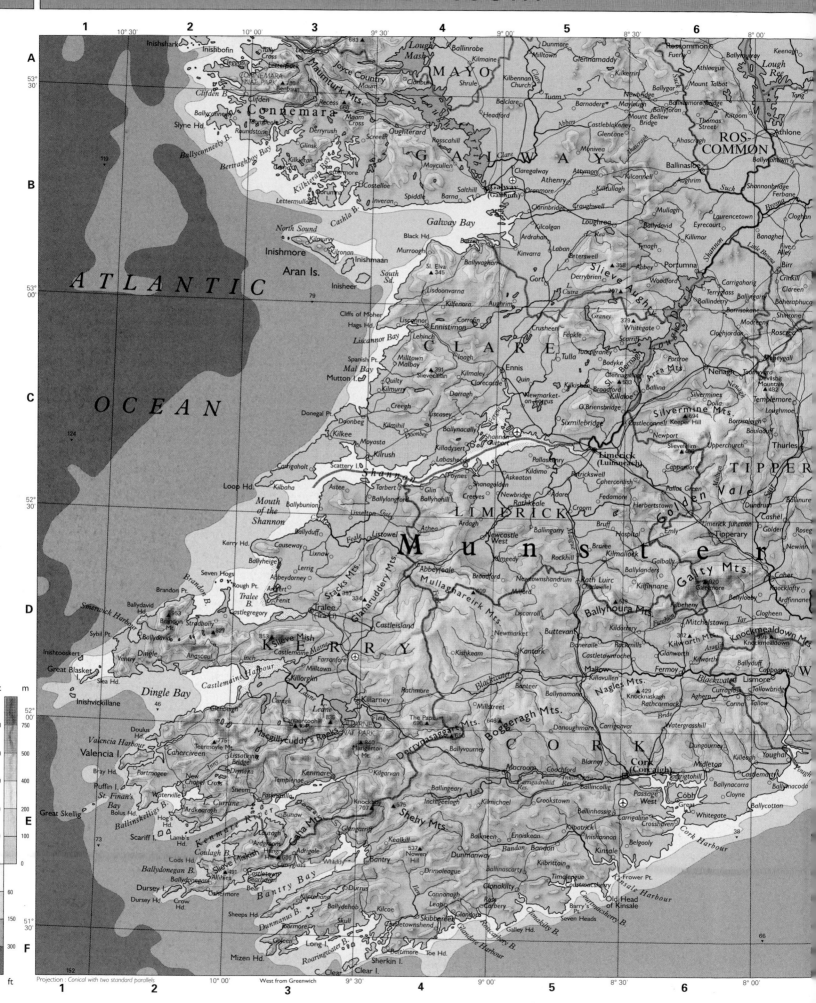

Projection : Conical with two standard parallels

West from Greenwich

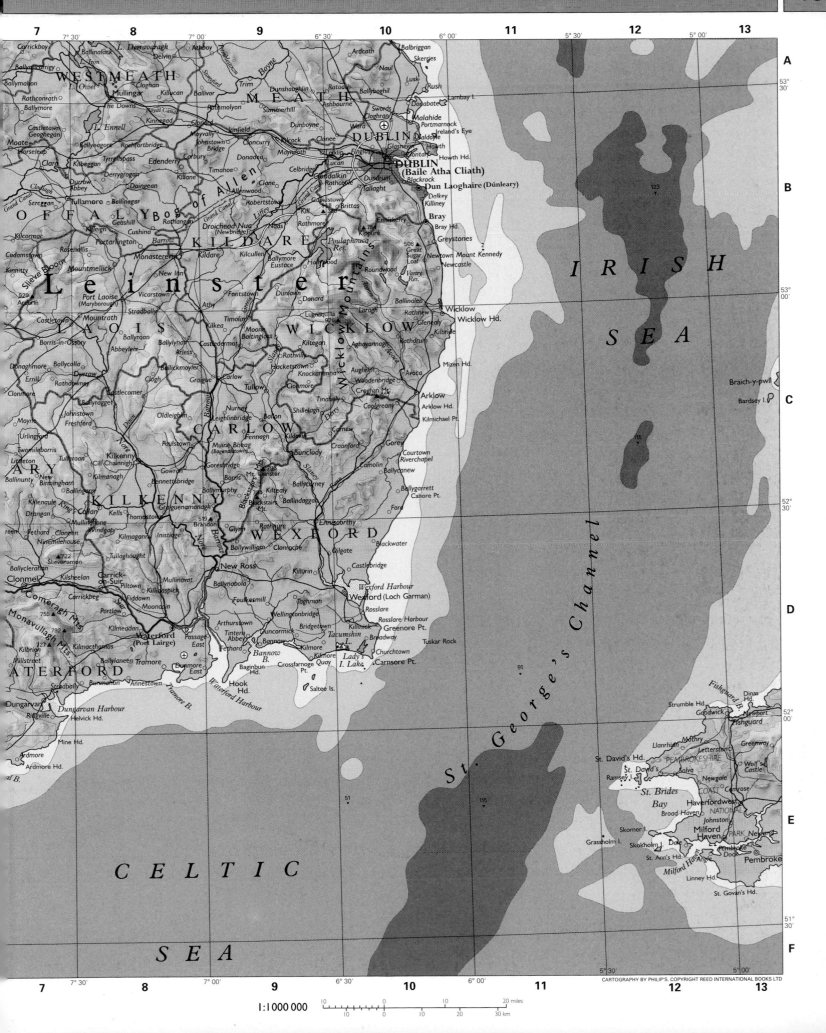

CELTIC

SEA

IRISH

SEA

St. George's Channel

CARTOGRAPHY BY PHILIP'S. COPYRIGHT REED INTERNATIONAL BOOKS LTD

1:1 000 000

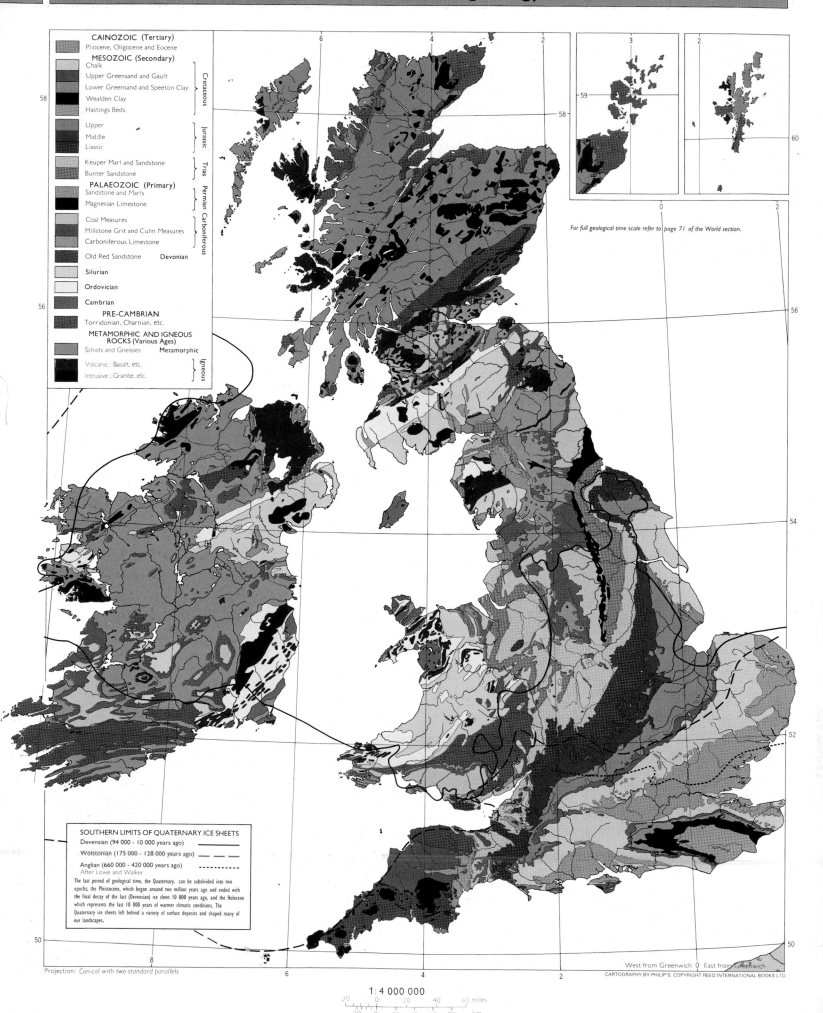

CAINOZOIC (Tertiary)
Pliocene, Oligocene and Eocene

MESOZOIC (Secondary)
Chalk
Upper Greensand and Gault
Lower Greensand and Speeton Clay   } Cretaceous
Wealden Clay
Hastings Beds

Upper
Middle   } Jurassic
Liassic

Keuper Marl and Sandstone   } Trias
Bunter Sandstone

PALAEOZOIC (Primary)
Sandstone and Marls   } Permian
Magnesian Limestone

Coal Measures
Millstone Grit and Culm Measures   } Carboniferous
Carboniferous Limestone

Old Red Sandstone   Devonian

Silurian

Ordovician

Cambrian

PRE-CAMBRIAN
Torridonian, Charnian, etc.

METAMORPHIC AND IGNEOUS ROCKS (Various Ages)
Schists and Gneisses   Metamorphic

Volcanic : Basalt, etc.   } Igneous
Intrusive : Granite, etc.

For full geological time scale refer to page 71 of the World section.

SOUTHERN LIMITS OF QUATERNARY ICE SHEETS
Devensian (94 000 - 10 000 years ago) ——————
Wolstonian (175 000 - 128 000 years ago) ——————
Anglian (660 000 - 420 000 years ago) ------------
After Lowe and Walker

The last period of geological time, the Quaternary, can be subdivided into two epochs; the Pleistocene, which began around two million years ago and ended with the final decay of the last (Devensian) ice sheet 10 000 years ago, and the Holocene which represents the last 10 000 years of warmer climatic conditions. The Quaternary ice sheets left behind a variety of surface deposits and shaped many of our landscapes.

West from Greenwich 0 East from Greenwich

Projection: *Conical with two standard parallels*

CARTOGRAPHY BY PHILIP'S. COPYRIGHT REED INTERNATIONAL BOOKS LTD.

1 : 4 000 000

20   0   20   40   60 miles
20 0 20 40 60 80 km

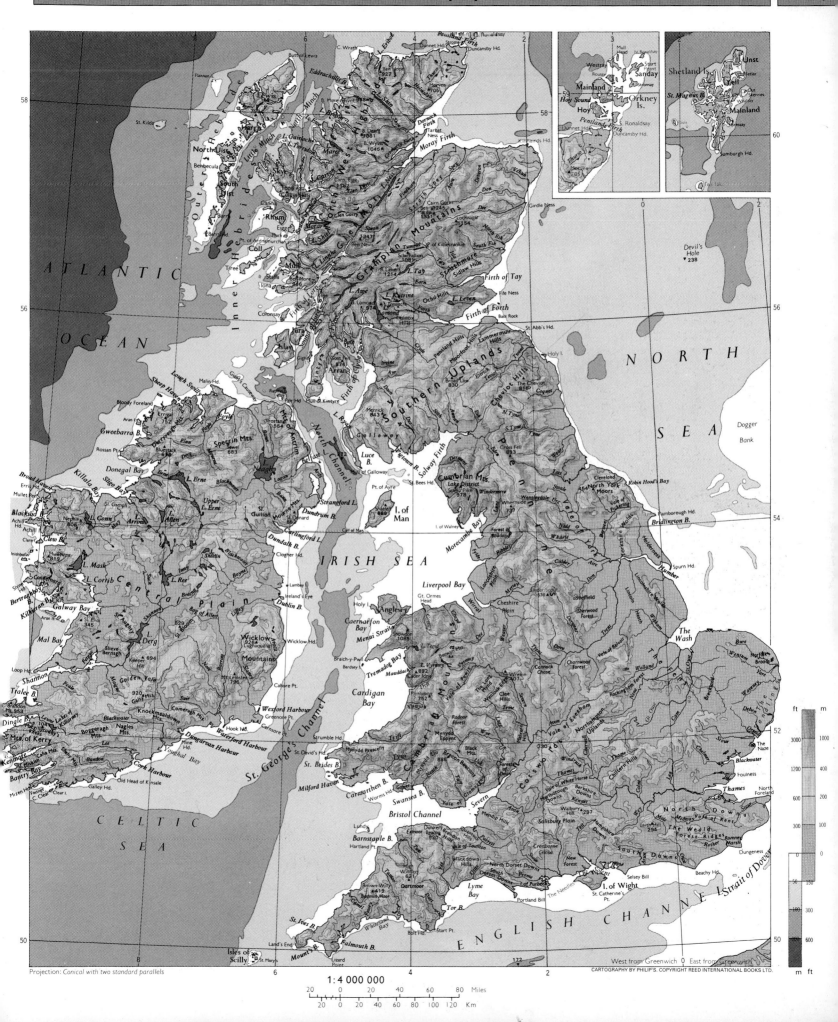

Projection: Conical with two standard parallels

1 : 4 000 000

```
20    0    20    40    60    80  Miles
20  0  20  40  60  80  100 120  Km
```

JANUARY TEMPERATURE
Actual surface temperature

°C
7
6
5
4
3
2
1
0

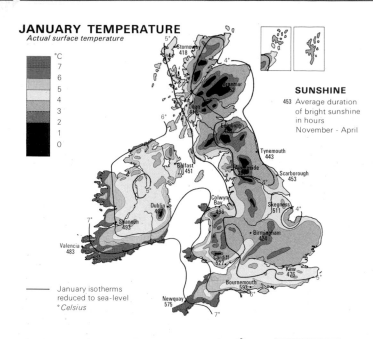

—— January isotherms reduced to sea-level °Celsius

SUNSHINE
453 Average duration of bright sunshine in hours November - April

JULY TEMPERATURE
Actual surface temperature

°C
17
16
15
14
13
12
11
10

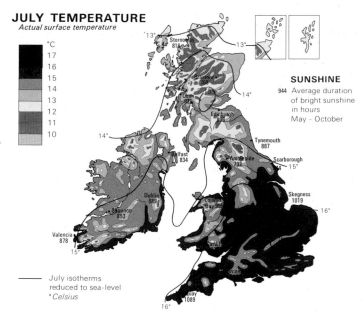

—— July isotherms reduced to sea-level °Celsius

SUNSHINE
944 Average duration of bright sunshine in hours May - October

ANNUAL RAINFALL

mm
2500
2000
1500
1000
750
625

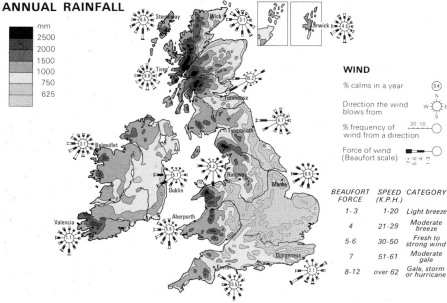

WIND

% calms in a year

Direction the wind blows from

% frequency of wind from a direction

Force of wind (Beaufort scale)

BEAUFORT FORCE	SPEED (K.P.H.)	CATEGORY
1-3	1-20	Light breeze
4	21-29	Moderate breeze
5-6	30-50	Fresh to strong wind
7	51-61	Moderate gale
8-12	over 62	Gale, storm or hurricane

SNOW
Average number of mornings with snow cover per year

more than 50
20-50
15-20
10-15
5-10
less than 5

(after Manley, 1970)

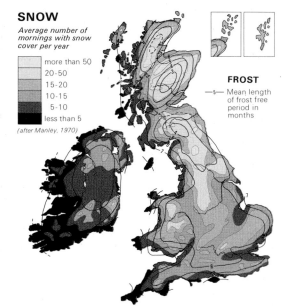

FROST
—5— Mean length of frost free period in months

VARIABILITY OF RAIN
The percentage frequency with which rainfall varies from the normal rainfall regime in an area: the higher the percentage figure, the more variable the rainfall.

over 20%
18-20%
16-18%
14-16%
12-14%
10-12%
under 10%

(after Gregory, 1955)

Regions of reliably high rainfall (more than 1250mm in at least 70% of the years)

Regions of occasionally low rainfall (less than 750mm in at least 30% of the years)

CLIMATE STATIONS
•T Climate stations which appear on page 19

1 : 12 000 000

SYNOPTIC CHART FOR A TYPICAL WINTER DEPRESSION
21st January 1971

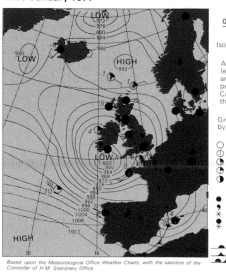

HOUR OF OBSERVATION
06h00 GREENWICH MEAN TIME

PRESSURE
Isobars are drawn at intervals of 4 mb.

WIND
Arrows fly with the wind. A full length feather represents 18 k.p.h. and a short feather 9 k.p.h. A solid pennant represents 90 k.p.h. Calm is indicated by a circle outside the weather symbol ◯

TEMPERATURE
Given in °C and is shown on the charts by a figure alongside the station circle.

CLOUD SYMBOLS
◯ Clear sky	◐ Sky ¾ covered
◔ Sky ⅛ covered	◕ Sky ⅞ covered
◑ Sky ¼ covered	● Sky ⅞ covered
◑ Sky ⅜ covered	● Sky covered
◑ Sky ½ covered	⊗ Sky obscured

WEATHER SYMBOLS
● Rain	△ Hail
⸴ Drizzle	▽ Shower
* Snow	℞ Thunderstorm
⁎ Rain and Snow	≡ Fog
	= Mist

FRONTS
Warm front on the surface
Cold front on the surface
Occluded front

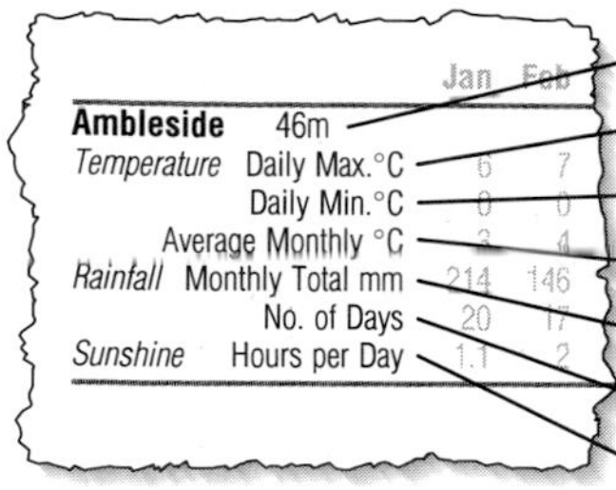

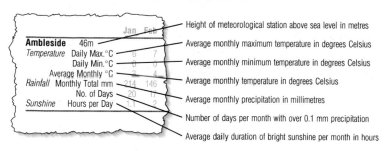

- Height of meteorological station above sea level in metres
- Average monthly maximum temperature in degrees Celsius
- Average monthly minimum temperature in degrees Celsius
- Average monthly temperature in degrees Celsius
- Average monthly precipitation in millimetres
- Number of days per month with over 0.1 mm precipitation
- Average daily duration of bright sunshine per month in hours

	Jan	Feb	Mar	Apr	May	June	July	Aug	Sep	Oct	Nov	Dec	Year
Ambleside 46m													
Temperature Daily Max.°C	6	7	9	12	16	19	20	19	17	13	9	7	13
Daily Min.°C	0	0	2	4	6	9	11	11	9	6	3	1	5
Average Monthly °C	3	4	6	8	11	14	15	15	13	10	6	4	9
Rainfall Monthly Total mm	214	146	112	101	90	111	134	139	184	196	209	215	1851
No. of Days	20	17	15	15	14	15	18	17	18	19	19	21	208
Sunshine Hours per Day	1.1	2	3.2	4.5	6	5.7	4.5	4.2	3.3	2.2	1.4	1	3.3
Belfast 4m													
Temperature Daily Max.°C	6	7	9	12	15	18	18	18	16	13	9	7	12
Daily Min.°C	2	2	3	4	6	9	11	11	9	7	4	3	6
Average Monthly °C	4	4	6	8	11	13	15	15	13	10	7	5	9
Rainfall Monthly Total mm	80	52	50	48	52	68	94	77	80	83	72	90	845
No. of Days	20	17	16	16	15	16	19	17	18	19	19	21	213
Sunshine Hours per Day	1.5	2.3	3.4	5	6.3	6	4.4	4.4	3.6	2.6	1.8	1.1	3.5
Belmullet 9m													
Temperature Daily Max.°C	8	9	10	12	14	16	17	17	16	14	10	9	12
Daily Min.°C	3	4	4	6	8	10	11	11	10	8	5	4	7
Average Monthly °C	5	6	7	9	11	13	14	14	13	11	8	6	10
Rainfall Monthly Total mm	108	64	82	70	75	80	76	95	108	116	127	131	1132
No. of Days	18	13	16	15	14	12	14	17	16	18	20	22	195
Sunshine Hours per Day	1.9	2.5	3.4	5.2	7	6	4.6	5.1	3.9	2.9	1.9	1.3	3.8
Birkenhead 60m													
Temperature Daily Max.°C	6	6	9	11	15	17	19	19	16	13	9	7	12
Daily Min.°C	2	2	3	5	8	11	13	13	11	8	5	3	7
Average Monthly °C	4	4	6	8	11	14	16	16	14	10	7	5	10
Rainfall Monthly Total mm	64	46	40	41	55	55	67	80	66	71	76	65	726
No. of Days	18	13	13	13	13	13	15	15	15	17	17	19	181
Sunshine Hours per Day	1.6	2.4	3.5	5.3	6.3	6.7	5.7	5.4	4.2	2.9	1.8	1.3	3.9
Birmingham 163m													
Temperature Daily Max.°C	5	6	9	12	16	19	20	20	17	13	9	6	13
Daily Min.°C	2	2	3	5	7	10	12	12	10	7	5	3	7
Average Monthly °C	3	4	6	8	11	15	16	16	14	10	7	5	10
Rainfall Monthly Total mm	74	54	50	53	64	50	69	69	61	69	84	67	764
No. of Days	17	15	13	13	14	13	15	14	14	15	17	18	178
Sunshine Hours per Day	1.4	2.1	3.2	4.6	5.4	6	5.4	5.1	3.9	2.8	1.6	1.2	3.6
Cambridge 12m													
Temperature Daily Max.°C	6	7	11	14	17	21	22	22	19	15	10	7	14
Daily Min.°C	1	1	2	4	7	10	12	12	10	6	4	2	6
Average Monthly °C	3	4	6	9	12	15	17	17	14	10	7	5	10
Rainfall Monthly Total mm	49	35	36	37	45	45	58	55	51	51	54	41	558
No. of Days	15	13	10	11	11	11	12	12	11	13	14	14	147
Sunshine Hours per Day	1.7	2.5	3.8	5.1	6.2	6.7	6	5.7	4.6	3.4	1.9	1.4	4.1
Cardiff 62m													
Temperature Daily Max.°C	7	7	10	13	16	19	20	21	18	14	10	8	14
Daily Min.°C	2	2	3	5	8	11	12	13	11	8	5	3	7
Average Monthly °C	4	5	7	9	12	15	16	17	14	11	8	6	10
Rainfall Monthly Total mm	108	72	63	65	76	63	89	97	99	109	116	108	1065
No. of Days	18	14	13	13	13	13	14	15	16	16	17	18	180
Sunshine Hours per Day	1.7	2.7	4	5.6	6.4	6.9	6.2	6	4.7	3.4	1.9	1.5	4.3
Craibstone 91m													
Temperature Daily Max.°C	5	6	8	10	13	16	18	17	15	12	8	6	11
Daily Min.°C	0	0	2	3	5	8	10	10	8	6	3	1	5
Average Monthly °C	3	3	5	7	9	12	14	13	12	9	6	4	8
Rainfall Monthly Total mm	78	55	53	51	63	54	95	75	67	92	93	80	856
No. of Days	19	16	15	15	14	14	18	15	16	18	19	18	197
Sunshine Hours per Day	1.8	2.9	3.5	4.9	5.9	6.1	5.1	4.8	4.3	3.1	2	1.5	3.8
Cromer 54m													
Temperature Daily Max.°C	6	7	9	12	15	18	21	20	18	14	10	8	13
Daily Min.°C	1	1	3	5	7	10	12	13	11	8	5	3	7
Average Monthly °C	4	4	6	8	11	14	16	16	15	11	7	5	10
Rainfall Monthly Total mm	58	46	37	39	48	39	63	56	54	61	64	53	618
No. of Days	18	16	13	13	11	11	13	12	14	16	18	18	173
Sunshine Hours per Day	1.8	2.6	4	5.4	6.4	6.8	6.3	5.8	5	3.6	2	1.9	4.3
Dublin 47m													
Temperature Daily Max.°C	8	8	10	13	15	18	20	19	17	14	10	8	14
Daily Min.°C	1	2	3	4	6	9	11	11	9	6	4	3	6
Average Monthly °C	4	5	7	8	11	14	15	15	13	10	7	6	10
Rainfall Monthly Total mm	67	55	51	45	60	57	70	74	72	70	67	74	762
No. of Days	13	10	10	11	10	11	13	12	12	11	12	14	139
Sunshine Hours per Day	1.9	2.5	3.4	5	6.2	6	4.8	4.9	3.9	3.2	2.1	1.6	3.8
Durham 102m													
Temperature Daily Max.°C	6	6	9	12	15	18	20	19	17	13	9	7	13
Daily Min.°C	0	0	1	3	6	9	11	10	9	6	3	2	5
Average Monthly °C	3	3	5	7	10	13	15	15	13	9	6	4	9
Rainfall Monthly Total mm	59	51	38	38	51	49	61	67	60	63	66	55	658
No. of Days	17	15	14	13	13	14	15	14	14	16	17	17	179
Sunshine Hours per Day	1.7	2.5	3.3	4.6	5.4	6	5.1	4.8	4.1	3	1.9	1.4	3.6
Lerwick 82m													
Temperature Daily Max.°C	5	5	6	8	11	13	14	14	13	10	8	6	9
Daily Min.°C	1	1	2	3	5	7	10	10	8	6	4	3	5
Average Monthly °C	3	3	4	5	8	10	12	12	11	8	6	4	7
Rainfall Monthly Total mm	109	87	69	68	52	55	72	71	87	104	111	118	1003
No. of Days	25	22	20	21	15	15	17	17	19	23	24	25	243
Sunshine Hours per Day	0.8	1.8	2.9	4.4	5.3	5.3	4	3.8	3.5	2.2	2.2	0.5	3
London (Kew) 5m													
Temperature Daily Max.°C	6	7	10	13	17	20	22	21	19	14	10	7	14
Daily Min.°C	2	2	3	6	8	12	14	13	11	8	5	4	7
Average Monthly °C	4	5	7	9	12	16	18	17	15	11	8	5	11
Rainfall Monthly Total mm	54	40	37	37	46	45	57	59	49	57	64	48	593
No. of Days	15	13	11	12	12	11	12	11	13	13	15	15	153
Sunshine Hours per Day	1.5	2.3	3.6	5.3	6.4	7.1	6.4	6.1	4.7	3.2	1.8	1.3	4.1
Oxford 63m													
Temperature Daily Max.°C	7	7	11	14	17	20	22	22	19	14	10	8	14
Daily Min.°C	1	1	2	5	7	10	12	12	10	7	4	2	6
Average Monthly °C	4	4	6	9	12	15	17	17	14	11	7	5	10
Rainfall Monthly Total mm	61	44	43	41	55	52	55	60	59	64	69	57	660
No. of Days	13	10	9	9	10	9	10	10	10	11	12	13	126
Sunshine Hours per Day	1.7	2.6	3.9	5.3	6.1	6.6	5.9	5.7	4.4	3.2	2.1	1.6	4.1
Plymouth 27m													
Temperature Daily Max.°C	8	8	10	12	15	18	19	19	18	15	11	9	14
Daily Min.°C	4	4	5	6	8	11	13	13	12	9	7	5	8
Average Monthly °C	6	6	7	9	12	15	16	16	15	12	9	7	11
Rainfall Monthly Total mm	99	74	69	53	63	53	70	77	78	91	113	110	950
No. of Days	19	15	14	12	12	12	14	14	15	16	17	18	178
Sunshine Hours per Day	1.9	2.9	4.3	6.1	7.1	7.4	6.4	6.4	5.1	3.7	2.2	1.7	4.6
Renfrew 6m													
Temperature Daily Max.°C	5	7	9	12	15	18	19	19	16	13	9	7	12
Daily Min.°C	1	1	2	4	6	9	11	11	9	6	4	2	6
Average Monthly °C	3	4	6	8	11	14	15	15	13	9	7	4	9
Rainfall Monthly Total mm	111	85	69	67	63	70	97	93	102	119	106	127	1109
No. of Days	19	16	15	15	14	15	17	17	17	18	18	20	201
Sunshine Hours per Day	1.1	2.1	2.9	4.7	6	6.1	5.1	4.4	3.7	2.3	1.4	0.8	3.4
St Helier 9m													
Temperature Daily Max.°C	9	8	11	13	16	19	21	21	19	16	12	10	15
Daily Min.°C	5	4	6	7	10	13	15	15	14	11	8	6	9
Average Monthly °C	7	6	8	10	13	16	18	18	17	13	10	8	12
Rainfall Monthly Total mm	89	68	57	43	44	39	48	67	69	77	101	99	801
No. of Days	19	15	13	12	11	10	11	12	15	15	17	19	169
Sunshine Hours per Day	2.3	3.1	5	6.7	7.8	8.5	7.8	7.6	5.6	4.1	2.5	1.8	5.3
St Mary's 50m													
Temperature Daily Max.°C	9	9	11	12	14	17	19	19	18	15	12	10	14
Daily Min.°C	6	6	7	7	9	12	13	14	13	11	9	7	9
Average Monthly °C	8	7	9	10	12	14	16	16	15	13	10	9	12
Rainfall Monthly Total mm	91	71	69	46	56	49	61	64	67	80	96	94	844
No. of Days	22	17	16	13	14	14	16	15	16	17	19	21	200
Sunshine Hours per Day	2	2.9	4.2	6.4	7.6	7.6	6.7	6.7	5.2	3.9	2.5	1.8	4.8
Southampton 20m													
Temperature Daily Max.°C	7	8	11	14	17	20	22	22	19	15	11	8	15
Daily Min.°C	2	2	3	5	8	11	13	13	11	7	5	3	7
Average Monthly °C	5	5	7	10	13	16	17	17	15	11	8	6	11
Rainfall Monthly Total mm	83	56	52	45	56	49	60	69	70	86	94	84	804
No. of Days	17	13	13	12	12	12	13	13	14	14	16	17	166
Sunshine Hours per Day	1.8	2.6	4	5.7	6.7	7.2	6.5	6.4	4.9	3.6	2.2	1.6	4.5
Tiree 9m													
Temperature Daily Max.°C	7	7	9	10	13	15	16	16	15	12	10	8	12
Daily Min.°C	4	3	4	5	7	10	11	11	10	8	6	5	7
Average Monthly °C	5	5	6	8	10	12	14	14	13	10	8	6	9
Rainfall Monthly Total mm	117	77	67	64	55	70	91	90	118	129	122	128	1128
No. of Days	23	19	17	17	15	16	20	18	20	23	22	24	234
Sunshine Hours per Day	1.3	2.6	3.7	5.7	7.5	6.8	5.2	5.3	4.2	2.6	1.6	0.9	4
Valencia 9m													
Temperature Daily Max.°C	9	9	11	13	15	17	18	18	17	14	12	10	14
Daily Min.°C	5	4	5	6	8	11	12	13	11	9	7	6	8
Average Monthly °C	7	7	8	9	11	0	15	15	14	12	9	8	11
Rainfall Monthly Total mm	165	107	103	75	86	81	107	95	122	140	151	168	1400
No. of Days	20	15	14	13	13	13	15	15	16	17	18	21	190
Sunshine Hours per Day	1.6	2.5	3.5	5.2	6.5	5.9	4.7	4.9	3.8	2.8	2	1.3	3.7
York 17m													
Temperature Daily Max.°C	6	7	10	13	16	19	21	21	18	14	10	7	13
Daily Min.°C	1	1	2	4	7	10	12	12	10	7	4	2	6
Average Monthly °C	3	4	6	9	12	15	17	16	14	10	7	5	10
Rainfall Monthly Total mm	59	46	37	41	50	50	62	68	55	56	65	50	639
No. of Days	17	15	13	13	13	14	15	14	14	15	17	17	177
Sunshine Hours per Day	1.3	2.1	3.2	4.7	6.1	6.4	5.6	5.1	4.1	2.8	1.6	1.1	3.7

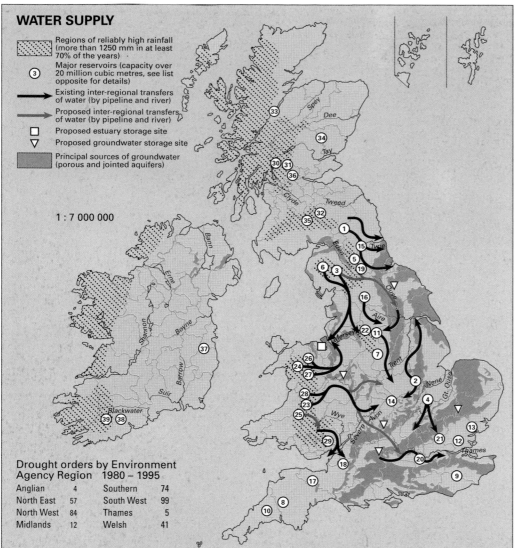

WATER SUPPLY

- Regions of reliably high rainfall (more than 1250 mm in at least 70% of the years)
- ③ Major reservoirs (capacity over 20 million cubic metres, see list opposite for details)
- → Existing inter-regional transfers of water (by pipeline and river)
- → Proposed inter-regional transfers of water (by pipeline and river)
- □ Proposed estuary storage site
- ▽ Proposed groundwater storage site
- Principal sources of groundwater (porous and jointed aquifers)

1 : 7 000 000

Drought orders by Environment Agency Region 1980 – 1995

Anglian	4	Southern	74
North East	57	South West	99
North West	84	Thames	5
Midlands	12	Welsh	41

Major reservoirs (with capacity in million m³)

England

1	Kielder Res.	198
2	Rutland Water	123
3	Haweswater	85
4	Grafham Water	59
5	Cow Green Res.	41
6	Thirlmere	41
7	Carsington Res.	36
8	Roadford Res.	35
9	Bewl Water Res.	31
10	Colliford Lake	29
11	Ladybower Res.	28
12	Hanningfield Res.	27
13	Abberton Res.	25
14	Draycote Water	23
15	Derwent Res.	22
16	Grimwith Res.	22
17	Wimbleball Lake	21
18	Chew Valley Lake	20
19	Balderhead Res.	20
20	Thames Valley (linked reservoirs)	
21	Lea Valley (linked reservoirs)	
22	Longendale (linked reservoirs)	

Wales

23	Elan Valley	99
24	Llyn Celyn	74
25	Llyn Brianne	62
26	Llyn Brenig	60
27	Llyn Vyrnwy	60
28	Llyn Clywedog	48
29	Llandegfedd Res.	22

Scotland

30	Loch Lomond	86
31	Loch Katrine	64
32	Megget Res.	64
33	Loch Ness	26
34	Blackwater Res.	25
35	Daer Res.	23
36	Carron Valley Res.	21

Ireland

37	Poulaphouca Res.	168
38	Inishcarra Res.	57
39	Carrigadrohid Res.	33

Average daily domestic water use in England and Wales

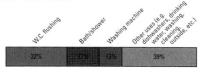

W.C. flushing	Bath/shower	Washing machine	Other uses (e.g. dishwashers, drinking water, washing, cleaning, outside, etc.)
32%	17%	12%	39%

Water abstractions in England and Wales (1995) 55 970 megalitres per day* of which:

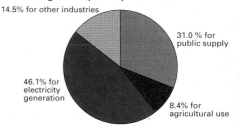

- 14.5% for other industries
- 31.0 % for public supply
- 46.1% for electricity generation
- 8.4% for agricultural use

*average daily domestic consumption per head 380 litres.

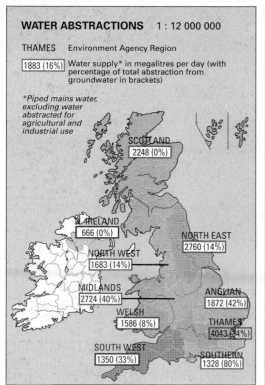

WATER ABSTRACTIONS   1 : 12 000 000

THAMES   Environment Agency Region

1883 (16%)   Water supply* in megalitres per day (with percentage of total abstraction from groundwater in brackets)

*Piped mains water, excluding water abstracted for agricultural and industrial use

- SCOTLAND 2248 (0%)
- IRELAND 666 (0%)
- NORTH EAST 2760 (14%)
- NORTH WEST 1683 (14%)
- MIDLANDS 2724 (40%)
- ANGLIAN 1872 (42%)
- WELSH 1586 (8%)
- THAMES 4043 (34%)
- SOUTH WEST 1350 (33%)
- SOUTHERN 1328 (80%)

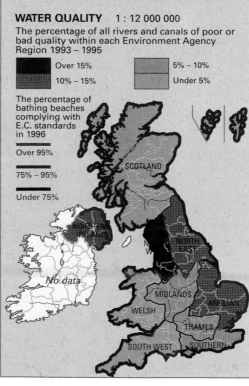

WATER QUALITY   1 : 12 000 000

The percentage of all rivers and canals of poor or bad quality within each Environment Agency Region 1993 – 1995

- Over 15%
- 10% – 15%
- 5% – 10%
- Under 5%

The percentage of bathing beaches complying with E.C. standards in 1996

- Over 95%
- 75% – 95%
- Under 75%

No data

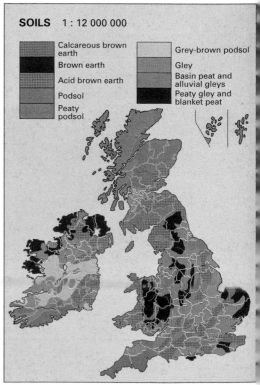

SOILS   1 : 12 000 000

- Calcareous brown earth
- Brown earth
- Acid brown earth
- Podsol
- Peaty podsol
- Grey-brown podsol
- Gley
- Basin peat and alluvial gleys
- Peaty gley and blanket peat

E.U. AIR QUALITY: Emissions in thousand tonnes

	Sulphur dioxide			Nitrogen oxides		
	1975	1985	1990	1975	1985	1990
Austria	–	195	90	–	245	221
Belgium	–	117	95	–	147	172
Denmark	418	339	183	182	294	270
Finland	–	382	260	–	252	290
France	3 329	1451	1200	1 608	1400	1487
Germany	3 325	2369	5633	2 532	2908	3033
Greece	–	–	–	–	308	338
Ireland	186	135	187	60	91	128
Italy	3 250	2244	1682	1 499	1736	2041
Luxembourg	–	17	10	–	22	–
Netherlands	386	261	204	447	578	575
Portugal	178	199	286	104	96	216
Spain	–	2191	2205	–	849	1247
Sweden	–	292	169	–	–	411
United Kingdom	5 310	3729	3754	2 365	2420	2731

ACID RAIN   1 : 12 000 000

Average acidity of precipitation in the U.K. (pH scale)

- 4.29 and under (most acidic)
- 4.30 – 4.39
- 4.40 – 4.49
- 4.50 – 4.59
- 4.60 – 4.69
- 4.70 – 4.79
- 4.80 and over (least acidic)

No data

E.S.As.
Environmentally Sensitive Areas in the U.K.

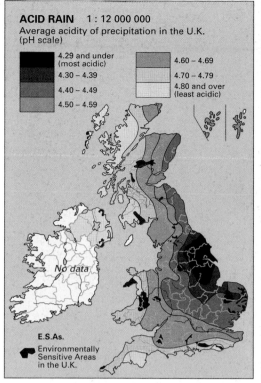

AIR QUALITY   1 : 12 000 000

Hourly average of tropospheric ozone (O_3) exceeding 100 parts per billion (summer 1990)*

- Over 45
- 30 – 45
- 15 – 30
- Under 15

Ground-level concentrations of smoke in the U.K., by region
U.K. average:
12 micrograms per m³

- Less than the U.K. average
- More than the U.K. average
- Over 3x the U.K. average

* W.H.O. recommends 75-100 ppb maximum

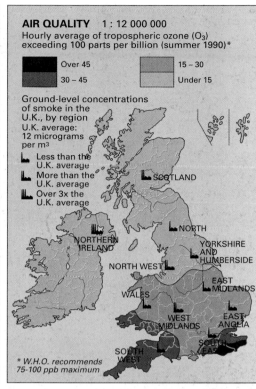

FORESTRY   1 : 12 000 000

The percentage of the total area covered by woodland and forest

- Over 20%
- 15% – 20%
- 10% – 15%
- 5% – 10%
- Under 5%
- △ 50%-80% coniferous
- △ Over 80% coniferous

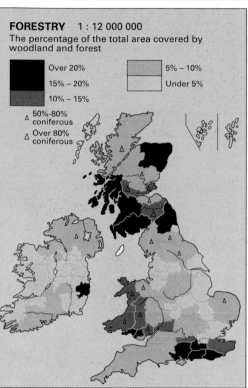

NATURAL VEGETATION   1 : 12 000 000

The plant cover associated with a particular environment if it is unaffected by human activity

- Oak
- Beech and Oak
- Ash and Oak
- Birch and Oakwood
- Scots Pine
- Heath, moorland, water meadows, fen, bog and marsh

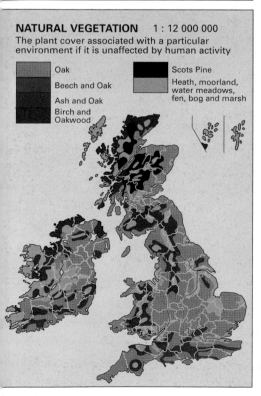

CONSERVATION   1 : 7 000 000

- National Parks
- Areas of Outstanding Natural Beauty
- National Scenic Areas
- Forest Parks and Special Protected Areas
- Green Belts (and the urban areas they surround)
- Heritage Coast (England and Wales)/Coastal Conservation Zones (Scotland)

∗ World Heritage Sites in the U.K.

(also designated, but not shown, St. Kilda, Outer Hebrides and Henderson Island, South Pacific Ocean)

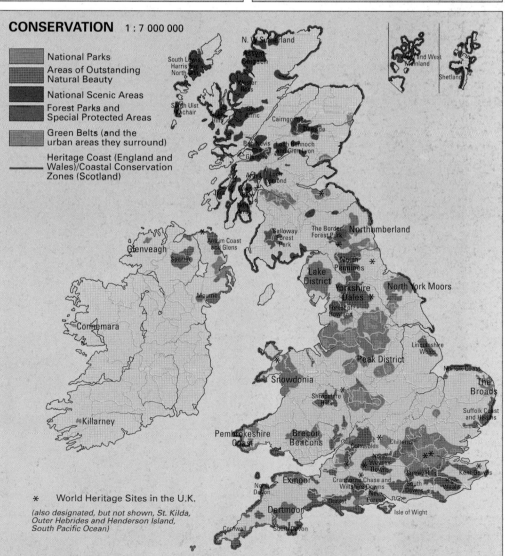

CARTOGRAPHY BY PHILIP'S. COPYRIGHT GEORGE PHILIP LTD

TYPES OF FARM

- ▨ Dairy cattle
- ▨ Beef cattle
- ▨ Sheep
- ● Pigs and/or Poultry
- ▨ Mixed farming
- ▨ Market gardening (fruit and vegetables)
- ▨ Cereals
- ▨ Other crops (mainly potatoes, sugar beet)
- — Northern limit of 9 month growing season
- ▨ Forests
- ▨ Built-up areas

1 : 7 000 000

▨ Areas with over 1000mm rainfall per year

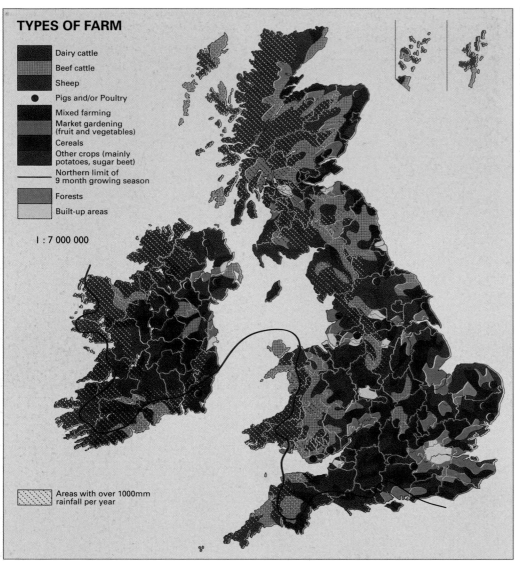

LAND UNDER AGRICULTURE 1 : 12 000 000
The percentage of the total land area used for farming in 1995

- ■ Over 80%
- ▨ 60% – 80%
- ▨ 40% – 60%
- ▨ 20% – 40%
- □ 0 – 20%

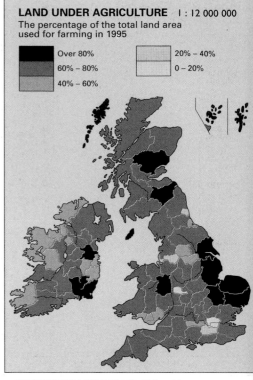

AGRICULTURAL LAND USE 1995 (U.K. only)

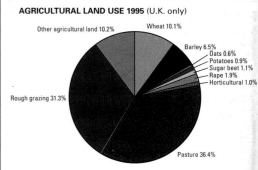

- Other agricultural land 10.2%
- Wheat 10.1%
- Barley 6.5%
- Oats 0.6%
- Potatoes 0.9%
- Sugar beet 1.1%
- Rape 1.9%
- Horticultural 1.0%
- Rough grazing 31.3%
- Pasture 36.4%

WHEAT 1 : 12 000 000
The percentage of the total farmland used for growing wheat in 1995

- ■ Over 40%
- ▨ 30% – 40%
- ▨ 20% – 30%
- ▨ 10% – 20%
- □ 0 – 10%

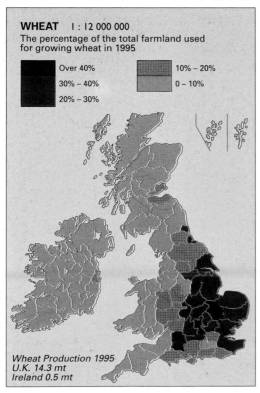

Wheat Production 1995
U.K. 14.3 mt
Ireland 0.5 mt

BARLEY 1 : 12 000 000
The percentage of the total farmland used for growing barley in 1995

- ■ Over 20%
- ▨ 10% – 20%
- □ 0 – 10%

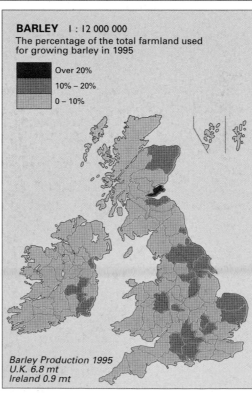

Barley Production 1995
U.K. 6.8 mt
Ireland 0.9 mt

PASTURE 1 : 12 000 000
The percentage of the total farmland used for grazing livestock in 1995

- ■ 80% – 100%
- ▨ 60% – 80%
- ▨ 40% – 60%
- ▨ 20% – 40%
- □ 0 – 20%

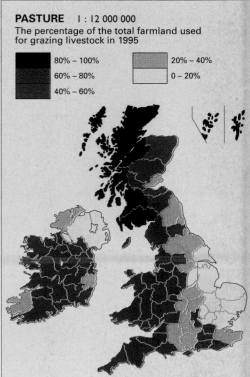

NUMBER AND SIZE OF AGRICULTURAL HOLDINGS IN THE U.K.

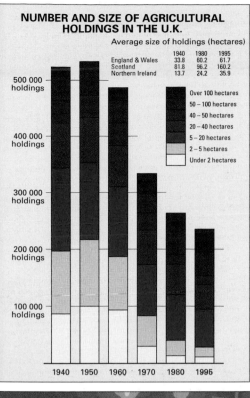

Average size of holdings (hectares)

	1940	1980	1995
England & Wales	33.8	60.2	61.7
Scotland	81.8	96.2	160.2
Northern Ireland	13.7	24.2	35.9

- Over 100 hectares
- 50 – 100 hectares
- 40 – 50 hectares
- 20 – 40 hectares
- 5 – 20 hectares
- 2 – 5 hectares
- Under 2 hectares

500 000 holdings
400 000 holdings
300 000 holdings
200 000 holdings
100 000 holdings

1940 1950 1960 1970 1980 1995

POTATOES   1 : 12 000 000
The percentage of the total farmland used for growing potatoes in 1995

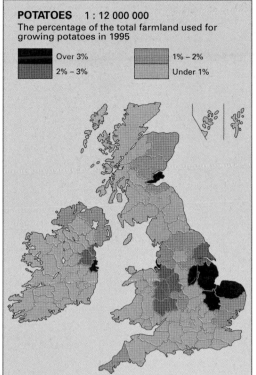

- Over 3%
- 2% – 3%
- 1% – 2%
- Under 1%

MARKET GARDENING   1 : 12 000 000
The percentage of the total farmland used for market gardening in 1995

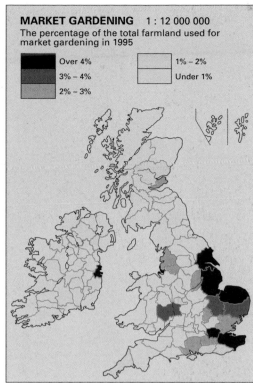

- Over 4%
- 3% – 4%
- 2% – 3%
- 1% – 2%
- Under 1%

FISHING

Quantities of fish landed at major ports (port districts in Scotland) in 1995

('000 tonnes)
100
50
25
10
5

Type of fish landed

- Demersal (Deep Sea Fish)
- Pelagic (Shallow Water Fish)
- Shellfish

Fishing Regions

IV	North Sea
VIa	West Scotland
VIIa	Irish Sea
VIIb/h/j	W. Ireland & Sole Bank
VIId/e	English Channel
VIIf/g	Bristol Ch. & S. E. Ireland

Fish landed according to region of capture (1995)

- Demersal
- Pelagic

1 fish represents 10 000 tonnes caught

—— Region boundary

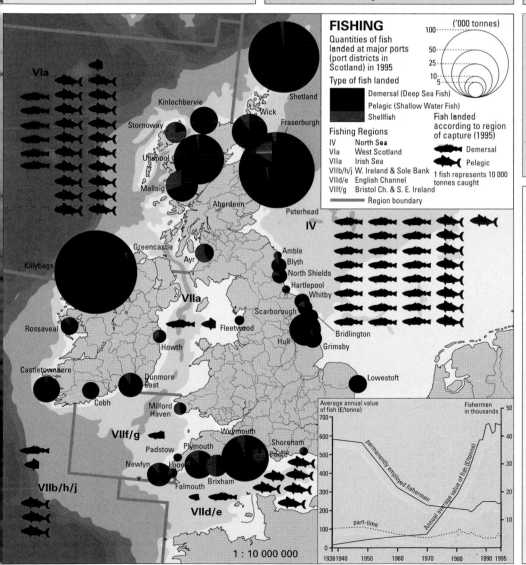

VIa
Kinlochbervie
Wick
Shetland
Stornoway
Fraserburgh
Ullapool
Mallaig
Aberdeen
Peterhead
IV
Greencastle
Ayr
Amble
Blyth
North Shields
Hartlepool
Whitby
VIIa
Scarborough
Killybegs
Bridlington
Fleetwood
Hull
Rossaveal
Grimsby
Howth
Castletownbere
Dunmore East
Lowestoft
Cobh
Milford Haven
VIIf/g
Weymouth
Shoreham
Padstow
Plymouth
Poole
Newlyn
Looe
Falmouth
Brixham
VIIb/h/j
VIId/e

1 : 10 000 000

Average annual value of fish (£/tonne)
700
600
500
400
300
200
100

permanently employed fishermen

Fishermen in thousands
50
40
30
20
10

Annual average value of fish (£/tonne)

part-time

1938 1940   1950   1960   1970   1980   1990 1995

1000 500 200 100 50 m

VALUE OF AGRICULTURAL OUTPUT (U.K. only)

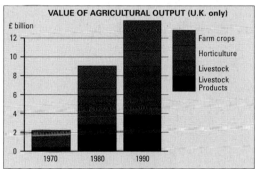

£ billion
12
10
8
6
4
2
0

1970   1980   1990

- Farm crops
- Horticulture
- Livestock
- Livestock Products

AGRICULTURAL LAND & LIVESTOCK, 1970-90 (U.K. only)

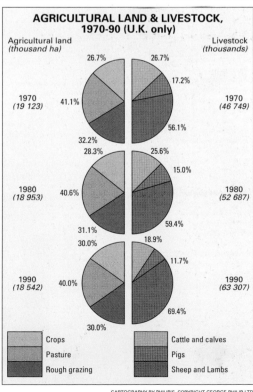

Agricultural land (thousand ha)   Livestock (thousands)

1970 (19 123)
26.7%
41.1%
32.2%

1970 (46 749)
26.7%
17.2%
56.1%

1980 (18 953)
28.3%
40.6%
31.1%

1980 (52 687)
25.6%
15.0%
59.4%

1990 (18 542)
30.0%
40.0%
30.0%

1990 (63 307)
18.9%
11.7%
69.4%

- Crops
- Pasture
- Rough grazing
- Cattle and calves
- Pigs
- Sheep and Lambs

EMPLOYMENT IN MANUFACTURING

The percentage of the workforce employed in manufacturing in 1996 (Ireland 1989)

- Over 30%
- 25% – 30%
- 20% – 25%
- 15% – 20%
- 12.5% – 15%
- Under 12.5%

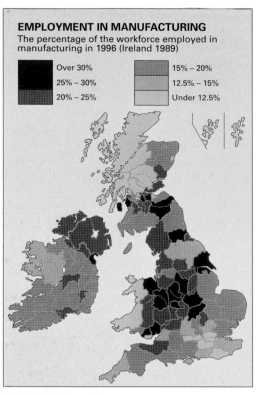

CHANGE IN MANUFACTURING EMPLOYMENT

The percentage change in the number of people employed in manufacturing 1980-89*

- Over 10% gain
- 0 – 10% gain
- 0 – 10% loss
- 10% – 20% loss
- 20% – 30% loss
- Over 30% loss

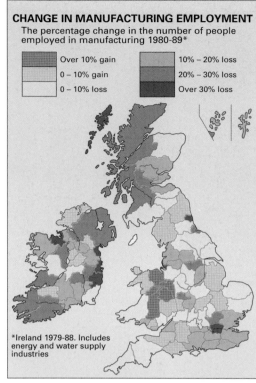

*Ireland 1979-88. Includes energy and water supply industries

LOCATION OF MANUFACTURING INDUSTRY

Heavy Industry
- ▲ Chemicals
- ■ Iron and Steel
- ● Motor vehicles

Light Industry
- ◆ Electrical Engineering

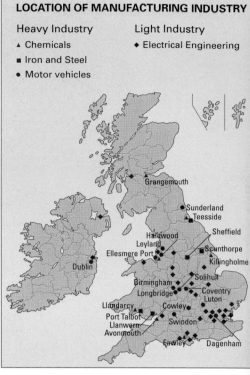

Grangemouth
Sunderland
Teesside
Sheffield
Halewood
Leyland
Scunthorpe
Ellesmere Port
Killingholme
Dublin
Solihull
Birmingham
Coventry
Longbridge
Luton
Llandarcy
Cowley
Llanwern
Port Talbot
Swindon
Avonmouth
Fawley
Dagenham

EMPLOYMENT IN AGRICULTURE

The percentage of the workforce employed in agriculture in 1996 (Ireland 1989)

- Over 25%
- 10% – 25%
- 2.5% – 10%
- 1% – 2.5%
- 0 – 1%

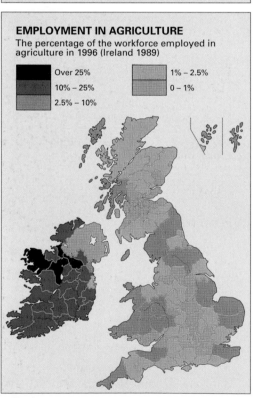

EMPLOYMENT IN SERVICES

The percentage of the workforce employed in the service industry in 1996 (Ireland 1989)

- Over 80%
- 70% – 80%
- 60% – 70%
- 50% – 60%
- Less than 50%

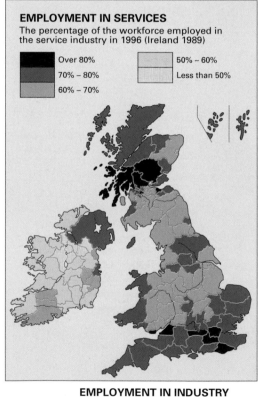

ASSISTED AREAS

These are areas in which extra financial support is focused to encourage economic growth

- Development areas in the U.K.
- Intermediate areas in the U.K.

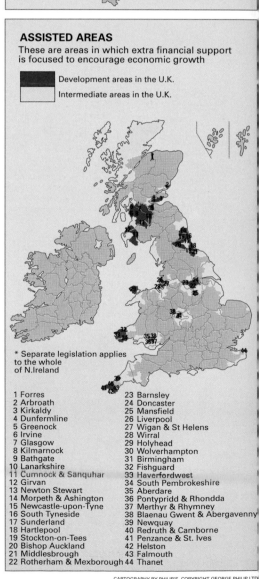

* Separate legislation applies to the whole of N.Ireland

1 Forres	23 Barnsley
2 Arbroath	24 Doncaster
3 Kirkaldy	25 Mansfield
4 Dunfermline	26 Liverpool
5 Greenock	27 Wigan & St Helens
6 Irvine	28 Wirral
7 Glasgow	29 Holyhead
8 Kilmarnock	30 Wolverhampton
9 Bathgate	31 Birmingham
10 Lanarkshire	32 Fishguard
11 Cumnock & Sanquhar	33 Haverfordwest
12 Girvan	34 South Pembrokeshire
13 Newton Stewart	35 Aberdare
14 Morpeth & Ashington	36 Pontypridd & Rhondda
15 Newcastle-upon-Tyne	37 Merthyr & Rhymney
16 South Tyneside	38 Blaenau Gwent & Abergavenny
17 Sunderland	39 Newquay
18 Hartlepool	40 Redruth & Camborne
19 Stockton-on-Tees	41 Penzance & St. Ives
20 Bishop Auckland	42 Helston
21 Middlesbrough	43 Falmouth
22 Rotherham & Mexborough	44 Thanet

EMPLOYMENT IN INDUSTRY

Employment in the U.K. by industry

- Services
- Transport
- Manufacturing
- Mining & energy supply
- Agriculture, forestry and fishing

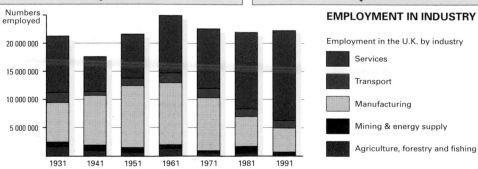

Numbers employed

20 000 000
15 000 000
10 000 000
5 000 000

1931 1941 1951 1961 1971 1981 1991

CARTOGRAPHY BY PHILIP'S. COPYRIGHT GEORGE PHILIP LTD

1 : 12 000 000

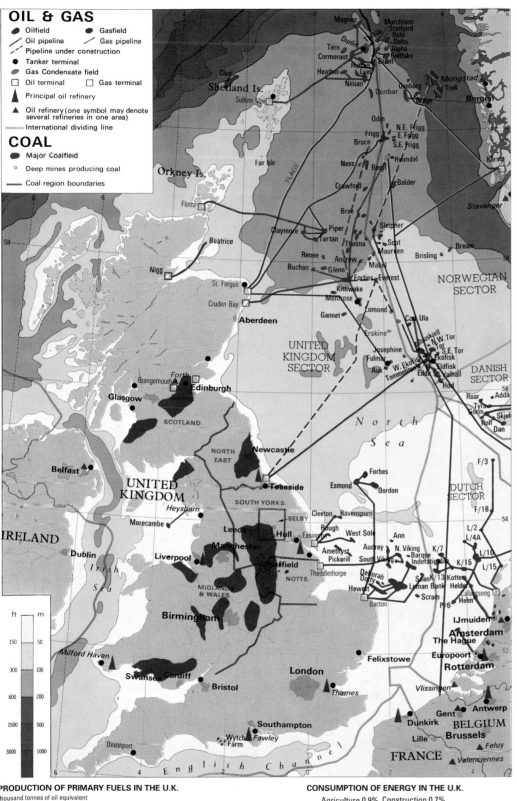

OIL & GAS

- Oilfield
- Gasfield
- Oil pipeline
- Gas pipeline
- Pipeline under construction
- Tanker terminal
- Gas Condensate field
- Oil terminal
- Gas terminal
- Principal oil refinery
- Oil refinery (one symbol may denote several refineries in one area)
- International dividing line

COAL

- Major Coalfield
- Deep mines producing coal
- Coal region boundaries

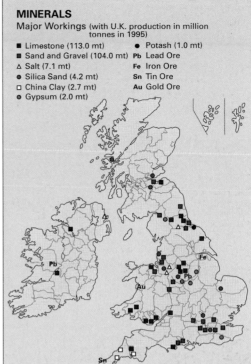

MINERALS

Major Workings (with U.K. production in million tonnes in 1995)

- Limestone (113.0 mt)
- Sand and Gravel (104.0 mt)
- Salt (7.1 mt)
- Silica Sand (4.2 mt)
- China Clay (2.7 mt)
- Gypsum (2.0 mt)
- Potash (1.0 mt)
- Pb Lead Ore
- Fe Iron Ore
- Sn Tin Ore
- Au Gold Ore

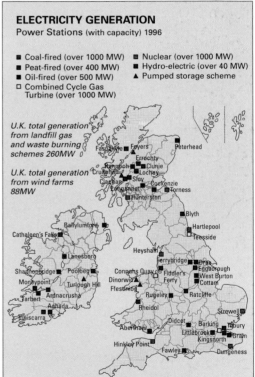

ELECTRICITY GENERATION

Power Stations (with capacity) 1996

- Coal-fired (over 1000 MW)
- Peat-fired (over 400 MW)
- Oil-fired (over 500 MW)
- Combined Cycle Gas Turbine (over 1000 MW)
- Nuclear (over 1000 MW)
- Hydro-electric (over 40 MW)
- Pumped storage scheme

U.K. total generation from landfill gas and waste burning schemes 260MW

U.K. total generation from wind farms 88MW

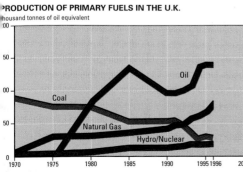

PRODUCTION OF PRIMARY FUELS IN THE U.K.

thousand tonnes of oil equivalent

Oil, Coal, Natural Gas, Hydro/Nuclear

1970 1975 1980 1985 1990 1995 1996 2000

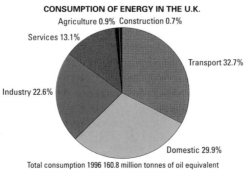

CONSUMPTION OF ENERGY IN THE U.K.

- Agriculture 0.9%
- Construction 0.7%
- Services 13.1%
- Transport 32.7%
- Industry 22.6%
- Domestic 29.9%

Total consumption 1996 160.8 million tonnes of oil equivalent

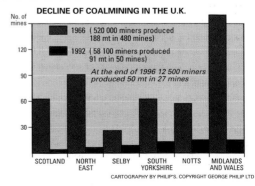

DECLINE OF COALMINING IN THE U.K.

No. of mines

1966 (520 000 miners produced 188 mt in 480 mines)
1992 (58 100 miners produced 91 mt in 50 mines)

At the end of 1996 12 500 miners produced 50 mt in 27 mines

SCOTLAND | NORTH EAST | SELBY | SOUTH YORKSHIRE | NOTTS | MIDLANDS AND WALES

CARTOGRAPHY BY PHILIP'S. COPYRIGHT GEORGE PHILIP LTD

The map shows the 6 counties in Northern Ireland, the 32 unitary authorities in Scotland, the 22 unitary authorities in Wales and the 87 unitary authorities in England as of 1st April 1998. Authorities which are too small to name on the map are numbered and listed separately.

The Channel Islands and the Isle of Man are dependencies of the Crown and have their own parliaments. They are not part of the United Kingdom.

●   Capital cities

○   Administrative headquarters in Ireland and selected headquarters in Great Britain

SCOTLAND
1. ABERDEEN CITY
2. DUNDEE CITY
3. WEST DUNBARTONSHIRE
4. EAST DUNBARTONSHIRE
5. CITY OF GLASGOW
6. INVERCLYDE
7. RENFREWSHIRE
8. EAST RENFREWSHIRE
9. NORTH LANARKSHIRE
10. FALKIRK
11. CLACKMANNANSHIRE
12. WEST LOTHIAN
13. CITY OF EDINBURGH
14. MIDLOTHIAN

WALES
15. SWANSEA
16. NEATH PORT TALBOT
17. BRIDGEND
18. RHONDDA CYNON TAFF
19. MERTHYR TYDFIL
20. CAERPHILLY
21. BLAENAU GWENT
22. TORFAEN
23. CARDIFF
24. NEWPORT

ENGLAND
25. HARTLEPOOL
26. DARLINGTON
27. STOCKTON-ON-TEES
28. MIDDLESBROUGH
29. REDCAR AND CLEVELAND
30. BLACKPOOL
31. BLACKBURN WITH DARWEN
32. HALTON
33. WARRINGTON
34. KINGSTON UPON HULL
35. NORTH EAST LINCOLNSHIRE
36. STOKE-ON-TRENT
37. TELFORD AND WREKIN
38. DERBY CITY
39. CITY OF NOTTINGHAM
40. LEICESTER CITY
41. RUTLAND
42. PETERBOROUGH
43. MILTON KEYNES
44. LUTON
45. NORTH SOMERSET
46. CITY OF BRISTOL
47. BATH AND NORTH EAST SOMERSET
48. SWINDON
49. READING
50. WOKINGHAM
51. WINDSOR AND MAIDENHEAD
52. SLOUGH
53. BRACKNELL FOREST
54. THURROCK
55. SOUTHEND-ON-SEA
56. MEDWAY TOWNS
57. PLYMOUTH
58. TORBAY
59. POOLE
60. BOURNEMOUTH
61. SOUTHAMPTON
62. PORTSMOUTH
63. BRIGHTON AND HOVE

ATLANTIC OCEAN

NORTH SEA

SHETLAND
Lerwick

ORKNEY
Kirkwall

WESTERN ISLES
Stornoway

SCOTLAND
HIGHLAND
MORAY
ABERDEENSHIRE
Aberdeen
Inverness
ANGUS
Dundee
PERTH & KINROSS
FIFE
Glenrothes
STIRLING
Stirling
ARGYLL AND BUTE
Glasgow
SOUTH LANARKSHIRE
NORTH AYRSHIRE
EAST AYRSHIRE
SOUTH AYRSHIRE
EAST LOTHIAN
Edinburgh
SCOTTISH BORDERS
Newtown St. Boswells
NORTHUMBERLAND
Morpeth

North

FRANCE

English Channel

CARTOGRAPHY BY PHILIP'S. COPYRIGHT GEORGE PHILIP LTD

Wes from Greenwich 0 East from Greeewich

ENGLAND

UNITED

KINGDOM

WALES

IRISH SEA

Channel

NORTHERN IRELAND

IRELAND

St. George's Channel

CELTIC SEA

Newcastle
UPON TYNE AND WEAR
Durham
DURHAM
NORTH YORKSHIRE
Northallerton
Carlisle
CUMBRIA
DUMFRIES AND GALLOWAY
Dumfries

ISLE OF MAN
Douglas

Belfast
ANTRIM
Antrim
Downpatrick
DOWN
Armagh
ARMAGH
Monaghan
MONAGHAN
Enniskillen
FERMANAGH
TYRONE
Omagh
Lifford
DONEGAL
Londonderry
Strabane

SLIGO
Sligo
LEITRIM
Carrickon Shannon
ROSCOMMON
Roscommon
MAYO
Castlebar
GALWAY
Galway
CLARE
Ennis
LIMERICK
Limerick
KERRY
Tralee
CORK
Cork

CAVAN
Cavan
LONGFORD
Longford
WESTMEATH
Mullingar
OFFALY
Tullamore
LAOIS
Port Laoise
TIPPERARY
Clonmel
WATERFORD
Waterford

MEATH
An Uaimh
Navas
KILDARE
Naas
CARLOW
Carlow
KILKENNY
Kilkenny
WEXFORD
Wexford
WICKLOW
Wicklow

DUBLIN
Dublin
Dundalk
LOUTH

EAST RIDING OF YORKSHIRE
Beverley
Hull
CITY OF YORK
York
NORTH LINCOLNSHIRE
Lincoln
LINCOLNSHIRE

LANCASHIRE
Preston
MERSEYSIDE
Liverpool
GREATER MANCHESTER
Manchester
WEST YORKSHIRE
Wakefield
SOUTH YORKSHIRE
Barnsley

CHESHIRE
Chester
DERBYSHIRE
Matlock
NOTTINGHAMSHIRE
Nottingham
LEICESTERSHIRE
Leicester

STAFFORDSHIRE
Stafford
WEST MIDLANDS
Birmingham
SHROPSHIRE
Shrewsbury

NORFOLK
Norwich
SUFFOLK
Ipswich
CAMBRIDGESHIRE
Cambridge
NORTHAMPTONSHIRE
Northampton
BEDFORD
Bedford
HERTFORD
Hartford
BUCKINGHAM
Aylesbury
OXFORDSHIRE
Oxford

ESSEX
Chelmsford
GREATER LONDON
London
Kingston
SURREY
KENT
Maidstone
EAST SUSSEX
Lewes
WEST SUSSEX
Chichester
HAMPSHIRE
Winchester
ISLE OF WIGHT
Newport
WEST BERKS
BERKS

WARWICKSHIRE
Warwick
WORCESTER
Worcester
HEREFORD
Hereford
GLOUCESTERSHIRE
Gloucester
SOUTH GLOUCESTER
Bristol
MONMOUTHSHIRE
WILTSHIRE
Trowbridge
SOMERSET
Taunton
DORSET
Dorchester

POWYS
CEREDIGION
GWYNEDD
ISLE OF ANGLESEY
CONWY
DENBIGH
FLINT
WREXHAM
CARMARTHEN
PEMBROKESHIRE
VALE OF GLAMORGAN
Cardiff

DEVON
Exeter
CORNWALL
Truro

Scilly Isles
(CORNWALL)

CHANNEL ISLANDS
Guernsey
St. Peter Port
Jersey
St. Helier

	Area in square kilometres
England	130,439
Wales	20,768
Scotland	77,167
Northern Ireland	13,483
United Kingdom	**241,857**
Isle of Man	**572**
Channel Islands	**195**
Ireland	**68,896**

AREA DATA

1 : 3 250 000

Projection: Conical with two standard parallels

25 0 25 50 75 miles
25 0 25 50 75 100 125 km

POPULATION DENSITY 1891

See map at right for reference to colours

Density in 1891 by country :
U.K. 142 people per km²
Ireland 49 people per km²

POPULATION DENSITY 1995

Persons per km²

- Over 1000
- 500 – 1000
- 200 – 500
- 100 – 200
- 50 – 100
- 25 – 50
- Under 25

The density for the whole of the U.K. is 241 people per km², the density for Ireland is 53.

1 : 7 000 000

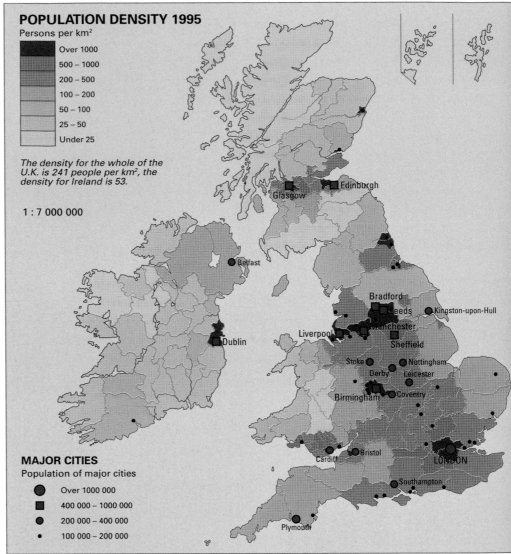

MAJOR CITIES

Population of major cities

- Over 1000 000
- 400 000 – 1000 000
- 200 000 – 400 000
- 100 000 – 200 000

AGE STRUCTURE OF THE U.K.

The bars represent the percentage of males and the percentage of females in the age group shown

- 1901
- 1990
- Projected 2150

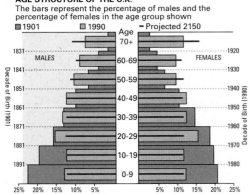

MALES   FEMALES

Age: 70+, 60-69, 50-59, 40-49, 30-39, 20-29, 10-19, 0-9

Decade of Birth (1901): 1831, 1841, 1851, 1861, 1871, 1881, 1891
Decade of Birth (1990): 1920, 1930, 1940, 1950, 1960, 1970, 1980

25% 20% 15% 10% 5%   5% 10% 15% 20% 25%

YOUNG PEOPLE 1 : 12 000 000

The percentage of the population under 15 years old in 1995 (Ireland 1991)

- Over 30%
- 25% – 30%
- 20% – 25%
- 19% – 20%
- 18% – 19%
- Under 18%

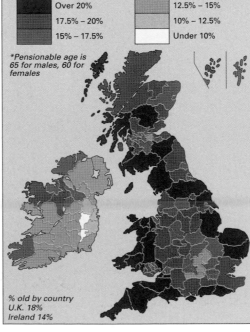

% young by country
U.K. 21%
Ireland 31%

OLD PEOPLE 1 : 12 000 000

The percentage of the population over pensionable age* in 1995 (Ireland 1991)

- Over 20%
- 17.5% – 20%
- 15% – 17.5%
- 12.5% – 15%
- 10% – 12.5%
- Under 10%

*Pensionable age is 65 for males, 60 for females

% old by country
U.K. 18%
Ireland 14%

URBANIZATION 1 : 12 000 000

The percentage of the population living in towns and cities (latest available year)

- Over 90%
- 80% – 90%
- 70% – 80%
- 60% – 70%
- 50% – 60%
- Under 50%

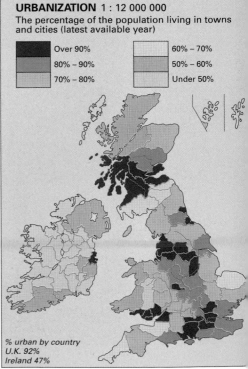

% urban by country
U.K. 92%
Ireland 47%

NATURAL POPULATION CHANGE

The difference between the number of births and the number of deaths per thousand inhabitants in 1995

- Over 10 more births
- 5 – 10 more births
- 2.5 – 5 more births
- 0 – 2.5 more births
- 0 – 2.5 more deaths
- Over 2.5 more deaths

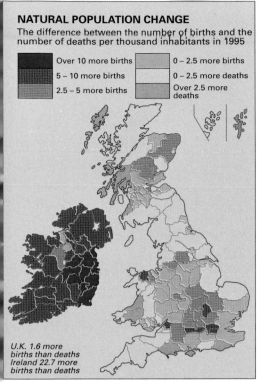

U.K. 1.6 more births than deaths
Ireland 22.7 more births than deaths

ETHNIC GROUP

Ethnic minorities as a % of total population in 1995/1996

- Over 6%
- 4% – 6%
- 2% – 4%
- 0 – 2%

Ethnic minority groups

- Indian/ Pakistani/ Bangladeshi
- W. Indian/ African
- Other

77 000 Total number of ethnic minority people in each region

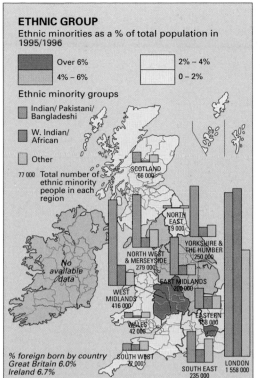

SCOTLAND 66 000
NORTH EAST 19 000
NORTH WEST & MERSEYSIDE 279 000
YORKSHIRE & THE HUMBER 250 000
WEST MIDLANDS 416 000
EAST MIDLANDS 200 000
WALES 42 000
EASTERN 158 000
SOUTH WEST 77 000
SOUTH EAST 235 000
LONDON 1 558 000

No available data

% foreign born by country
Great Britain 6.0%
Ireland 6.7%

MIGRATION 1 : 12 000 000

The difference between the number moving in and the number moving away (per 1000 inhabitants)*

- Over 15 moved in
- 10 – 15 moved in
- 5 – 10 moved in
- 0 – 5 moved in
- 0 – 5 moved away
- 5 – 10 moved away

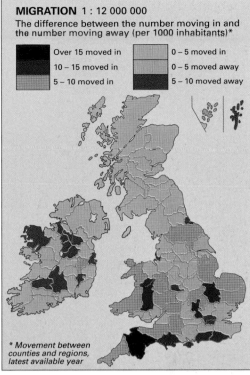

* Movement between counties and regions, latest available year

U.K. VITAL STATISTICS, 1900-2000

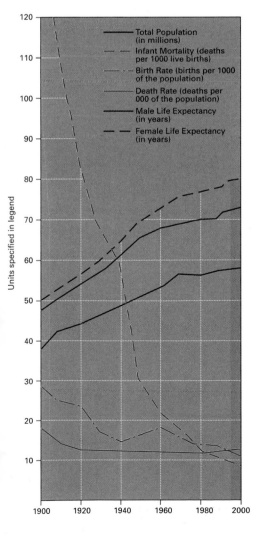

- Total Population (in millions)
- Infant Mortality (deaths per 1000 live births)
- Birth Rate (births per 1000 of the population)
- Death Rate (deaths per 000 of the population)
- Male Life Expectancy (in years)
- Female Life Expectancy (in years)

POPULATION CHANGE 1961-1991

The percentage change in the number of people between 1961 and 1991

- Over 30% gain
- 25% – 30% gain
- 20% – 25% gain
- 15% – 20% gain
- 10% – 15% gain
- 5% – 10% gain
- 0 – 5% gain
- 0 – 5% loss
- 5% – 10% loss
- Over 10% loss

1 : 7 000 000

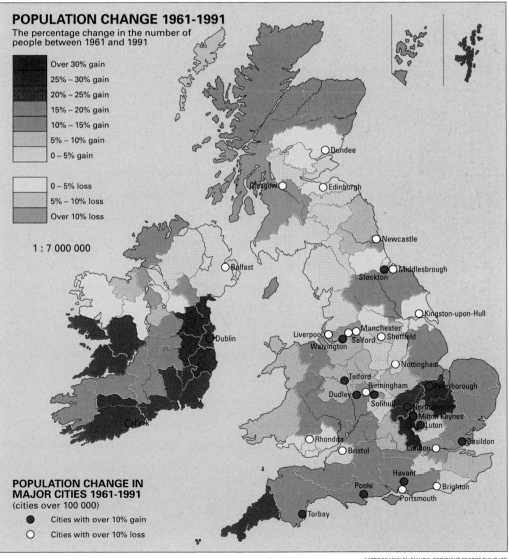

POPULATION CHANGE IN MAJOR CITIES 1961-1991
(cities over 100 000)

- ● Cities with over 10% gain
- ○ Cities with over 10% loss

CARTOGRAPHY BY PHILIP'S. COPYRIGHT GEORGE PHILIP LTD

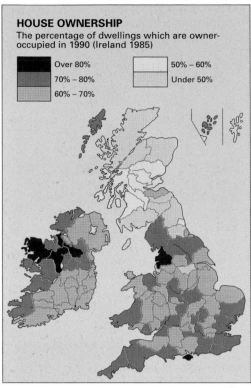

HOUSE OWNERSHIP

The percentage of dwellings which are owner-occupied in 1990 (Ireland 1985)

- Over 80%
- 70% – 80%
- 60% – 70%
- 50% – 60%
- Under 50%

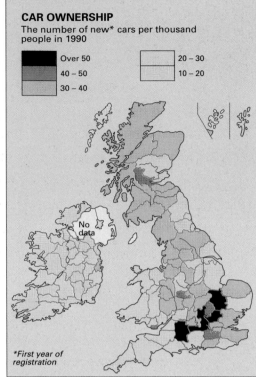

CAR OWNERSHIP

The number of new* cars per thousand people in 1990

- Over 50
- 40 – 50
- 30 – 40
- 20 – 30
- 10 – 20

No data

*First year of registration

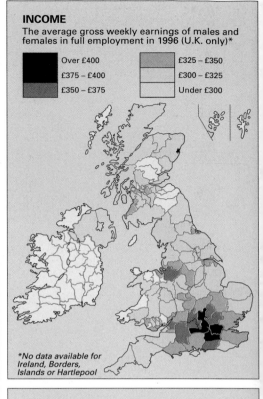

INCOME

The average gross weekly earnings of males and females in full employment in 1996 (U.K. only)*

- Over £400
- £375 – £400
- £350 – £375
- £325 – £350
- £300 – £325
- Under £300

*No data available for Ireland, Borders, Islands or Hartlepool

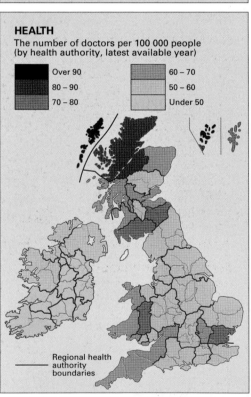

HEALTH

The number of doctors per 100 000 people (by health authority, latest available year)

- Over 90
- 80 – 90
- 70 – 80
- 60 – 70
- 50 – 60
- Under 50

— Regional health authority boundaries

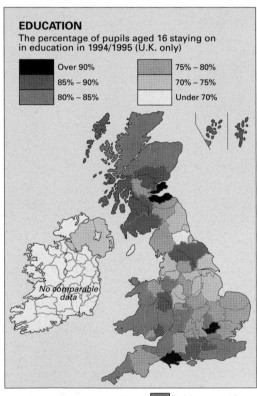

EDUCATION

The percentage of pupils aged 16 staying on in education in 1994/1995 (U.K. only)

- Over 90%
- 85% – 90%
- 80% – 85%
- 75% – 80%
- 70% – 75%
- Under 70%

No comparable data

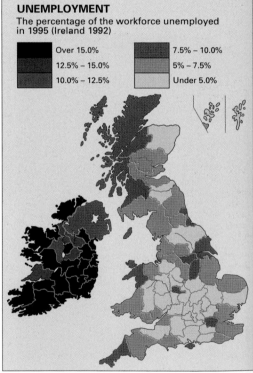

UNEMPLOYMENT

The percentage of the workforce unemployed in 1995 (Ireland 1992)

- Over 15.0%
- 12.5% – 15.0%
- 10.0% – 12.5%
- 7.5% – 10.0%
- 5% – 7.5%
- Under 5.0%

HOUSEHOLD EXPENDITURE: E.U. COMPARISON, 1992

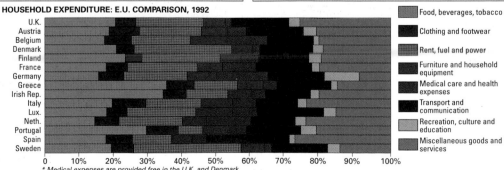

U.K.
Austria
Belgium
Denmark
Finland
France
Germany
Greece
Irish Rep.
Italy
Lux.
Neth.
Portugal
Spain
Sweden

0   10%   20%   30%   40%   50%   60%   70%   80%   90%   100%

* Medical expenses are provided free in the U.K. and Denmark

- Food, beverages, tobacco
- Clothing and footwear
- Rent, fuel and power
- Furniture and household equipment
- Medical care and health expenses
- Transport and communication
- Recreation, culture and education
- Miscellaneous goods and services

% OF U.K. HOUSEHOLDS OWNING DOMESTIC APPLIANCES

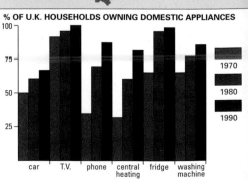

100
75
50
25

car   T.V.   phone   central heating   fridge   washing machine

1970
1980
1990

CARTOGRAPHY BY PHILIP'S. COPYRIGHT GEORGE PHILIP LTD

U.K. TRADE
TOP TEN TRADING PARTNERS 1996

One container represents 1% of the total value of imports or 1% of the total value of exports

IMPORTS

Germany £27.2b

Total Imports 1996 £184billion

Total Exports 1996 £167billion

U.S.A. £22.8b

France £17.7b

Netherlands £12.4b

Japan £9.0b

Italy £8.8b

Belgium/Lux. £8.6b

Irish Republic £7.2b

Switzerland £5.4b

Norway £5.0b

EXPORTS

Germany £20.8b

U.S.A. £19.8b

France £17.1b

Netherlands £13.5b

Irish Republic £8.7b

Belgium/Lux. £8.5b

Italy £8.0b

Spain £6.7b

Sweden £4.4b

Japan £4.3b

TYPE OF GOODS

- Machinery and Transport Equipment
- Road Vehicles
- Other manufactured Goods
- Chemicals
- Food and Live Animals
- Mineral fuels, Lubricants, etc.
- Other Goods

U.K. TOTAL FOREIGN TRADE 1970-1996 (£ million)

	Imports	Exports		Imports	Exports
1970	£9 051m	£8 063m	**1986**	£84 790m	£78 331m
1974	£23 117m	£16 494m	**1990**	£126 165m	£103 655m
1978	£40 969m	£37 368m	**1994**	£149 468m	£134 663m
1982	£56 940m	£55 538m	**1996**	£183 893m	£167 413m

TOURISM
TOP 20 TOURIST ATTRACTIONS (U.K. 1996)

- Theme Park
- Museum
- Country Park
- Historic Property

	Visitors
Blackpool Pleasure Beach	7 500 000
British Museum, London	6 228 275
Strathclyde Country Park	5 500 000
National Gallery, London	5 000 000
Palace Pier, Brighton	4 250 000
Alton Towers, Staffs.	2 749 000
Madame Tussauds, London	2 715 000
Tower of London	2 539 000
Westminster Abbey, London	2 500 000
Eastbourne Pier	2 200 000
York Minster	2 200 000
Tate Gallery, London	2 002 000
St. Pauls Cathedral, London	2 000 000
Pleasureland, Southport	2 000 000
Canterbury Cathedral	1 700 000
Chessington World of Adventures, Surrey	1 700 000
Natural History Museum, London	1 607 255
Science Museum, London	1 548 286
Sandwell Valley Country Park	1 500 000
Legoland, Windsor	1 420 511

FOREIGN VISITORS TO THE U.K.

Nature of visit
- Business
- Leisure

Country of origin
- North America
- Western Europe
- Other

No. of visits (millions): 18, 15, 12, 9, 6, 3, 0 — 1970, 1980, 1990

INCOME FROM TOURISM

SCOTLAND, NORTHERN IRELAND, NORTHUMBRIA, CUMBRIA, NORTH WEST, YORKSHIRE AND HUMBERSIDE, EAST MIDLANDS, HEART OF ENGLAND, EAST ANGLIA, WALES, WEST COUNTRY, SOUTHERN, SOUTH EAST, LONDON

The percentage of total U.K. income from tourism by region in 1995

- Over 25%
- 10% – 25%
- 5% – 10%
- 2.5% – 5%
- 0 – 2.5%

Total income from tourism
U.K. 1995   £24.8 billion
Ireland 1990   £7.7 billion

VISITS ABROAD BY U.K. RESIDENTS

Top 10 countries visited, 1996

No. of U.K. visitors (millions): 0 1 2 3 4 5 6 7 8 9 10

- France
- Spain
- Irish Rep.
- U.S.A.
- Germany
- Italy
- Belgium
- Netherlands
- Greece
- Portugal

Total visits by area, 1996
North America	3 597 000
Western Europe E.C.	31 054 000
Western Europe (non E.C.)	2 987 000
Rest of World	4 931 000

DEPENDENCE ON TRADE WITH THE U.K.

Trade with the U.K. as a percentage of each country's total trade

- Over 10%
- 7.5% – 10%
- 5.0% – 7.5%
- 2.5% – 5.0%
- 1.0% – 2.5%
- Under 1.0%

CHANGES IN TRADE WITH THE U.K.

Percentage change in exports and imports for selected countries 1985-1990

Change: 1000%, 500%, 100%, 50%

Increase 1985-1990

Exports Imports to U.K. from U.K.

Decrease 1985-1990

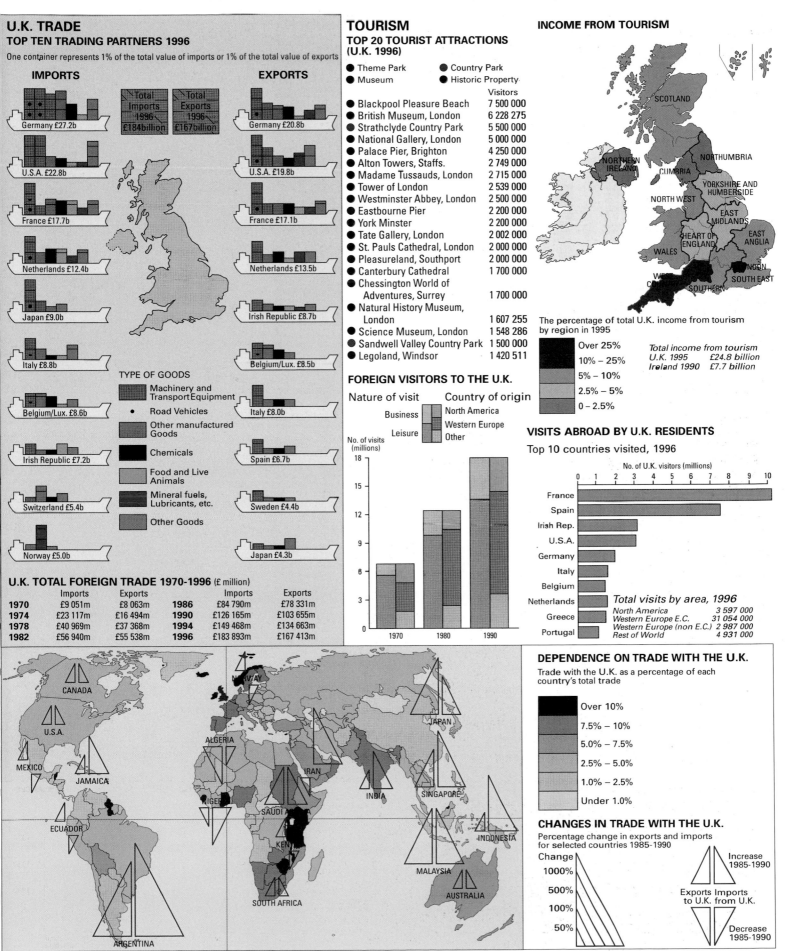

CANADA, U.S.A., MEXICO, JAMAICA, ECUADOR, ARGENTINA, NORWAY, ALGERIA, NIGERIA, SOUTH AFRICA, KENYA, SAUDI ARABIA, IRAN, INDIA, SINGAPORE, INDONESIA, MALAYSIA, AUSTRALIA, JAPAN

CARTOGRAPHY BY PHILIP'S. COPYRIGHT GEORGE PHILIP LTD

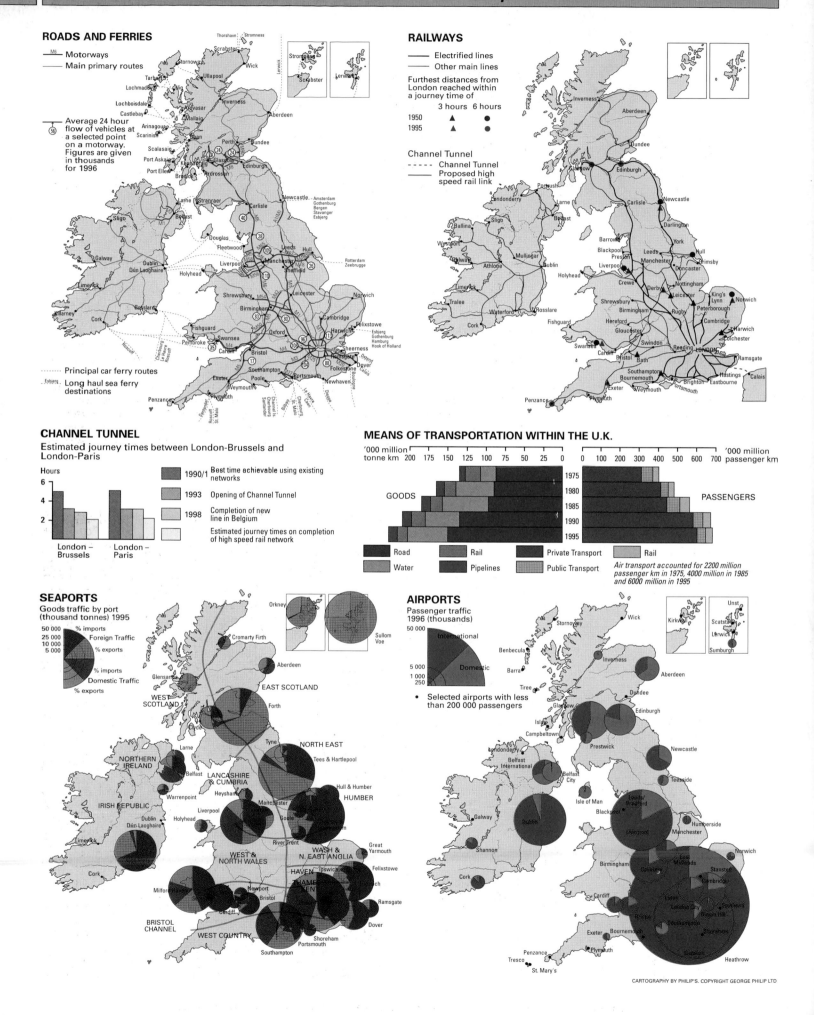

ROADS AND FERRIES

— M6 Motorways
— Main primary routes

⌖ (56) Average 24 hour flow of vehicles at a selected point on a motorway. Figures are given in thousands for 1996

····· Principal car ferry routes
- - - Esbjerg Long haul sea ferry destinations

RAILWAYS

— Electrified lines
— Other main lines

Furthest distances from London reached within a journey time of
	3 hours	6 hours
1950	▲	●
1995	▲	●

Channel Tunnel
- - - Channel Tunnel
— Proposed high speed rail link

CHANNEL TUNNEL

Estimated journey times between London-Brussels and London-Paris

Hours

■ 1990/1 Best time achievable using existing networks
■ 1993 Opening of Channel Tunnel
■ 1998 Completion of new line in Belgium
□ Estimated journey times on completion of high speed rail network

London – Brussels   London – Paris

MEANS OF TRANSPORTATION WITHIN THE U.K.

'000 million tonne km   200 175 150 125 100 75 50 25 0   0 100 200 300 400 500 600 700   '000 million passenger km

GOODS

PASSENGERS

1975
1980
1985
1990
1995

■ Road   ■ Rail   ■ Private Transport   □ Rail
■ Water   ■ Pipelines   ▦ Public Transport

Air transport accounted for 2200 million passenger km in 1975, 4000 million in 1985 and 6000 million in 1995

SEAPORTS

Goods traffic by port (thousand tonnes) 1995

50 000
25 000
10 000
5 000

% imports — Foreign Traffic — % exports
% imports — Domestic Traffic — % exports

AIRPORTS

Passenger traffic 1996 (thousands)

50 000 International
5 000
1 000
250 Domestic

• Selected airports with less than 200 000 passengers

CARTOGRAPHY BY PHILIP'S. COPYRIGHT GEORGE PHILIP LTD

INDEX TO BRITISH ISLES MAPS

This index lists the major placenames which appear on the large-scale maps of the British Isles (pages *2–15* with the yellow band). Placenames for the rest of the world can be found in the World Index, with the turquoise band.

The first number beside each name in the index gives the map page on which that feature or place will be found. The letter and figure immediately after the page number give the grid square within which the feature is situated. The letter represents the latitude and the figure the longitude. In some cases the feature may fall within the specified square, while the name is outside. This is usually the case only with very large features. Rivers are indexed to their mouths or confluence.

The 'geographical co-ordinates' which follow the letter-figure references give the latitude and longitude of each place. The first co-ordinate indicates latitude – the distance north of the Equator. The second co-ordinate indicates longitude – the distance east or west of the Greenwich Meridian. Both latitude and longitude are measured in degrees and minutes (there are 60 minutes in a degree).

Thus the entry in the index for Runcorn reads:

Runcorn............. **7 F3**   53 20N   2 44W

This indicates that Runcorn appears on map page 7 in grid square F3 at latitude 53 degrees, 20 minutes north and at longitude 2 degrees, 44 minutes west. To find Runcorn by using the geographical co-ordinates, look at the edges of the map. The degrees of latitude are indicated by blue figures on the left-hand edge of the map and the degrees of longitude are marked on the bottom edge of the map. Runcorn will be found where lines extended from the two points on the map edge would cross on the map.

An open square □ indicates that the name refers to an administrative unit such as a county or region; rivers are indicated by an arrow →. Names composed of a proper name (Wight) and a description (Isle of) are positioned alphabetically by the proper name. All names beginning St. are alphabetized under Saint. A list of abbreviations used can be found in the World Index at the end of the atlas.

Place names on the turquoise-coded World Map section are to be found in the index at the rear of the book.

Ben Klibreck 3 F9 58 14N 4 25W
Ben Lawers 4 A7 56 33N 4 13W
Ben Lomond 4 B6 56 12N 4 39W
Ben Loyal 3 F9 58 25N 4 25W
Ben Lui 4 B6 56 24N 4 50W
Ben Macdhui 3 H10 57 4N 3 40W
Ben Mholach 2 F4 58 14N 6 33W
Ben Mhor 2 H3 57 16N 7 21W
Ben More, *Arg. & Bute* 4 B3 56 26N 6 2W
Ben More, *Stirl.* 4 B6 56 23N 4 31W
Ben More Assynt 3 F8 58 7N 4 51W
Ben Nevis 3 J7 56 48N 5 2W
Ben Rinnes 3 H11 57 25N 3 15W
Ben Stack 3 F8 58 20N 4 58W
Ben Tharsuinn 3 G9 57 47N 4 20W
Ben Venue 4 B7 56 13N 4 28W
Ben Vorlich 4 B7 56 22N 4 15W
Ben Wyvis 3 G8 57 40N 4 35W
Benbane Hd. 13 A9 55 15N 6 30W
Benbaun 12 D2 53 30N 9 50W
Benbecula 2 H3 57 26N 7 21W
Benderloch 4 A5 56 30N 5 22W
Beneraird 4 D6 55 4N 4 57W
Bennane Hd. 4 D6 55 8N 4 59W
Bentley 7 E6 53 33N 1 9W
Benwee Hd. 12 C2 54 20N 9 50W
Berkeley 8 C4 51 41N 2 28W
Berkhamsted 9 C7 51 45N 0 33W
Berkshire Downs 8 C5 51 30N 1 30W
Berry Hd. 11 G7 50 24N 3 29W
Berst Ness 3 D12 59 16N 3 0W
Bertraghboy B. 14 B3 53 22N 9 54W
Berwick-upon-Tweed 6 A5 55 47N 2 0W
Berwyn Mts. 10 B7 52 54N 3 26W
Betws-y-Coed 10 A6 53 4N 3 49W
Beverley 7 E8 53 52N 0 26W
Bewdley 8 B4 52 23N 2 19W
Bexhill 9 E9 50 51N 0 29 E
Bexley 9 D9 51 26N 0 10 E
Bicester 8 C6 51 53N 1 9W
Biddulph 7 F4 53 8N 2 11W
Bidean nam Bian 4 A5 56 39N 5 6W
Bideford 11 E5 51 1N 4 13W
Bideford B. = Barnstaple B. 11 E5 51 5N 4 20W
Bigbury B. 11 G6 50 18N 3 58W
Biggar 5 C8 55 38N 3 31W
Biggleswade 9 B8 52 6N 0 16W
Billericay 9 C9 51 38N 0 25 E
Billinge Hill 7 E3 53 32N 2 42W
Billingham 6 C6 54 36N 1 18W
Billingshurst 9 D8 51 2N 0 28W
Bilston 7 G4 52 34N 2 5W
Bingley 7 E5 53 51N 1 50W
Birdlip 8 C4 51 50N 2 7W
Birkenhead 7 F2 53 24N 3 1W
Birmingham 8 B5 52 30N 1 55W
Birr 14 B7 53 7N 7 55W
Birtley 6 C5 54 53N 1 34W
Bishop Auckland 6 C5 54 40N 1 40W
Bishop's Stortford 9 C9 51 52N 0 11 E
Bishop's Waltham 8 E6 50 57N 1 13W
Bla Bheinn 2 H5 57 14N 6 7W
Black Combe 6 D2 54 16N 3 20W
Black Hd., *Ant.* 13 B10 54 56N 5 42W
Black Hd., *Clare* 14 B4 53 9N 9 18W
Black Hd., *Corn.* 11 H3 50 0N 5 6W
Black Isle 3 G9 57 35N 4 15W
Black Mts. 10 D7 51 52N 3 5W
Black Mt. = Mynydd Du 10 D6 51 45N 3 45W
Blackburn 7 E4 53 44N 2 30W
Blackdown Hill 8 D7 51 4N 0 41W
Blackdown Hills 8 E2 50 57N 3 15W
Blackhill 7 E5 53 32N 1 53W
Blackhope Scar 5 C9 55 44N 3 5W
Blackmoor Vale 8 E4 50 54N 2 28W
Blackpool 7 E2 53 48N 3 3W
Blacksod B. 12 C2 54 6N 10 0W
Blacksod Pt. 12 C1 54 7N 10 5W
Blackstairs Mt. 15 C9 52 33N 6 50W
Blackwater →, *Essex* 9 C10 51 44N 0 53 E
Blackwater →, *Munst.* 14 E7 51 55N 7 50W
Blackwater →, *Tyrone* 13 B8 54 31N 6 35W
Blackwood 10 D7 51 40N 3 13W
Blaenau Ffestiniog 10 B6 52 59N 3 57W
Blaenau Gwent □ 10 D7 51 47N 3 12W
Blaenavon 10 D7 51 46N 3 5W
Blaina 10 D7 51 46N 3 10W
Blair Atholl 3 J10 56 46N 3 50W
Blairgowrie 5 A9 56 36N 3 20W
Blakeney 9 A11 52 57N 1 0 E
Blandford Forum 8 E4 50 52N 2 10W
Blarney 14 E5 51 57N 8 35W
Blaydon 6 C5 54 56N 1 47W
Bletchley 9 C7 51 59N 0 44W
Bloody Foreland 12 A5 55 10N 8 18W
Bluemull Sd. 2 A16 60 45N 1 0W
Blyth 6 B5 55 8N 1 32W
Blyth Bridge 7 G4 52 58N 2 4W
Boderg, L. 12 D6 53 55N 8 0W
Bodmin 11 G4 50 28N 4 44W
Bodmin Moor 11 F4 50 33N 4 36W
Boggeragh Mts. 14 D5 52 2N 8 55W
Bognor Regis 9 E7 50 47N 0 40W
Bogrie Hill 5 D8 55 8N 3 54W
Boisdale, L. 2 H3 57 9N 7 19W
Boldon 6 C6 54 57N 1 26W
Bolsover 7 F6 53 14N 1 18W
Bolt Hd. 11 G6 50 13N 3 48W
Bolt Tail 11 G6 50 13N 3 55W
Bolton 7 E4 53 35N 2 26W
Bolus Hd. 14 E2 51 48N 10 20W
Bo'ness 5 B8 56 1N 3 38W
Bonnyrigg 5 C9 55 52N 3 8W
Bootle, *Cumb.* 6 D2 54 17N 3 24W
Bootle, *Mersey.* 7 F2 53 28N 3 1W
Borehamwood 9 C8 51 40N 0 15W
Boroughbridge 6 D6 54 6N 1 23W
Borth 10 C5 52 29N 4 3W
Boscastle 11 F4 50 42N 4 42W
Boston 7 G8 52 59N 0 2W
Bourne 7 G8 52 46N 0 22W
Bournemouth 8 E5 50 43N 1 53W
Bourton-on-the-Water 8 C5 51 53N 1 45W
Bowland, Forest of 7 E3 54 0N 2 30W
Bowmore 4 C3 55 45N 6 18W
Bowness-on-Windermere 6 D3 54 22N 2 56W
Box Hill 9 D8 51 16N 0 16W
Boyle 12 D5 53 58N 8 19W
Boyne → 13 D9 53 43N 6 15W
Bracadale, L. 2 H4 57 20N 6 30W
Brackley 8 B6 52 3N 1 9W
Bracknell 9 D7 51 24N 0 45W
Bradda Hd. 13 C12 54 6N 4 46W
Bradford 7 E5 53 47N 1 45W
Bradford on Avon 8 D4 51 20N 2 15W
Bradwell-on-Sea 9 C10 51 44N 0 55 E
Braemar 3 J11 57 0N 3 25W
Braeriach 3 H10 57 4N 3 44W
Braich-y-pwll 10 B4 52 47N 4 46W
Braintree 9 C10 51 53N 0 34 E
Brampton 6 C3 54 56N 2 43W
Branderburgh 3 G11 57 43N 3 17W
Brandon, *Durham* 6 C5 54 46N 1 37W
Brandon, *Kilk.* 15 C9 52 31N 6 58W
Brandon, *Suffolk* 9 B10 52 27N 0 37 E
Brandon B. 14 D2 52 17N 10 8W
Brandon Mt. 14 D2 52 15N 10 15W
Brandon Pt. 14 D2 52 18N 10 10W
Braunton 11 E5 51 6N 4 9W
Bray 15 B10 53 12N 6 6W
Bray Hd., *Kerry* 14 E2 51 52N 10 26W
Bray Hd., *Wick.* 15 B10 53 12N 6 2W
Breadalbane 4 A7 56 30N 4 15W
Brechin 5 A10 56 44N 2 40W
Breckland 9 B10 52 30N 0 40 E
Brecon 10 D7 51 57N 3 23W
Brecon Beacons 10 D7 51 53N 3 27W
Bredon Hill 8 B4 52 3N 2 2W
Brendon Hills 8 D2 51 6N 3 25W
Brenig, L. 10 A6 53 6N 3 30W
Brent 9 C8 51 33N 0 18W
Brentwood 9 C9 51 37N 0 19 E
Bressay Sd. 2 B15 60 8N 1 10W
Brianne, L. 10 C6 52 8N 3 45W
Bridge of Don 3 H13 57 10N 2 8W
Bridgend 11 D6 51 30N 3 35W
Bridgnorth 7 G4 52 33N 2 25W
Bridgwater 8 D3 51 7N 3 0W
Bridlington 6 D8 54 6N 0 11W
Bridport 8 E3 50 43N 2 45W
Brierfield 7 E4 53 49N 2 15W
Brierley Hill 8 B4 52 29N 2 7W
Brigg 7 E8 53 33N 0 30W
Brighouse 7 E5 53 42N 1 47W
Brightlingsea 9 C11 51 49N 1 1 E
Brighton 9 E8 50 50N 0 9W
Bristol 8 D3 51 26N 2 35W
Bristol Channel 11 E4 51 18N 4 30W
Brixham 11 G6 50 24N 3 31W
Brize Norton 8 C5 51 46N 1 35W
Broad B. 2 F5 58 14N 6 16W
Broad Haven 12 C2 54 20N 9 55W
Broad Law 5 C9 55 31N 3 22W
Broad Sd. 11 H1 49 56N 6 19W
Broadstairs 9 D11 51 21N 1 28 E
Broadway 8 B5 52 2N 1 51W
Broadwindsor 8 E3 50 49N 2 49W
Brockenhurst 8 E5 50 49N 1 34W
Brodick 4 C5 55 34N 5 9W
Bromfield 8 B3 52 25N 2 45W
Bromley 9 D9 51 20N 0 5 E
Bromsgrove 8 B4 52 20N 2 3W
Bromyard 8 B4 52 12N 2 30W
Broom, L. 2 G7 57 55N 5 15W
Brora 3 F10 58 3N 3 50W
Brosna → 14 B7 53 8N 8 0W
Brotton 6 C7 54 34N 0 55W
Brough 6 C4 54 32N 2 19W
Brough Hd. 3 D11 59 8N 3 20W
Broughty Ferry 5 B10 56 29N 2 50W
Brown Clee Hill 8 B3 52 28N 2 36W
Brown Willy 11 F4 50 35N 4 34W
Brownhills 7 G5 52 38N 1 57W
Broxburn 5 C9 55 56N 3 23W
Bruernish Pt. 2 J3 57 0N 7 22W
Bruton 8 D4 51 6N 2 28W
Brynmawr 10 D7 51 48N 3 11W
Buchan 3 G13 57 32N 2 8W
Buchan Ness 3 H14 57 29N 1 48W
Buckfastleigh 11 G6 50 28N 3 47W
Buckhaven 5 B9 56 10N 3 2W
Buckie 3 G12 57 40N 2 58W
Buckingham 9 C7 52 0N 0 59W
Buckinghamshire □ 9 C7 51 50N 0 55W
Buckley 10 A7 53 10N 3 5W
Buddon Ness 5 B10 56 29N 2 42W
Bude 11 F4 50 49N 4 33W
Budle B. 6 A5 55 37N 1 45W
Budleigh Salterton 11 F7 50 37N 3 19W
Buie, L. 4 B4 56 20N 5 55W
Builth Wells 10 C7 52 10N 3 26W
Bulkington 8 B6 52 29N 1 25W
Bunclody 15 C9 52 40N 6 40W
Buncrana 12 A7 55 8N 7 28W
Bundoran 12 C5 54 24N 8 17W
Bungay 9 B11 52 27N 1 26 E
Burford 8 C5 51 48N 1 38W
Burgess Hill 9 E8 50 57N 0 7W
Burghead B. 3 G10 57 40N 3 33W
Burnham 9 C7 51 32N 0 40W
Burnham Market 9 A10 52 57N 0 43 E
Burnham-on-Crouch 9 C10 51 37N 0 50 E
Burnham-on-Sea 8 D3 51 14N 3 0W
Burnley 7 E4 53 47N 2 14W
Burntisland 5 B9 56 4N 3 14W
Burntwood 7 G5 52 41N 1 55W
Burrow Hd. 4 E7 54 40N 4 23W
Burry Port 10 D5 51 41N 4 17W
Burscough Bridge 7 E3 53 36N 2 52W
Burton Latimer 9 B7 52 23N 0 41W
Burton upon Trent 7 G5 52 48N 1 39W
Bury 7 E4 53 36N 2 19W
Bury St. Edmunds 9 B10 52 15N 0 42 E
Bushey 9 C8 51 38N 0 20W
Bushmills 13 A8 55 14N 6 32W
Bute 4 C5 55 48N 5 2W
Bute, Kyles of 4 C5 55 55N 5 10W
Bute, Sd. of 4 C5 55 43N 5 8W
Buttevant 14 D5 52 14N 8 40W
Buxton 7 F5 53 16N 1 54W
Byfleet 9 D7 51 20N 0 32W

C

Cader Idris 10 B6 52 43N 3 56W
Caernarfon 10 A5 53 8N 4 17W
Caernarfon B. 10 A4 53 4N 4 40W
Caernarvon = Caernarfon 10 A5 53 8N 4 17W
Caerphilly 11 D7 51 34N 3 13W
Caha Mts. 14 E3 51 45N 9 40W
Caher 14 D7 52 23N 7 56W
Cahirciveen 14 E2 51 57N 10 13W
Cahore Pt. 15 C10 52 34N 6 11W
Cairn Gorm 3 H10 57 7N 3 40W
Cairn Table 5 C8 55 30N 4 0W
Cairngorm Mts. 3 H10 57 6N 3 42W
Cairnsmore of Fleet 4 E7 54 59N 4 20W
Caister-on-Sea 9 A12 52 38N 1 43 E
Caithness 3 F10 58 25N 3 35W
Caithness, Ord of 3 F10 58 9N 3 37W
Calder → 7 E6 53 44N 1 21W
Caledonian Canal 2 J7 56 50N 5 6W
Caliach Pt. 4 A3 56 37N 6 20W
Callan 15 C8 52 33N 7 25W
Callander 4 B7 56 15N 4 14W
Calne 8 D5 51 26N 2 0W
Cam → 9 B9 52 21N 0 16 E
Camberley 9 D7 51 20N 0 44W
Camborne 11 G3 50 13N 5 18W
Cambrian Mts. 10 C6 52 25N 3 52W
Cambridge 9 B9 52 13N 0 8 E
Cambridgeshire □ 9 B9 52 12N 0 7 E
Camden 9 C8 51 33N 0 10W
Camelford 11 F4 50 37N 4 41W
Campbeltown 4 D4 55 25N 5 36W
Canbane East 13 D7 53 45N 7 6W
Canna, Sd. of 2 H5 57 1N 6 30W
Cannock 7 G4 52 42N 2 2W
Cannock Chase 7 G5 52 43N 2 0W
Canterbury 9 D11 51 17N 1 5 E
Canvey 9 C10 51 32N 0 35 E
Caolisport, L. 4 C4 55 54N 5 40W
Cardiff 11 E7 51 28N 3 11W
Cardigan 10 C4 52 6N 4 41W
Cardigan B. 10 B4 52 30N 4 30W
Carisbrooke 8 E6 50 42N 1 19W
Carlingford L. 13 C9 54 2N 6 5W
Carlisle 6 C3 54 54N 2 55W
Carlow 15 C9 52 50N 6 58W
Carlow □ 15 C9 52 43N 6 50W
Carlton 7 G6 52 58N 1 6W
Carluke 5 C8 55 44N 3 50W
Carmarthen 10 D5 51 52N 4 20W
Carmarthen B. 10 D4 51 40N 4 30W
Carmarthenshire □ 10 D5 51 55N 4 13W
Carmel Hd. 10 A4 53 24N 4 34W
Carn Ban 3 H9 57 6N 4 15W
Carn Eige 2 H7 57 17N 5 9W
Carn Glas-choire 3 H10 57 20N 3 50W
Carn Mor 3 H11 57 14N 3 13W
Carn na Saobhaidhe 3 H9 57 12N 4 20W
Carndonagh 13 A7 55 15N 7 16W
Carnedd Llewelyn 10 A6 53 9N 3 58W
Carnforth 6 D3 54 8N 2 47W
Carnoustie 5 A10 56 30N 2 41W
Carnsore Pt. 15 D10 52 10N 6 20W
Carra, L. 12 D3 53 41N 9 12W
Carrauntoohill 14 E3 52 0N 9 49W
Carrick 4 D6 55 12N 4 38W
Carrick-on-Shannon 12 D5 53 57N 8 7W
Carrick-on-Suir 15 D8 52 22N 7 30W
Carrickfergus 13 B10 54 43N 5 50W
Carrickmacross 13 D8 53 58N 6 43W
Carrigan Hd. 12 B4 54 38N 8 40W
Carron → 2 H7 57 30N 5 30W
Carron, L. 2 H6 57 22N 5 35W
Carstairs 5 C8 55 42N 3 41W
Cashel 14 C7 52 31N 7 53W
Cashla B. 14 B3 53 12N 9 37W
Castle Cary 8 D3 51 5N 2 32W
Castle Donington 7 G6 52 50N 1 20W
Castle Douglas 5 E8 54 57N 3 57W
Castlebar 12 D3 53 52N 9 17W
Castleblaney 13 C8 54 7N 6 44W
Castlederg 12 B6 54 43N 7 35W
Castleford 7 E6 53 43N 1 21W
Castleisland 14 D4 52 14N 9 28W
Castlemaine Harbour 14 D3 52 8N 9 50W
Castlepollard 12 D7 53 40N 7 20W
Castlerea 12 D5 53 47N 8 30W
Castletown 13 C12 54 4N 4 40W
Castletown Bearhaven 14 E3 51 40N 9 54W
Caterham 9 D8 51 16N 0 4W
Cavan 12 D7 54 0N 7 22W
Cavan □ 13 D7 53 58N 7 10W
Ceananus Mor 13 D8 53 42N 6 53W
Cefn-mawr 10 B7 52 58N 3 3W
Cefnffordd 10 D6 51 42N 3 39W
Celbridge 15 B9 53 20N 6 33W
Cellar Hd. 2 F5 58 25N 6 10W
Celyn, L. 10 B6 52 56N 3 42W
Cemaes Hd. 10 C4 52 7N 4 44W
Ceredigion □ 10 C6 52 16N 3 58W
Chadwell St. Mary 9 D9 51 28N 0 22 E
Chandler's Ford 8 E6 50 59N 1 23W
Channel Is. 11 J9 49 30N 2 40W
Chapel en le Frith 7 F5 53 19N 1 54W
Chard 8 E3 50 52N 2 59W
Charlbury 8 C6 51 52N 1 29W
Charlestown of Aberlour 3 H11 57 27N 3 13W
Charleville = Rath Luirc 14 D5 52 21N 8 40W
Charlton Kings 8 C4 51 52N 2 3W
Charnwood Forest 7 G6 52 43N 1 18W
Chatham 9 D10 51 22N 0 32 E
Chatteris 9 B9 52 27N 0 3 E
Cheadle, *Gt. Man.* 7 F4 53 23N 2 14W
Cheadle, *Staffs.* 7 G5 52 59N 1 59W
Cheddar 8 D3 51 16N 2 47W
Chelmsford 9 C9 51 44N 0 29 E
Cheltenham 8 C4 51 55N 2 5W
Chepstow 10 D8 51 38N 2 40W
Chertsey 9 D7 51 23N 0 30W
Cherwell → 8 C6 51 46N 1 18W
Chesham 9 C7 51 42N 0 36W
Cheshire □ 7 F3 53 14N 2 30W
Cheshunt 9 C8 51 42N 0 1W
Chesil Beach 11 F8 50 37N 2 33W
Chester 7 F3 53 12N 2 53W
Chester-le-Street 6 C5 54 53N 1 34W
Chesterfield 7 F6 53 14N 1 26W
Cheviot Hills 6 B3 55 20N 2 30W
Chichester 9 E7 50 50N 0 47W
Chicken Hd. 2 F5 58 10N 6 15W
Chigwell 9 C9 51 37N 0 4 E
Chiltern Hills 9 C7 51 44N 0 42W
Chippenham 8 D4 51 27N 2 7W
Chipping Norton 8 C5 51 56N 1 32W
Chipping Ongar 9 C9 51 42N 0 11 E
Chipping Sodbury 8 C4 51 31N 2 23W
Chobham 9 D7 51 20N 0 36W
Chorley 7 E3 53 39N 2 39W
Chorleywood 9 C8 51 39N 0 29W
Christchurch 8 E5 50 44N 1 45W
Chulmleigh 11 F6 50 55N 3 52W
Church Stretton 8 A3 52 32N 2 49W
Churchdown 8 C4 51 53N 2 9W
Chwarel y Fan 10 D7 51 56N 3 5W
Cill Chainnigh = Kilkenny 15 C8 52 40N 7 17W
Cinderford 8 C3 51 49N 2 30W
Cirencester 8 C5 51 43N 1 59W
Clach Leathad 4 A6 56 36N 4 52W
Clackmannan □ 5 B8 56 9N 3 49W
Clacton-on-Sea 9 C11 51 47N 1 10 E
Clara 15 B7 53 20N 7 38W
Clare □ 14 C4 52 45N 9 0W
Clare → 14 B4 53 22N 9 5W
Clare I. 12 D2 53 48N 10 0W
Clay Cross 7 F6 53 11N 1 26W
Clear, C. 14 F3 51 26N 9 30W
Cleator Moor 6 C2 54 31N 3 30W
Clee Hills 8 B3 52 26N 2 35W
Cleethorpes 7 E8 53 33N 0 2W
Cleeve Cloud 8 C5 51 56N 1 57W
Clent Hills 8 B4 52 25N 2 6W
Clevedon 8 D3 51 26N 2 52W
Cleveland Hills 6 D6 54 25N 1 11W
Cleveleys 7 E2 53 53N 3 3W
Clew B. 12 D2 53 54N 9 50W
Clifden 12 E1 53 30N 10 2W
Clifden B. 12 E1 53 29N 10 5W
Clift Sd. 2 B15 60 4N 1 17W
Clisham 2 G4 57 57N 6 50W
Clitheroe 7 E4 53 52N 2 23W
Clogher Hd. 13 D9 53 48N 6 15W
Clonakilty 14 E5 51 37N 8 53W
Clondalkin 15 B10 53 20N 6 25W
Clones 13 C7 54 10N 7 13W
Clonmel 15 D7 52 22N 7 42W
Clovelly 11 F5 51 0N 4 25W
Clun Forest 8 B2 52 27N 3 7W
Clwyd → 10 A6 53 20N 3 30W
Clydach 10 D6 51 42N 3 54W
Clyde → 4 C7 55 56N 4 29W
Clyde, Firth of 4 D6 55 20N 5 0W
Clydebank 4 C7 55 54N 4 25W
Clydesdale 5 C8 55 42N 3 50W
Clywedog, L. 10 C6 52 29N 3 40W
Cnoc Moy 4 D4 55 23N 5 44W
Coalisland 13 B8 54 33N 6 42W
Coalville 7 G6 52 43N 1 21W
Coatbridge 4 C7 55 52N 4 2W
Cóbh 14 E6 51 50N 8 18W
Cockenzie 5 C10 55 58N 2 59W
Cockermouth 6 C2 54 40N 3 22W
Cods Hd. 14 E2 51 40N 10 7W
Coigach 2 G7 57 55N 5 10W
Colchester 9 C10 51 54N 0 55 E
Cold Fell 6 C3 54 54N 2 40W
Coldstream 5 C11 55 39N 2 14W
Coleraine 13 A8 55 8N 6 40W
Coleshill 8 B5 52 30N 1 42W
Colgrave Sd. 2 A16 60 35N 1 0W
Colinton 5 C9 55 54N 3 15W
Coll 4 A2 56 40N 6 35W
Collier Law 6 C5 54 47N 1 59W
Collooney 12 C5 54 11N 8 28W
Colne 7 E4 53 51N 2 11W
Colonsay 4 B3 56 4N 6 12W
Colwyn Bay 10 A6 53 17N 3 44W
Combe Martin 11 E5 51 12N 4 2W
Comber 13 B10 54 33N 5 45W
Comeragh Mts. 15 D7 52 17N 7 35W
Congleton 7 F4 53 10N 2 12W
Conisbrough 7 F6 53 29N 1 12W
Coniston 6 D2 54 22N 3 6W
Conn, L. 12 C3 54 3N 9 15W
Connacht 12 D4 53 45N 8 40W
Connah's Quay 10 A7 53 13N 3 6W
Connel 4 B5 56 27N 5 24W
Connemara 12 E2 53 29N 9 45W
Cononbridge 3 G9 57 32N 4 30W
Consett 6 C5 54 52N 1 50W
Conway = Conwy 10 A6 53 17N 3 50W
Conwy 10 A6 53 17N 3 50W
Conwy □ 10 A6 53 10N 3 44W
Conwy B. 10 A6 53 17N 3 57W
Cookstown 13 B8 54 40N 6 43W
Cootehill 13 C7 54 5N 7 5W
Coquet → 6 B5 55 18N 1 45W
Corbridge 6 C5 54 58N 2 0W
Corby 9 A7 52 30N 0 41W
Corby Glen 7 G7 52 49N 0 31W
Corcaigh = Cork 14 E6 51 54N 8 30W
Corfe Castle 8 E4 50 37N 2 3W
Cork 14 E6 51 54N 8 30W
Cork □ 14 E5 51 50N 8 50W
Cork Harbour 14 E6 51 46N 8 16W
Corn Hill 12 D6 53 48N 7 43W
Cornwall □ 11 G4 50 26N 4 40W
Cornwall, C. 11 G2 50 8N 5 42W
Corrib, L. 14 B4 53 5N 9 10W
Corringham 9 C10 51 30N 0 26 E
Corry Mt. 12 C5 54 8N 8 8W
Corryvreckan, G. of 4 B4 56 10N 5 44W
Corsewall Pt. 4 E5 55 0N 5 10W
Corsham 8 D4 51 25N 2 11W
Coseley 7 G4 52 33N 2 6W
Cot Nab 7 D7 54 1N 0 45W
Cotswold Hills 8 C4 51 42N 2 10W
Cottingham 7 E8 53 47N 0 23W
Coul Pt. 4 C2 55 50N 6 30W
Coupar Angus 5 A9 56 33N 3 17W
Courtmacsherry B. 14 E5 51 37N 8 37W
Cove 4 B6 56 2N 4 50W
Coventry 8 B6 52 25N 1 28W
Cow Green Res. 6 C4 54 40N 2 20W
Cowal 4 B5 56 5N 5 8W
Cowdenbeath 5 B9 56 7N 3 20W
Cowes 8 E6 50 45N 1 18W
Craigavon 13 C9 54 28N 6 20W
Craignish, L. 4 B4 56 11N 5 32W
Crail 5 B10 56 16N 2 38W
Cramlington 6 B5 55 5N 1 36W
Cranborne Chase 8 E4 50 56N 2 6W
Cranbrook 9 D10 51 6N 0 33 E
Cranfield Pt. 13 C9 54 1N 6 3W
Cranleigh 9 D8 51 8N 0 29W
Crawley 9 D8 51 7N 0 10W
Creag Meagaidh 3 J8 56 57N 4 38W
Crediton 11 F6 50 47N 3 39W
Cree → 4 E7 54 51N 4 24W
Creran, L. 4 A5 56 30N 5 20W
Crewe 7 F4 53 6N 2 28W
Crewkerne 8 E3 50 53N 2 48W
Criccieth 10 B5 52 55N 4 15W
Cricklade 8 C5 51 38N 1 50W
Crieff 5 B8 56 22N 3 50W
Criffell 5 E8 54 56N 3 38W
Crinan Canal 4 B5 56 4N 5 30W
Croagh Patrick 12 D2 53 46N 9 40W
Croghan Mt. 15 C10 52 48N 6 20W
Crohy Hd. 12 B5 54 55N 8 28W
Cromarty 3 G9 57 40N 4 2W
Cromarty Firth 3 G9 57 40N 4 15W
Cromdale, Hills of 3 H11 57 20N 3 28W
Cromer 9 A11 52 56N 1 18 E
Crook 6 C5 54 43N 1 45W
Crosby 7 E2 53 30N 3 2W
Cross Fell 6 C4 54 44N 2 29W
Crossfarnoge Pt. 15 D9 52 10N 6 37W
Crosshaven 14 E6 51 48N 8 19W
Crossmaglen 13 C8 54 5N 6 37W
Crow Hd. 14 E2 51 34N 10 9W
Crow Sd. 11 H1 49 56N 6 16W
Crowborough 9 D9 51 3N 0 9 E
Crowthorne 9 D7 51 22N 0 50W
Croydon 9 D8 51 18N 0 5W
Cruden Bay 3 H14 57 25N 1 50W
Cuckfield 9 D8 51 1N 0 8W
Cuffley 9 C8 51 43N 0 9W
Cuilcagh 12 C6 54 12N 7 50W
Cuillin Hills 2 H5 57 14N 6 15W
Cuillin Sd. 2 H5 57 4N 6 20W
Cullen 3 G12 57 45N 2 50W
Cullin, L. 12 D3 53 58N 9 12W
Culloden 3 H9 57 29N 4 7W
Cullompton 11 F7 50 52N 3 23W
Culm → 11 F6 50 46N 3 31W
Culter Fell 5 C8 55 35N 3 30W
Cults 3 H13 57 8N 2 10W
Culvain 2 J7 56 55N 5 19W
Cumbernauld 5 C8 55 57N 3 58W
Cumbrae Is. 4 C6 55 46N 4 54W
Cumbria □ 6 C3 54 35N 2 55W
Cumbrian Mts. 6 D2 54 30N 3 0W
Cumnock 4 D7 55 27N 4 18W
Cunninghame 4 C6 55 38N 4 35W
Cupar 5 B9 56 20N 3 3W
Cupidstown Hill 15 B9 53 15N 6 31W
Currane, L. 14 E2 51 50N 10 8W
Cwmbran 10 D7 51 39N 3 3W

D

Daingean 15 B8 53 18N 7 15W
Dalbeattie 5 E8 54 55N 3 50W
Dalkeith 5 C9 55 54N 3 5W
Dalmellington 4 D7 55 20N 4 25W
Dalry 4 C6 55 44N 4 42W
Dalton-in-Furness 6 D2 54 9N 3 10W
Danbury 9 C10 51 43N 0 34 E
Darlington 6 C5 54 33N 1 33W
Dart → 11 G6 50 24N 3 36W
Dartford 9 D9 51 26N 0 15 E
Dartmoor 11 F6 50 36N 4 0W
Dartmouth 11 G6 50 21N 3 35W
Darton 7 E5 53 36N 1 32W

Place names on the turquoise-coded World Map section are to be found in the index at the rear of the book.

Darvel 4 C7 55 37N 4 20W
Darwen 7 E4 53 42N 2 29W
Daventry 8 B6 52 16N 1 10W
Dawlish 11 F7 50 34N 3 28W
Dawros Hd. 12 B4 54 48N 8 32W
Deal 9 D11 51 13N 1 25 E
Dean, Forest of 8 C3 51 50N 2 35W
Dearne 7 E6 53 32N 1 17W
Dee →, *Aberds.* 3 H13 57 4N 2 7W
Dee →, *Flints.* 10 A7 53 15N 3 7W
Deer Sd. 3 E12 58 58N 2 50W
Denbigh 10 A7 53 12N 3 26W
Denbighshire □ 10 A7 53 8N 3 22W
Denby Dale 7 E5 53 35N 1 40W
Dennis Hd. 3 D13 59 23N 2 26W
Denny 5 B8 56 1N 3 55W
Denton 7 F4 53 26N 2 10W
Derby 7 G6 52 27N 1 28W
Derbyshire □ 7 F6 53 0N 1 30W
Derg, L. 14 C6 53 0N 8 20W
Derravaragh, L. 12 D7 53 38N 7 22W
Derry =
Londonderry 12 B7 55 0N 7 23W
Derry → 15 C9 52 43N 6 35W
Derrynsaggart Mts. 14 E4 51 58N 9 15W
Derwent →,
Derby 7 G6 52 53N 1 17W
Derwent →,
N. Yorks. 7 E7 53 45N 0 57W
Desborough 9 B7 52 27N 0 50W
Deveron → 3 G12 57 40N 2 31W
Devilsbit 14 C7 52 50N 7 58W
Devizes 8 D5 51 21N 2 0W
Devon □ 11 F6 50 50N 3 40W
Devonport 11 G5 50 23N 4 11W
Dewsbury 7 E5 53 42N 1 38W
Didcot 8 C6 51 36N 1 14W
Dinas Hd. 10 C4 52 2N 4 56W
Dingle 14 D2 52 9N 10 17W
Dingle B. 14 D2 52 3N 10 20W
Dingwall 3 G9 57 36N 4 26W
Dinnington 7 F6 53 21N 1 12W
Diss 9 B11 52 23N 1 6 E
Ditchling Beacon 9 E8 50 49N 0 7W
Dizzard Pt. 11 F4 50 46N 4 38W
Dodman Pt. 11 G4 50 13N 4 49W
Dolgellau 10 B6 52 44N 3 53W
Dolgelley =
Dolgellau 10 B6 52 44N 3 53W
Dollar 5 B8 56 9N 3 41W
Don →, *Aberds.* 3 H13 57 14N 2 5W
Don →,
S. Yorks. 7 E7 53 41N 0 51W
Donaghadee 13 B10 54 38N 5 32W
Doncaster 7 E6 53 31N 1 9W
Donegal 12 B5 54 39N 8 8W
Donegal □ 12 B6 54 53N 8 0W
Donegal B. 12 B4 54 30N 8 35W
Donegal Harbour 12 B5 54 35N 8 15W
Donna Nook 7 F9 53 29N 0 9 E
Dooega Hd. 12 D1 53 54N 10 3W
Doon, L. 4 D7 55 15N 4 22W
Dorchester 8 E4 50 42N 2 28W
Dorking 9 D8 51 14N 0 20W
Dornoch 3 G9 57 52N 4 5W
Dornoch Firth 3 G10 57 52N 4 0W
Dorridge 8 B5 52 22N 1 45W
Dorset □ 8 E4 50 48N 2 25W
Douglas 13 C13 54 9N 4 29W
Doulus Hd. 14 E2 51 57N 10 19W
Doune 4 B7 56 12N 4 3W
Dounreay 3 E10 58 34N 3 44W
Dove → 7 G5 52 51N 1 36W
Dover 9 D11 51 7N 1 19 E
Dovey = Dyfi → 10 B6 52 32N 4 0W
Down □ 13 C10 54 20N 5 47W
Downham Market 9 A9 52 36N 0 22 E
Downpatrick 13 C10 54 20N 5 43W
Downpatrick Hd. 12 C3 54 20N 9 21W
Driffield 7 D8 54 1N 0 25W
Drogheda 13 D9 53 45N 6 20W
Droichead Atha =
Drogheda 13 D9 53 45N 6 20W
Droichead Nua 15 B9 53 11N 6 50W
Droitwich 8 B4 52 16N 2 10W
Dromore 12 B7 54 31N 7 28W
Dronfield 7 F6 53 18N 1 29W
Druridge B. 6 B5 55 16N 1 32W
Drygarn Fawr 10 C6 52 13N 3 39W
Dublin 15 B10 53 20N 6 18W
Dublin □ 15 B10 53 24N 6 20W
Dudley 8 A4 52 30N 2 5W
Dufftown 3 H11 57 26N 3 9W
Dukinfield 7 F4 53 29N 2 5W
Dulas B. 10 A5 53 22N 4 16W
Dumbarton 4 C6 55 58N 4 35W
Dumfries 5 D8 55 4N 3 37W
Dumfries &
Galloway □ 5 D8 55 5N 4 0W
Dún Dealgan =
Dundalk 13 C9 54 1N 6 25W
Dun Laoghaire 15 B10 53 17N 6 9W
Dunaff Hd. 12 A6 55 18N 7 30W
Dunany Pt. 13 D9 53 51N 6 15W
Dunbar 5 C10 56 0N 2 32W
Dunblane 5 B8 56 10N 3 58W
Duncansby Hd. 3 E12 58 39N 3 0W
Dundalk 13 C9 54 1N 6 25W
Dundalk B. 13 D9 53 55N 6 15W
Dundee 5 B10 56 29N 3 0W
Dundrum 13 C10 54 17N 5 50W
Dunfermline 5 B9 56 5N 3 28W
Dungannon 13 B8 54 30N 6 47W
Dungarvan 15 D7 52 6N 7 40W
Dungarvan Harbour 15 D7 52 5N 7 35W
Dungeness 9 E10 50 54N 0 59 E
Dunipace 5 B8 56 4N 3 55W
Dunkeld 5 A8 56 34N 3 36W
Dunkery Beacon 8 D1 51 15N 3 37W
Dúnleary = Dun
Laoghaire 15 B10 53 17N 6 9W
Dunmanway 14 E4 51 43N 9 8W
Dunnet B. 3 E11 58 37N 3 23W
Dunoon 4 C6 55 57N 4 56W
Duns 5 C11 55 47N 2 20W
Dunstable 9 C7 51 53N 0 31W
Dunster 8 D2 51 11N 3 28W
Dunvegan Hd. 2 G4 57 30N 6 42W
Durham 6 C5 54 47N 1 34W
Durham □ 6 C5 54 42N 1 45W
Durlston Hd. 8 E5 50 35N 1 58W
Durness 3 E8 58 34N 4 45W
Dursley 8 C4 51 41N 2 21W
Dury Voe 2 B15 60 20N 1 8W
Dyce 3 H13 57 12N 2 11W
Dyfi → 10 B6 52 32N 4 0W
Dymchurch 9 D11 51 2N 1 0 E

E

Ealing 9 C8 51 30N 0 19W
Earadale Pt. 4 D4 55 24N 5 50W
Earby 7 E4 53 55N 2 8W
Earl Shilton 7 G6 52 35N 1 20W
Earlsferry 5 B10 56 11N 2 50W
Earn → 5 B9 56 20N 3 19W
Earn, L. 4 B7 56 23N 4 14W
Easington 6 C6 54 50N 1 24W
Easington Colliery 6 C6 54 49N 1 19W
East Ayrshire □ 4 D7 55 26N 4 11W
East Cowes 8 E6 50 45N 1 17W
East Dereham 9 A10 52 40N 0 57 E
East
Dunbartonshire □
4 C7 55 57N 4 20W
East Grinstead 9 D9 51 8N 0 0 E
East Kilbride 4 C7 55 46N 4 10W
East Linton 5 C10 56 0N 2 40W
East Lothian □ 5 C10 55 57N 2 48W
East
Renfrewshire □ 4 C7 55 48N 4 23W
East Retford =
Retford 7 F7 53 19N 0 55W
East Riding of
Yorkshire □ 7 E8 53 52N 0 26W
East Sussex □ 9 E9 51 0N 0 20 E
East Wittering 9 E7 50 46N 0 53W
Eastbourne 9 E9 50 46N 0 18 E
Easter Ross 3 G8 57 50N 4 35W
Eastleigh 8 E6 50 58N 1 21W
Eastwood 7 F6 53 2N 1 17W
Eaval 2 G3 57 33N 7 12W
Ebbw Vale 10 D7 51 47N 3 12W
Eccleshall 7 G4 52 52N 2 14W
Eckington 7 F6 53 19N 1 21W
Eday Sd. 3 D12 59 12N 2 45W
Eddrachillis B. 2 F7 58 16N 5 10W
Eddystone 11 G5 50 11N 4 16W
Eden → 6 C2 54 57N 3 2W
Edenbridge 9 D9 51 12N 0 4 E
Edenderry 15 B8 53 21N 7 3W
Edge Hill 8 B6 52 7N 1 28W
Edinburgh 5 C9 55 57N 3 12W
Egham 9 D7 51 25N 0 33W
Egremont 6 D1 54 28N 3 33W
Eigg 2 J5 56 54N 6 10W
Eil, L. 2 J7 56 50N 5 15W
Eishort, L. 2 H6 57 9N 6 0W
Elan → 10 C6 52 17N 3 30W
Elan Valley
Reservoirs 10 C6 52 12N 3 42W
Elgin 3 G11 57 39N 3 20W
Elie 5 B10 56 11N 2 50W
Elland 7 E5 53 41N 1 49W
Ellesmere Port 7 F3 53 17N 2 55W
Ellon 3 H13 57 21N 2 5W
Ely 9 B9 52 24N 0 16 E
Emsworth 9 E7 50 51N 0 56W
Enard B. 2 F7 58 5N 5 20W
Enfield 9 C8 51 39N 0 4W
Ennell, L. 12 E7 53 29N 7 25W
Ennis 14 C5 52 51N 8 59W
Enniscorthy 15 D9 52 30N 6 35W
Enniskillen 12 C6 54 20N 7 40W
Ennistimon 14 C4 52 56N 9 18W
Eport, L. 2 G3 57 33N 7 10W
Epping 9 C9 51 42N 0 8 E
Epsom 9 D8 51 19N 0 16W
Eriboll, L. 3 F8 58 28N 4 41W
Ericht, L. 3 J9 56 50N 4 25W
Eriskay, Sd. of 2 H3 57 5N 7 20W
Erisort L. 2 F4 58 5N 6 30W
Erne → 12 C5 54 30N 8 16W
Erne, Lower L. 12 C6 54 26N 7 46W
Erne, Upper L. 12 C7 54 14N 7 22W
Errigal 12 A5 55 2N 8 8W
Erris Hd. 12 C2 54 19N 10 0W
Erskine 4 C7 55 52N 4 27W
Esha Ness 2 A14 60 30N 1 36W
Esher 9 D8 51 21N 0 22W
Esk → 5 E9 54 58N 3 4W
Eskdale 5 D9 55 12N 3 4W
Essex □ 9 C9 51 55N 0 30 E
Eston 6 C6 54 33N 1 6W
Etive, L. 4 A5 56 30N 5 12W
Ettrick Water → 5 C10 55 31N 2 55W
Evesham 8 B5 52 6N 1 57W
Ewe, L. 2 G6 57 49N 5 38W
Ewell 9 D8 51 20N 0 15W
Exe → 11 F7 50 38N 3 27W
Exeter 11 F6 50 43N 3 31W
Exmoor 11 E6 51 10N 3 59W
Exmouth 11 F7 50 37N 3 26W
Eye, *Cambs.* 7 G8 52 36N 0 11W
Eye, *Suffolk* 9 B11 52 19N 1 9 E
Eye Pen. 2 F5 58 13N 6 10W
Eyemouth 5 C11 55 53N 2 5W
Eynhallow Sd. 3 D11 59 8N 3 7W
Eynort, L. 2 H3 57 13N 7 18W

F

Fair Hd. 13 A9 55 14N 6 10W
Fair Isle 2 C14 59 32N 1 36W
Fairford 8 C5 51 42N 1 48W
Fakenham 9 A10 52 50N 0 51 E
Faldingworth 7 F8 53 21N 0 22W
Falkirk 5 B8 56 1N 3 47W
Falkland 5 B9 56 15N 3 13W
Falmouth 11 G3 50 9N 5 5W
Fanad Hd. 12 A6 55 17N 7 40W
Faraid Hd. 3 E8 58 35N 4 48W
Fareham 8 E6 50 52N 1 11W
Faringdon 8 C5 51 39N 1 34W
Farnborough 9 D7 51 17N 0 46W
Farne Is. 6 A5 55 38N 1 37W
Farnham 9 D7 51 13N 0 49W
Farnworth 7 E4 53 33N 2 24W
Fauldhouse 5 C8 55 50N 3 44W
Faversham 9 D10 51 18N 0 54 E
Fawley 8 E6 50 49N 1 20W
Feale → 14 D3 52 26N 9 40W
Featherbed Moss 7 E5 53 31N 1 56W
Felixstowe 9 C11 51 58N 1 22 E
Felton 6 B5 55 18N 1 42W
Fergus → 14 C5 52 45N 9 0W
Fermanagh □ 12 C6 54 21N 7 40W
Fermoy 14 D6 52 4N 8 18W
Ferndown 8 E5 50 48N 1 53W
Ferryhill 6 C5 54 42N 1 32W
Fethaland, Pt. of 2 A15 60 39N 1 20W
Ffestiniog 10 B6 52 58N 3 56W
Fife □ 5 B9 56 13N 3 2W
Fife Ness 5 B10 56 17N 2 35W
Filey 6 D8 54 13N 0 18W
Filton 8 C3 51 30N 2 34W
Findhorn → 3 G10 57 38N 3 38W
Findochty 3 G12 57 42N 2 53W
Finn → 12 B6 54 50N 7 55W
Fionn L. 2 G7 57 46N 5 30W
Fishguard 10 D4 51 59N 4 59W
Fitful Hd. 2 C15 59 54N 1 20W
Five Sisters 2 H7 57 11N 5 21W
Flamborough Hd. 6 D8 54 8N 0 4W
Fleet 9 D7 51 16N 0 50W
Fleet, L. 3 G9 57 57N 4 2W
Fleetwood 7 E2 53 55N 3 1W
Flint 10 A7 53 15N 3 7W
Flintshire □ 10 A7 53 15N 3 10W
Flitwick 9 C8 51 59N 0 30W
Flodden 6 A4 55 37N 2 8W
Foinaven 3 F8 58 30N 4 53W
Folkestone 9 D11 51 5N 1 11 E
Fordingbridge 8 E5 50 56N 1 48W
Foreland Pt. 11 E6 51 14N 3 47W
Forfar 5 A10 56 40N 2 53W
Formartine 3 H13 57 20N 2 15W
Formby 7 E2 53 33N 3 3W
Forres 3 G10 57 37N 3 38W
Fort Augustus 3 H8 57 9N 4 40W
Fort William 2 J7 56 48N 5 8W
Forth 5 B8 56 8N 3 48W
Forth, Firth of 5 B10 56 5N 2 55W
Fortrose 3 G9 57 35N 4 10W
Fortuneswell 11 F9 50 33N 2 26W
Foulness I. 9 C10 51 36N 0 55 E
Fowey 11 G4 50 20N 4 39W
Fowey → 11 G4 50 20N 4 39W
Foyle → 13 B7 55 0N 7 13W
Foyle, L. 13 A7 55 6N 7 8W
Foynes 14 C4 52 37N 9 5W
Framlingham 9 B11 52 14N 1 20 E
Fraserburgh 3 G13 57 41N 2 3W
Frimley 9 D7 51 18N 0 43W
Frinton-on-Sea 9 C11 51 50N 1 16 E
Frodsham 7 F3 53 17N 2 45W
Frome 8 D4 51 16N 2 17W
Frome → 8 E4 50 44N 2 5W
Frower Pt. 14 E6 51 40N 8 30W
Fulwood 7 E3 53 47N 2 41W
Furness 6 D2 54 14N 3 8W
Fyne, L. 4 C5 56 0N 5 20W

G

Gaillimh = Galway 14 B4 53 16N 9 4W
Gainsborough 7 F7 53 23N 0 46W
Gairloch 2 G6 57 42N 5 40W
Gairloch, L. 2 G6 57 43N 5 45W
Galashiels 5 C10 55 37N 2 50W
Gallan Hd. 2 F3 58 14N 7 2W
Galley Hd. 14 E5 51 32N 8 56W
Galloway 4 D7 55 1N 4 25W
Galloway, Mull of 4 E6 54 38N 4 50W
Galston 4 C7 55 36N 4 22W
Galty Mts. 14 D6 52 22N 8 10W
Galtymore 14 D6 52 22N 8 12W
Galway 14 B4 53 16N 9 4W
Galway □ 14 B4 53 16N 9 3W
Galway B. 14 B4 53 10N 9 20W
Gamlingay 9 B8 52 9N 0 11W
Gara, L. 12 D5 53 57N 8 26W
Garforth 7 E6 53 48N 1 22W
Garioch 3 H12 57 18N 2 40W
Garron Pt. 13 A10 55 3N 6 0W
Garry, L. 3 H8 57 5N 4 52W
Garstang 7 E3 53 53N 2 47W
Gatehouse of Fleet 4 E7 54 53N 4 10W
Gateshead 6 C5 54 57N 1 37W
Gatley 7 F4 53 25N 2 15W
Gerrans B. 11 G4 50 12N 4 57W
Gerrards Cross 9 C7 51 35N 0 32W
Giants Causeway 13 A8 55 15N 6 30W
Gibraltar Pt. 7 F9 53 6N 0 20 E
Gill, L. 12 C5 54 15N 8 25W
Gillingham, *Dorset,* 8 D4 51 2N 2 15W
Gillingham, *Kent,* 9 D10 51 23N 0 34 E
Girdle Ness 3 H13 57 9N 2 2W
Girvan 4 D6 55 15N 4 50W
Gisborough Moor 6 D7 54 30N 1 2W
Glanaruddery Mts. 14 D4 52 20N 9 27W
Glandore Harbour 14 E4 51 33N 9 8W
Glas Maol 3 J11 56 52N 3 20W
Glasgow 4 C7 55 52N 4 14W
Glastonbury 8 D3 51 9N 2 42W
Glen Affric 3 H8 57 15N 5 0W
Glen B. 12 B4 54 43N 8 45W
Glen Garry, *Highl.* 2 H7 57 3N 5 7W
Glen Garry,
Perth & Kinr. 3 J9 56 47N 4 5W
Glen Mor 3 H8 57 12N 4 37W
Glen Shiel 2 H7 57 8N 5 20W
Glencoe 4 A5 56 40N 5 6W
Gleneagles 5 B8 56 16N 3 44W
Glengad Hd. 13 A7 55 19N 7 11W
Glengarriff 14 E3 51 45N 9 33W
Glennamaddy 12 D4 53 37N 8 33W
Glenrothes 5 B9 56 12N 3 11W
Glenties 12 B5 54 48N 8 18W
Glossop 7 F5 53 27N 1 56W
Gloucester 8 C4 51 52N 2 15W
Gloucestershire □ 8 C4 51 44N 2 10W
Goat Fell 4 C5 55 37N 5 11W
Godalming 9 D7 51 12N 0 37W
Goil, L. 4 B6 56 8N 4 52W
Golden Vale 14 C6 52 33N 8 17W
Golspie 3 G10 57 58N 3 58W
Goodwick 10 C3 52 1N 5 0W
Goole 7 E7 53 42N 0 52W
Gorebridge 5 C9 55 51N 3 2W
Gorey 15 C10 52 41N 6 18W
Goring-by-Sea 9 E8 50 49N 0 26W
Gorleston 9 A12 52 35N 1 44 E
Gorseinon 10 D5 51 40N 4 2W
Gort 14 B5 53 4N 8 50W
Gosport 8 E6 50 48N 1 8W
Gourock 4 C6 55 58N 4 49W
Gower 11 D5 51 35N 4 10W
Grafham Water 9 B8 52 18N 0 17W
Gragareth 6 D4 54 12N 2 29W
Grampian
Highlands =
Grampian Mts. 3 J10 56 50N 4 0W
Grampian Mts. 3 J10 56 50N 4 0W
Granard 12 D6 53 47N 7 30W
Grand Union Canal 9 B7 52 5N 0 52W
Grange-over-Sands 6 D3 54 12N 2 55W
Grangemouth 5 B8 56 1N 3 43W
Grantham 7 G7 52 55N 0 39W
Grantown-on-Spey 3 H10 57 19N 3 36W
Grassington 6 D5 54 5N 2 0W
Gravesend 9 D9 51 25N 0 22 E
Grays 9 D9 51 28N 0 23 E
Great Blasket I. 14 D1 52 5N 10 30W
Great Driffield =
Driffield 7 D8 54 1N 0 25W
Great Dunmow 9 C9 51 52N 0 22 E
Great Harwood 7 E4 53 47N 2 25W
Great I. 14 E6 51 52N 8 15W
Great Malvern 8 B4 52 7N 2 19W
Great Ormes Hd. 10 A6 53 20N 3 52W
Great Ouse → 9 A9 52 47N 0 22 E
Great Shunner Fell 6 D4 54 22N 2 16W
Great Stour =
Stour → 9 D11 51 15N 1 20 E
Great Sugar Loaf 15 B10 53 10N 6 10W
Great Torrington 11 F5 50 57N 4 9W
Great Whernside 6 D5 54 9N 1 59W
Great Yarmouth 9 A12 52 40N 1 45 E
Greater London □ 9 C8 51 30N 0 5W
Greater
Manchester □ 7 E4 53 30N 2 15W
Green Lowther 5 D8 55 22N 3 44W
Greenholm 4 C7 55 40N 4 20W
Greenock 4 C6 55 57N 4 46W
Greenore 13 C9 54 2N 6 8W
Greenore Pt. 15 D10 52 15N 6 20W
Greenstone Pt. 2 G6 57 55N 5 38W
Greenwich 9 D9 51 28N 0 0 E
Greian Hd. 2 H2 57 1N 7 30W
Gretna 5 E9 54 59N 3 4W
Gretna Green 5 E9 55 0N 3 3W
Greystones 15 B10 53 9N 6 4W
Griminish Pt. 2 G3 57 40N 7 29W
Grimsby 7 E8 53 35N 0 5W
Gruinard B. 2 G6 57 56N 5 35W
Gruinart, L. 4 C3 55 50N 6 20W
Gruting Voe 2 B14 60 12N 1 32W
Guernsey 11 J8 49 30N 2 35W
Guildford 9 D7 51 14N 0 34W
Guisborough 6 C6 54 32N 1 2W
Guiseley 7 E5 53 52N 1 43W
Gullane 5 B10 56 2N 2 50W
Gurnard's Hd. 11 G2 50 12N 5 37W
Gweebarra B. 12 B5 54 52N 8 21W
Gweedore 12 A5 55 4N 8 15W
Gwynedd □ 10 B6 52 52N 3 59W

H

Hackley Hd. 3 H14 57 19N 1 58W
Hackney 9 C8 51 33N 0 2W
Haddington 5 C10 55 57N 2 48W
Hadleigh, *Essex,* 9 C10 51 33N 0 37 E
Hadleigh, *Suffolk,* 9 B10 52 3N 0 58 E
Hags Hd. 14 C4 52 57N 9 28W
Hailsham 9 E9 50 52N 0 17 E
Halberry Hd. 3 F11 58 20N 3 11W
Halesowen 8 B4 52 27N 2 2W
Halesworth 9 B12 52 21N 1 31 E
Halifax 7 E5 53 43N 1 51W
Halkirk 3 E11 58 30N 3 30W
Halstead 9 C10 51 59N 0 39 E
Halton □ 7 F3 53 22N 2 44W
Haltwhistle 6 C4 54 58N 2 27W
Hambleton Hills 6 D6 54 17N 1 12W
Hamilton 4 C7 55 47N 4 2W
Hammersmith and
Fulham 9 D8 51 30N 0 15W
Hampshire □ 8 D6 51 3N 1 20W
Hampshire Downs 8 D6 51 10N 1 10W
Handa I. 2 F7 58 23N 5 10W
Haringey 9 C8 51 35N 0 7W
Harlech 10 B5 52 52N 4 7W
Harleston 9 B11 52 25N 1 18 E
Harlow 9 C9 51 47N 0 9 E
Harpenden 9 C8 51 48N 0 20W
Harris 2 G4 57 50N 6 55W
Harris, Sd. of 2 G3 57 44N 7 6W
Harrogate 7 E5 53 59N 1 32W
Harrow 9 C8 51 35N 0 15W
Hartland Pt. 11 E4 51 2N 4 32W
Hartlepool 6 C6 54 42N 1 11W
Harwich 9 C11 51 56N 1 18 E
Haslemere 9 D7 51 5N 0 41W
Haslingden 7 E4 53 43N 2 20W
Hastings 9 E10 50 51N 0 36 E
Hatfield, *Herts.* 9 C8 51 46N 0 11W
Hatfield, *S. Yorks.* 7 E7 53 34N 0 59W
Havant 9 E7 50 51N 0 59W
Haverfordwest 10 D4 51 48N 4 59W
Haverhill 9 B9 52 6N 0 27 E
Havering 9 C9 51 33N 0 20 E
Haweswater 6 C3 54 32N 2 48W
Hawick 5 D10 55 25N 2 48W
Hawkhurst 9 D10 51 2N 0 31 E
Hay-on-Wye 10 C7 52 4N 3 9W
Hayle 11 G3 50 12N 5 25W
Haywards Heath 9 D8 51 1N 0 6W
Hazel Grove 7 F4 53 23N 2 7W
Healaval Bheag 2 H4 57 24N 6 41W
Heanor 7 F6 53 1N 1 20W
Heathfield 9 E9 50 58N 0 18 E
Heaval 2 J3 56 58N 7 30W
Hebburn 6 C5 54 59N 1 30W
Hebden Bridge 7 E5 53 45N 2 0W
Hecla 2 H3 57 18N 7 15W
Hednesford 7 G5 52 43N 2 0W
Hedon 7 E8 53 44N 0 11W
Helensburgh 4 B6 56 1N 4 44W
Helli Ness 2 B15 60 3N 1 10W
Helmsdale 3 F10 58 8N 3 43W
Helmsley 6 D6 54 15N 1 2W
Helston 11 G3 50 7N 5 17W
Helvellyn 6 C2 54 31N 3 1W
Helvick Hd. 15 D7 52 3N 7 33W
Hemel Hempstead 9 C8 51 45N 0 28W
Hemsworth 7 E6 53 37N 1 21W
Henfield 9 E8 50 56N 0 17W
Hengoed 10 D7 51 39N 3 14W
Henley-on-Thames 9 C7 51 32N 0 53W
Hereford 8 B3 52 4N 2 42W
Herefordshire □ 8 B3 52 10N 2 30W
Herma Ness 2 A16 60 50N 0 54W
Herne Bay 9 D11 51 22N 1 8 E
Hertford 9 C8 51 47N 0 4W
Hertfordshire □ 9 C8 51 51N 0 5W
Hessle 7 E8 53 44N 0 28W
Heswall 7 F2 53 19N 3 6W
Hetton-le-Hole 6 C6 54 49N 1 26W
Hexham 6 C4 54 58N 2 7W
Heysham 6 D3 54 5N 2 53W
Heywood 7 E4 53 35N 2 13W
High Pike 6 C2 54 43N 3 4W
High Willhays 11 F6 50 41N 3 59W
High Wycombe 9 C7 51 37N 0 45W
Higham Ferrers 9 B7 52 18N 0 36W
Highbridge 8 D3 51 13N 2 59W
Highland □ 3 H7 57 30N 5 0W
Highworth 8 C5 51 38N 1 42W
Hillingdon 9 C8 51 33N 0 29W
Hilpsford Pt. 6 D2 54 4N 3 12W
Hinckley 7 G6 52 33N 1 21W
Hindley 7 E3 53 32N 2 35W
Hinkley Pt. 8 D2 51 13N 3 9W
Hitchin 9 C8 51 57N 0 16W
Hockley 9 C10 51 35N 0 39 E
Hoddesdon 9 C8 51 45N 0 1W
Hog's Back 9 D7 51 13N 0 40W
Hogs Hd. 14 E2 51 46N 10 13W
Holbeach 7 G9 52 48N 0 1 E
Holborn Hd. 3 E10 58 37N 3 30W
Holderness 7 E8 53 45N 0 5W
Holmfirth 7 E5 53 34N 1 48W
Holsworthy 11 F5 50 48N 4 21W
Holt 9 A11 52 55N 1 4 E
Holy I., *Angl.* 10 A4 53 17N 4 37W
Holy I., *Northumb.* 6 A5 55 42N 1 48W
Holyhead 10 A4 53 18N 4 38W
Holywell 10 A7 53 16N 3 14W
Honiton 11 F7 50 48N 3 11W
Hook 9 D7 51 17N 0 55W
Hook Hd. 15 D9 52 8N 6 57W
Horden 6 C6 54 45N 1 17W
Horley 9 D8 51 10N 0 10W
Horn Hd. 12 A6 55 13N 8 0W
Horncastle 7 F8 53 13N 0 8W
Horndean 8 E6 50 50N 1 0W
Hornsea 7 E8 53 55N 0 10W
Horsforth 7 E5 53 50N 1 39W
Horsham 9 D8 51 4N 0 20W
Horwich 7 E3 53 37N 2 33W
Houghton-le-Spring 6 C6 54 51N 1 28W
Houghton Regis 9 C7 51 54N 0 32W
Hounslow 9 D8 51 29N 0 20W
Hourn, L. 2 H6 57 7N 5 35W
Hove 9 E8 50 50N 0 10W
Howden 7 E7 53 45N 0 52W
Howth Hd. 15 B10 53 21N 6 3W
Hoy Sd. 3 E11 58 57N 3 20W
Hoylake 7 F2 53 24N 3 11W
Hucknall 7 F6 53 3N 1 12W
Huddersfield 7 E5 53 38N 1 49W
Hull = Kingston
upon Hull 7 E8 53 45N 0 20W
Humber → 7 E8 53 40N 0 10W
Hungerford 8 D5 51 25N 1 30W
Hungry Hill 14 E3 51 41N 9 48W
Hunstanton 9 A9 52 57N 0 30 E
Hunterston 4 C6 55 43N 4 55W

Place names on the turquoise-coded World Map section are to be found in the index at the rear of the book.

Huntingdon   **Narberth**

Place names on the turquoise-coded World Map section are to be found in the index at the rear of the book.

Narrows   **Slieve Elva**

Place names on the turquoise-coded World Map section are to be found in the index at the rear of the book.

Slieve Foye   **Youghal**

Place names on the turquoise-coded World Map section are to be found in the index at the rear of the book.

WORLD MAPS

SETTLEMENTS

⬠ PARIS   ■ Berne   ◉ Livorno   ◉ Brugge   ⊙ Algeciras   ⊙ Frejus   ○ Oberammergau   ○ Thira

Settlement symbols and type styles vary according to the scale of each map and indicate the importance
of towns on the map rather than specific population figures

∴ Ruins or Archæological Sites   �’ Wells in Desert

ADMINISTRATION

——— International Boundaries   ⬭ National Parks   Administrative
                                                                        Area Names
– – – International Boundaries   Country Names
      (Undefined or Disputed)   KENT
                                            NICARAGUA
········ Internal Boundaries   CALABRIA

International boundaries show the *de facto* situation where there are rival claims to territory

COMMUNICATIONS

——— Principal Roads   ✿ Airfields   ⌇ Other Railways

⌒ Other Roads   ⌒ Principal Railways   ⌐---⌐ Railway Tunnels

-·-·- Trails and Seasonal Roads   ----- Railways   ▭▭▭ Principal Canals
                                        Under Construction
≍ Passes

PHYSICAL FEATURES

⤳ Perennial Streams   ⬬ Intermittent Lakes   ▲ 8848 Elevations in metres

----- Intermittent Streams   ⸛ Swamps and Marshes   ▼ 8050 Sea Depths in metres

⬭ Perennial Lakes   ▭ Permanent Ice   1134 Height of Lake Surface
                                    and Glaciers   Above Sea Level
                                                                 in metres

ELEVATION AND DEPTH TINTS

Height of Land Above Sea Level   Land Below Sea Level   Depth of Sea

in metres   6000 4000 3000 2000 1500 1000 400 200 0
in feet   6000 12 000 15 000 18 000 24 000   in feet
             18 000 12 000 9000 6000 4500 3000 1200 600
                                                                0 200 2000 4000 5000 6000 8000   in metres

Some of the maps have different contours to highlight and clarify the principal relief features

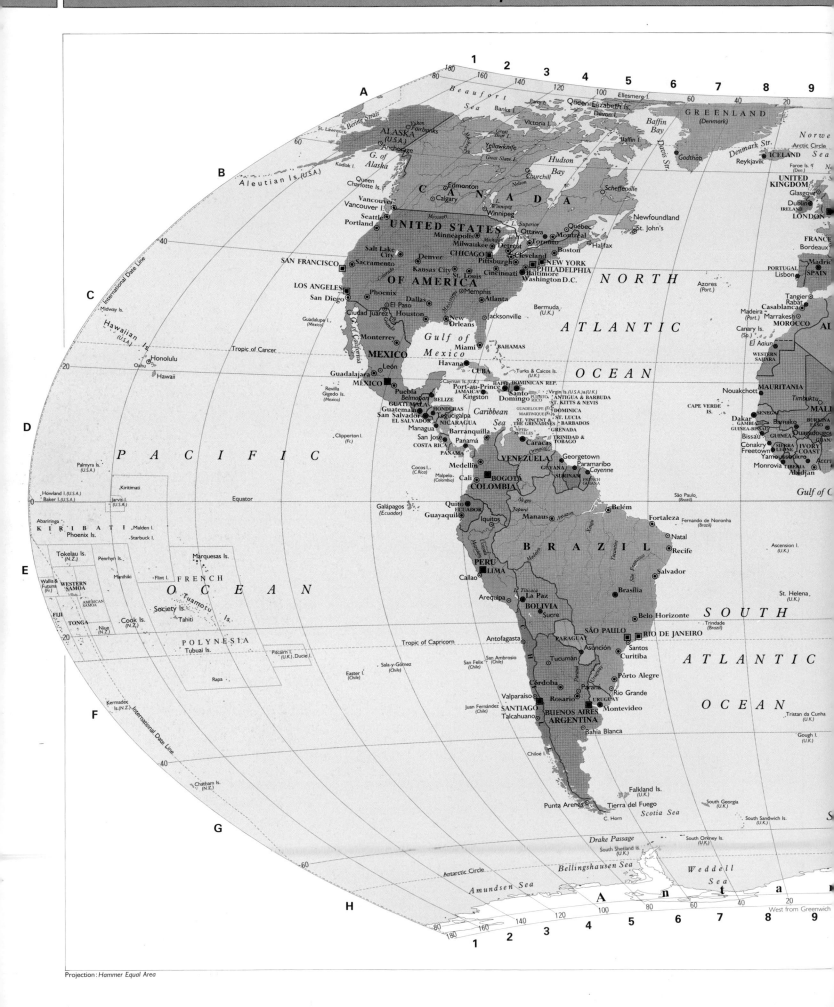

Projection: *Hammer Equal Area*

ARCTIC OCEAN

Svalbard (Norw.)
Barents Sea
Novaya Zemlya
Kara Sea
Severnaya Zemlya
Laptev Sea
New Siberian Is.
East Siberian Sea
Wrangel I.
Arctic Circle

NORWAY   SWEDEN   FINLAND
Murmansk   Arkhangelsk
Norilsk
Verkhoyansk
Yakutsk
Magadan
Bering Sea
Sea of Okhotsk
Petropavlovsk-Kamchatskiy

Oslo   Helsinki
Stockholm   EST.
ST. PETERSBURG
Perm   Yekaterinburg
Tomsk   Krasnoyarsk
L. Baikal
Okhotsk
Sakhalin
Komsomolsk
Khabarovsk
International Date Line

DENMARK
Copenhagen   LATVIA LITH.
MOSCOW
Kazan   Omsk   Novosibirsk
Irkutsk   Ulan Ude
Amur
Kuril

Amsterdam   Hamburg   Minsk   BELARUS
Berlin   Warsaw
Volga   Samara   Chelyabinsk
Barnaul
Ulan Bator
Harbin
Changchun
Vladivostok
Sapporo

Brussels   Prague   POLAND
GERMANY   Kiev   UKRAINE
Saratov   Aqmola
KAZAKSTAN
Karaganda
MONGOLIA
SHENYANG
NORTH KOREA
Pyongyang
SEOUL
JAPAN

PARIS   LUX.   AUSTRIA   Budapest   ROMANIA
Odessa   Volgograd   Astrakhan   L. Balkhash   Alma Ata
BEIJING   TIANJIN
SOUTH KOREA
Dalian
TŌKYŌ

Lyons   Milan   Belgrade   BULGARIA   Black Sea
GEORGIA   Tbilisi   Baku   UZBEKISTAN   Bishkek   KYRGYZSTAN   Tashkent
Ürümqi
Taiyuan
Osaka
Kitakyushu

Marseilles   ITALY   YUG.   Sofia   Bucharest
ARM. AZER.   Yerevan   TURKMENISTAN   Samarkand   Dushanbe   TAJIKISTAN
CHINA
Lanzhou
Xi'an
Nanjing
Kitakyushu

Barcelona   Naples   Rome   GREECE   ISTANBUL   Ankara   Izmir
TURKEY   Ashkhabad
Mashhad
Huang He
SHANGHAI
East China Sea

Algiers   Sardinia   MALTA   Athens   CYPRUS   SYRIA   TEHRĀN
AFGHANISTAN
Chengdu
CHONGQING
Wuhan
PACIFIC OCEAN

Tunis   Sicily   Crete   Mediterranean Sea   Beirut   Damascus   Baghdād
Tabriz
Islamabad
Lahore
TIBET
Lhasa
Fuzhou
Taipei

TUNISIA   Tripoli   Benghazi   Alexandria   Jerusalem   ISR.   JORDAN   IRAQ   IRAN
Kābul
DELHI
New Delhi
NEPAL
Katmandu
Kunming
GUANGZHOU
TAIWAN
Bonin Is. (Japan)

GERIA   CAIRO
Amman   KUWAIT   The Gulf   Shirāz
Esfahān
PAKISTAN
Kanpur
BANGLA-
DESH
DACCA
CALCUTTA
HONG KONG
Tropic of Cancer

LIBYA   EGYPT   Aswān
Riyadh   BAHRAIN   QATAR   Abu Dhabi   U.A.E.
Ahmadabad
Nagpur
INDIA
Hainan
South
China
Sea
Volcano Is. (Japan)
Marcus I. (Japan)

NIGER   CHAD   SUDAN   SAUDI ARABIA   Mecca   Muscat   OMAN
KARACHI
MUMBAI (Bombay)
Hyderabad
BURMA MYANMAR
Rangoon
Hanoi
Vientiane
Wake I. (U.S.A.)

Niamey   Kano   Omdurman   Khartoum   Red Sea
Arabian Sea
Bay of Bengal
THAILAND
VIET-
NAM
MANILA
NORTHERN MARIANAS (U.S.A.)

NIGERIA   Abuja   Ndjamena   Asmara   ERITREA   YEMEN   Aden   G. of Aden
Bangalore
CHENNAI (Madras)
BANGKOK
CAMBODIA
PHILIPPINES
GUAM (U.S.A.)

Ibadan   CENTRAL AFRICAN REP.   Addis Ababa   DJIBOUTI   Socotra (Yemen)
Lakshadweep Is. (India)
Andaman Is. (India)
Phnom Penh
Ho Chi Minh City
MARSHALL IS.

Lagos   CAMEROON   Douala   Bangui   SOMALI   ETHIOPIA   SOMALI REP.
Colombo
SRI LANKA
Nicobar Is. (India)
MALAYSIA
Yap
FEDERATED STATES
Truk
Pohnpei

EQUATORIAL GUINEA   SAO TOME & PRINCIPE   Libreville   GABON   UGANDA   KENYA
Mogadishu
MALDIVES
Medan
Kuala Lumpur
PEN. MALAYSIA
BRUNEI
PALAU
OF MICRONESIA
Caroline Is.

CONGO (ZAIRE)   Kampala   Kigali RWANDA   Nairobi
Equator
SINGAPORE
Borneo
SABAH
Gilbert Is.

Brazzaville   Kinshasa   BURUNDI   Dodoma   Mombasa   SEYCHELLES   Diego Garcia   Chagos Arch. (U.K.)
Palembang
Banjarmasin
IRIAN JAYA
NAURU
KIRIBATI

CABINDA (Angola)   Kananga   Zanzibar   Tanganyika   Amirante Is.
INDIAN OCEAN
JAKARTA
INDONESIA
PAPUA NEW GUINEA
New Ireland
SOLOMON IS.

Luanda   Lubumbashi   TANZANIA   Dar es Salaam   Aldabra Is.
Bandung
Surabaya
Java
Ujung Pandang
Port Moresby
New Britain
Santa Cruz I.

ANGOLA   Benguela   ZAMBIA   Lilongwe MALAWI   COMOROS   Mayotte (Fr.)   Cargados Carajos
Agalega Is.
Timor
Arafura Sea
C. York
Darwin
TUVALU

NAMIBIA   Windhoek   ZIMBABWE   Harare   MOZAMBIQUE   MADAGASCAR   Antananarivo   Rodriguez   MAURITIUS
Cocos Is. (Austral.)
Christmas I. (Austral.)
Cairns
VANUATU

Gaborone   BOTSWANA   Pretoria   Maputo   RÉUNION (Fr.)
Tropic of Capricorn
Port Hedland
Alice Springs
AUSTRALIA
Townsville
Rockhampton
NEW CALEDONIA (Fr.)
FIJI
Suva

Johannesburg   SWAZILAND   LESOTHO   Durban   Amsterdam I. (Fr.)   St. Paul (Fr.)
Geraldton
Kalgoorlie-Boulder
Brisbane
Lord Howe I. (Austral.)

SOUTH AFRICA   Cape Town   C. of Good Hope   Port Elizabeth
Prince Edward Is. (S.Africa)   Crozet Is. (Fr.)   Kerguelen (Fr.)
Perth
Fremantle
Great Australian Bight
Adelaide
Newcastle
Sydney
Canberra
Norfolk I. (Austral.)

McDonald I.   Heard I. (Austral.)
Melbourne
Tasman Sea
Auckland
North I.
NEW ZEALAND

SOUTHERN OCEAN
Tasmania
Wellington
Hobart
Christchurch
South I.
Dunedin
Stewart I.
Bounty Is. (N.Z.)
Antipodes Is. (N.Z.)

Bouvet I. (Norw.)
Antarctic Circle
Campbell I. (N.Z.)
Auckland Is. (N.Z.)
Macquarie Is. (Austral.)
Ross Sea

Antarctica

Hanoi ● Capital Cities

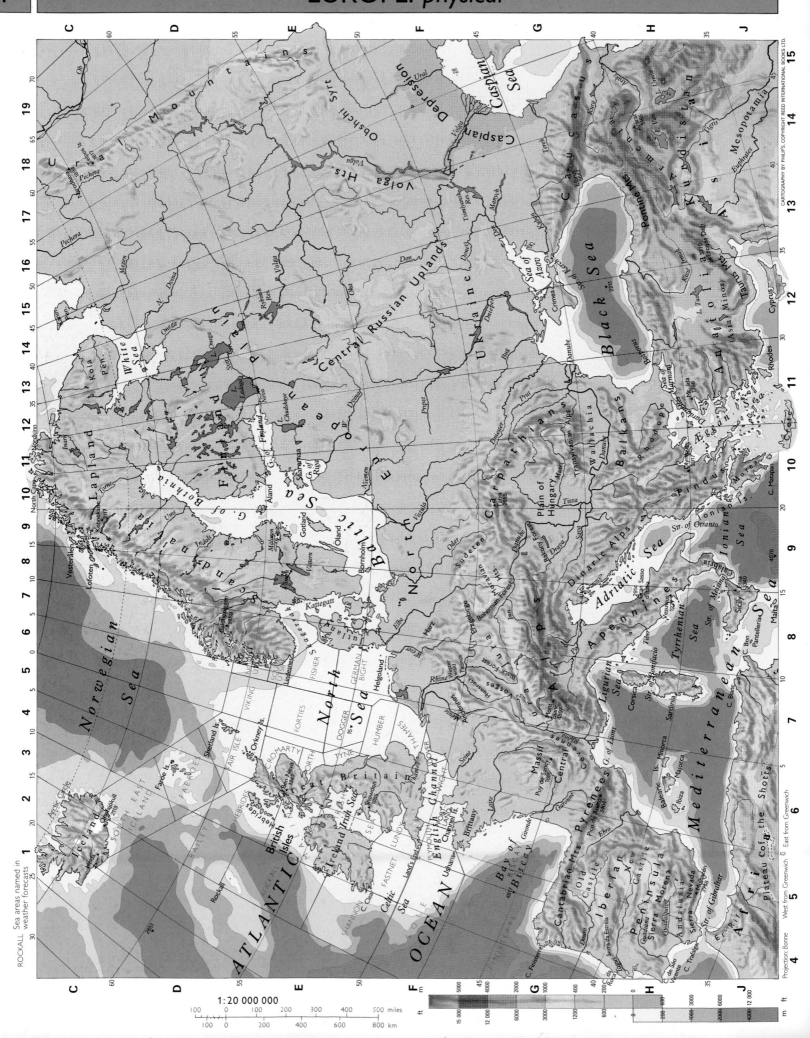

ROCKALL Sea areas named in weather forecasts

CARTOGRAPHY BY PHILIP'S, COPYRIGHT REED INTERNATIONAL BOOKS LTD.

1:20 000 000

100   0   100   200   300   400   500 miles

100   0   200   400   600   800 km

West from Greenwich   0   East from Greenwich

Projection: Bonne

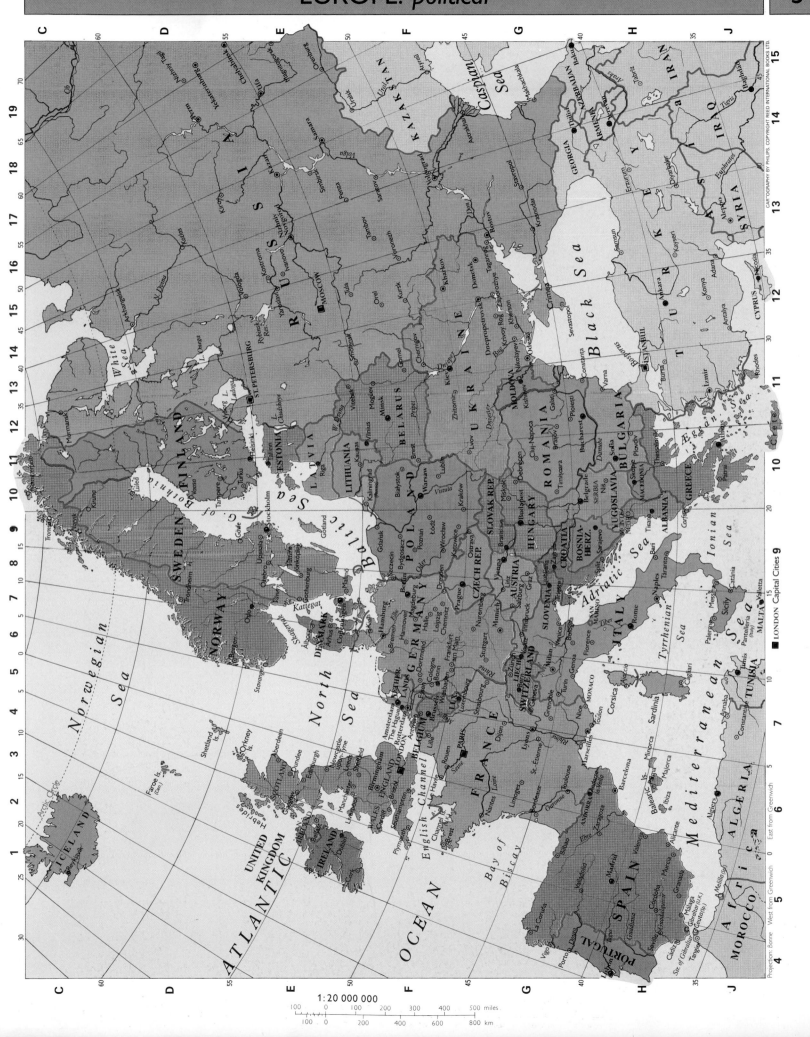

■ LONDON Capital Cities

Projection: Bonne   West from Greenwich   0   East from Greenwich

1:20 000 000

100   0   100   200   300   400   500 miles

100   0   200   400   600   800 km

ICELAND
On the same scale   West from Greenwich

Projection: Conical with two standard parallels

East from Greenwich

1:10 000 000

COPYRIGHT. GEORGE PHILIP & SON, LTD.

ATLANTIC OCEAN

NORWAY

Shetland Is.
Yell · Unst · Fetlar
Foula · Mainland · Lerwick

Fair Isle

Orkney Is.
Westray · Sanday
Mainland · Stronsay
Hoy · Kirkwall
South Ronaldsay

Pentland Firth

C. Wrath
Thurso · Wick
Laxig
Helmsdale

Lewis · Stornoway
North Minch
Golspie

St. Kilda
Harris
North Uist
Benbecula
South Uist
Barra

Outer Hebrides
Inner Hebrides

NORTH WEST HIGHLANDS

Ullapool
Invergordon · Dingwall · Nairn · Elgin · Buckie · Banff · Fraserburgh · Peterhead
L. Ness · Inverness · Huntly · Inverurie
Aviemore · Spey · Don · Aberdeen

SCOTLAND
GRAMPIAN Mts.

Skye
Rhum
Eigg
Coll
Tiree
Mull
Tobermory
Oban
Colonsay

Ben Nevis · Fort William
Dee · Ballater · Stonehaven

Perth · Dundee · St. Andrews
Forfar · Arbroath · Montrose

NORTH SEA

L. Lomond · Stirling · Glenrothes · Kirkcaldy
Greenock · Paisley · Glasgow · Edinburgh · Dunfermline
Jura · East Kilbride · Hamilton · Dunbar
Islay · Arran · Kilmarnock · Galashiels · Berwick-upon-Tweed
Campbeltown · Irvine · Ayr · Jedburgh · Hawick · Alnwick
SOUTHERN UPLANDS · Cheviot Hills

Malin Hd.
Buncrana
Letterkenny · Coleraine
Aran I. · Londonderry · Ballymena · Larne
Donegal · NORTHERN IRELAND · Antrim · Bangor
Lower L. Erne · Omagh · Lough Neagh · Belfast
Enniskillen · Portadown · Lisburn · Lurgan
Clones · Armagh · Newry

Dumfries
Kirkcudbright
Stranraer · Workington · Carlisle · Hexham · Gateshead · Newcastle-upon-Tyne · South Shields
Mull of Galloway · Whitehaven · Durham · Sunderland · Hartlepool · Redcar
Cumbrian Mts. · Darlington · Middlesbrough · Stockton-on-Tees · Scarborough

UNITED KINGDOM

Douglas · I. of Man
Barrow-in-Furness · Lancaster
PENNINES · Harrogate · York · Beverley · Bridlington
Keighley · Leeds · Kingston upon Hull
Blackpool · Burnley · Bradford · Huddersfield · Scunthorpe · Grimsby
Preston · Halifax · Barnsley · Doncaster
Blackburn · Bolton · Rotherham · Sheffield · Lincoln · Louth · Skegness
Oldham · Mansfield · The Wash · Cromer

IRISH SEA
IRELAND

Ballina
Castlebar · Lough Mask · Lough Conn
Westport · Roscommon · Longford
CONNEMARA · Lough Corrib · Athlone · Mullingar · Boyne
Galway B. · Lough Ree · Drogheda
Aran Is. · Ballinasloe · Tullamore · Liffey · Dublin · Dun Laoghaire
Ennis · Lough Derg · Port Laoise · Athy · Bray
Limerick · Thurles · Carlow · Kilkenny · Arklow
Tipperary · Wexford · Rosslare

Holyhead · Anglesey · Liverpool · Manchester · Stockport · Sheffield
Bangor · Warrington · Crewe · Chesterfield
Colwyn Bay · Chester · Derby · Nottingham · Grantham · Boston
Snowdon · Wrexham · Stoke-on-Trent · Stafford · Trent · Norwich
CAMBRIAN Mts. · Shrewsbury · Telford · Leicester · Peterborough · Great Yarmouth · Lowestoft
Welshpool · Wolverhampton · Nuneaton · Corby · Thetford
Cardigan Bay · Aberystwyth · BIRMINGHAM · Coventry · Rugby · Northampton · Bury St. Edmunds · Ipswich
WALES · Redditch · Royal Leamington Spa · Bedford · Cambridge · Felixstowe
Hereford · Worcester · Milton Keynes · Stevenage · Harwich
Carmarthen · Brecon · Cheltenham · Gloucester · Luton · Harlow · Colchester
Llanelli · Merthyr Tydfil · Neath · Rhondda · Cwmbran · Oxford · Hemel Hempstead · Watford · Basildon · Southend-on-Sea
Swansea · Port Talbot · Newport · High Wycombe · Slough · LONDON · Chatham · Margate
Cardiff · Bristol · Newbury · Reading · Maidstone · Canterbury · Dover
Barry · Bath · Basingstoke · Guildford · Reigate · Ashford · Folkestone
Bristol Channel · Weston-super-Mare · Salisbury · Winchester · Crawley · Hastings
Barnstaple · EXMOOR · Taunton · Yeovil · Fareham · Brighton · Eastbourne sur-Mer
Bude · Southampton · Havant · Worthing
Newquay · Exeter · DARTMOOR · Exmouth · Bournemouth · Poole · Newport · Portsmouth
Truro · St. Austell · Torbay · Weymouth · Isle of Wight
Land's End · Plymouth
Penzance
Isles of Scilly

ENGLAND

Dingle · Tralee · Listowel
Kilrush · Killarney · Mallow
Shannon · Macgillycuddy's Reeks · Blackwater · Dungarvan
Carrauntohill · Clonmel · Waterford · Youghal
Bantry · Bandon · Cork · Cobh · Kinsale
C. Clear

MUNSTER
Nenagh · Carrick-on-Suir

CELTIC SEA

St. George's Channel

Fishguard
Haverfordwest · Milford Haven · Pembroke

Cardigan Bay

WICKLOW Mts.

NETHERLANDS
The Hague
Haarlem
Texel
Den Helder
Alkmaar
Hoek van Holland
ROTTERDAM
Dordrecht
Vlissingen
Zeebrugge
Oostende
ANTWERP
Gent · Brugge · Mechelen
BELGIUM
BRUSSELS
Tournai
Lille · Roubaix
Béthune · Lens · Valenciennes
Bruay-en-Artois · Douai · Cambrai
St. Omer
Calais · Gravelines · Dunkerque
Boulogne · Le Touquet-Paris-Plage
Grisnez
Str. of Dover
Abbeville
Le Tréport · Dieppe
Amiens
PICARDIE
St. Quentin

English Channel

Channel Is. (U.K.)
Alderney
Guernsey · St. Peter Port · Sark
Jersey · St. Helier

C. de la Hague
Pte. de Barfleur
Cherbourg
COTENTIN
Valognes
Bayeux · Caen
St. Lô
Carteret

FRANCE
Pays de Caux
Fécamp
Le Havre · Rouen
Bolbec · Elbeuf
Trouville-sur-Mer · Lisieux
Seine

Bergen
Stord
Bømlo
Haugesund
Kopervik
Åkrahamn
Sandnes
Bryne
Nærbø
Stavanger
Oslo

Norwich

ft m
3000 1000
1500 500
600 200
0 0
50 150
100 300
200 600
500 1500
1000 3000
2000 6000
m ft

Projection: Conical with two standard parallels

1 : 5 000 000

50 0 50 100 miles
50 0 50 100 150 km

West from Greenwich
East from Greenwich

CARTOGRAPHY BY PHILIP'S.
COPYRIGHT REED INTERNATIONAL BOOKS LTD

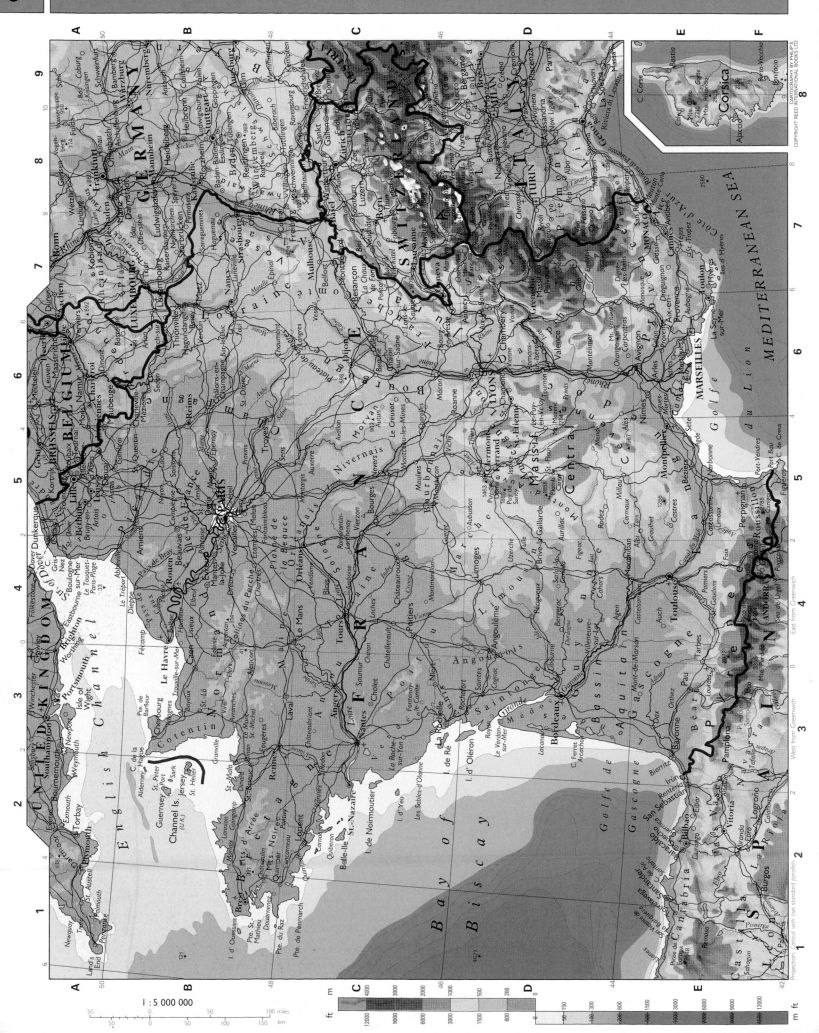

1 : 5 000 000

Projection: Conical with two standard parallels

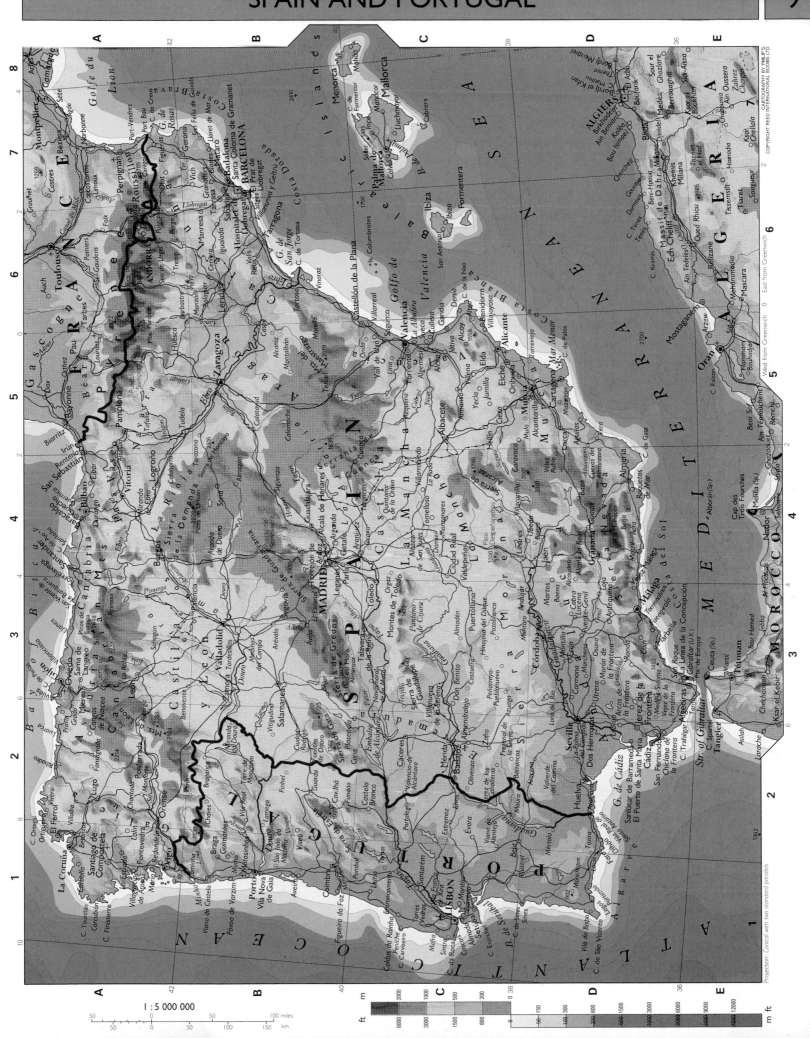

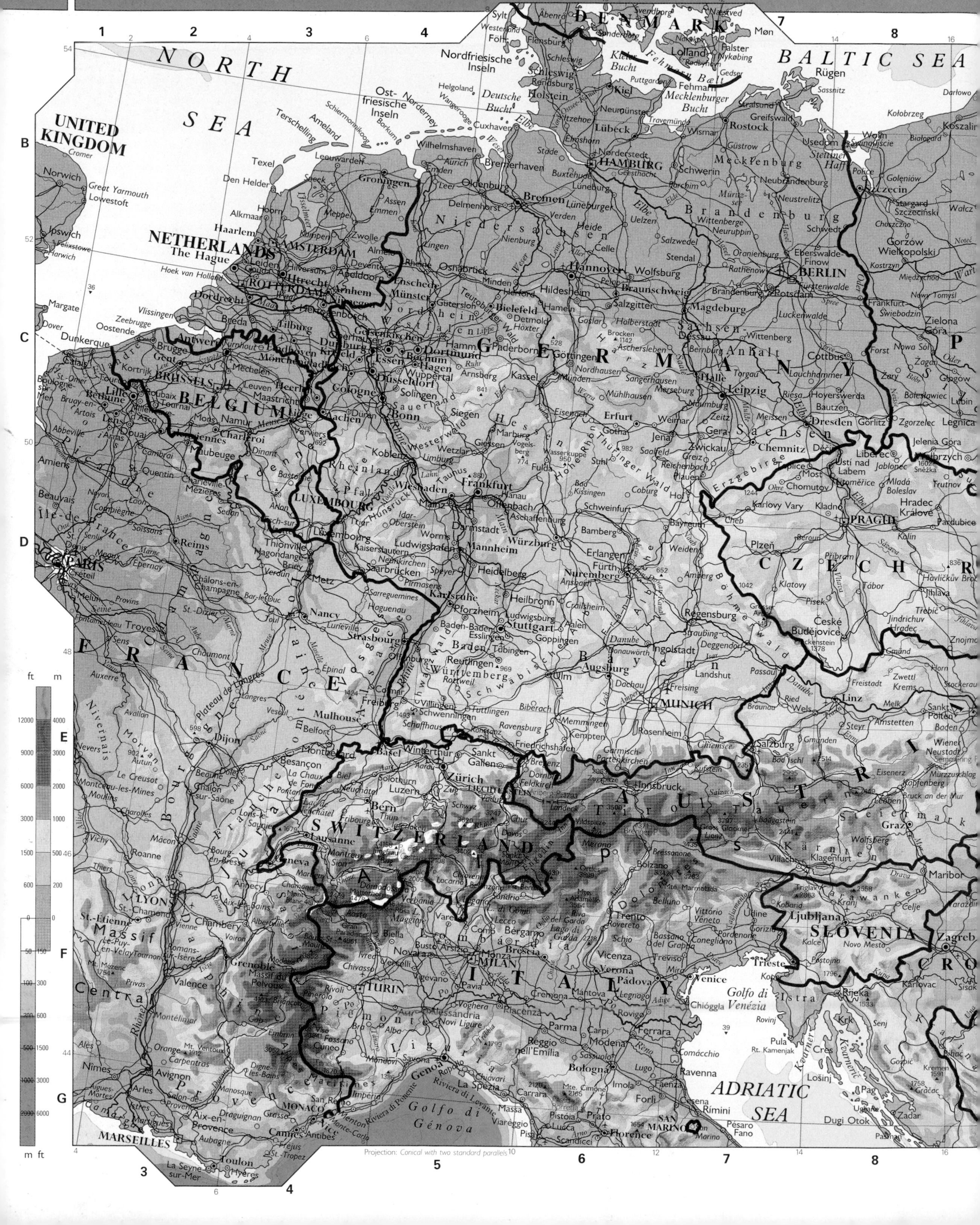

NORTH SEA

BALTIC SEA

UNITED KINGDOM

DENMARK

NETHERLANDS
The Hague

BELGIUM

LUXEMBOURG

GERMANY

FRANCE

SWITZERLAND

ITALY

AUSTRIA

CZECH

SLOVENIA

ADRIATIC SEA

Golfo di Venézia

Golfo di Génova

Nordfriesische Inseln

Ostfriesische Inseln

Mecklenburger Bucht

Deutsche Bucht

HAMBURG
BREMEN
HANNOVER
BERLIN
Magdeburg
Leipzig
Dresden
PRAGUE
Nuremberg
MUNICH
Stuttgart
Frankfurt
Cologne
BRUSSELS
AMSTERDAM
ROTTERDAM
PARIS
Strasbourg
Dijon
LYONS
TURIN
MILAN
Genoa
MARSEILLES
MONACO
Nice
Florence
SAN MARINO
Venice
Ljubljana
Zagreb
Trieste
Graz
Salzburg
Innsbruck
Linz
Zürich
Bern
Geneva
Basel
Luzern
Grenoble
Bologna
Verona
Padova
Rimini
Ancona

Projection: Conical with two standard parallels

Grid references (top): 3, 4, 5, 6, 7
Left margin letters: B, C, D, E, F, G
Numbers: 1, 2

Scale bar (left):
ft / m
12000 / 4000
9000 / 3000
6000 / 2000
3000 / 1000
1500 / 500
600 / 200
0 / 0
50 / 150
100 / 300
200 / 600
500 / 1500
1000 / 3000
2000 / 6000
3000 / 9000
4000 / 12000
m / ft

Countries / regions:
FRANCE, SWITZERLAND, AUSTRIA, SLOVENIA, CROATIA, ALGERIA, TUNISIA, MALTA, ITALY

Seas:
LIGURIAN SEA, TYRRHENIAN SEA, ADRIATIC SEA, MEDITERRANEAN, Golfo di Génova, Golfo di Venézia, Golfo di Táranto

Major cities:
LYONS, Grenoble, Valence, MARSEILLES, Toulon, MONACO, TURIN, MILAN, Genoa, Bologna, Florence, ROME, VATICAN CITY, NAPLES, Venice, Trieste, Ljubljana, Zagreb, Palermo, Messina, Catánia, Siracusa, Cagliari, Sássari, Bari, Táranto, Tunis, Constantine, Valletta

Islands:
Corsica, Sardinia, Elba, Sicily (SICILIA), Capraia, Pianosa, Montecristo, Giglio, Ísole Ponziane, Capri, Ischia, Ísole Eólie, Strómboli, Lipari, Vulcano, Salina, Ustica (Italy), Ísole Égadi, Favignana, Pantelleria (Italy), Ísole Pelagie (Italy), Lampedusa, I. Linosa, Lampione, Gozo

Projection: Conical with two standard parallels

Bottom grid numbers: 2, 3, 10, 4, 12, 5, 14, 6, 16, 7

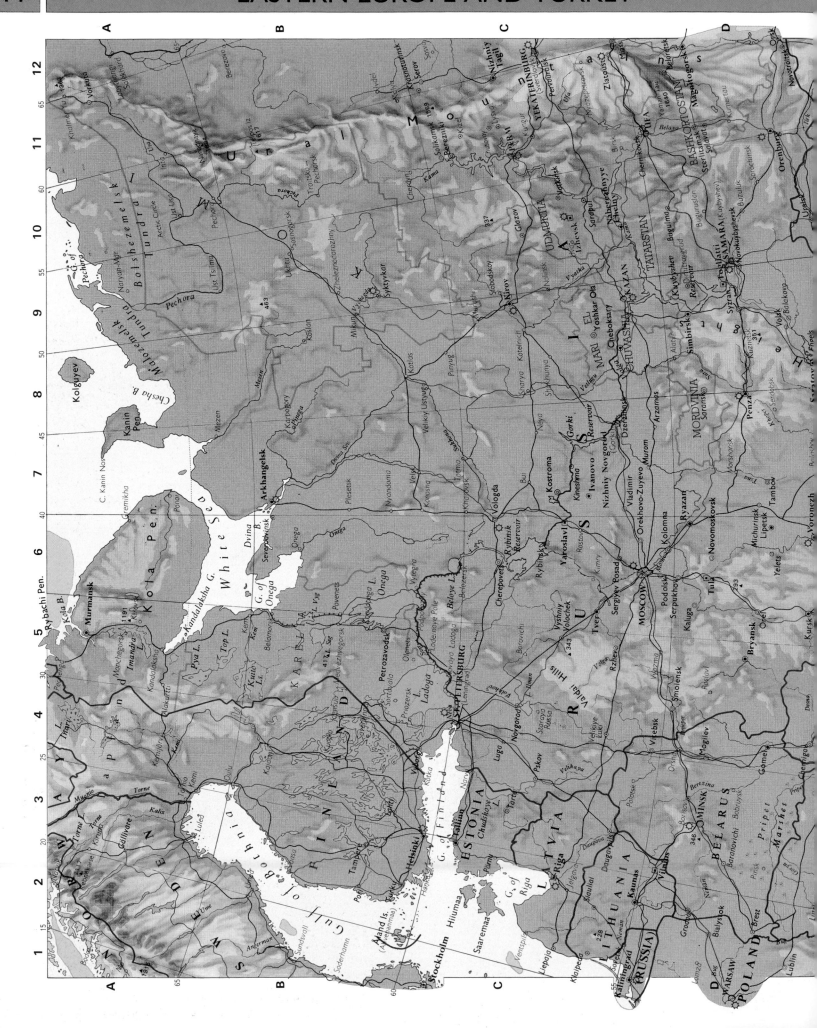

1. Crimea (Ukr.)
2. Adygea (Russ.)
3. Karachey-Cherkessia (Russ.)
4. Kabardino-Balkana (Russ.)
5. North Osetia (Russ.)
6. Ingushetia (Russ.)
7. Chechenia (Russ.)
8. Nakhichevan (Azer.)

1:10 000 000

50 0 50 100 150 200 250 miles
50 0 50 100 150 200 250 300 350 400 km

Projection: Conical with two standard parallels

Division between Greeks and Turks in Cyprus, Turks to the North

East from Greenwich

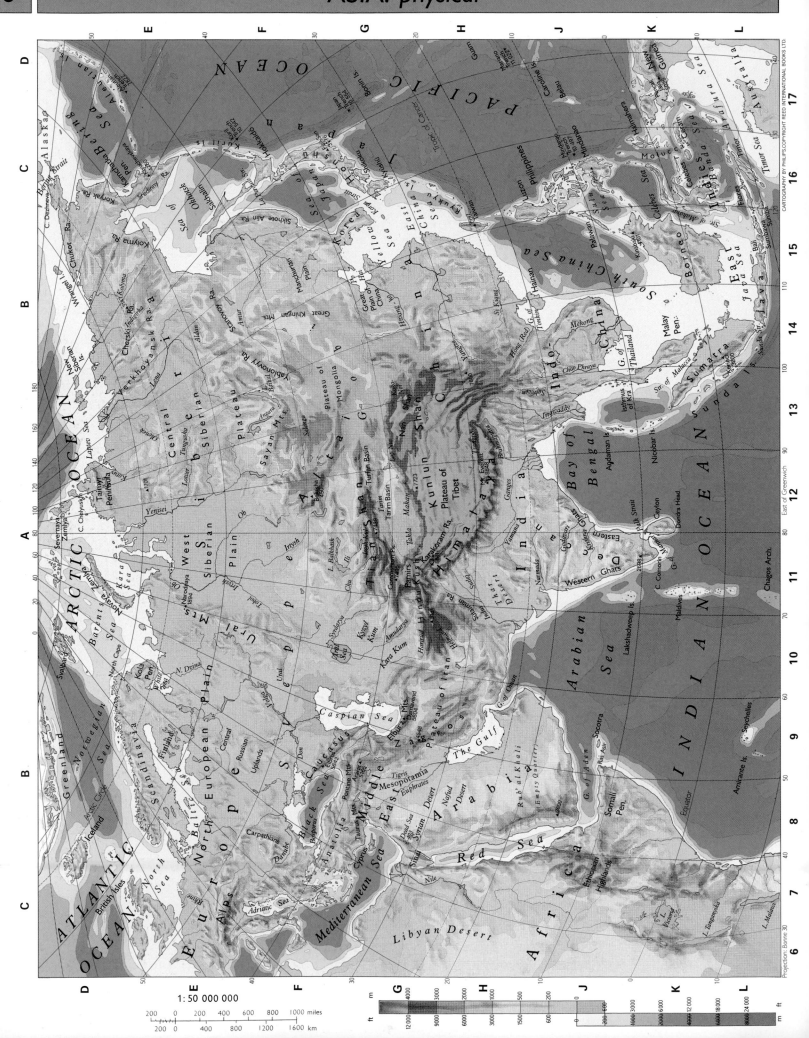

1:50 000 000

Projection: Bonne 30

East of Greenwich

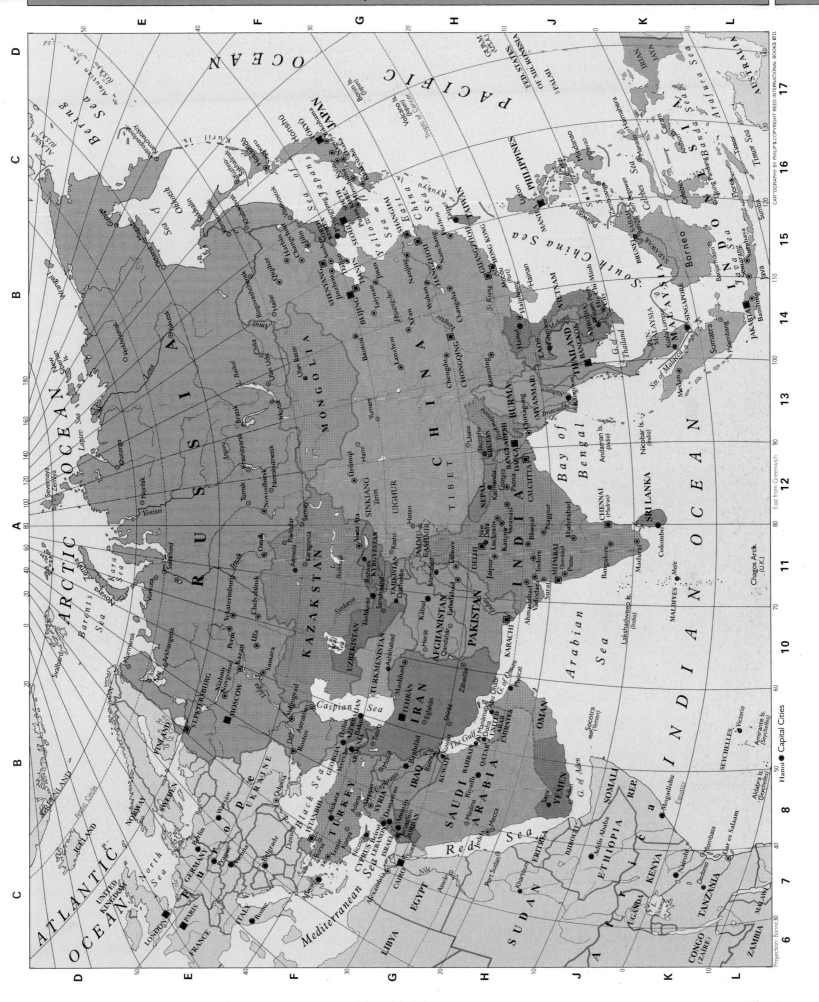

Hanoi ● Capital Cities

Projection: Bonne

East from Greenwich

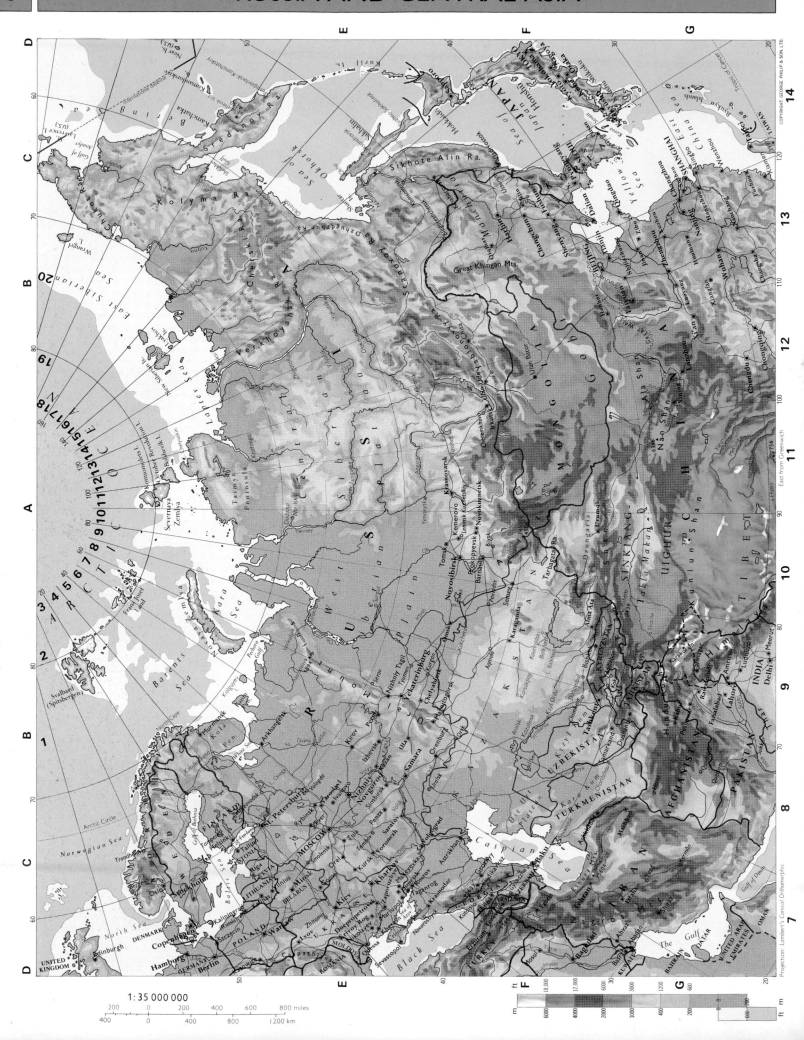

1:35 000 000

Projection: Lambert's Conical Orthomorphic

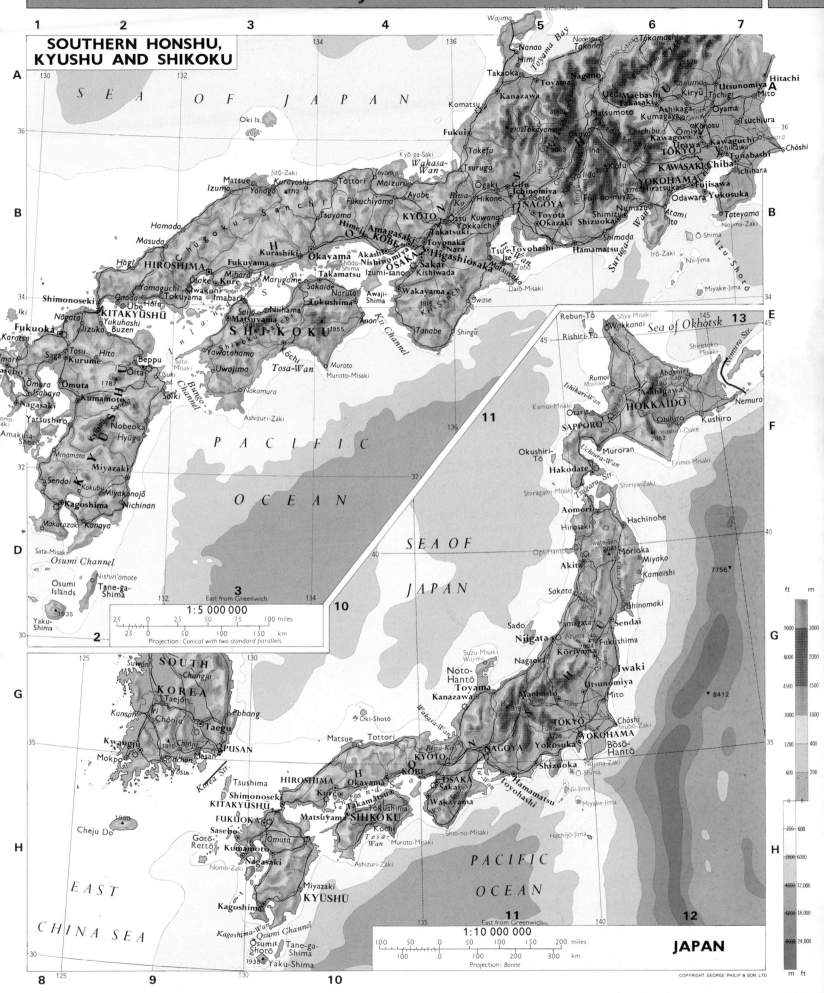

SOUTHERN HONSHU, KYUSHU AND SHIKOKU

1:5 000 000

Projection: Conical with two standard parallels

1:10 000 000

JAPAN

Projection: Bonne

COPYRIGHT. GEORGE PHILIP & SON. LTD.

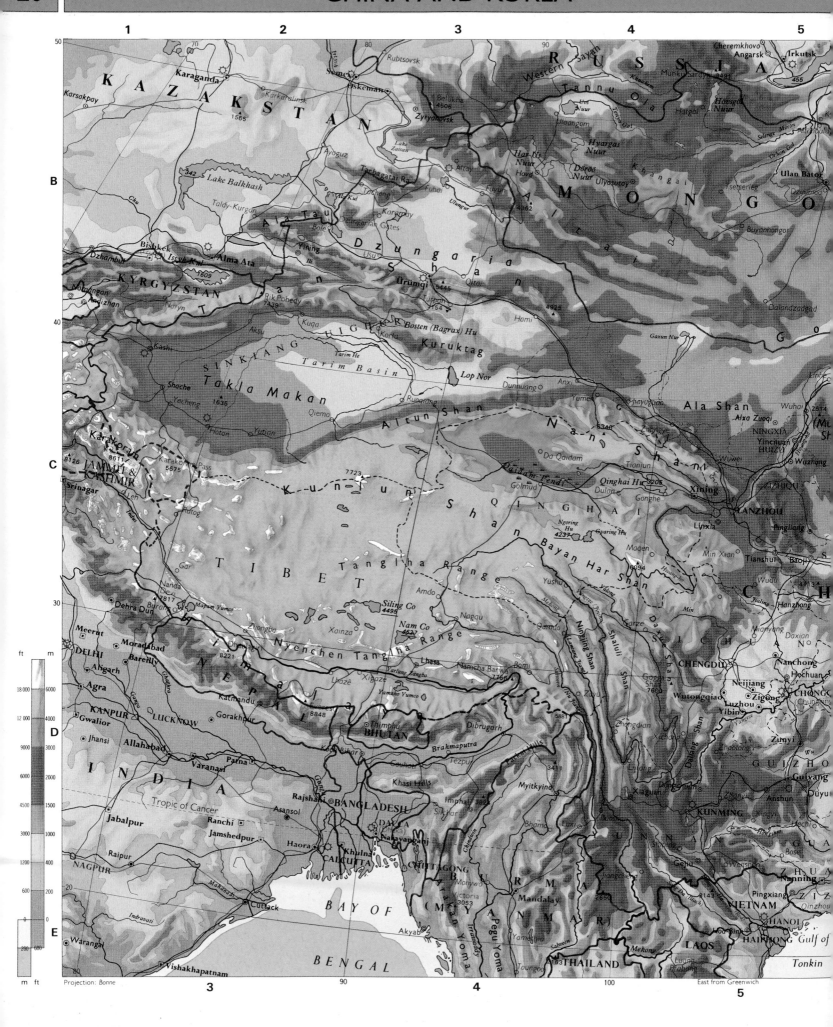

COPYRIGHT GEORGE PHILIP & SON LTD.

1:15 000 000

100   0   100   200   300   400 miles

100   0   100   200   300   400   500   600 km

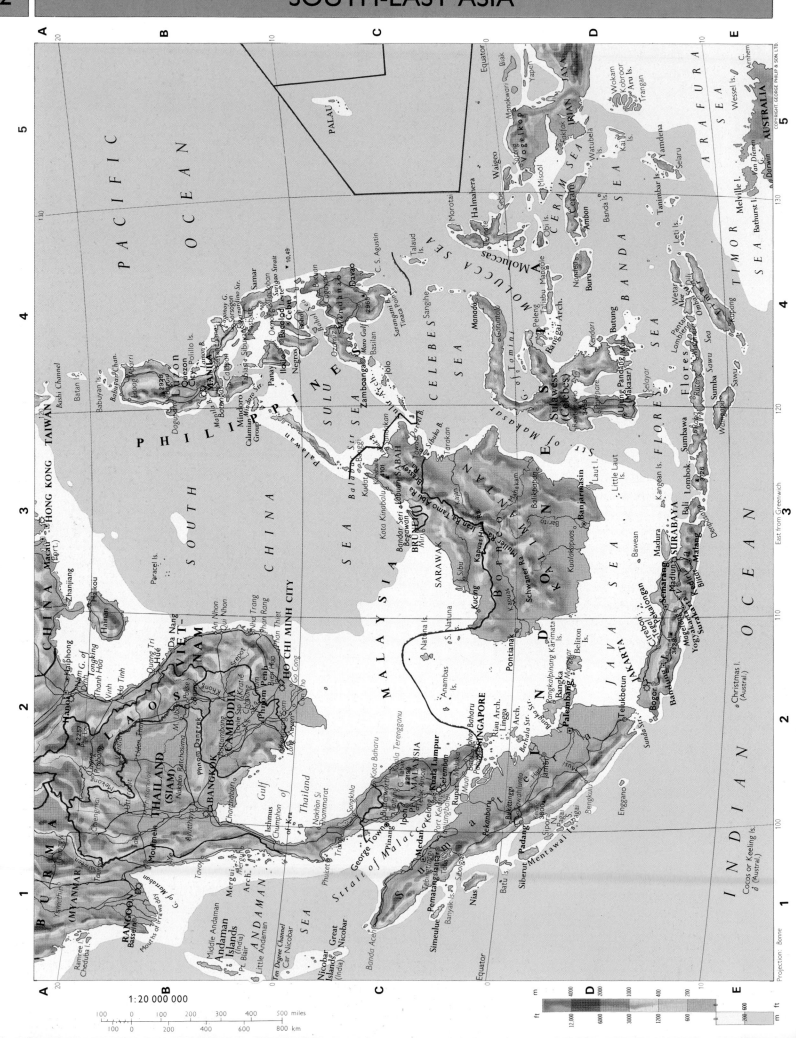

Projection: Bonne

1:20 000 000

East from Greenwich

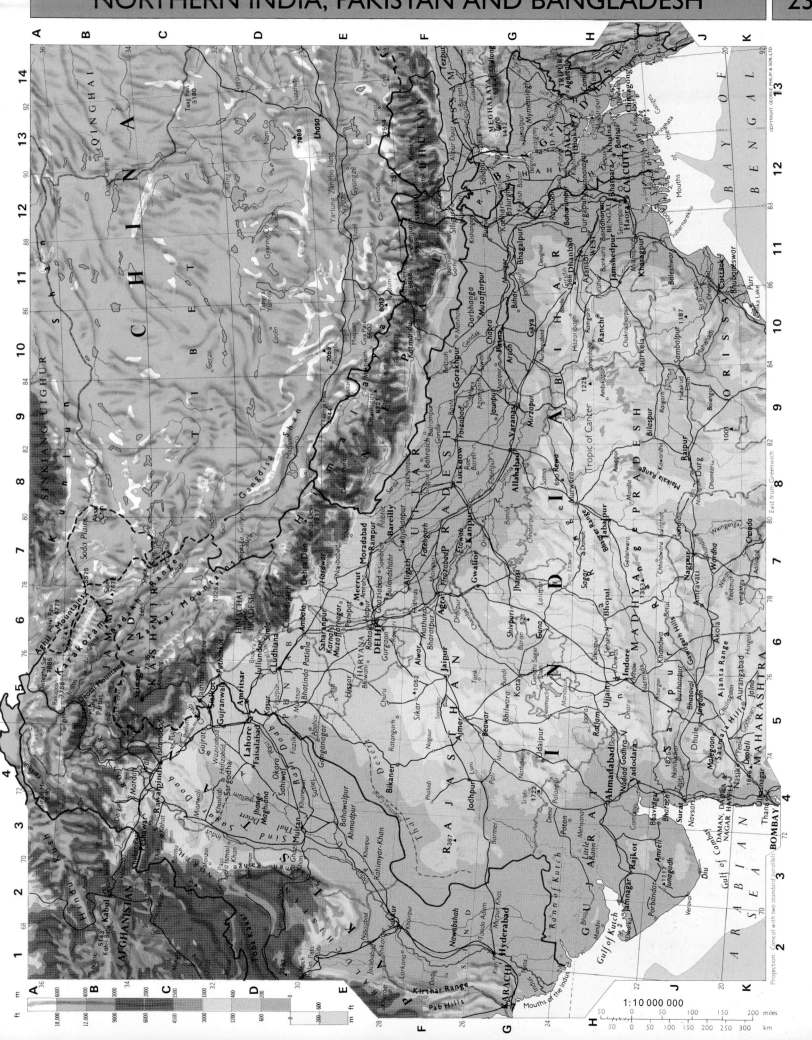

Projection: Conical with two standard parallels

1:10 000 000

COPYRIGHT GEORGE PHILIP & SON LTD.

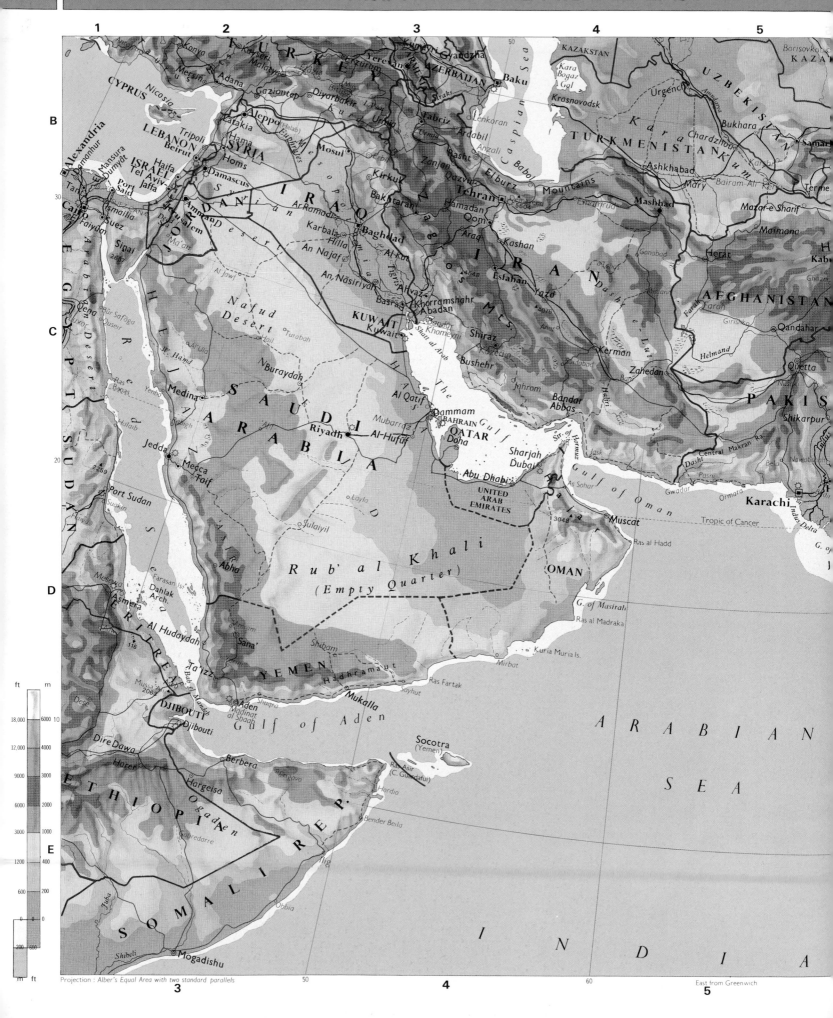

Projection : Alber's Equal Area with two standard parallels

East from Greenwich

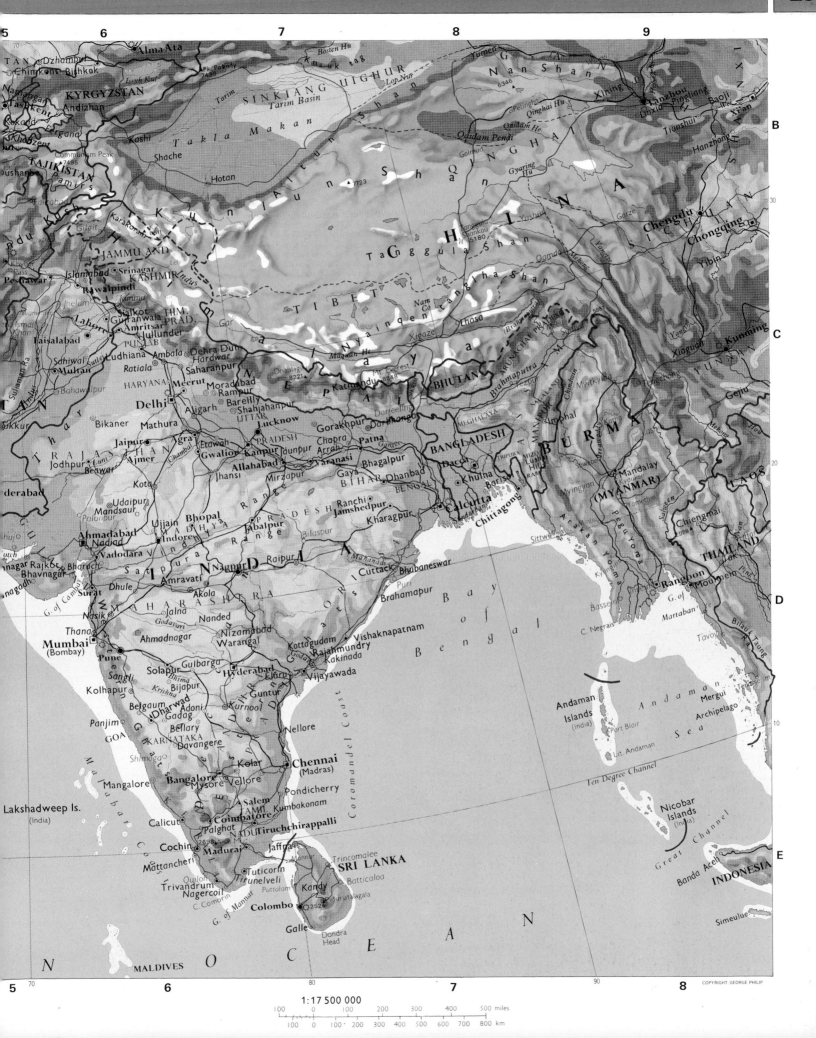

COPYRIGHT GEORGE PHILIP

1:17 500 000

100   0   100   200   300   400   500 miles

100   0   100   200   300   400   500   600   700   800 km

AFRICA : *physical*

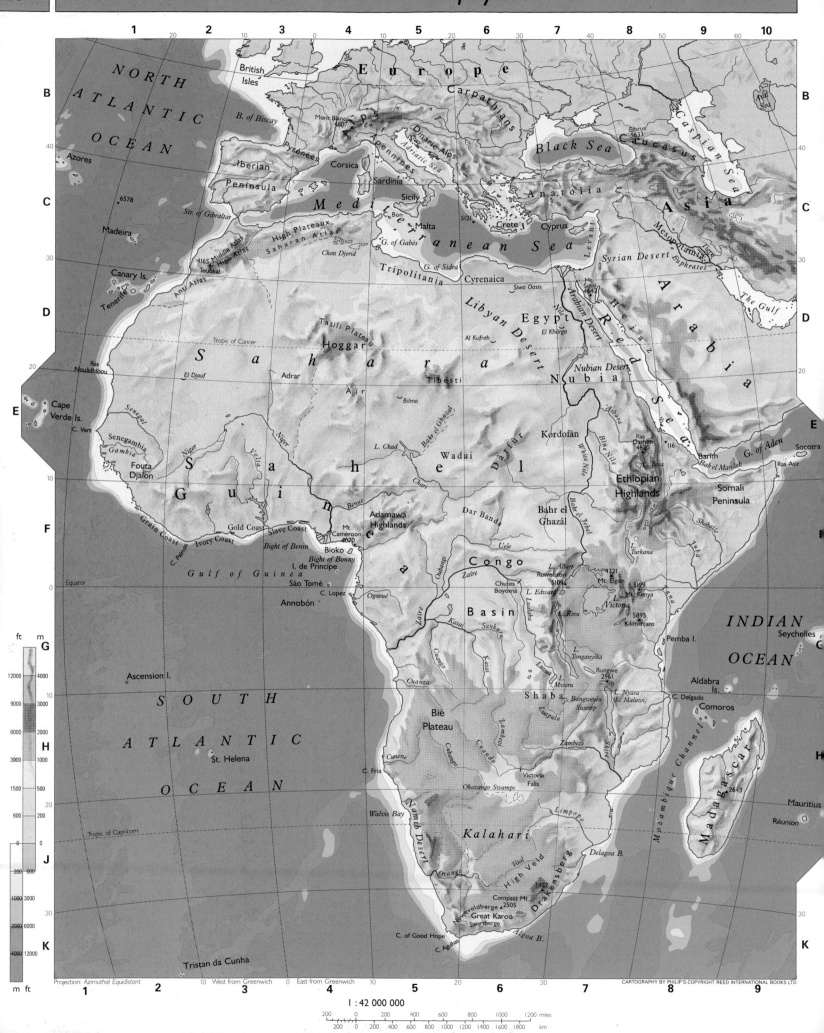

CARTOGRAPHY BY PHILIP'S. COPYRIGHT REED INTERNATIONAL BOOKS LTD

1 : 42 000 000

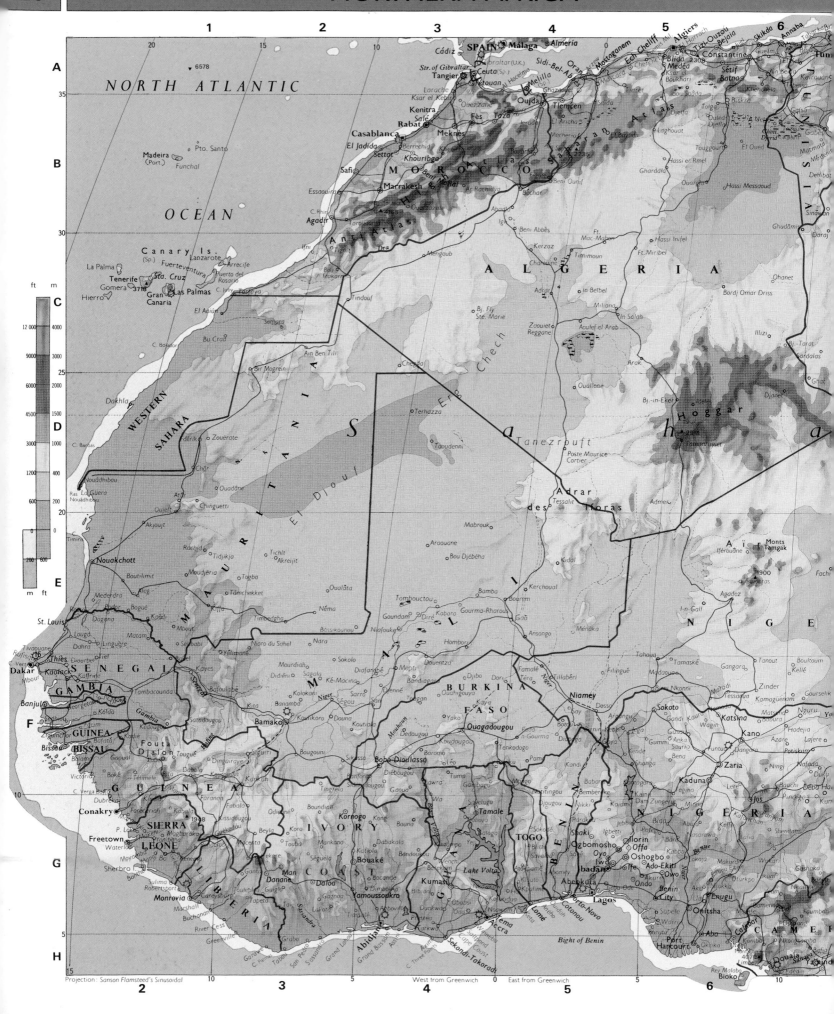

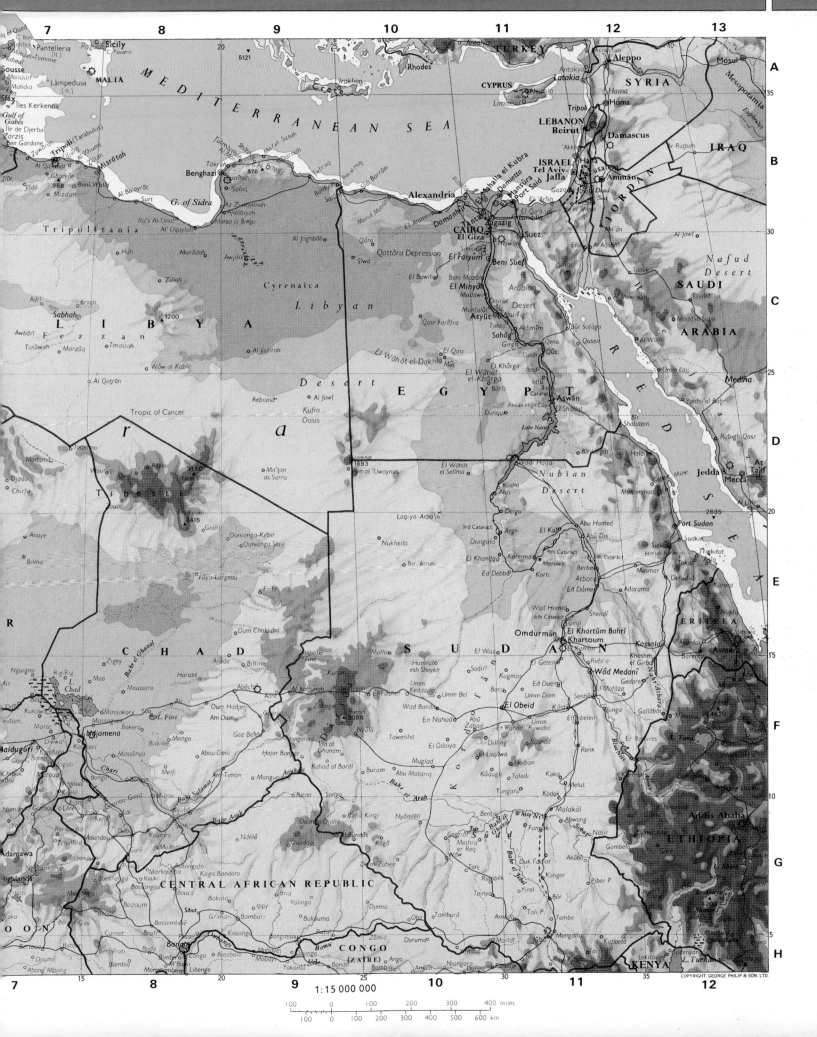

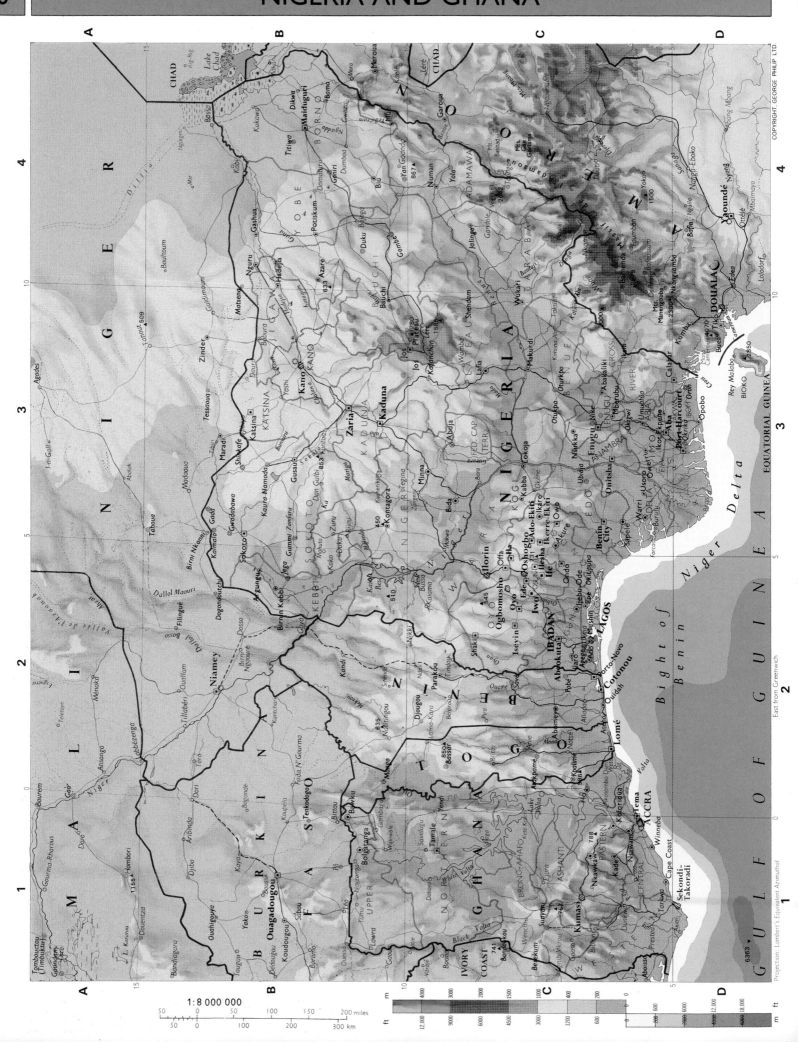

1:8 000 000

Projection: Lambert's Equivalent Azimuthal

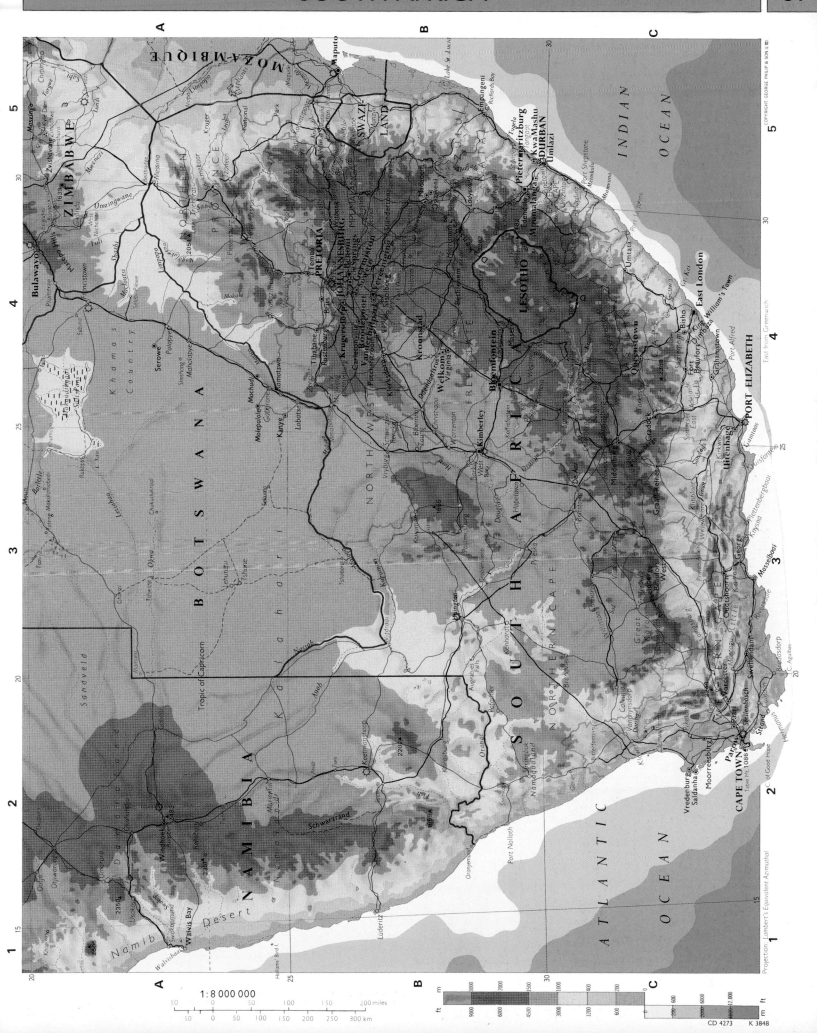

1 : 8 000 000

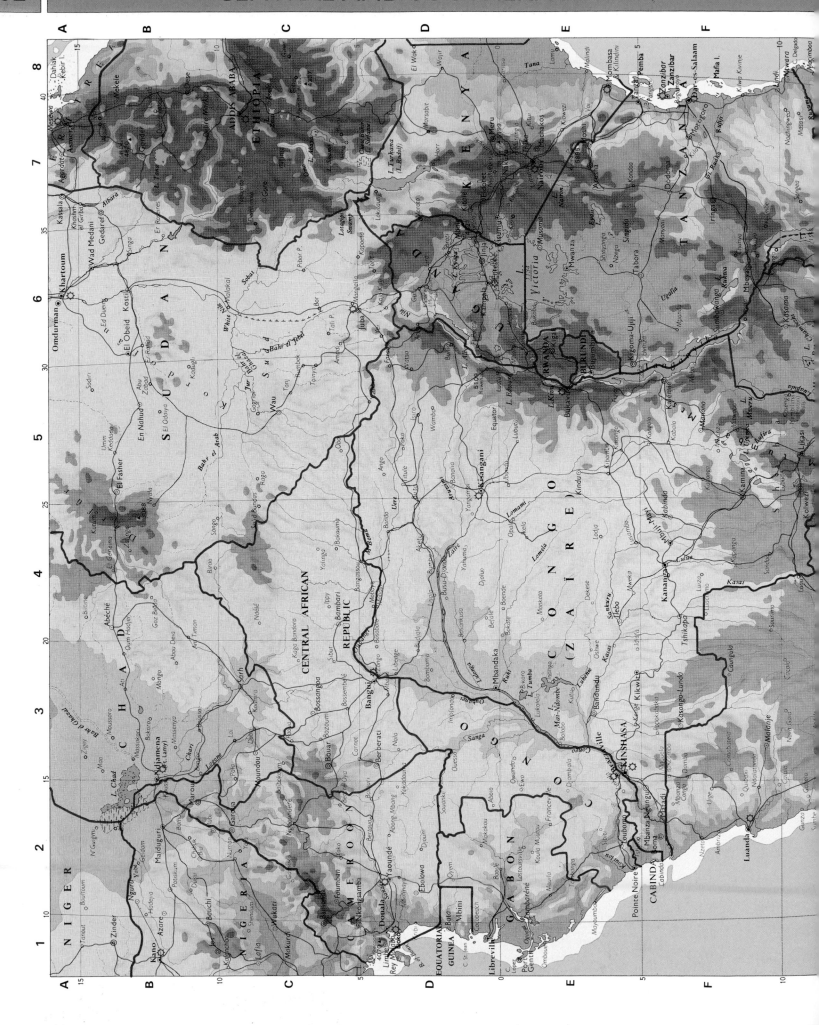

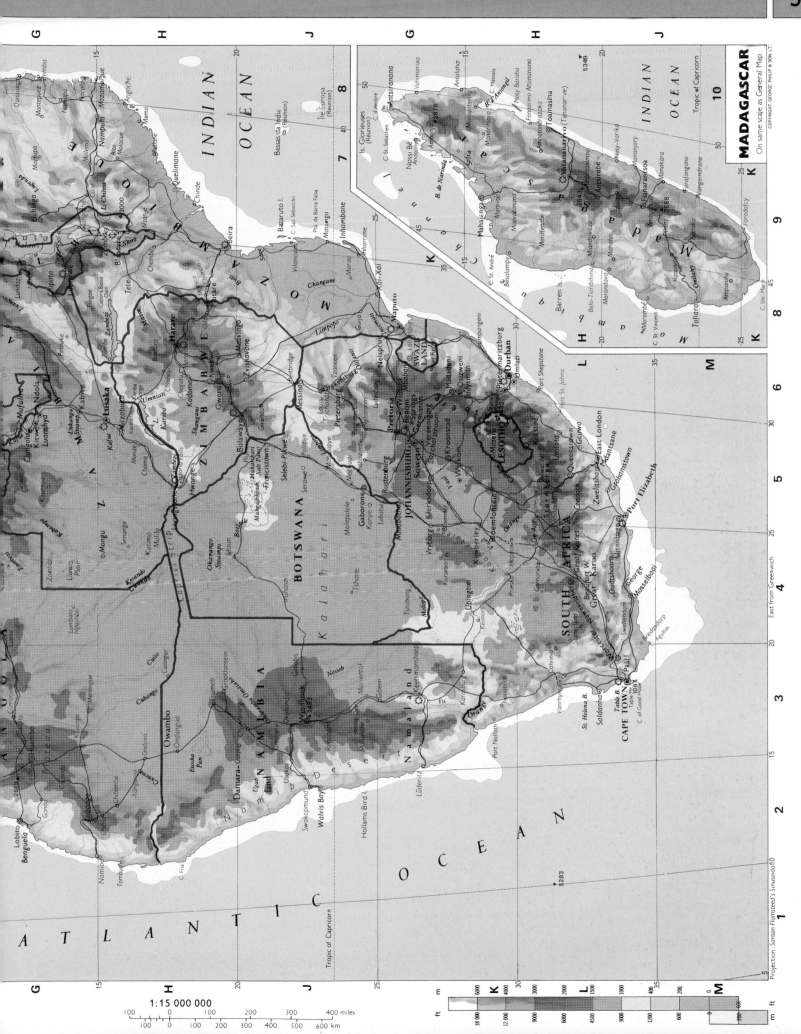

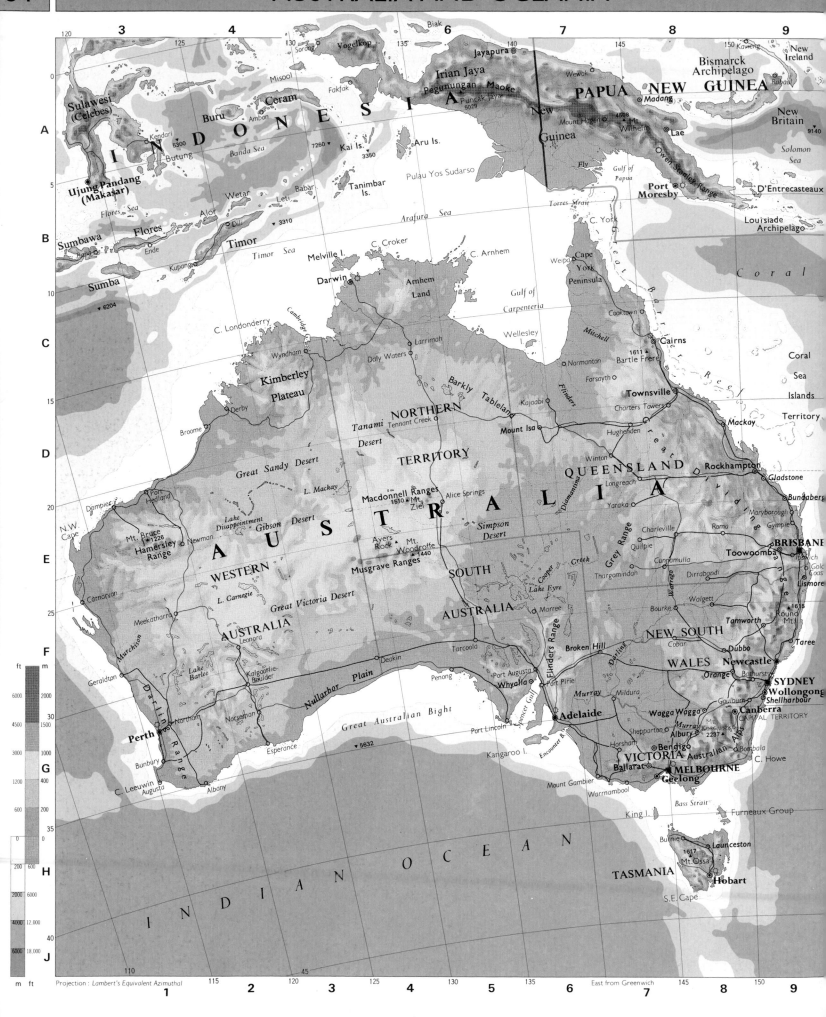

Projection : Lambert's Equivalent Azimuthal   East from Greenwich

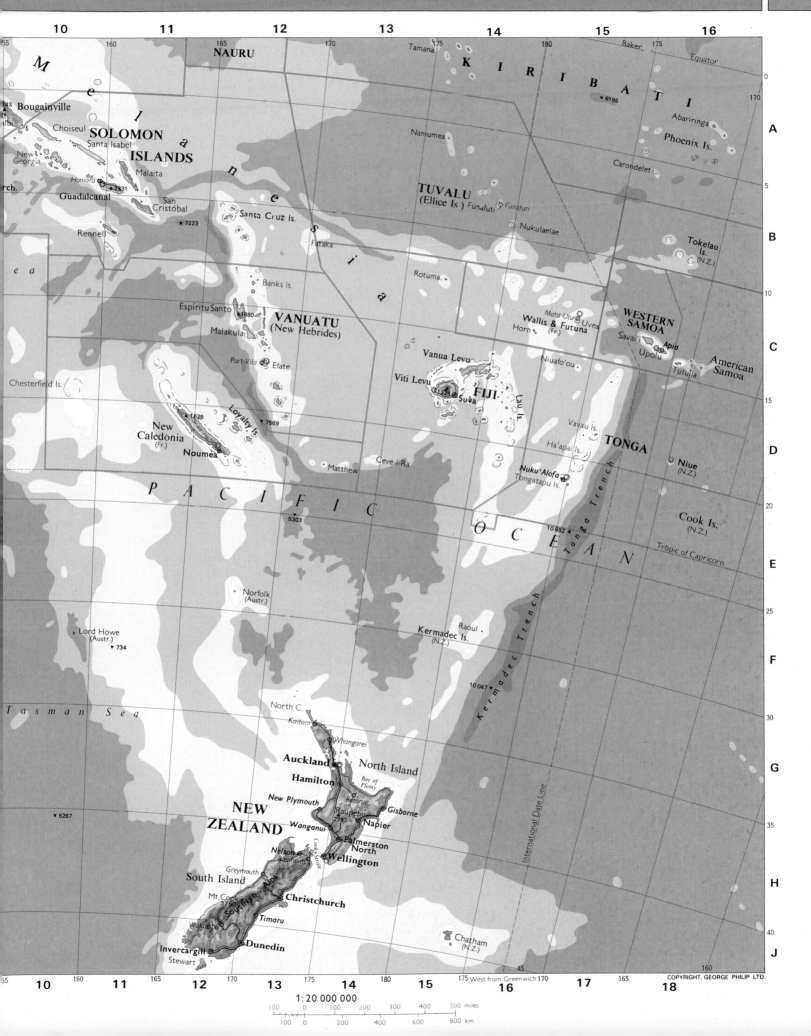

10 160 **11** 165 **12** 170 **13** 175 **14** 180 **15** Baker 175 **16** Equator 170

NAURU   Tamana   KIRIBATI   ▼6195   Abariringa   0

M   ▲743 Bougainville   Phoenix Is.   A
albi   Choiseul   Namumea   170
New   SOLOMON   Santa Isabel   e   Carondelet   5
Georgia   Honiara ▲2331   ISLANDS   Malaita   TUVALU   Tokelau   B
Guadalcanal   San   l   (Ellice Is) Funafuti ○Funafuti   Is.
Cristóbal   a   Nukulaelae   (N.Z.)

rch.   Rennell   ▼7223   Santa Cruz Is.   n   Rotuma.   10
ea   Fataka   e   Mata Utu ○ Uvea   WESTERN   C
Banks Is.   s   Wallis & Futuna   SAMOA
Espíritu Santo   i   Horn (Fr.)   Savai'i   Apia
▲1880   VANUATU   a   Niuafo'ou   Upolu ○○   American   15
Malakula   (New Hebrides)   Tutuila   Samoa
Chesterfield Is.   Port-Vila ○ Efate   Vanua Levu   C
New   Viti Levu   Lau Is.
▲1628   Loyalty Is.   Suva   FIJI   Vavau Is.   TONGA   D
Caledonia   ▼7569   Ha'apai Is.   ○ Niue
(Fr.)   Nouméa   Matthew   Ceve-i-Ra   Nuku'Alofa   (N.Z.)
Tongatapu Is.   20

P A C I F I C   Cook Is.
▼5303   O C E A N   10 882 ▼   (N.Z.)   E
Tropic of Capricorn   25

Norfolk   Kermadec   Raoul   F
(Austr.)   Trench
Lord Howe   Kermadec Is.   10 047 ▼   30
(Austr.)   (N.Z.)
▼734

Tasman Sea   North C.   G
Kaitaia   Whangarei   International Date Line
Auckland   North Island   35
Hamilton   Bay of
NEW   New Plymouth   Plenty   Gisborne
▼5267   ZEALAND   Ruapehu   Rotorua   Napier   40
2797   Wanganui   Palmerston
Nelson   Cook Strait   North   Wellington   H
Greymouth   Blenheim
South Island   Mt.Cook   Christchurch
3759   Southern Alps   Timaru   Chatham   J
Wakatipu   (N.Z.)
Invercargill ○ Dunedin
Stewart

10 160 **11** 165 **12** 170 **13** 175 **14** 180 **15** 175 West from Greenwich 170 **17** 165 **18** 160

1 : 20 000 000

100   0   100   200   300   400   500 miles
100   0   200   400   600   800 km

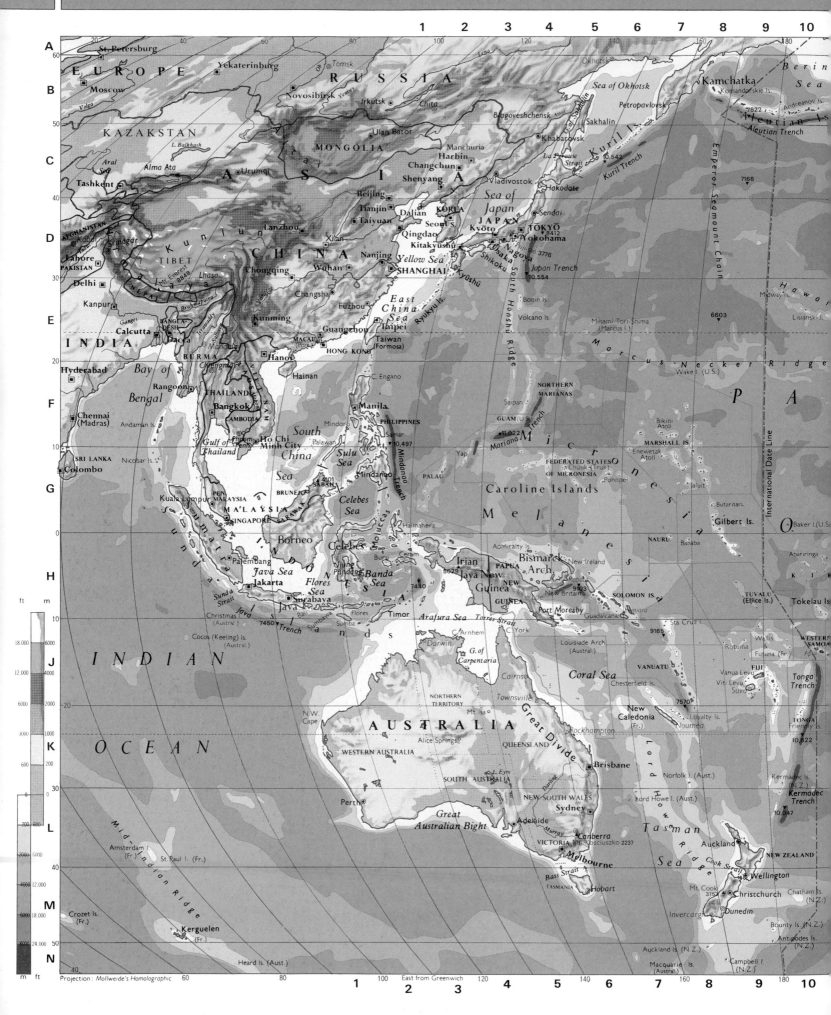

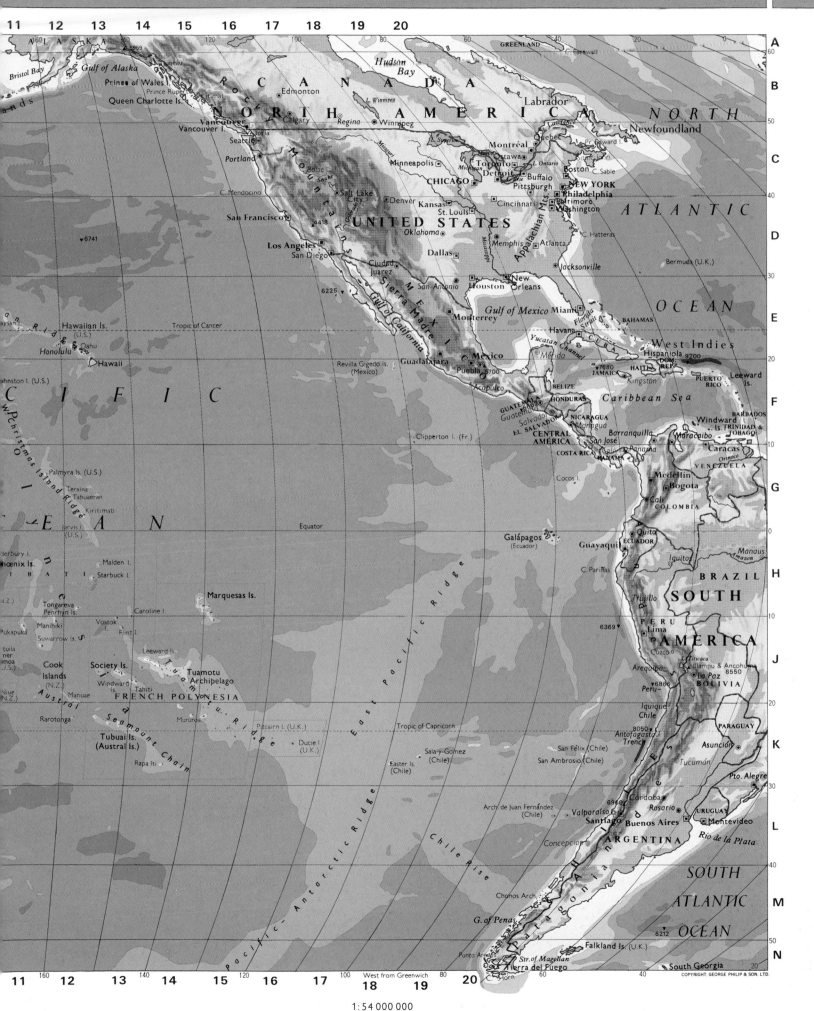

1:54 000 000

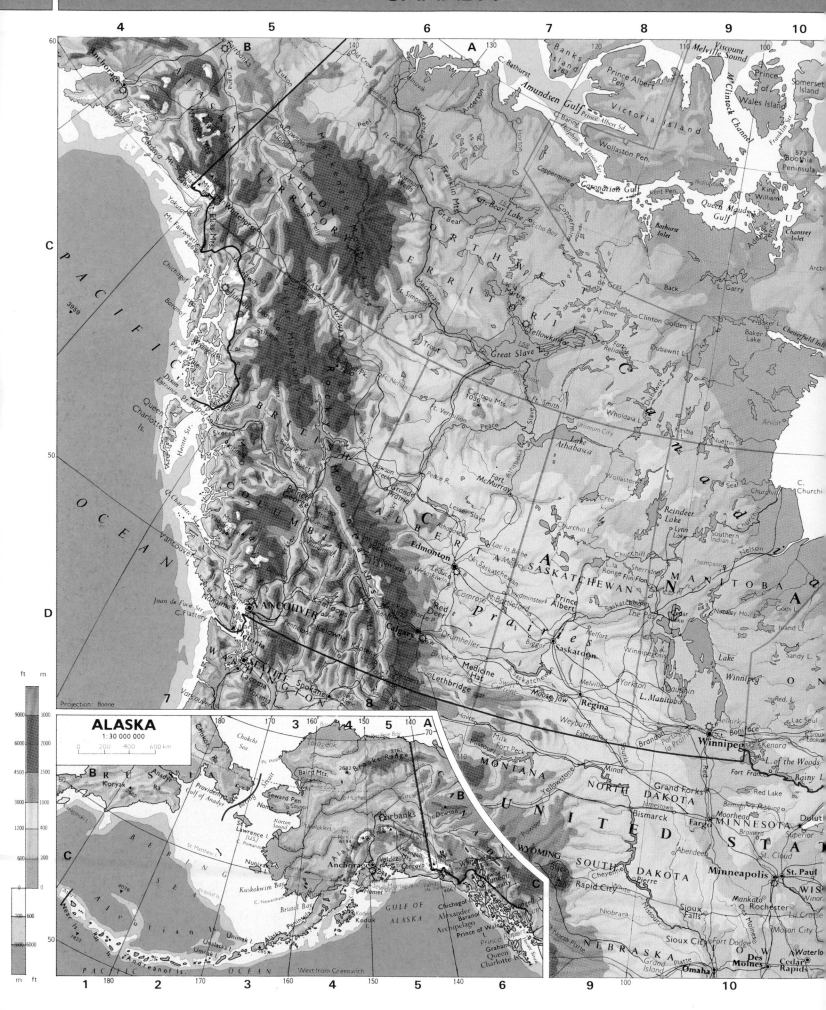

ft   m

9000 3000

6000 2000

4500 1500

3000 1000

1200   400

600   200

0   0

       200 600

       2000 6000

m   ft

Projection: Bonne

ALASKA
1:30 000 000
0   200   400   600 km

1:15 000 000

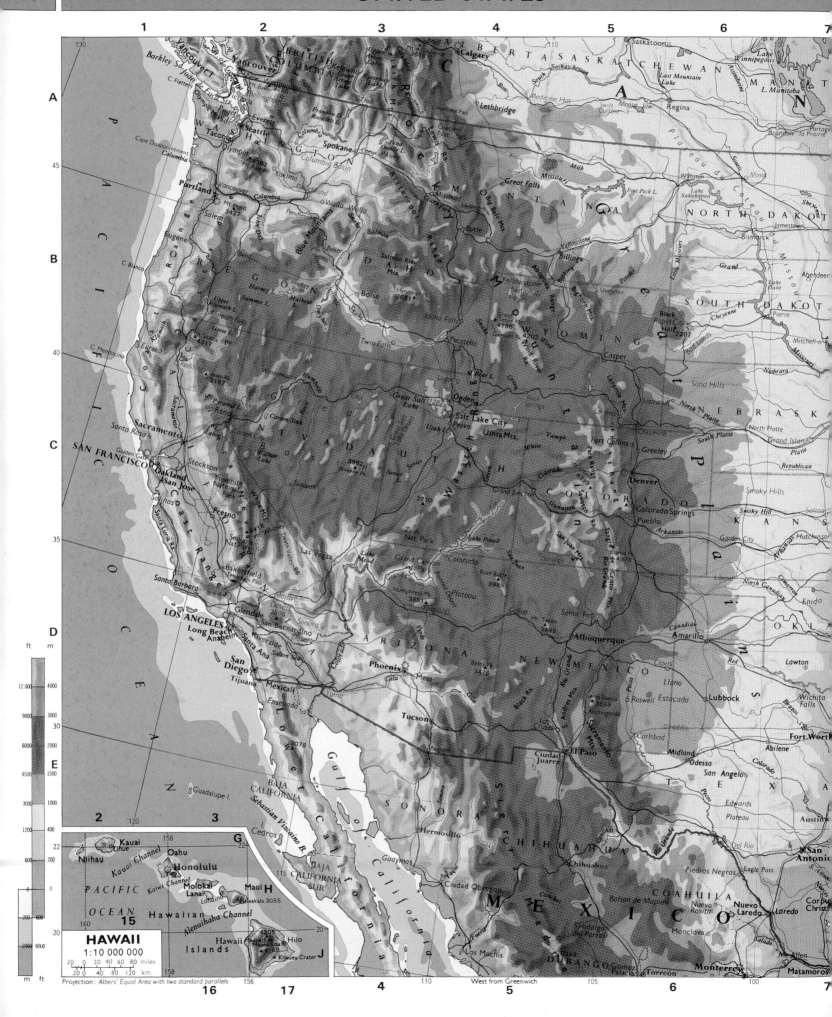

HAWAII
1:10 000 000

Projection : Albers' Equal Area with two standard parallels

1:12 000 000

50   0   50   100   150   200   250   300 miles

50   0   50 100 150 200 250 300 350 400 450 500 km

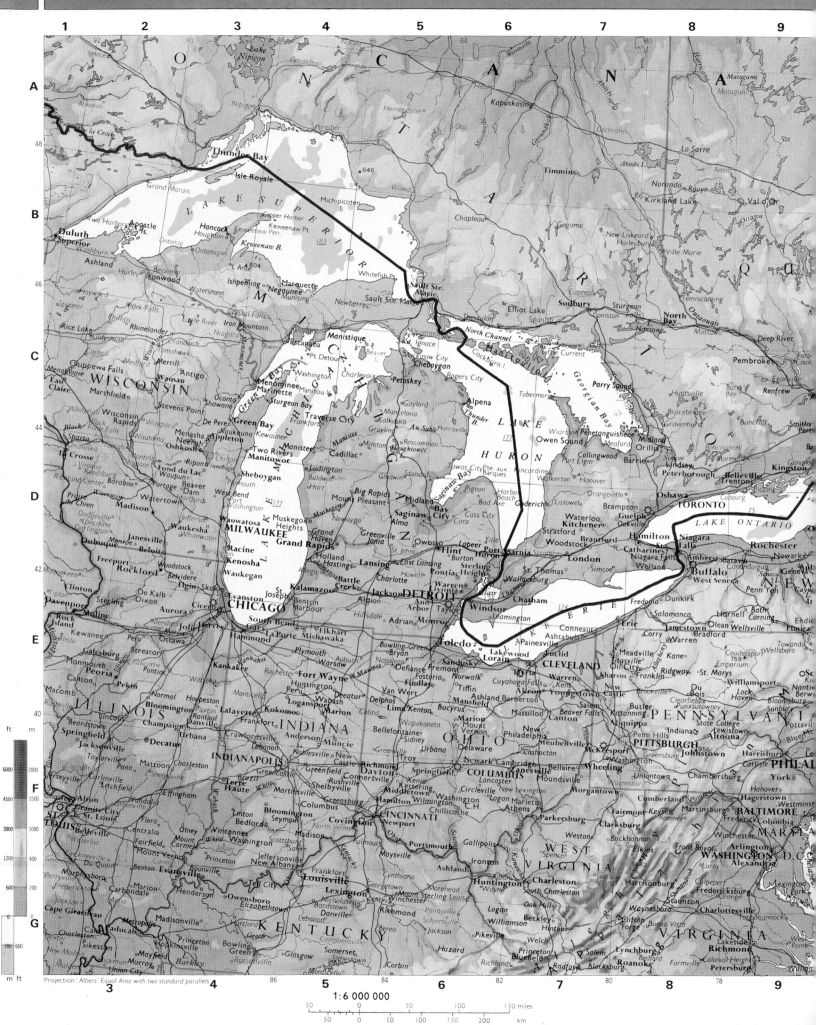

10   11   12   13   14   15   16   17

D   A

556   Chibougamau   Chibougamau I.

Pipmuacan I.

Gouin
Res.

Dolbeau

Port-Cartier   West Pt.   64   62   60

Anticosti I.

Jupiter   Heath Pt.

C. North

GULF OF
ST. LAWRENCE   48

Cap Chat

Matane   Shickshock Mts.   Gaspé

1310

Gaspé Peninsula   C. Gaspé   672

St. Félicien   St. Jean
Roberval   Chicoutimi
Jonquière   Saguenay

Rimouski

Dalhousie   Chaleur Bay

Magdalen
Is.
(Quebec)

Cape Breton
Island

Rivière du Loup   Campbellton   Bathurst   Miramichi B.   North Pt.   Tignish   PRINCE EDWARD
ISLAND   532   Glace Bay
Sydney

Edmundston   819   Newcastle   Chatham   Northumberland Str.   Summerside   Bras d'Or

La Tuque   Forks   N E W   Charlottetown   East Pt.

Q U E B E C   Kent   Van
Eagle   Buren   Grand
Lake   Falls   Chipman   Springhill   New Glasgow   Chedabucto B.

Grand-Mère   Montmagny   St. John   Allagash   Caribou   B R U N S W I C K   Moncton   Stellarton   Canso
Shawinigan   Lévis   Presque Isle   Grand L.   Sussex   N
Cap-de-la-Madeleine   Quebec   Louzon   Eagle L.   Chamberlain   Houlton   Fredericton   O   Kentville   Darmouth
Trois-Rivières   Ste-Marie   L.   Chesuncook   1605   Patten   V   Truro   Halifax
Louiseville   Plessisville   St-George   Mt. Katahdin   Chiputneticook   A   S
L'Annonciation   968   Victoriaville   Thetford   1606   Lake   St. Stephen   Digby   C   Bridgewater
Joliette   Mines   Moosehead   Millinocket   Saint   Bay of Fundy   O   Rossignol Res.
Sorel   Drummondville   Lac-   L.   John   T   Shelburne
St-Jérôme   St-   Asbestos   Mégantic   Greenville   Mottawamkeag   I
Hawkesbury   Hyacinthe   M A I N E   Lincoln   St. Stephen   A
Buckingham   MONTREAL   Granby   Sherbrooke   Old Town   Machias   Yarmouth   C. Sable
Hull   Lachine   Magog   Richardson   Davei   Grand
Ottawa   St-Jean   Coaticook   Lakes   Bangor   Foxcroft   Manan I.
Carleton   Beauharnois   Colebrook   Skowhegan   Brewer   Ellsworth   44
Place   Cornwall   Cowansville   Newport   Rangeley   Mt. Desert
Malone   St. Albans   Island Pond   Kennebec   Waterville   Belfast
Massena   Plattsburg   Farmington   Augusta   Penobscot B.
Ogdensburg   Potsdam   Champlain   Lancaster   Rumford   Gardiner   Rockland
Gouverneur   Burlington   Winooski   St.   Berlin   Lewiston
Saranac Lakes   Montpelier   Johnsbury   Auburn
Watertown   Barre   NEW HAMPSHIRE   Washington   Brunswick
Lowville   Adirondack Mts.   1629   Middlebury   1917   Conway   Bath
Lake Pleasant   Ticonderoga   Rutland   Lebanon   Laconia   Saco
Lake George   WHITE MTS.   Biddeford
VERMONT   Concord   Rochester
Oswego   Granville   Claremont   Dover
Oneida   Rome   Springfield   Franklin   Portsmouth
Oneonta   Glens   Hudson   Manchester   C. Ann
Utica   Falls   Keene   Nashua   Newburyport
Syracuse   Gloversville   Saratoga Springs   Brattleboro   Lawrence   Lowell
Schenectady   Amsterdam   Greenfield   Fitchburg   Salem
Cortland   Norwich   Albany   Pittsfield   Leominster   M A S S   Cambridge   BOSTON
Johnson City   Catskill   Northampton   Worcester   Quincy   Cape Cod
Binghamton   1281   Chicopee   Brockton
Y O R K   Kingston   Springfield   Woonsocket   Taunton
Carbondale   Poughkeepsie   Hartford   Pawtucket   Fall River
Dunmore   Newburgh   Waterbury   New Britain   Providence   New Bedford
Scranton   Middletown   Beacon   Meriden   CONN.   R.I.   Martha's
Wilkes   Danbury   New   New   Vineyard   Nantucket
Barre   Hazleton   Paterson   Haven   London   Block I.
Bethlehem   Mount   Stamford   Long   Island
Easton   Yonkers   Vernon   Bridgeport   Riverhead
Shenandoah   Jersey City   Newark   NEW YORK
Allentown   Reading   Elizabeth   New Brunswick   42
Pottstown   Norristown   New Brunswick   Long Branch
PHILADELPHIA   Trenton   Asbury Park
Lancaster   Camden   NEW
Chester   Wilmington   JERSEY
Bridgeton   Vineland
Millville   Atlantic City   40
MD   Dover   Ocean City
Salisbury   Milford   Cape May   A T L A N T I C
Snow Hill   Cape Henlopen
DELAWARE   O C E A N   38
Cambridge
Seaford

10   74   West from Greenwich   72   12   70   13

14   66   15   64   16   62   17

GREENLAND
(Denmark)

Arctic Circle

C A N A D A   Godthåb   60

Vancouver   Edmonton   Winnipeg   50
Seattle   Ottawa   Montreal
SAN FRANCISCO   Toronto   Boston   40
LOS ANGELES   CHICAGO   Detroit   NEW YORK   PHILADELPHIA
Denver   St. Louis   Washington D.C.
U N I T E D   S T A T E S   Bermuda
(U.K.)
Atlanta   30
Houston   New   Miami   BAHAMAS
M E X I C O   Orleans
Monterrey   Havana   DOMINICAN
REP.
Guadalajara   JAMAICA   HAITI   PUERTO
20   Kingston   RICO
MEXICO   BELIZE   HONDURAS
GUATEMALA
Guatemala   NICARAGUA
EL SALVADOR   10
COSTA RICA   Panamá

120   110   100   90   80

**NORTH AMERICA
Political 1 : 70 000 000**

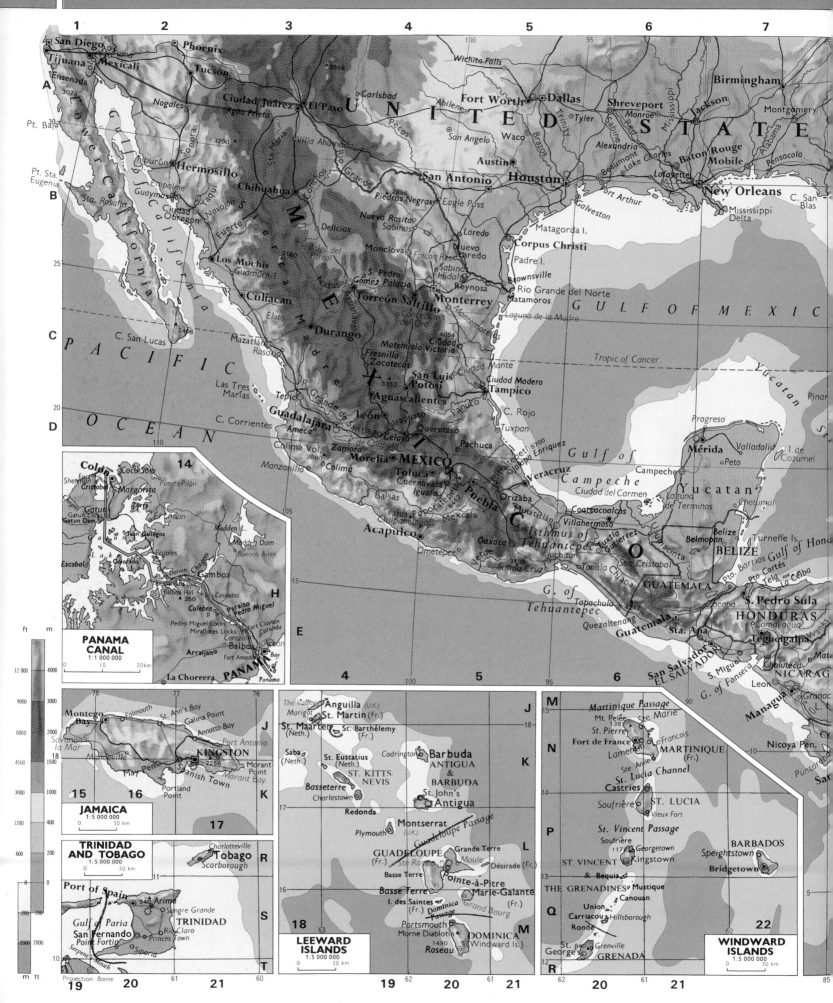

8 9 10 11 12 13

Columbus
Atlanta
Augusta
Macon
Columbus
Savannah
Albany
C. Fear
Charleston

Bermuda (U.K.)
Hamilton

A T L A N T I C   O C E A N

A

B

Jacksonville
Daytona Beach
Orlando
C. Canaveral
West Palm Beach
St. Tampa
Petersburg
L. Okeechobee
Grand
Bahama
I.
Freeport
Gt. Abaco I.
Miami
Fort
Lauderdale
New Providence I.
C. Sable
Key West
Nassau
Eleuthera I.
Cat I.
S. Salvador
BAHAMAS
Andros I.

Tropic of Cancer

C

Havana
Matanzas
Cárdenas
Sagua la Grande
Sta. Clara
Rio
C
U
B
A
Morón
Camagüey
Long I.
Acklins
Gt. Inagua
I.
Mayaguana
Turks &
Caicos Is.
(U.K.)

GREATER

Cienfuegos
Sancti Spíritus
Ciego de Ávila
Manzanillo
Bayamo
2000
Holguin
Santiago
de Cuba
Guantánamo
Windward Passage
Cap Haïtien
Gonaïves
Santiago
San Francisco
de Macorís
PUERTO RICO (U.S.A.)
St. Thomas (U.S.A.)
Charlotte Amalie
Virgin Is. (U.K.)
San Juan
Anguilla
St. Martin (Fr. & Neth.)
ST. KITTS-NEVIS

I. de Juventud
Grand Cayman
(U.K.)
Montego Bay
JAMAICA
Kingston
Santiago
de Cuba
Les Cayes
Port au Prince
2280
DOMINICAN
REP.
La Romana
Barahona
Santo Domingo
Mona Passage
Mayagüez
1338
Ponce
Aguas
St. Croix
(U.S.A.)
ANTIGUA &
BARBUDA
St. John's
Montserrat (U.K.)
Guadeloupe (Fr.)
Pointe à Pitre

D

N.
Hispaniola
Haïti
A N T I L L E S
Leeward
Islands
LESSER
DOMINICA

Martinique (Fr.)
Fort de France
A N T I L L E S
Windward
ST. VINCENT
&
THE GRENADINES
Islands
ST. LUCIA
BARBADOS
Bridgetown
GRENADA

E

Caratasca Lagoon
C. Gracias á Dios

C A R I B B E A N   S E A

Mosquito
Coast
Providencia
(Col.)
San Andrés
(Col.)
Bluefields

Pta. Gallinas
Pen. de la
Guajira
Santa Marta
BARRANQUILLA
Gulf of Venezuela
Aruba (Neth.)
Curaçao
Willemstad
Bonaire
NETH.
ANTILLES
Pen. de
Paraguaná
La Blanquilla
(Ven.)
Margarita
La Tortuga
(Ven.)
Carúpano
Port of Spain
Tobago
TRINIDAD & TOBAGO

Limón
Colón
PANAMA
Panama
G. of
Darién
Cartagena
Sincelejo
5800
Sierra Nevada
de Santa Marta
Punto
Fijo
Coro
MARACAIBO
Cabimas
Maracay
Valencia
Caracas
Barcelona
2596
Cumaná
San Fernando
G. of
Paria
Delta of the
Orinoco

F

Vol. Barú
3374
David
Azuero
Pen.
Coiba
G. of
Panama
Atrato
Quibdó
Medellín
Manizales
Pereira
3560
Barrancabermeja
Cauca
Cúcuta
4100
San Cristóbal
Bucaramanga
Mérida
Valera
L. de
Maracaibo
Cord. de Mérida
Barinas
Arauca
Apure
Arauca
San Fernando
de Apure
Barquisimeto
El Tigre
Orinoco
Ciudad
Bolívar
Ciudad
Guayana
Georgetown
New
Amsterdam

Buenaventura
Cali
3750
Armenia
Tolima 5215
Girardot
Bogotá
C O L O M B I A
Meta
Pto. Ayacucho
2285
V E N E Z U E L A
Caura
Caroní
Angel
Falls
2560
Roraima
2810
Sierra Pacaraima
Cuyuni
Essequibo
G U Y A N A
Courantyne
280
SURINAM

Popayán
4546
Guaviare
Guaviare
Casiquiare
Sa. Parú

B R A Z I L

G

West from Greenwich 80 9 75 10 70 11 65 12 13 COPYRIGHT. GEORGE PHILIP & SON. LTD.

1:15 000 000
100   0   100   200   300   400 miles
100   0   100   200   300   400   500   600 km

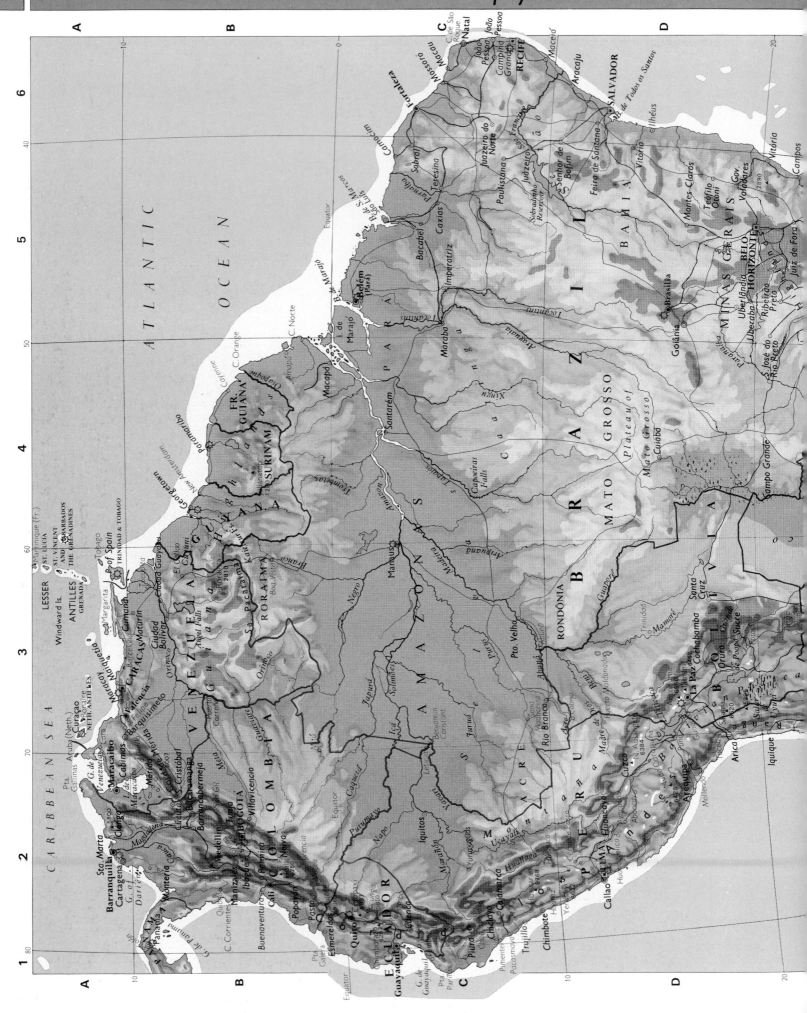

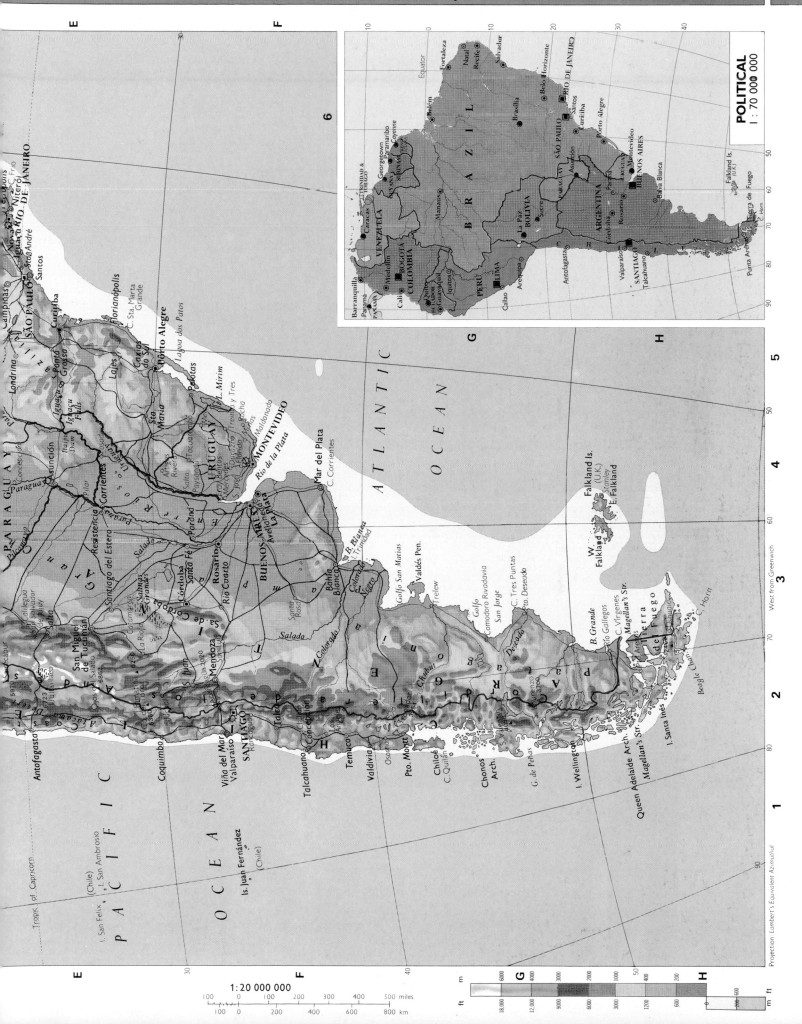

POLITICAL
1 : 70 000 000

Projection Lambert's Equivalent Azimuthal

1:20 000 000

100   0   100   200   300   400   500 miles

100   0   200   400   600   800 km

Legend

- Ice cap
- Permanent ice shelf
- Maximum extent of sea ice
- March (Summer) extent of sea ice
- ▲ 3488 / 3700   Surface elevation and depth of ice (in metres)
- ● Stanley (U.K.)   Permanent bases

Projection: Zenithal Equidistant

1:35 000 000

200 0 200 400 600 800 miles
400 0 400 800 1200 km

COPYRIGHT. GEORGE PHILIP & SON LTD.

West from Greenwich   East from Greenwich

Arctic (upper map)

NORTH AMERICA · CANADA · ARCTIC OCEAN · ASIA · RUSSIA

Greenland (Denmark) (KALAALLIT NUNAAT)

NORWAY

Hudson Bay · Baffin Bay · Davis Str. · Labrador · Denmark Strait

Beaufort Sea · Canada Basin · Alpha Cordillera · Makarov Basin · Lomonosov Ridge · Fram Basin · Nansen Cordillera · Nansen Basin · Amundsen Basin

Kara Sea · Barents Sea · Laptev Sea · Greenland Sea · McKinley Sea

Victoria Island · Banks I. · Melville I. · Parry Is. · Ellesmere I. · Ellef Ringnes I. · Sverdrup Is. · Axel Heiberg I. · Devon I. · Somerset · Southampton I. · Melville Pen. · King William · Pr. of Wales I. · Bathurst I. · Boothia Pen.

Franz Josef Land · Severnaya Zemlya · Novaya Zemlya · New Siberian Is. · Wrangel I. · Taimyr Peninsula · Central Siberian Plateau · Ural Mts.

North Pole · Magnetic Pole 1990

Svalbard (Norway) · Vestspitsbergen · Jan Mayen · Bear I.

Gunnbjørn Field 3700 · Mont Forel 3360

Antarctica (lower map)

ANTARCTICA · East Antarctica · West Antarctica

INDIAN OCEAN · PACIFIC OCEAN · ATLANTIC

Weddell Sea · Ross Sea · Amundsen Sea · Bellingshausen Sea · Davis Sea · Drake Passage

Queen Maud Land · Enderby Ld. · Kemp Land · Mac-Robertson Land · Queen Mary Land · Wilkes Land · Marie Byrd Land · Coats Land · Palmer Land · Graham Land · Edward VII

Antarctic Peninsula · Alexander I. · Charcot I. · Thurston I. · Peter I Øy (Nor.) · Berkner I. · Roosevelt I.

Ross Ice Shelf · Ronne Ice Shelf · Filchner Ice Shelf · Amery Ice Shelf · West Ice Shelf · Shackleton Ice Shelf · Abbot Ice Shelf · Larsen Ice Shelf · George VI Ice Shelf

Falkland Is. (U.K.) · South Georgia · South Orkney Is. (U.K.) · South Shetland Is. · Elephant I. · Clarence I. · Coronation I. · Signy I. (U.K.) · Orcadas (Arg.) · Tierra del Fuego · C. de Hornos

South Pole · Amundsen-Scott (U.S.A.) 2773 / 2407

Transantarctic Mountains · Ellsworth Mts. · Vinson Massif 4897 · Pensacola Mountains · Prince Charles Mts. · Queen Maud Mts. · Queen Alexandra Ra. · Mt. Markham 4349 · Mt. Erebus 4023 · Mt. Lister 3743 · Mt. Sidley 4181

Permanent bases: Halley Bay (U.K.) · Faraday (U.K.) · Rothera (U.K.) · Palmer (U.S.A.) · Siple (U.S.A.) · Byrd · Mawson (Austr.) · Davis (Austr.) · Casey (Austr.) · Mizuho (Japan) · Syowa (Japan) · Mirny · Molodezhnaya · Zhongshan (China) · Dumont d'Urville (Fr.) · McMurdo (U.S.A.) · Scott (N.Z.) · Dakshin Gangotri (India) · Georg von Neumayer (Germany) · Marambio (Arg.) · Esperanza (Arg.) · Gen. Bernardo O'Higgins (Chile) · Capitan Arturo Prat (Chile)

Magnetic Pole 1990

Antarctic Circle

West from Greenwich · East from Greenwich

WORLD
THEMATIC MAPS

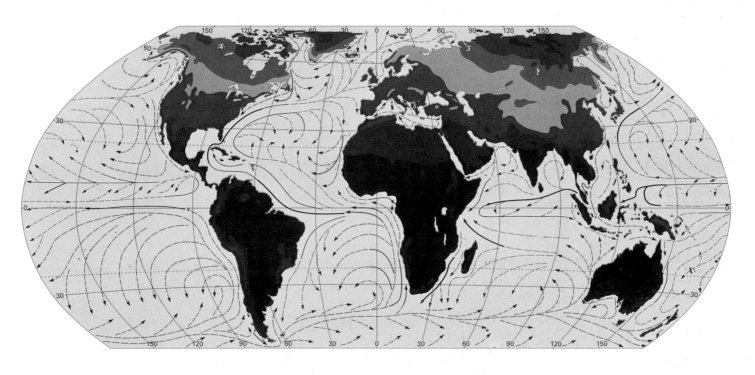

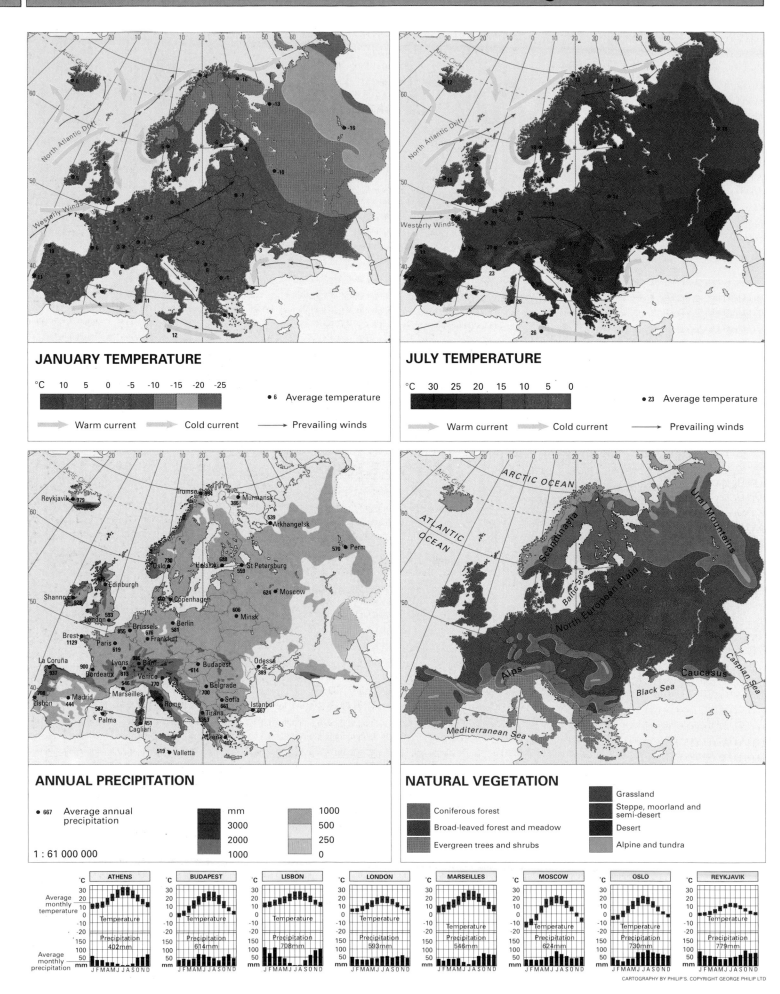

JANUARY TEMPERATURE

°C 10 5 0 -5 -10 -15 -20 -25

● 6 Average temperature

→ Warm current   → Cold current   → Prevailing winds

JULY TEMPERATURE

°C 30 25 20 15 10 5 0

● 23 Average temperature

→ Warm current   → Cold current   → Prevailing winds

ANNUAL PRECIPITATION

● 667 Average annual precipitation

1 : 61 000 000

mm
3000
2000
1000

1000
500
250
0

NATURAL VEGETATION

Coniferous forest
Broad-leaved forest and meadow
Evergreen trees and shrubs

Grassland
Steppe, moorland and semi-desert
Desert
Alpine and tundra

CARTOGRAPHY BY PHILIP'S. COPYRIGHT GEORGE PHILIP LTD

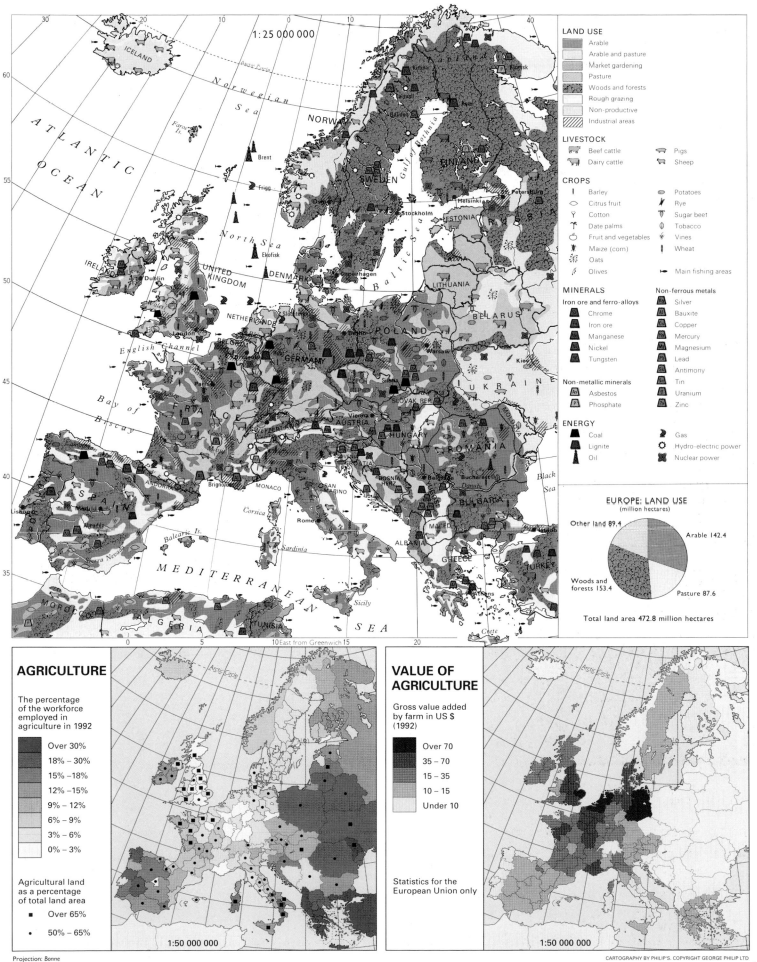

1:25 000 000

LAND USE
- Arable
- Arable and pasture
- Market gardening
- Pasture
- Woods and forests
- Rough grazing
- Non-productive
- Industrial areas

LIVESTOCK
- Beef cattle
- Dairy cattle
- Pigs
- Sheep

CROPS
- Barley
- Citrus fruit
- Cotton
- Date palms
- Fruit and vegetables
- Maize (corn)
- Oats
- Olives
- Potatoes
- Rye
- Sugar beet
- Tobacco
- Vines
- Wheat
- Main fishing areas

MINERALS

Iron ore and ferro-alloys
- Chrome
- Iron ore
- Manganese
- Nickel
- Tungsten

Non-metallic minerals
- Asbestos
- Phosphate

Non-ferrous metals
- Silver
- Bauxite
- Copper
- Mercury
- Magnesium
- Lead
- Antimony
- Tin
- Uranium
- Zinc

ENERGY
- Coal
- Lignite
- Oil
- Gas
- Hydro-electric power
- Nuclear power

EUROPE: LAND USE
(million hectares)

- Other land 89.4
- Arable 142.4
- Woods and forests 153.4
- Pasture 87.6

Total land area 472.8 million hectares

AGRICULTURE

The percentage of the workforce employed in agriculture in 1992

- Over 30%
- 18% – 30%
- 15% –18%
- 12% –15%
- 9% – 12%
- 6% – 9%
- 3% – 6%
- 0% – 3%

Agricultural land as a percentage of total land area
- ■ Over 65%
- • 50% – 65%

1:50 000 000

VALUE OF AGRICULTURE

Gross value added by farm in US $ (1992)

- Over 70
- 35 – 70
- 15 – 35
- 10 – 15
- Under 10

Statistics for the European Union only

1:50 000 000

Projection: *Bonne*

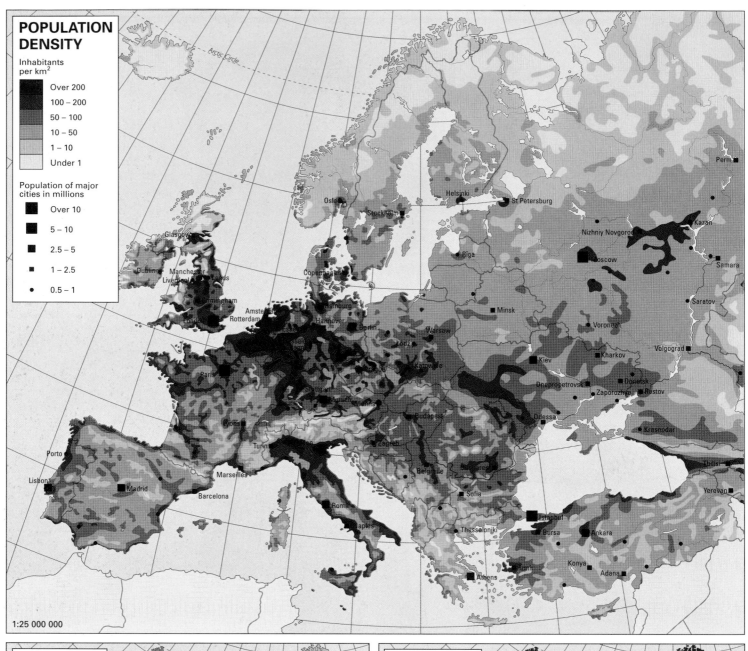

POPULATION DENSITY

Inhabitants per km²

- Over 200
- 100 – 200
- 50 – 100
- 10 – 50
- 1 – 10
- Under 1

Population of major cities in millions

- Over 10
- 5 – 10
- 2.5 – 5
- 1 – 2.5
- 0.5 – 1

1:25 000 000

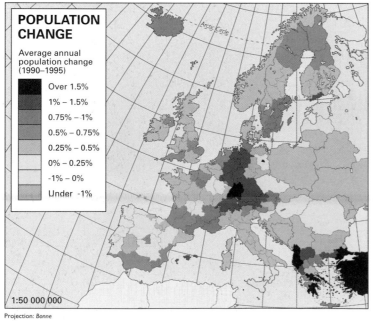

POPULATION CHANGE

Average annual population change (1990–1995)

- Over 1.5%
- 1% – 1.5%
- 0.75% – 1%
- 0.5% – 0.75%
- 0.25% – 0.5%
- 0% – 0.25%
- -1% – 0%
- Under -1%

1:50 000 000

Projection: *Bonne*

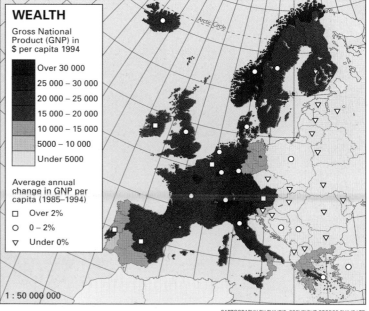

WEALTH

Gross National Product (GNP) in $ per capita 1994

- Over 30 000
- 25 000 – 30 000
- 20 000 – 25 000
- 15 000 – 20 000
- 10 000 – 15 000
- 5000 – 10 000
- Under 5000

Average annual change in GNP per capita (1985–1994)

- ☐ Over 2%
- ○ 0 – 2%
- ▽ Under 0%

1 : 50 000 000

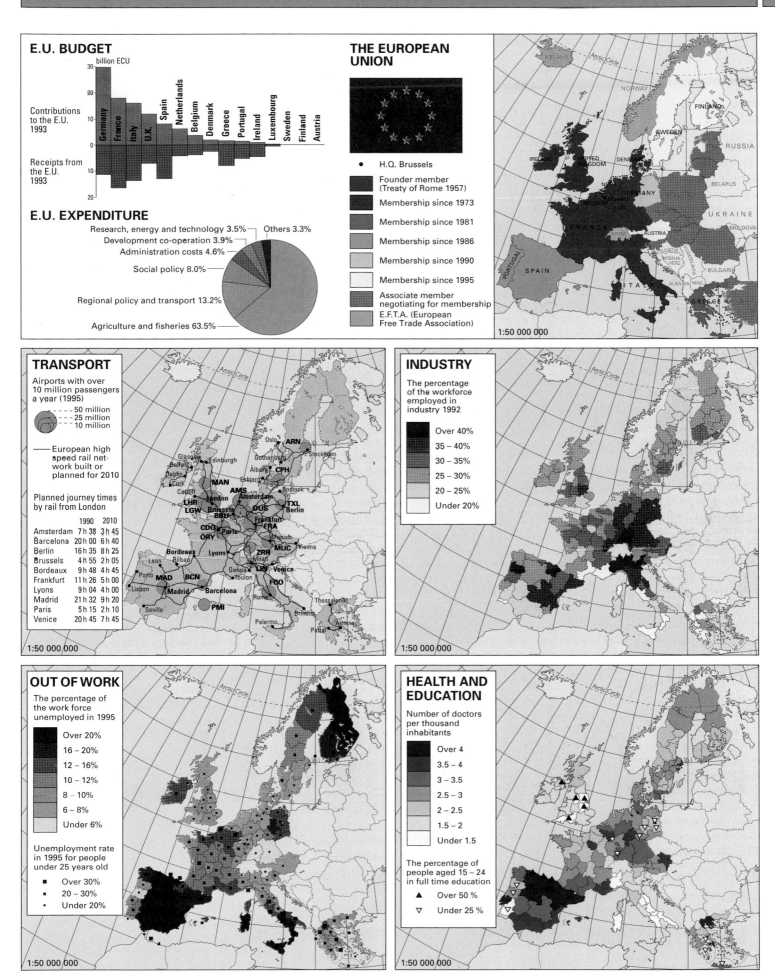

E.U. BUDGET

billion ECU

Contributions to the E.U. 1993

Receipts from the E.U. 1993

Germany, France, Italy, U.K., Spain, Netherlands, Belgium, Denmark, Greece, Portugal, Ireland, Luxembourg, Sweden, Finland, Austria

E.U. EXPENDITURE

Research, energy and technology 3.5%
Development co-operation 3.9%
Administration costs 4.6%
Social policy 8.0%
Regional policy and transport 13.2%
Agriculture and fisheries 63.5%
Others 3.3%

THE EUROPEAN UNION

- H.Q. Brussels
- Founder member (Treaty of Rome 1957)
- Membership since 1973
- Membership since 1981
- Membership since 1986
- Membership since 1990
- Membership since 1995
- Associate member negotiating for membership
- E.F.T.A. (European Free Trade Association)

1:50 000 000

TRANSPORT

Airports with over 10 million passengers a year (1995)

- 50 million
- 25 million
- 10 million

European high speed rail network built or planned for 2010

Planned journey times by rail from London

	1990	2010
Amsterdam	7h 38	3h 45
Barcelona	20h 00	6h 40
Berlin	16h 35	8h 25
Brussels	4h 55	2h 05
Bordeaux	9h 48	4h 45
Frankfurt	11h 26	5h 00
Lyons	9h 04	4h 00
Madrid	21h 32	9h 20
Paris	5h 15	2h 10
Venice	20h 45	7h 45

1:50 000 000

INDUSTRY

The percentage of the workforce employed in industry 1992

- Over 40%
- 35 – 40%
- 30 – 35%
- 25 – 30%
- 20 – 25%
- Under 20%

1:50 000 000

OUT OF WORK

The percentage of the work force unemployed in 1995

- Over 20%
- 16 – 20%
- 12 – 16%
- 10 – 12%
- 8 – 10%
- 6 – 8%
- Under 6%

Unemployment rate in 1995 for people under 25 years old

- ■ Over 30%
- ▪ 20 – 30%
- • Under 20%

1:50 000 000

HEALTH AND EDUCATION

Number of doctors per thousand inhabitants

- Over 4
- 3.5 – 4
- 3 – 3.5
- 2.5 – 3
- 2 – 2.5
- 1.5 – 2
- Under 1.5

The percentage of people aged 15 – 24 in full time education

- ▲ Over 50 %
- ▽ Under 25 %

1:50 000 000

Projection: Bonne

CARTOGRAPHY BY PHILIP'S. COPYRIGHT GEORGE PHILIP LTD

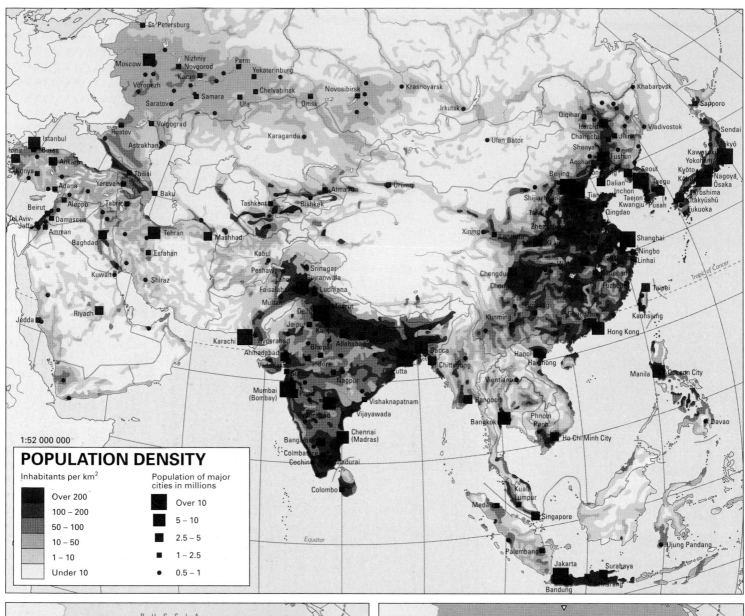

POPULATION DENSITY

1:52 000 000

Inhabitants per km²

	Over 200
	100 – 200
	50 – 100
	10 – 50
	1 – 10
	Under 10

Population of major cities in millions

	Over 10
	5 – 10
	2.5 – 5
	1 – 2.5
	0.5 – 1

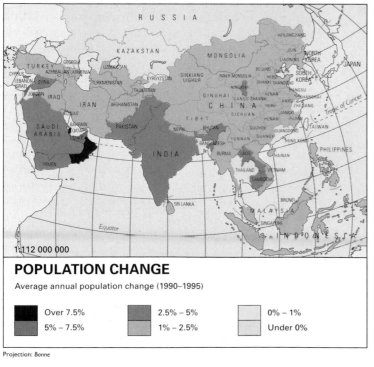

POPULATION CHANGE

1:112 000 000

Average annual population change (1990–1995)

	Over 7.5%		2.5% – 5%
	5% – 7.5%		1% – 2.5%

	0% – 1%
	Under 0%

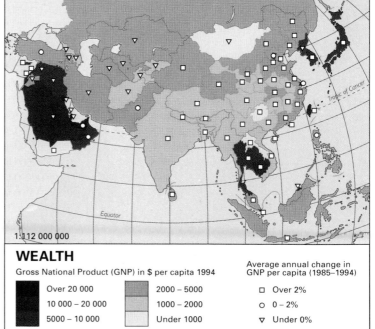

WEALTH

1:112 000 000

Gross National Product (GNP) in $ per capita 1994

	Over 20 000		2000 – 5000
	10 000 – 20 000		1000 – 2000
	5000 – 10 000		Under 1000

Average annual change in GNP per capita (1985–1994)

□	Over 2%
○	0 – 2%
▽	Under 0%

Projection: *Bonne*

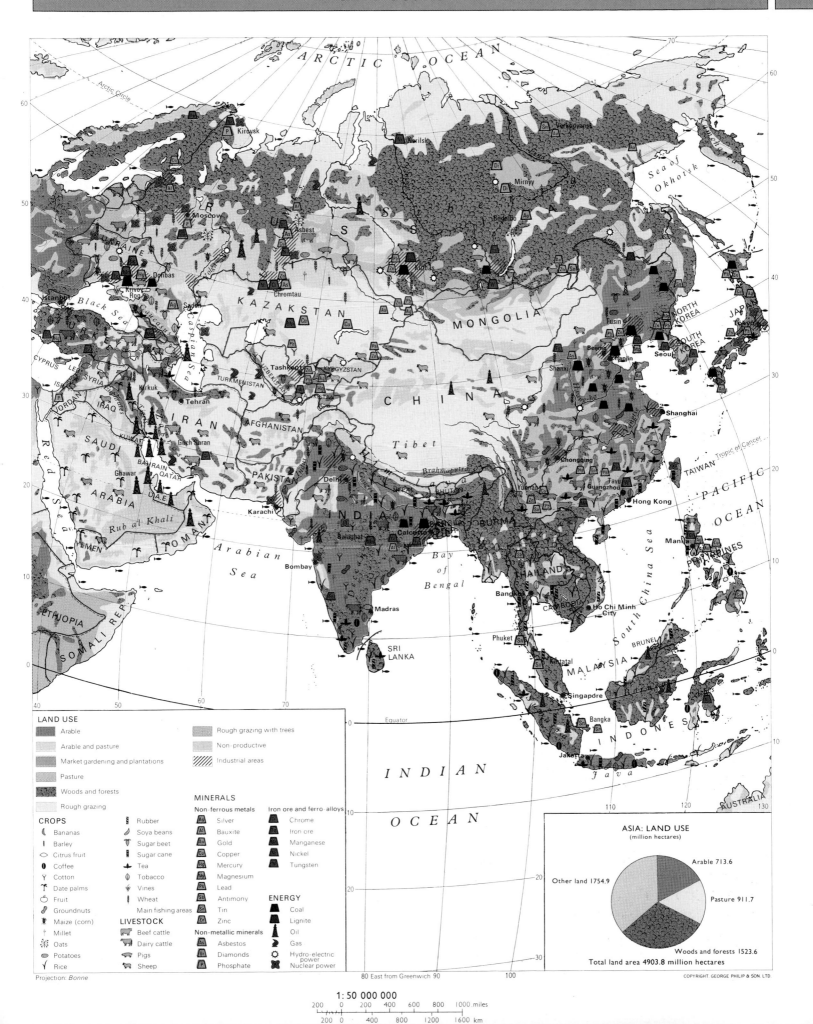

ARCTIC OCEAN

Arctic Circle

Sea of Okhotsk

Kirovsk
Norilsk
Verkhoyansk
Moscow
Asbest
Mirny
Bodaibo
UKRAINE
Donbas
Krivoy Rog
Chromtau
Kuzbas
Istanbul
Black Sea
CYPRUS
SYRIA
Caucasus
KAZAKHSTAN
MONGOLIA
NORTH KOREA
JAPAN
Tokyo
Fusin
Beijing
Tianjin
Seoul
SOUTH KOREA
Tashkent
KYRGYZSTAN
Shanxi
Huang-ho
Kirkuk
Tehran
TURKMENISTAN
UZBEKISTAN
Shanghai
JORDAN
IRAQ
IRAN
AFGHANISTAN
Gach Saran
CHINA
Tibet
Chongqing
ISRAEL
LEB
KUWAIT
SAUDI
Brahmaputra
TAIWAN
Tropic of Cancer
PACIFIC OCEAN
BAHRAIN
QATAR
Ganges
NEPAL
BHUTAN
Yunnan
Guangzhou
Ghawar
UAE
Delhi
Hong Kong
ARABIA
PAKISTAN
Karachi
INDIA
BURMA
Manila
OMAN
Rub al Khali
Calcutta
PHILIPPINES
YEMEN
Balaghat
Arabian Sea
Deccan
Bombay
Bay of Bengal
THAILAND
Bangkok
South China Sea
CAMBODIA
Ho Chi Minh City
ETHIOPIA
SOMALI REP.
Madras
Phuket
BRUNEI
SRI LANKA
Natal
MALAYSIA
Singapore
INDONESIA
Equator
Bangka
Java
Jakarta
INDIAN OCEAN
AUSTRALIA

LAND USE

- Arable
- Arable and pasture
- Market gardening and plantations
- Pasture
- Woods and forests
- Rough grazing
- Rough grazing with trees
- Non-productive
- Industrial areas

CROPS
- Bananas
- Barley
- Citrus fruit
- Coffee
- Cotton
- Date palms
- Fruit
- Groundnuts
- Maize (corn)
- Millet
- Oats
- Potatoes
- Rice
- Rubber
- Soya beans
- Sugar beet
- Sugar cane
- Tea
- Tobacco
- Vines
- Wheat
- Main fishing areas

LIVESTOCK
- Beef cattle
- Dairy cattle
- Pigs
- Sheep

MINERALS

Non-ferrous metals
- Ag Silver
- Al Bauxite
- Au Gold
- Cu Copper
- Mercury
- Magnesium
- Pb Lead
- Antimony
- Sn Tin
- Zn Zinc

Non-metallic minerals
- As Asbestos
- Di Diamonds
- P Phosphate

Iron ore and ferro-alloys
- Chrome
- Iron ore
- Manganese
- Nickel
- Tungsten

ENERGY
- Coal
- Lignite
- Oil
- Gas
- Hydro-electric power
- Nuclear power

Projection: Bonne

80 East from Greenwich 90   100

COPYRIGHT GEORGE PHILIP & SON LTD.

ASIA: LAND USE
(million hectares)

Other land 1754.9
Arable 713.6
Pasture 911.7
Woods and forests 1523.6

Total land area 4903.8 million hectares

1:50 000 000

200 0 200 400 600 800 1000 miles
200 0 400 800 1200 1600 km

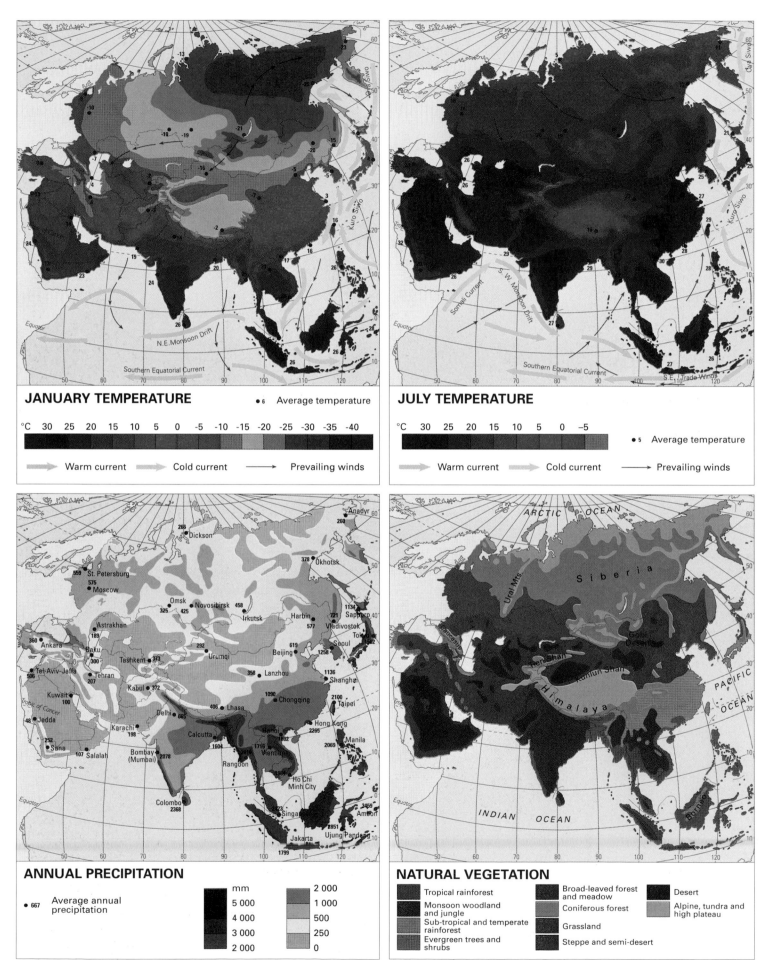

JANUARY TEMPERATURE

• 6 Average temperature

°C 30 25 20 15 10 5 0 -5 -10 -15 -20 -25 -30 -35 -40

→ Warm current   → Cold current   → Prevailing winds

JULY TEMPERATURE

°C 30 25 20 15 10 5 0 -5

• 5 Average temperature

→ Warm current   → Cold current   → Prevailing winds

ANNUAL PRECIPITATION

• 667 Average annual precipitation

mm
5 000
4 000
3 000
2 000

2 000
1 000
500
250
0

NATURAL VEGETATION

Tropical rainforest

Monsoon woodland and jungle

Sub-tropical and temperate rainforest

Evergreen trees and shrubs

Broad-leaved forest and meadow

Coniferous forest

Grassland

Steppe and semi-desert

Desert

Alpine, tundra and high plateau

Projection: *Modified Hammer Equal Area*   1 : 105 000 000

CARTOGRAPHY BY PHILIP'S. COPYRIGHT GEORGE PHILIP LTD

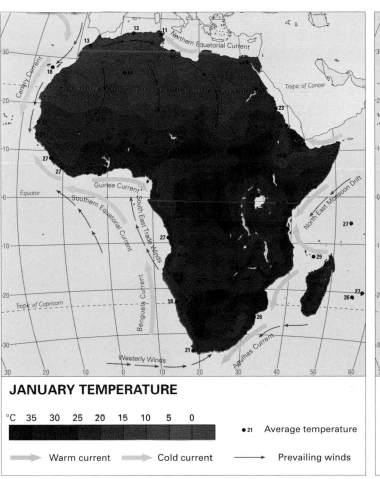

JANUARY TEMPERATURE

°C 35 30 25 20 15 10 5 0

• 21 Average temperature

➡ Warm current   ➡ Cold current   → Prevailing winds

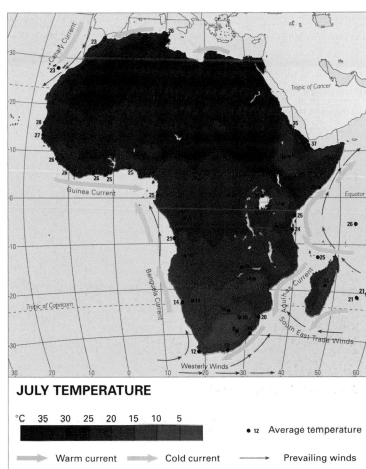

JULY TEMPERATURE

°C 35 30 25 20 15 10 5

• 12 Average temperature

➡ Warm current   ➡ Cold current   → Prevailing winds

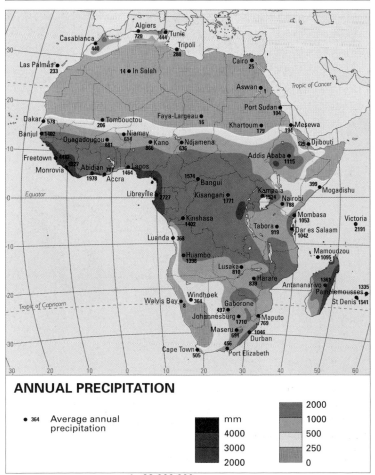

ANNUAL PRECIPITATION

• 364 Average annual precipitation

mm	
	2000
4000	1000
3000	500
2000	250
	0

Projection: *Modified Hammer Equal Area*   1 : 93 000 000

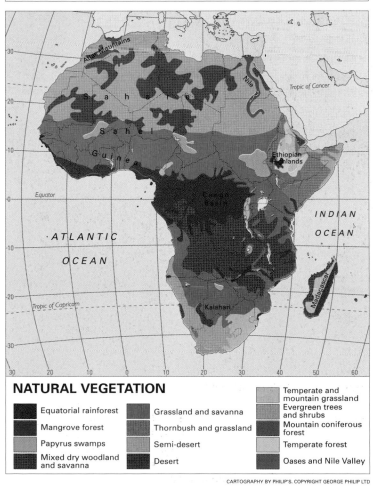

NATURAL VEGETATION

- Equatorial rainforest
- Mangrove forest
- Papyrus swamps
- Mixed dry woodland and savanna
- Grassland and savanna
- Thornbush and grassland
- Semi-desert
- Desert
- Temperate and mountain grassland
- Evergreen trees and shrubs
- Mountain coniferous forest
- Temperate forest
- Oases and Nile Valley

CARTOGRAPHY BY PHILIP'S. COPYRIGHT GEORGE PHILIP LTD

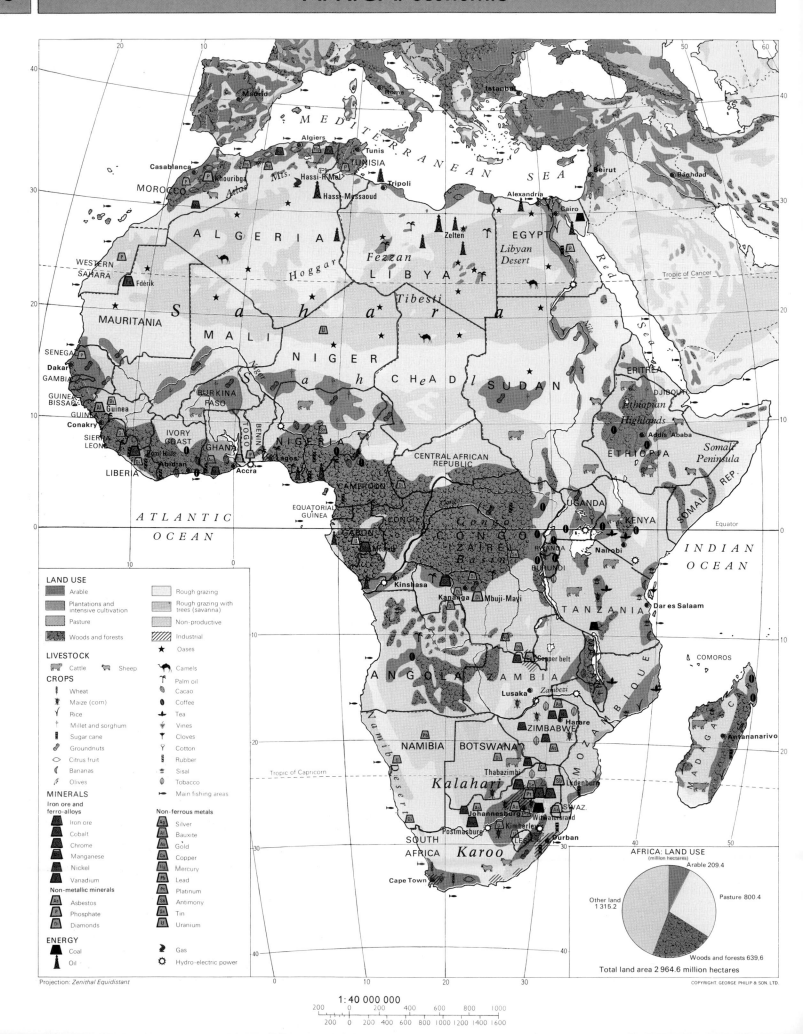

LAND USE

- Arable
- Plantations and intensive cultivation
- Pasture
- Woods and forests
- Rough grazing
- Rough grazing with trees (savanna)
- Non-productive
- Industrial

LIVESTOCK

- Cattle
- Sheep

CROPS

- Wheat
- Maize (corn)
- Rice
- Millet and sorghum
- Sugar cane
- Groundnuts
- Citrus fruit
- Bananas
- Olives
- Camels
- Palm oil
- Cacao
- Coffee
- Tea
- Vines
- Cloves
- Cotton
- Rubber
- Sisal
- Tobacco
- Main fishing areas

Oases

MINERALS

Iron ore and ferro-alloys

- Iron ore
- Cobalt
- Chrome
- Manganese
- Nickel
- Vanadium

Non-metallic minerals

- As Asbestos
- P Phosphate
- Di Diamonds

Non-ferrous metals

- Ag Silver
- Al Bauxite
- Au Gold
- Cu Copper
- Hg Mercury
- Pb Lead
- Pt Platinum
- Sb Antimony
- Sn Tin
- U Uranium

ENERGY

- Coal
- Oil
- Gas
- Hydro-electric power

AFRICA: LAND USE
(million hectares)

- Arable 209.4
- Pasture 800.4
- Woods and forests 639.6
- Other land 1 315.2

Total land area 2 964.6 million hectares

Projection: *Zenithal Equidistant*

1:40 000 000

COPYRIGHT. GEORGE PHILIP & SON. LTD.

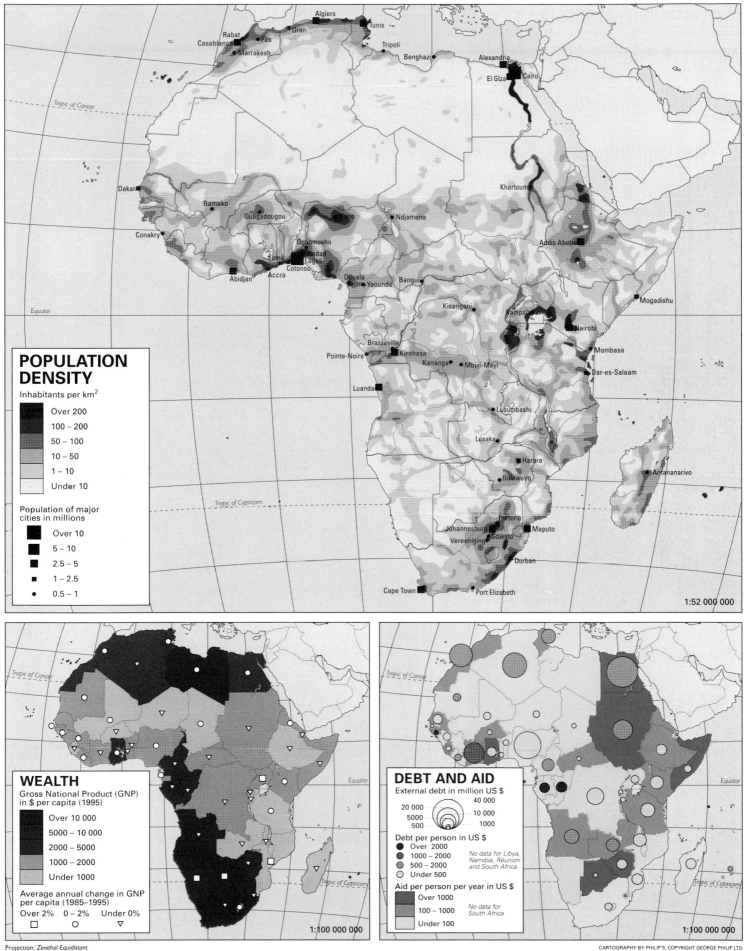

POPULATION DENSITY

Inhabitants per km²

- Over 200
- 100 – 200
- 50 – 100
- 10 – 50
- 1 – 10
- Under 10

Population of major cities in millions

- Over 10
- 5 – 10
- 2.5 – 5
- 1 – 2.5
- 0.5 – 1

Algiers
Rabat
Casablanca
Fes
Oran
Marrakesh
Tunis
Tripoli
Benghazi
Alexandria
El Giza
Cairo
Khartoum
Dakar
Bamako
Ouagadougou
Kano
Ndjamena
Conakry
Ogbomosho
Ibadan
Addis Ababa
Tome
Lagos
Cotonou
Abidjan
Accra
Douala
Yaoundé
Bangui
Kisangani
Mogadishu
Kampala
Nairobi
Brazzaville
Mombasa
Pointe-Noire
Kinshasa
Kananga
Mbuji-Mayi
Dar-es-Salaam
Luanda
Lubumbashi
Lusaka
Harare
Antananarivo
Bulawayo
Pretoria
Johannesburg
Maputo
Vereeniging
Soweto
Durban
Cape Town
Port Elizabeth

Tropic of Cancer
Equator
Tropic of Capricorn

1:52 000 000

WEALTH

Gross National Product (GNP) in $ per capita (1995)

- Over 10 000
- 5000 – 10 000
- 2000 – 5000
- 1000 – 2000
- Under 1000

Average annual change in GNP per capita (1985–1995)

Over 2%   0 – 2%   Under 0%
□   ○   ▽

Tropic of Cancer
Equator
Tropic of Capricorn

1:100 000 000

DEBT AND AID

External debt in million US $

- 20 000 / 40 000
- 5000 / 10 000
- 500 / 1000

Debt per person in US $

- Over 2000
- 1000 – 2000
- 500 – 2000
- Under 500

No data for Libya, Namibia, Réunion and South Africa

Aid per person per year in US $

- Over 1000
- 100 – 1000
- Under 100

No data for South Africa

Tropic of Cancer
Equator
Tropic of Capricorn

1:100 000 000

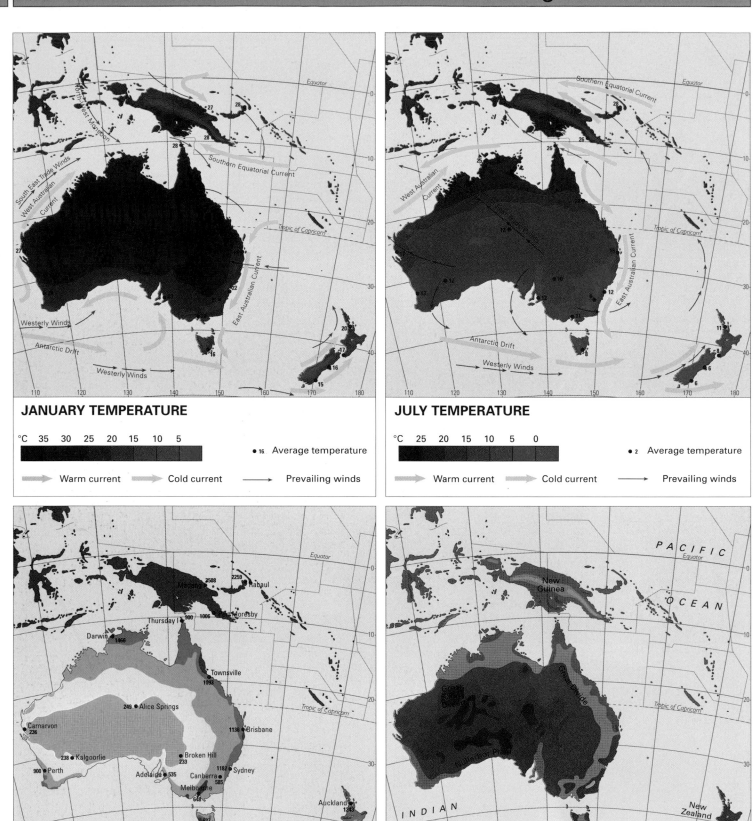

JANUARY TEMPERATURE

°C 35 30 25 20 15 10 5

● 16 Average temperature

Warm current   Cold current   Prevailing winds

JULY TEMPERATURE

°C 25 20 15 10 5 0

● 2 Average temperature

Warm current   Cold current   Prevailing winds

ANNUAL PRECIPITATION

● 627 Average annual precipitation

mm	
3000	1000
2000	500
1000	250
	0

NATURAL VEGETATION

Tropical rainforest	Evergreen trees and shrubs	Desert
Temperate rainforest	Grassland and savanna	Alpine
Sub-tropical and temperate woodland	Semi-desert	

Projection: *Modified Hammer Equal Area*   1 : 67 000 000

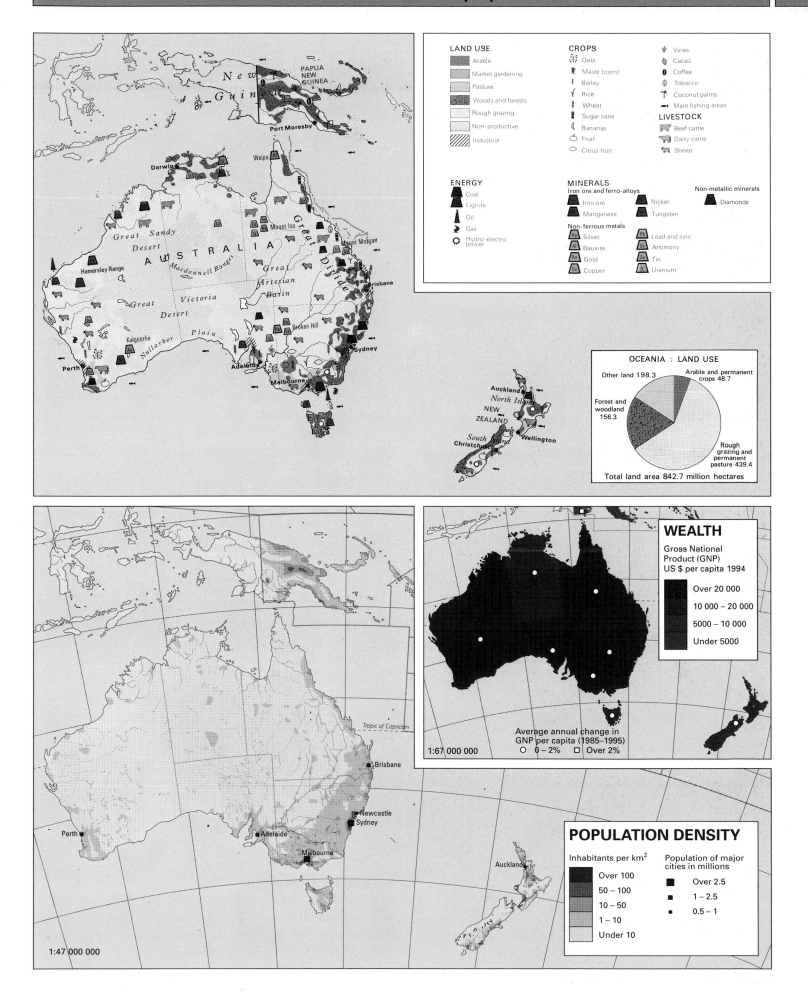

LAND USE

- Arable
- Market gardening
- Pasture
- Woods and forests
- Rough grazing
- Non-productive
- Industrial

CROPS

- Oats
- Maize (corn)
- Barley
- Rice
- Wheat
- Sugar cane
- Bananas
- Fruit
- Citrus fruit
- Vines
- Cacao
- Coffee
- Tobacco
- Coconut palms
- Main fishing areas

LIVESTOCK

- Beef cattle
- Dairy cattle
- Sheep

ENERGY

- Coal
- Lignite
- Oil
- Gas
- Hydro-electric power

MINERALS

Iron ore and ferro-alloys

- Iron ore
- Manganese
- Nickel
- Tungsten

Non-ferrous metals

- Ag Silver
- Al Bauxite
- Au Gold
- Cu Copper
- Pb Lead and zinc
- Sb Antimony
- Sn Tin
- U Uranium

Non-metallic minerals

- Diamonds

OCEANIA : LAND USE

- Other land 198.3
- Arable and permanent crops 48.7
- Forest and woodland 156.3
- Rough grazing and permanent pasture 439.4

Total land area 842.7 million hectares

Map 1 labels (Land use / economic)

New Guinea
PAPUA NEW GUINEA
Port Moresby
Darwin
Weipa
Mount Isa
Mount Morgan
Hamersley Range
Great Sandy Desert
AUSTRALIA
Macdonnell Ranges
Great Artesian Basin
Great Victoria Desert
Brisbane
Great Dividing
Kalgoorlie
Nullarbor Plain
Broken Hill
Sydney
Perth
Adelaide
Melbourne
Auckland
North Island
NEW ZEALAND
South Island
Christchurch
Wellington

WEALTH

Gross National Product (GNP) US $ per capita 1994

- Over 20 000
- 10 000 – 20 000
- 5000 – 10 000
- Under 5000

1:67 000 000

Average annual change in GNP per capita (1985–1995)

- ○ 0 – 2%
- □ Over 2%

POPULATION DENSITY

Inhabitants per km²

- Over 100
- 50 – 100
- 10 – 50
- 1 – 10
- Under 10

Population of major cities in millions

- Over 2.5
- 1 – 2.5
- 0.5 – 1

Map labels (population)

Brisbane
Newcastle
Sydney
Perth
Adelaide
Melbourne
Tropic of Capricorn
Auckland

1:47 000 000

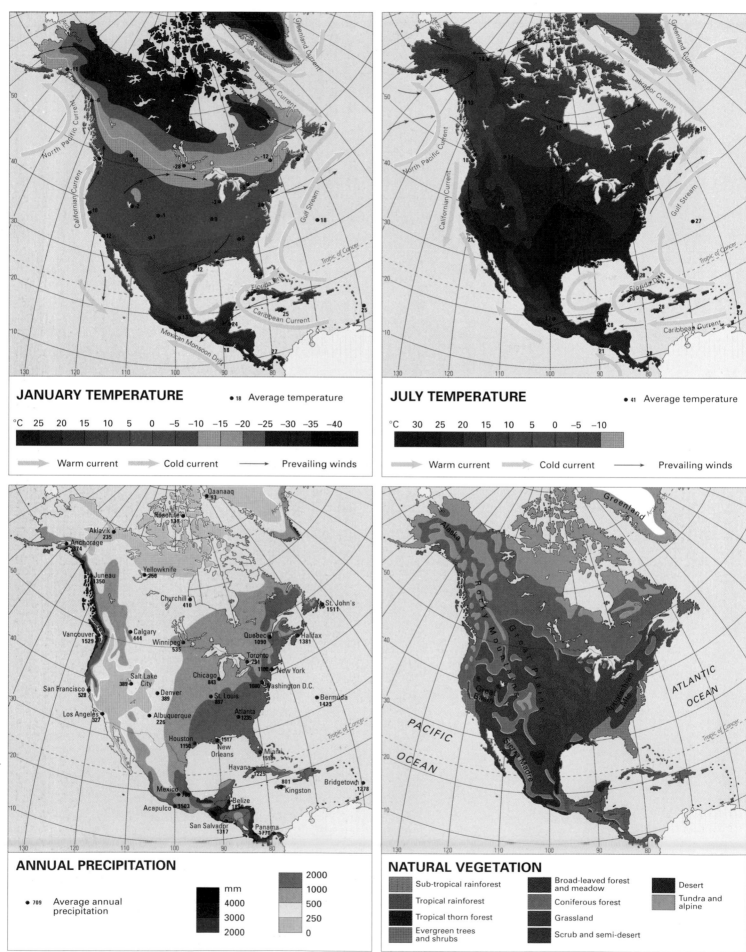

JANUARY TEMPERATURE

● 18 Average temperature

°C 25 20 15 10 5 0 −5 −10 −15 −20 −25 −30 −35 −40

→ Warm current → Cold current → Prevailing winds

JULY TEMPERATURE

● 41 Average temperature

°C 30 25 20 15 10 5 0 −5 −10

→ Warm current → Cold current → Prevailing winds

ANNUAL PRECIPITATION

● 709 Average annual precipitation

mm
4000
3000
2000

2000
1000
500
250
0

Projection: *Modified Hammer Equal Area*

1 : 84 000 000

NATURAL VEGETATION

Sub-tropical rainforest
Tropical rainforest
Tropical thorn forest
Evergreen trees and shrubs
Broad-leaved forest and meadow
Coniferous forest
Grassland
Scrub and semi-desert
Desert
Tundra and alpine

CARTOGRAPHY BY PHILIP'S. COPYRIGHT GEORGE PHILIP LTD

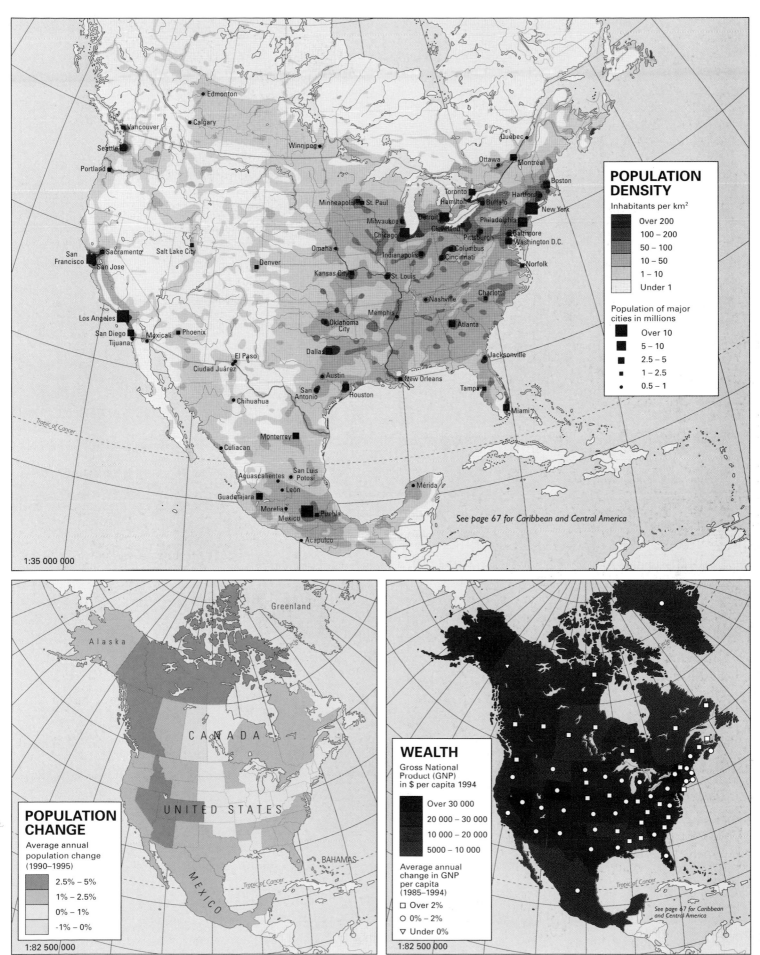

POPULATION DENSITY

Inhabitants per km²

- Over 200
- 100 – 200
- 50 – 100
- 10 – 50
- 1 – 10
- Under 1

Population of major cities in millions

- Over 10
- 5 – 10
- 2.5 – 5
- 1 – 2.5
- 0.5 – 1

See page 67 for Caribbean and Central America

1:35 000 000

POPULATION CHANGE

Average annual population change (1990–1995)

- 2.5% – 5%
- 1% – 2.5%
- 0% – 1%
- -1% – 0%

1:82 500 000

WEALTH

Gross National Product (GNP) in $ per capita 1994

- Over 30 000
- 20 000 – 30 000
- 10 000 – 20 000
- 5000 – 10 000

Average annual change in GNP per capita (1985–1994)

- □ Over 2%
- ○ 0% – 2%
- ▽ Under 0%

See page 67 for Caribbean and Central America

1:82 500 000

Projection: Polyconic

CARTOGRAPHY BY PHILIP'S. COPYRIGHT GEORGE PHILIP LTD

NORTH AMERICA: *economic*

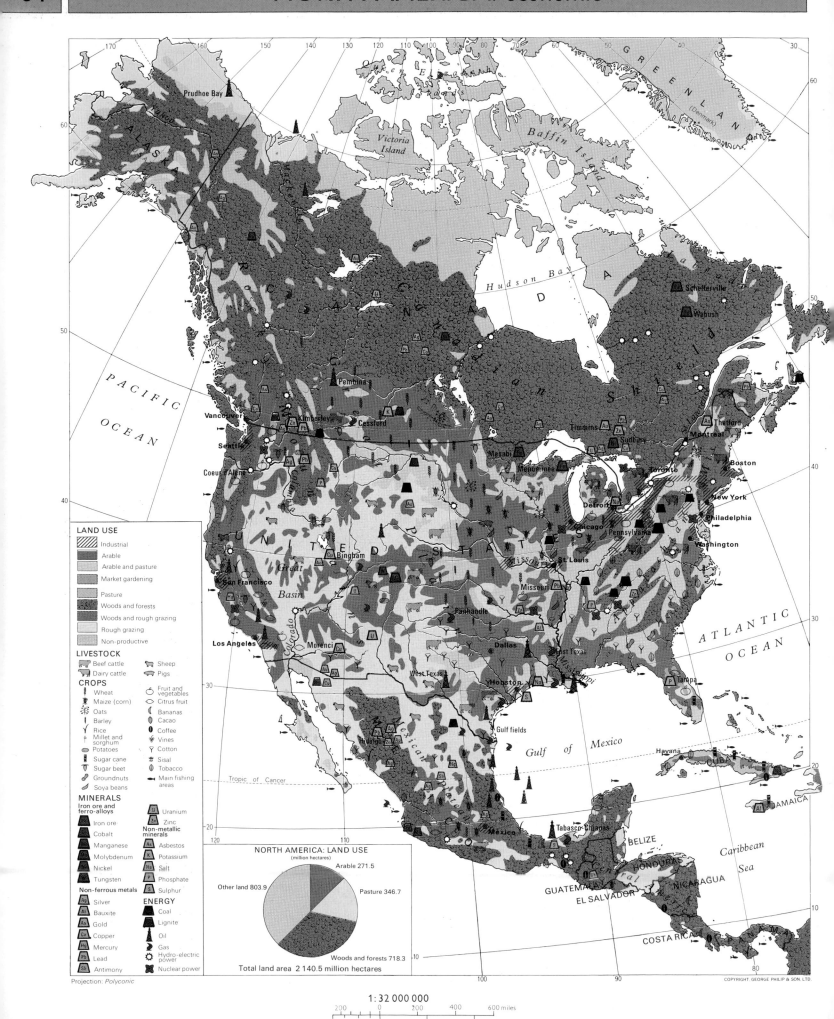

LAND USE

- Industrial
- Arable
- Arable and pasture
- Market gardening
- Pasture
- Woods and forests
- Woods and rough grazing
- Rough grazing
- Non-productive

LIVESTOCK

- Beef cattle
- Sheep
- Dairy cattle
- Pigs

CROPS

- Wheat
- Maize (corn)
- Oats
- Barley
- Rice
- Millet and sorghum
- Potatoes
- Sugar cane
- Sugar beet
- Groundnuts
- Soya beans
- Fruit and vegetables
- Citrus fruit
- Bananas
- Cacao
- Coffee
- Vines
- Cotton
- Sisal
- Tobacco
- Main fishing areas

MINERALS

Iron ore and ferro-alloys

- Iron ore
- Cobalt
- Manganese
- Molybdenum
- Nickel
- Tungsten

Non-ferrous metals

- Ag Silver
- Al Bauxite
- Au Gold
- Cu Copper
- Hg Mercury
- Pb Lead
- Sb Antimony
- U Uranium
- Zn Zinc

Non-metallic minerals

- As Asbestos
- K Potassium
- Na Salt
- P Phosphate
- S Sulphur

ENERGY

- Coal
- Lignite
- Oil
- Gas
- Hydro-electric power
- Nuclear power

NORTH AMERICA: LAND USE
(million hectares)

- Arable 271.5
- Pasture 346.7
- Woods and forests 718.3
- Other land 803.9

Total land area 2 140.5 million hectares

Projection: *Polyconic*

COPYRIGHT GEORGE PHILIP & SON LTD.

1 : 32 000 000

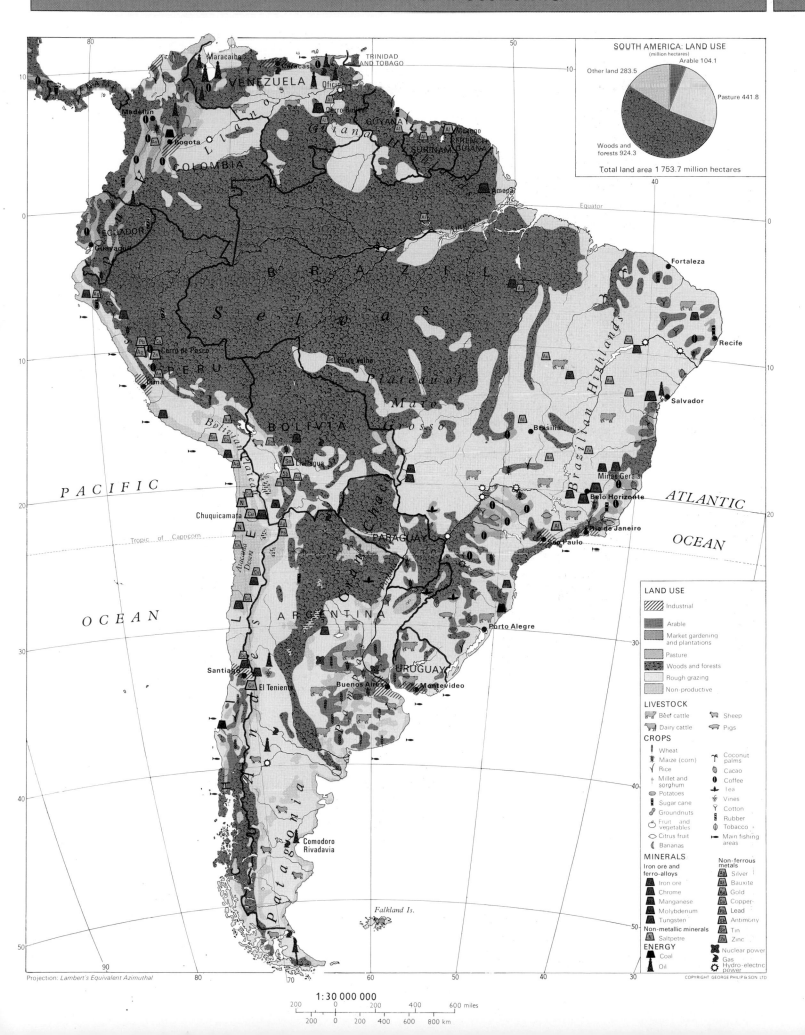

SOUTH AMERICA: LAND USE
(million hectares)
Arable 104.1
Other land 283.5
Pasture 441.8
Woods and forests 924.3
Total land area 1 753.7 million hectares

LAND USE
Industrial
Arable
Market gardening and plantations
Pasture
Woods and forests
Rough grazing
Non-productive

LIVESTOCK
Beef cattle   Sheep
Dairy cattle   Pigs

CROPS
Wheat   Coconut palms
Maize (corn)   Cacao
Rice   Coffee
Millet and sorghum   Tea
Potatoes   Vines
Sugar cane   Cotton
Groundnuts   Rubber
Fruit and vegetables Tobacco
Citrus fruit   Main fishing areas
Bananas

MINERALS
Iron ore and ferro-alloys   Non-ferrous metals
Iron ore   Silver
Chrome   Bauxite
Manganese   Gold
Molybdenum   Copper
Tungsten   Lead
Non-metallic minerals Antimony
Saltpetre   Tin
                     Zinc
ENERGY
Coal   Nuclear power
Oil   Gas
                     Hydro-electric power

Projection: *Lambert's Equivalent Azimuthal*

COPYRIGHT GEORGE PHILIP & SON LTD

1:30 000 000
200   0   200   400   600 miles
200 0 200 400 600 800 km

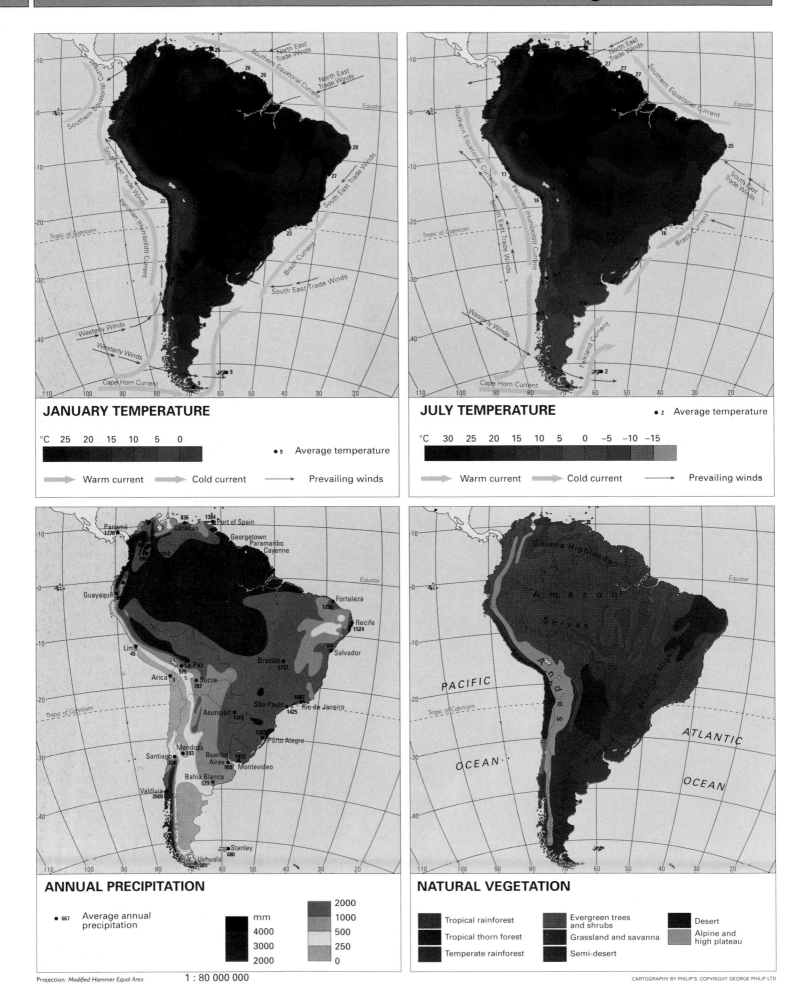

JANUARY TEMPERATURE

°C 25 20 15 10 5 0

• 9   Average temperature

Warm current   Cold current   Prevailing winds

JULY TEMPERATURE

• 2   Average temperature

°C 30 25 20 15 10 5 0 −5 −10 −15

Warm current   Cold current   Prevailing winds

ANNUAL PRECIPITATION

• 667   Average annual precipitation

	mm
	4000
	3000
	2000
2000	
1000	
500	
250	
0	

NATURAL VEGETATION

Tropical rainforest

Tropical thorn forest

Temperate rainforest

Evergreen trees and shrubs

Grassland and savanna

Semi-desert

Desert

Alpine and high plateau

Projection: *Modified Hammer Equal Area*   1 : 80 000 000

CARTOGRAPHY BY PHILIP'S. COPYRIGHT GEORGE PHILIP LTD

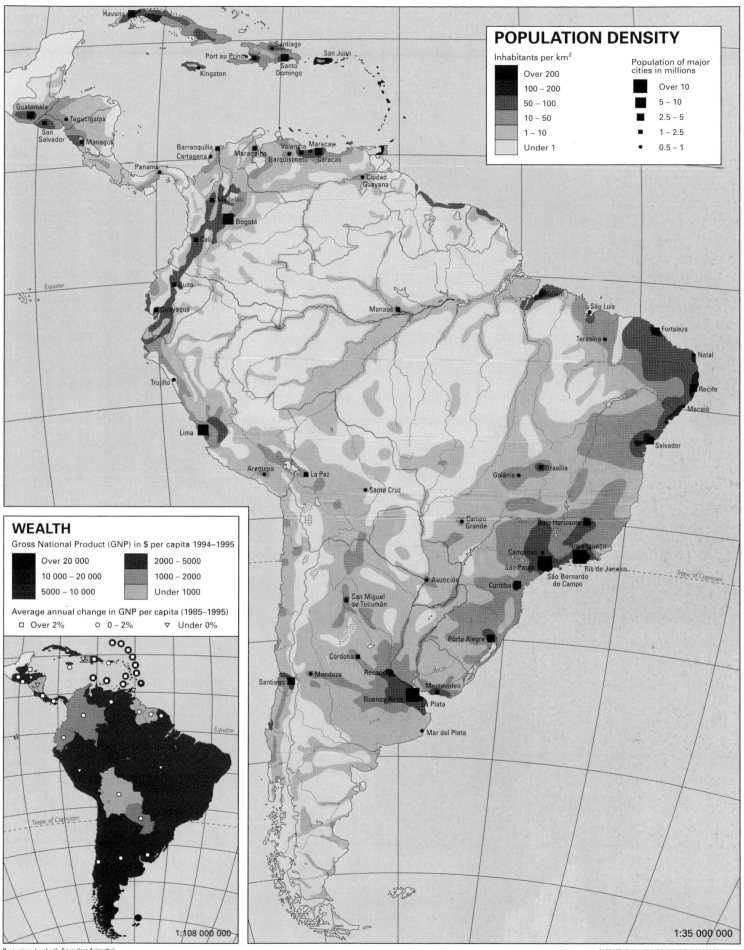

POPULATION DENSITY

Inhabitants per km²

- Over 200
- 100 – 200
- 50 – 100
- 10 – 50
- 1 – 10
- Under 1

Population of major cities in millions

- Over 10
- 5 – 10
- 2.5 – 5
- 1 – 2.5
- 0.5 – 1

WEALTH

Gross National Product (GNP) in $ per capita 1994–1995

- Over 20 000
- 10 000 – 20 000
- 5000 – 10 000
- 2000 – 5000
- 1000 – 2000
- Under 1000

Average annual change in GNP per capita (1985–1995)

- ☐ Over 2%
- ○ 0 – 2%
- ▽ Under 0%

1:108 000 000

Projection: *Lambert's Equivalent Azimuthal*

1:35 000 000

CARTOGRAPHY BY PHILIP'S. COPYRIGHT GEORGE PHILIP LTD

Havana
Santiago
Port au Prince
Kingston
San Juan
Santo Domingo
Guatemala
Tegucigalpa
San Salvador
Managua
Panama
Barranquilla
Cartagena
Maracaibo
Valencia Maracay
Barquisimeto Caracas
Ciudad Guayana
Medellín
Bogotá
Cali
Quito
Guayaquil
Manaus
Belém
São Luís
Fortaleza
Teresina
Natal
Trujillo
Recife
Maceió
Lima
Salvador
Arequipa
La Paz
Brasília
Goiânia
Santa Cruz
Campo Grande
Belo Horizonte
Campinas
Nova Iguaçu
São Paulo
Rio de Janeiro
Asunción
Curitiba
São Bernardo do Campo
San Miguel de Tucumán
Pôrto Alegre
Córdoba
Santiago
Mendoza
Rosario
Montevideo
Buenos Aires
La Plata
Mar del Plata

Equator

Tropic of Capricorn

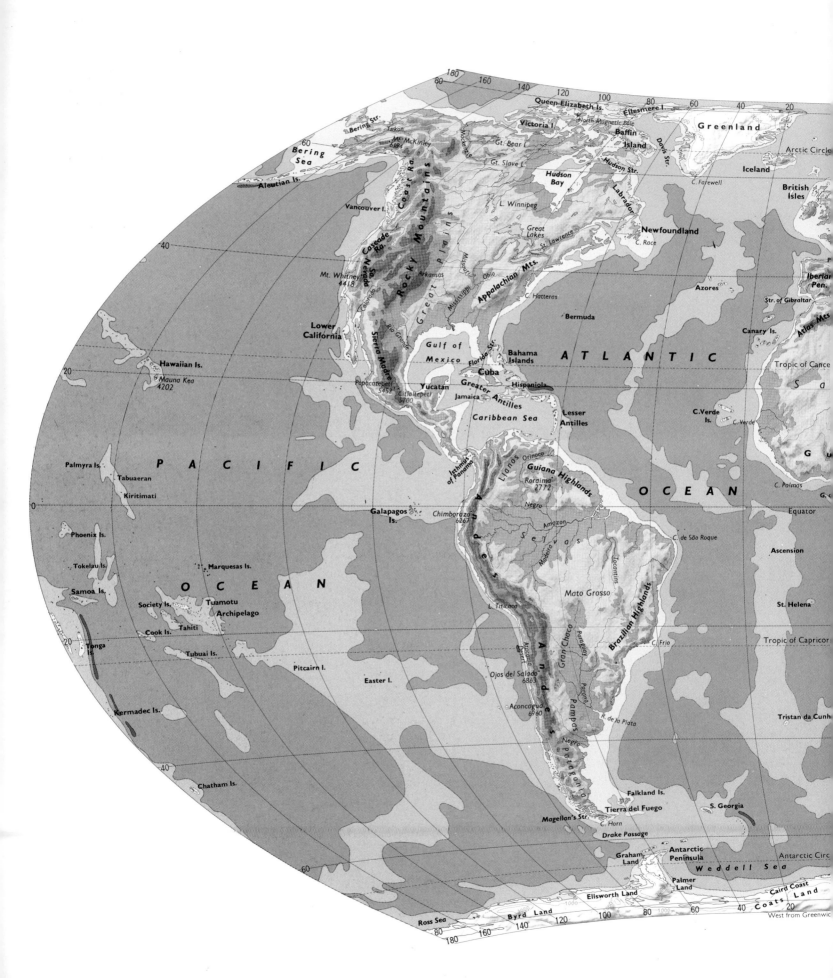

Projection: Hammer Equal Area

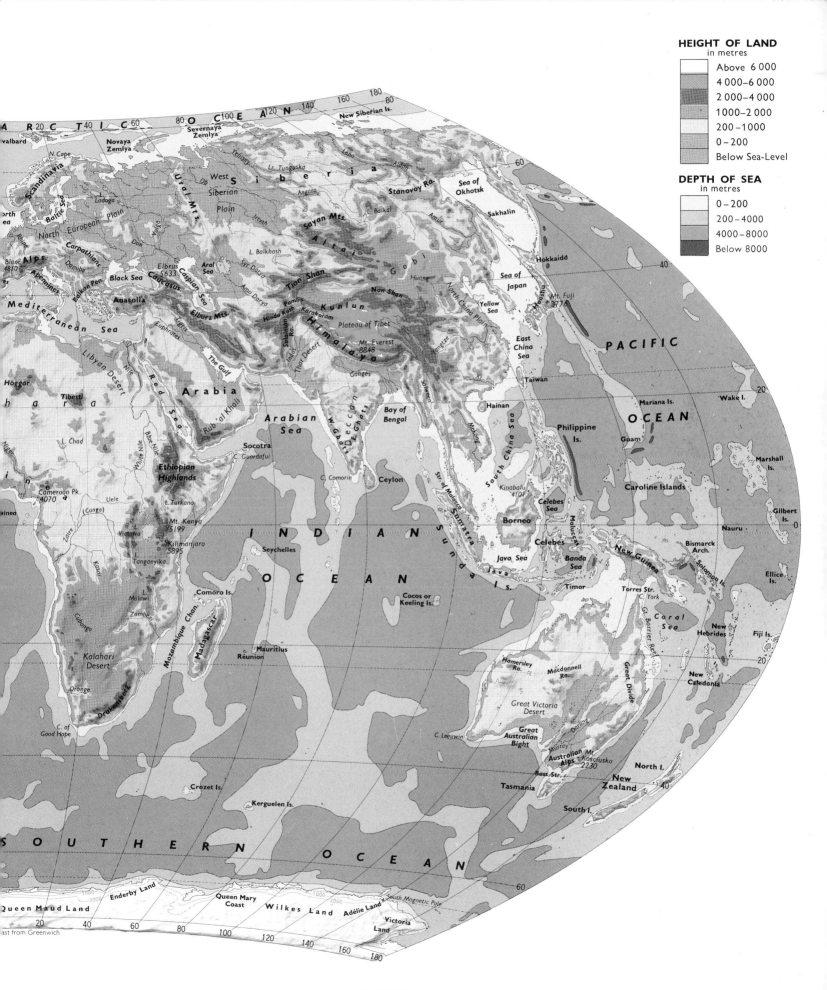

HEIGHT OF LAND
in metres

Above 6 000
4 000–6 000
2 000–4 000
1000–2 000
200–1000
0–200
Below Sea-Level

DEPTH OF SEA
in metres

0–200
200–4000
4000–8000
Below 8000

1:80 000 000

Copyright, George Philip & Son, Ltd.

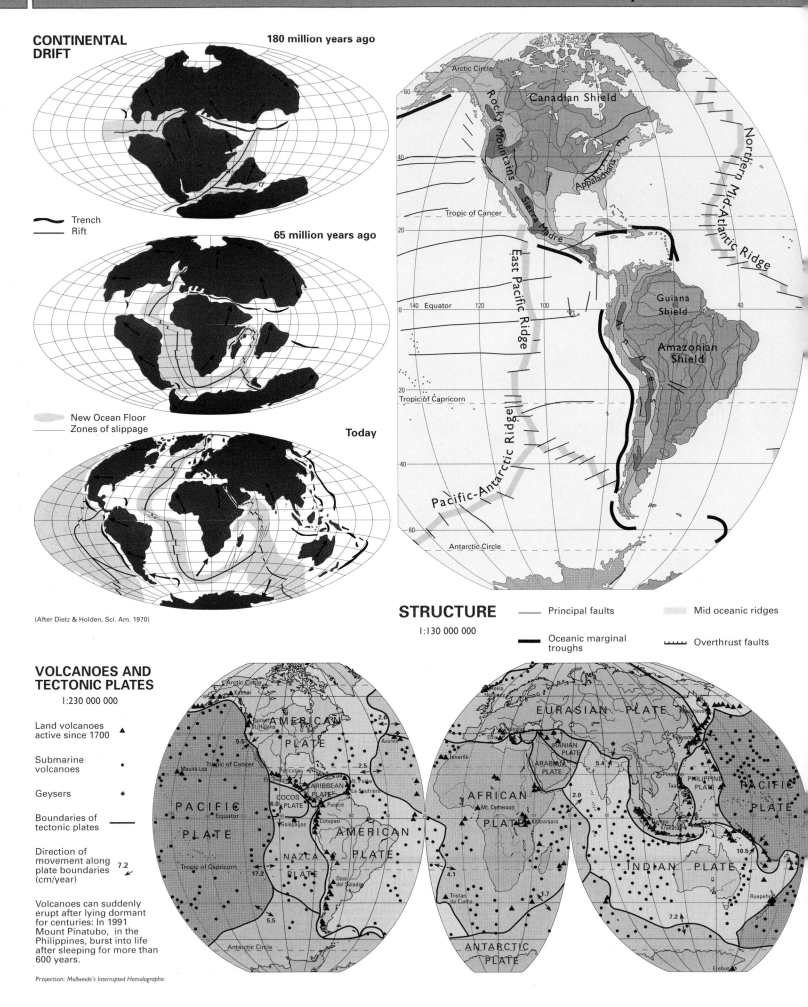

CONTINENTAL DRIFT

180 million years ago

65 million years ago

Today

~ Trench
— Rift

New Ocean Floor
Zones of slippage

(After Dietz & Holden, Sci. Am. 1970)

STRUCTURE
1:130 000 000

— Principal faults
— Oceanic marginal troughs
▒ Mid oceanic ridges
⊥⊥⊥ Overthrust faults

VOLCANOES AND TECTONIC PLATES
1:230 000 000

▲ Land volcanoes active since 1700

• Submarine volcanoes

+ Geysers

— Boundaries of tectonic plates

7.2 → Direction of movement along plate boundaries (cm/year)

Volcanoes can suddenly erupt after lying dormant for centuries: In 1991 Mount Pinatubo, in the Philippines, burst into life after sleeping for more than 600 years.

Projection: *Mollweide's Interrupted Homolographic*

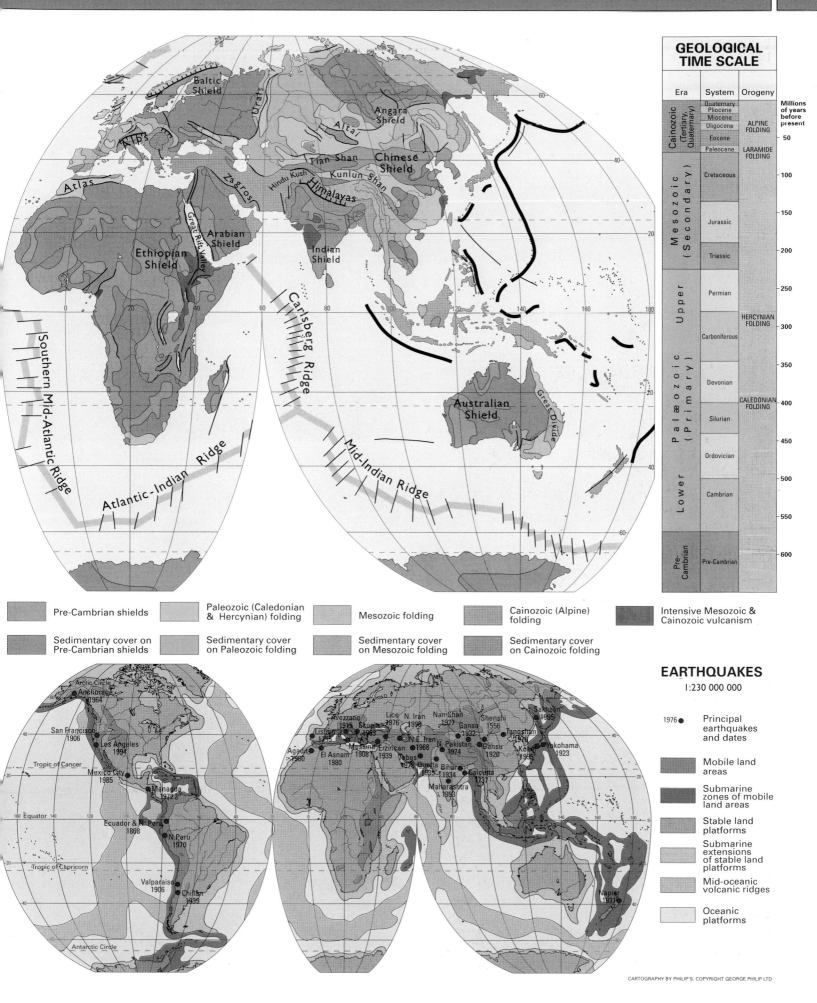

GEOLOGICAL TIME SCALE

Era	System	Orogeny	Millions of years before present
Cainozoic (Tertiary, Quaternary)	Quaternary		
	Pliocene	ALPINE FOLDING	
	Miocene		
	Oligocene		50
	Eocene		
	Paleocene	LARAMIDE FOLDING	
Mesozoic (Secondary)	Cretaceous		100
			150
	Jurassic		
	Triassic		200
Upper Paleozoic (Primary)	Permian		250
	Carboniferous	HERCYNIAN FOLDING	300
	Devonian		350
Lower Paleozoic (Primary)	Silurian	CALEDONIAN FOLDING	400
	Ordovician		450
	Cambrian		500
			550
Pre-Cambrian	Pre-Cambrian		600

Pre-Cambrian shields

Paleozoic (Caledonian & Hercynian) folding

Mesozoic folding

Cainozoic (Alpine) folding

Intensive Mesozoic & Cainozoic vulcanism

Sedimentary cover on Pre-Cambrian shields

Sedimentary cover on Paleozoic folding

Sedimentary cover on Mesozoic folding

Sedimentary cover on Cainozoic folding

EARTHQUAKES

1:230 000 000

1976 ● Principal earthquakes and dates

Mobile land areas

Submarine zones of mobile land areas

Stable land platforms

Submarine extensions of stable land platforms

Mid-oceanic volcanic ridges

Oceanic platforms

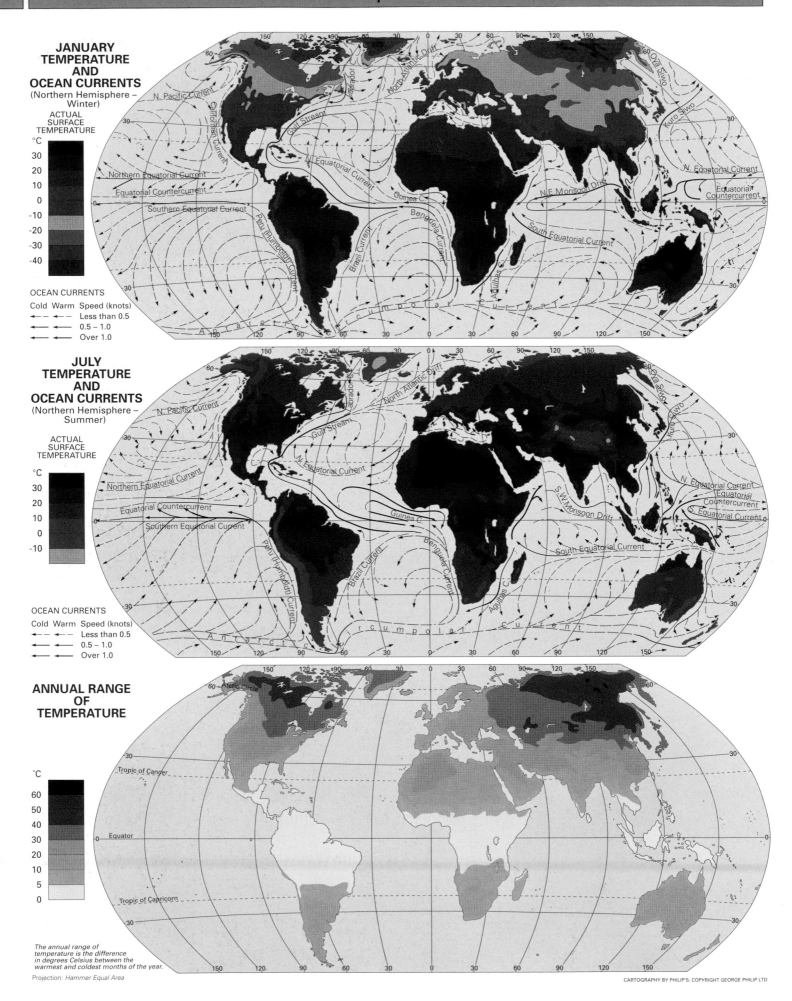

JANUARY TEMPERATURE AND OCEAN CURRENTS
(Northern Hemisphere – Winter)

ACTUAL SURFACE TEMPERATURE
°C
30
20
10
0
-10
-20
-30
-40

OCEAN CURRENTS
Cold Warm Speed (knots)
Less than 0.5
0.5 – 1.0
Over 1.0

JULY TEMPERATURE AND OCEAN CURRENTS
(Northern Hemisphere – Summer)

ACTUAL SURFACE TEMPERATURE
°C
30
20
10
0
-10

OCEAN CURRENTS
Cold Warm Speed (knots)
Less than 0.5
0.5 – 1.0
Over 1.0

ANNUAL RANGE OF TEMPERATURE

°C
60
50
40
30
20
10
5
0

The annual range of temperature is the difference in degrees Celsius between the warmest and coldest months of the year.

Projection: Hammer Equal Area

CARTOGRAPHY BY PHILIP'S. COPYRIGHT GEORGE PHILIP LTD

1 : 190 000 000

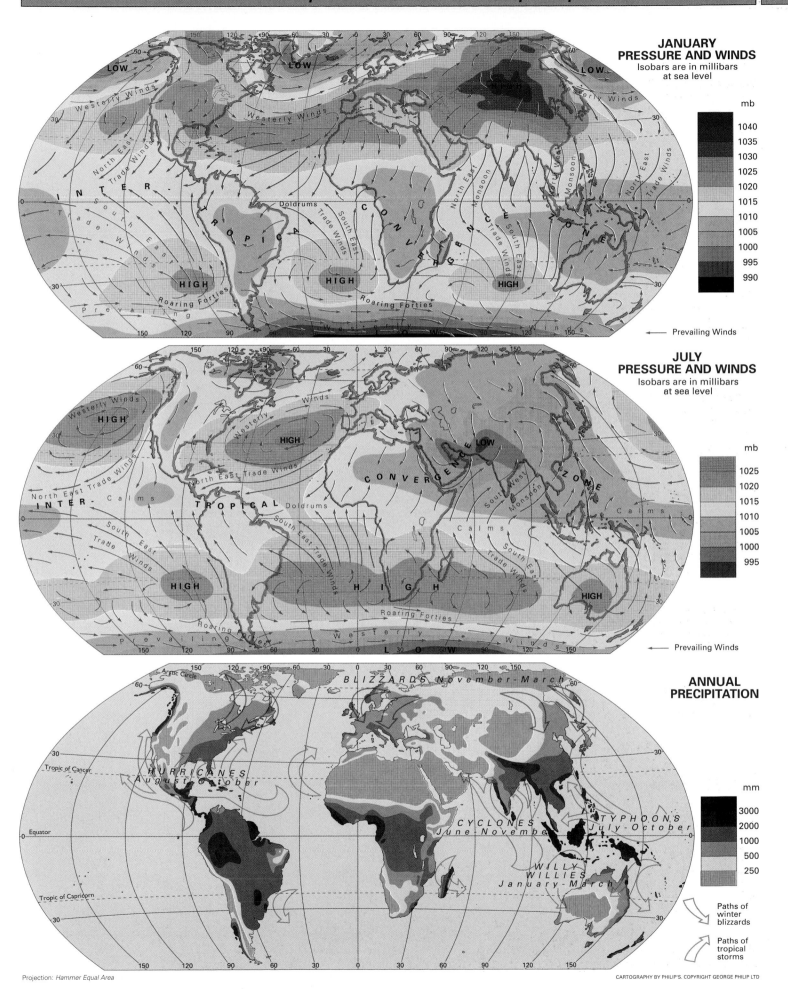

JANUARY PRESSURE AND WINDS
Isobars are in millibars at sea level

mb
1040
1035
1030
1025
1020
1015
1010
1005
1000
995
990

← Prevailing Winds

JULY PRESSURE AND WINDS
Isobars are in millibars at sea level

mb
1025
1020
1015
1010
1005
1000
995

← Prevailing Winds

ANNUAL PRECIPITATION

mm
3000
2000
1000
500
250

⇨ Paths of winter blizzards

⇨ Paths of tropical storms

Projection: *Hammer Equal Area*

CARTOGRAPHY BY PHILIP'S. COPYRIGHT GEORGE PHILIP LTD

1 : 190 000 000

CLIMATIC REGIONS   *after Köppen*

Köppen's classification recognises five major climatic regions corresponding broadly to the five principal vegetation types and these are designated by the letters A, B, C, D and E. Each one of these are subdivided on the basis of temperature and rainfall. This map shows a climate graph for a selected place within each of the 12 sub-regions.

TROPICAL RAINY CLIMATES A

Af	Rain Forest Climate	All mean monthly temperatures above 18°C and an annual variation in temperature of less than 6°C
Am	Monsoon Climate	
Aw	Savanna Climate	All monthly temperatures above 18°C but with an annual variation in temperature of less than 12°C

DRY CLIMATES B

| BS | Steppe Climate | The principal difference between this grouping and groups A, C, D and E is the combination of a wide range of temperatures with low rainfall |
| BW | Desert Climate | |

WARM TEMPERATE RAINY CLIMATES C

The climatic group is separated from group A by having the mean temperature of the coolest month below 18°C but above -3°C. The mean temperature of the warmest month is over 10°C.

Cw	Dry Winter Climate	The wettest month of summer has at least ten times as much rain as the driest winter month
Cs	Dry Summer Climate (Mediterranean)	The wettest month of winter has at least three times as much rain as the driest month of summer. The driest summer month itself has less than 30mm rainfall.
Cf	Climate with no Dry Season	Even rainfall throughout the year.

COLD TEMPERATE RAINY CLIMATES D

| Dw | Dry Winter Climate | The mean temperature of the coldest month is below -3°C but the mean temperature of the warmest month is still over 10°C. |
| Df | Climate with no Dry Season | |

POLAR CLIMATES E

| ET | Tundra Climate | The mean temperature of the warmest month is below 10°C giving permanently frozen subsoil. |
| EF | Polar Climate | The mean temperature of the warmest month is below 0°C giving permanently ice and snow. |

The classification is in some cases subdivided by the addition of the following letters after the major types :-

	a	Hot summer – mean temperature of the hottest month above 22°C and with more than four months of over 10°C.
Used with groups C and D	b	Warm summer – mean temperature of the hottest month below 22°C but still with more than four months of over 10°C.
	c	Cool short summer – mean temperature of the hottest month below 22°C but with less than four months of over 10°C.
Used with group D	d	Cool short summer and cold winter – mean temperature of the hottest month below 22°C and of the coolest month below -38°C
Used with group B	h	Hot dry climate – mean annual temperature above 18°C.
	k	Cool dry climate – mean annual temperature below 18°C.
Used with group E	H	Polar climate due to elevation being over 1500m.

QUEBEC D
°C
30 20 10 0 -10 -20 -30 -40
Temperature
350 300 250 200 150 100 50 mm
Precipitation 1053mm
J F M A M J J A S O N D

EDMONTON BS
°C
30 20 10 0 -10 -20 -30 -40
Temperature
350 300 250 200 150 100 50 mm
Precipitation 460mm
J F M A M J J A S O N D

LA PAZ ET
°C
30 20 10 0 -10 -20 -30 -40
Temperature
350 300 250 200 150 100 50 mm
Precipitation 575mm
J F M A M J J A S O N D

— Colour of climate region on map
— Average monthly daily maximum temperature
— Average monthly temperature
— Average monthly daily minimum temperature
— Average annual rainfall
— Average monthly rainfall
— Months of the year

EISMITTE EF
°C
30 20 10 0 -10 -20 -30 -40
Temperature
350 300 250 200 150 100 50 mm
Precipitation 109mm
J F M A M J J A S O N D

BUENOS AIRES Cf
°C
30 20 10 0 -10 -20 -30 -40
Temperature
350 300 250 200 150 100 50 mm
Precipitation 950mm
J F M A M J J A S O N D

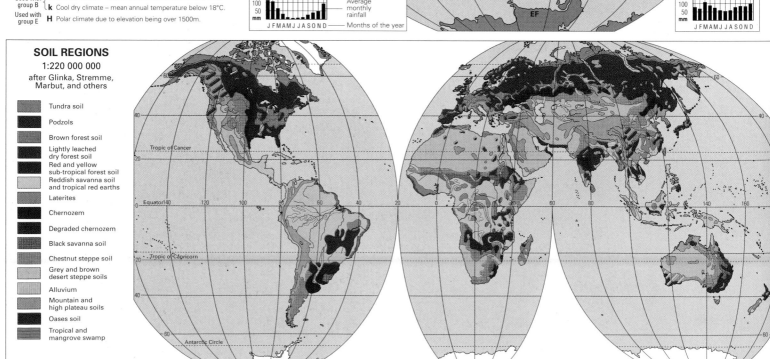

SOIL REGIONS

1:220 000 000

after Glinka, Stremme, Marbut, and others

- Tundra soil
- Podzols
- Brown forest soil
- Lightly leached dry forest soil
- Red and yellow sub-tropical forest soil
- Reddish savanna soil and tropical red earths
- Laterites
- Chernozem
- Degraded chernozem
- Black savanna soil
- Chestnut steppe soil
- Grey and brown desert steppe soils
- Alluvium
- Mountain and high plateau soils
- Oases soil
- Tropical and mangrove swamp

Projection: *Interrupted Mollweide's Homolographic*

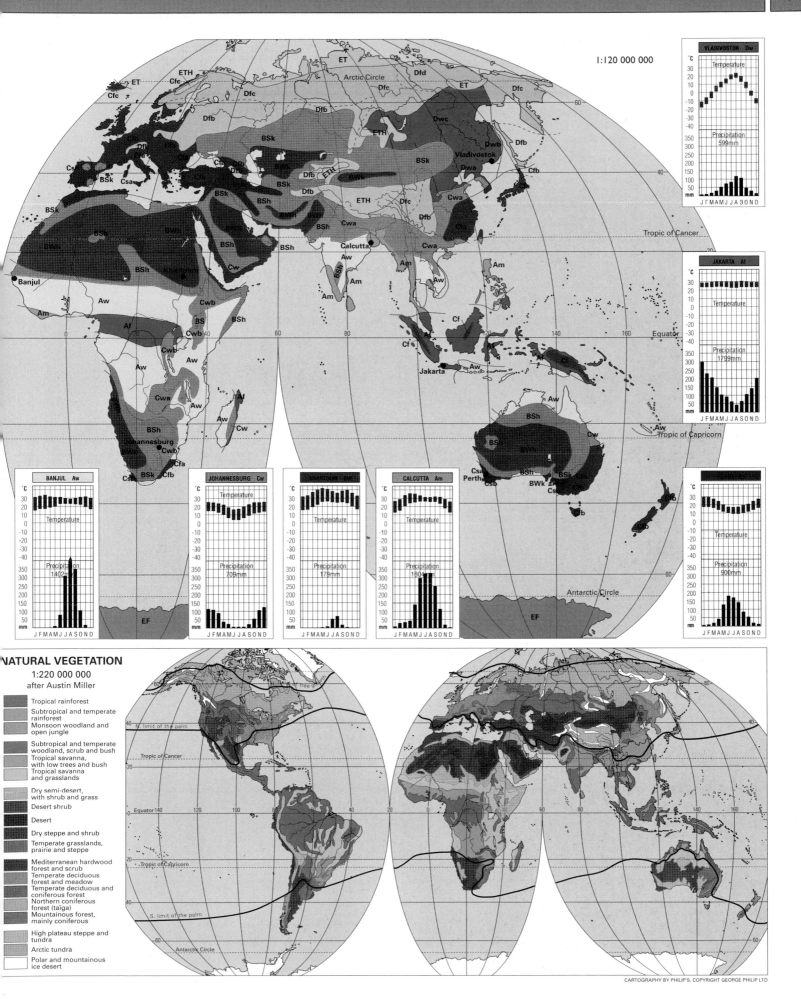

Addis Ababa Ethiopia 2410m
- Height of meteorological station above sea level in metres
- Temperature Daily Max.°C — Average monthly maximum temperature in degrees Celsius
- Daily Min.°C — Average monthly minimum temperature in degrees Celsius
- Average Monthly °C — Average monthly temperature in degrees Celsius
- *Rainfall* Monthly Total mm — Average monthly precipitation in millimetres
- *Sunshine* Hours per Day — Average daily duration of bright sunshine per month in hours

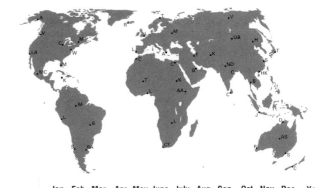

	Jan	Feb	Mar	Apr	May	June	July	Aug	Sep	Oct	Nov	Dec	Year
Addis Ababa Ethiopia 2410m													
Temperature Daily Max.°C	23	24	25	24	25	23	20	20	21	22	23	22	23
Daily Min.°C	6	7	9	10	9	10	11	11	10	7	5	5	8
Average Monthly °C	14	15	17	17	17	16	16	15	15	14	14	15
Rainfall Monthly Total mm	13	35	67	91	81	117	247	255	167	29	8	5	1115
Sunshine Hours per Day	8.7	8.2	7.6	8.1	6.5	4.8	2.8	3.2	5.2	7.6	6.7	7	6.4
Alice Springs Australia 580m													
Temperature Daily Max.°C	35	35	32	27	23	19	19	23	27	31	33	35	28
Daily Min.°C	21	20	17	12	8	5	4	6	10	15	18	20	13
Average Monthly °C	28	27	25	20	15	12	12	14	18	23	26	27	21
Rainfall Monthly Total mm	44	33	27	10	15	13	7	8	7	18	29	38	249
Sunshine Hours per Day	10.3	10.4	9.3	9.2	8	8	8.9	9.8	10	9.7	10.1	10	9.5
Anchorage USA 183m													
Temperature Daily Max.°C	-7	-3	0	7	13	18	19	17	13	6	-2	-6	-6
Daily Min.°C	-15	-12	-9	-2	4	8	10	9	5	-2	-9	-14	-2
Average Monthly °C	-11	-7	-4	3	9	13	15	13	9	2	-5	-10	-4
Rainfall Monthly Total mm	20	18	13	11	13	25	47	64	64	47	28	24	374
Sunshine Hours per Day	2.4	4.1	6.6	8.3	8.3	9.2	8.5	6	4.4	3.1	2.6	1.6	5.4
Athens Greece 107m													
Temperature Daily Max.°C	13	14	16	20	25	30	33	33	29	24	19	15	23
Daily Min.°C	6	7	8	11	16	20	23	23	19	15	12	8	14
Average Monthly °C	10	10	12	16	20	25	28	28	24	20	15	11	18
Rainfall Monthly Total mm	62	37	37	23	23	14	6	7	15	51	56	71	402
Sunshine Hours per Day	3.9	5.2	5.8	7.7	8.9	10.7	11.9	11.5	9.4	6.8	4.8	3.8	7.3
Bahrain City Bahrain 2m													
Temperature Daily Max.°C	20	21	25	29	33	36	37	38	36	32	27	22	30
Daily Min.°C	14	15	18	22	25	29	31	32	29	25	22	16	23
Average Monthly °C	17	18	21	25	29	32	34	35	32	29	25	19	26
Rainfall Monthly Total mm	18	12	10	9	2	0	0	0	0	0.4	3	16	70
Sunshine Hours per Day	5.9	6.9	7.9	8.8	10.6	13.2	12.1	12	12	10.3	7.7	6.4	9.5
Bangkok Thailand 10m													
Temperature Daily Max.°C	32	33	34	35	34	33	32	32	32	31	31	31	33
Daily Min.°C	20	23	24	26	25	25	25	24	24	24	23	20	24
Average Monthly °C	26	28	29	30	30	29	28	28	28	28	27	26	28
Rainfall Monthly Total mm	9	30	36	82	165	153	168	183	310	239	55	8	1438
Sunshine Hours per Day	8.2	8	8	10	7.5	6.1	4.7	5.2	5.2	6.1	7.3	7.8	7
Brasilia Brazil 910m													
Temperature Daily Max.°C	28	28	28	28	27	27	27	29	30	29	28	27	28
Daily Min.°C	18	18	18	17	15	13	13	14	16	18	18	18	16
Average Monthly °C	23	23	23	22	21	20	20	21	23	24	23	22	22
Rainfall Monthly Total mm	252	204	227	93	17	3	6	3	30	127	255	343	1560
Sunshine Av. Monthly Dur.	5.8	5.7	6	7.4	8.7	9.3	9.6	9.8	7.9	6.5	4.8	4.4	7.2
Buenos Aires Argentina 25m													
Temperature Daily Max.°C	30	29	26	22	18	14	14	16	18	21	25	28	22
Daily Min.°C	17	17	16	12	9	5	6	6	8	10	14	16	11
Average Monthly °C	23	23	21	17	13	10	10	11	13	15	19	22	16
Rainfall Monthly Total mm	79	71	109	89	76	61	56	61	79	86	84	99	950
Sunshine Hours per Day	9.2	8.5	7.5	6.8	4.9	3.5	3.8	5.2	6	6.8	8.1	8.5	6.6
Cairo Egypt 75m													
Temperature Daily Max.°C	19	21	24	28	32	35	35	35	33	30	26	21	28
Daily Min.°C	9	9	12	14	18	20	22	22	20	18	14	10	16
Average Monthly °C	14	15	18	21	25	28	29	28	26	24	20	16	22
Rainfall Monthly Total mm	4	4	3	1	2	1	0	0	1	1	3	7	27
Sunshine Hours per Day	6.9	8.4	8.7	9.7	10.5	11.9	11.7	11.3	10.4	9.4	8.3	6.4	9.5
Calcutta India 5m													
Temperature Daily Max.°C	27	29	34	36	35	34	32	32	32	32	29	26	31
Daily Min.°C	13	15	21	24	25	26	26	26	26	23	18	13	21
Average Monthly °C	20	22	27	30	30	30	29	29	29	28	23	20	26
Rainfall Monthly Total mm	10	30	34	44	140	297	325	332	253	114	20	5	1604
Sunshine Hours per Day	8.6	8.7	8.9	9	8.7	5.4	4.1	4.1	5.1	6.5	8.3	8.4	7.1
Cape Town South Africa 44m													
Temperature Daily Max.°C	26	26	25	23	20	18	17	18	19	21	24	25	22
Daily Min.°C	15	15	14	11	9	7	7	7	8	10	13	15	11
Average Monthly °C	21	20	20	17	14	13	12	12	14	16	18	20	16
Rainfall Monthly Total mm	12	19	17	42	67	98	68	76	36	45	12	13	505
Sunshine Hours per Day	11.4	10.2	9.4	7.7	6.1	5.7	6.4	6.6	7.6	8.6	10.2	10.9	8.4
Casablanca Morocco 59m													
Temperature Daily Max.°C	17	18	20	21	22	24	26	26	26	24	21	18	22
Daily Min.°C	8	9	11	12	15	18	19	20	18	15	12	10	14
Average Monthly °C	13	13	15	16	18	21	23	23	22	20	17	14	18
Rainfall Monthly Total mm	78	61	54	37	20	3	0	1	6	28	58	94	440
Sunshine Hours per Day	5.2	6.3	7.3	9	9.4	9.7	10.2	9.7	9.1	7.4	5.9	5.3	7.9
Chicago USA 186m													
Temperature Daily Max.°C	0.6	1.5	6.4	14.1	20.6	26.4	28.9	28	23.8	17.4	8.4	2.1	14.9
Daily Min.°C	-7	-6	-2	5	11	16	20	19	14	8	0	-5	-6
Average Monthly °C	-3	-2	2	9	16	21	24	23	19	13	4	-2	4
Rainfall Monthly Total mm	47	41	70	77	96	103	86	80	69	71	56	48	844
Sunshine Hours per Day	4	5	6.6	6.9	8.9	10.2	10	9.2	8.2	6.9	4.5	3.7	7
Christchurch New Zealand 5m													
Temperature Daily Max.°C	21	21	19	17	13	11	10	11	14	17	19	21	16
Daily Min.°C	12	12	10	7	4	2	1	3	5	7	8	11	7
Average Monthly °C	16	16	15	12	9	6	6	7	9	12	13	16	11
Rainfall Monthly Total mm	56	46	43	46	76	69	61	58	51	51	51	61	669
Sunshine Hours per Day	7	6.5	5.6	4.7	4.3	3.9	4.1	4.7	5.6	6.1	6.9	6.3	5.5
Colombo Sri Lanka 10m													
Temperature Daily Max.°C	30	31	31	31	30	30	29	29	30	29	29	30	30
Daily Min.°C	22	22	23	24	25	25	25	25	24	24	23	22	24
Average Monthly °C	26	26	27	28	28	27	27	27	27	27	26	26	27
Rainfall Monthly Total mm	101	66	118	230	394	220	140	102	174	348	333	142	2368
Sunshine Hours per Day	7.9	9	8.1	7.2	6.4	5.4	6.1	6.3	6.2	6.5	6.4	7.8	6.9
Darwin Australia 30m													
Temperature Daily Max.°C	32	32	33	33	33	31	31	32	33	34	34	33	33
Daily Min.°C	25	25	25	24	23	21	19	21	23	25	26	26	24
Average Monthly °C	29	29	29	29	28	26	25	26	28	29	30	29	28
Rainfall Monthly Total mm	405	309	279	77	8	2	0	1	15	48	108	214	1466
Sunshine Hours per Day	5.8	5.8	6.6	9.8	9.3	10	9.9	10.4	10.1	9.4	9.6	6.8	8.6
Harbin China 175m													
Temperature Daily Max.°C	-14	-9	0	12	21	26	29	27	20	12	-1	-11	9
Daily Min.°C	-26	-23	-12	-1	7	14	18	16	8	0	-12	-22	-3
Average Monthly °C	-20	-16	-6	6	14	20	23	22	14	6	-7	-17	3
Rainfall Monthly Total mm	4	6	17	23	44	92	167	119	52	36	12	5	577
Sunshine Hours per Day	6.4	7.8	8	7.8	8.3	8.6	8.6	8.2	7.2	6.9	6.1	5.7	7.5
Hong Kong China 35m													
Temperature Daily Max.°C	18	18	20	24	28	30	31	31	30	27	24	20	25
Daily Min.°C	13	13	16	19	23	26	26	26	25	23	19	15	20
Average Monthly °C	16	15	18	22	25	28	28	28	27	25	21	17	23
Rainfall Monthly Total mm	30	60	70	133	332	479	286	415	364	33	46	17	2265
Sunshine Hours per Day	4.7	3.5	3.1	3.8	5	5.4	6.8	6.5	6.6	7	6.2	5.5	5.3
Honolulu Hawaii 5m													
Temperature Daily Max.°C	26	26	26	27	28	29	29	29	30	29	28	26	28
Daily Min.°C	19	19	19	20	21	22	23	23	23	22	21	20	21
Average Monthly °C	23	22	23	23	24	26	26	26	26	24	23	24
Rainfall Monthly Total mm	96	84	73	33	25	8	11	23	25	47	55	76	556
Sunshine Hours per Day	7.3	7.7	8.3	8.6	8.8	9.1	9.4	9.3	9.2	8.3	7.5	6.2	8.3
Jakarta Indonesia 10m													
Temperature Daily Max.°C	29	29	30	31	31	31	31	31	31	31	30	29	30
Daily Min.°C	23	23	23	24	24	23	23	23	23	23	23	23	23
Average Monthly °C	26	26	27	27	27	27	27	27	27	27	27	26	27
Rainfall Monthly Total mm	300	300	211	147	114	97	64	43	66	112	142	203	1799
Sunshine Av. Monthly Dur.	6.1	6.5	7.7	8.5	8.4	8.5	9.1	9.5	9.6	9	7.7	7.1	8.1
Kabul Afghanistan 1791 m													
Temperature Daily Max.°C	2	4	12	19	26	31	33	33	30	22	17	8	20
Daily Min.°C	-8	-6	1	6	11	13	16	15	11	6	1	-3	5
Average Monthly °C	-3	-1	6	13	18	22	25	24	20	14	9	3	12
Rainfall Monthly Total mm	28	61	72	117	33	1	7	1	0	1	37	14	372
Sunshine Av. Monthly Dur.	5.9	6	5.7	6.8	10.1	11.5	11.4	11.2	9.8	9.4	7.8	6.1	8.5
Khartoum Sudan 380m													
Temperature Daily Max.°C	32	33	37	40	42	41	38	36	38	39	35	32	37
Daily Min.°C	16	17	20	23	26	27	26	25	25	25	21	17	22
Average Monthly °C	24	25	28	32	34	34	32	30	32	32	28	25	30
Rainfall Monthly Total mm	0	0	0	1	7	5	56	80	28	2	0	0	179
Sunshine Av. Monthly Dur.	10.6	11.2	10.4	10.8	10.4	10.1	8.6	8.6	9.6	10.3	10.8	10.6	10.2

	Jan	Feb	Mar	Apr	May	June	July	Aug	Sep	Oct	Nov	Dec	Year
ngston Jamaica 35m													
mperature Daily Max.°C	30	30	30	31	31	32	32	32	32	31	31	31	31
Daily Min.°C	20	20	20	21	22	24	23	23	23	23	22	21	22
Average Monthly °C	25	25	25	26	26	28	28	28	27	27	26	26	26
infall Monthly Total mm	23	15	23	31	102	89	38	91	99	180	74	36	801
nshine Av. Monthly Dur.	8.3	8.8	8.7	8.7	8.3	7.8	8.5	8.5	7.6	7.3	8.3	7.7	8.2
gos Nigeria 40m													
mperature Daily Max.°C	32	33	33	32	31	29	28	28	29	30	31	32	31
Daily Min.°C	22	23	23	23	23	22	22	21	22	22	23	22	22
Average Monthly °C	27	28	28	28	27	26	25	24	25	26	27	27	26
infall Monthly Total mm	28	41	99	99	203	300	180	56	180	190	63	25	1464
nshine Av. Monthly Dur.	5.9	6.8	6.3	6.1	5.6	3.8	2.8	3.3	3	5.1	6.6	6.5	5.2
ma Peru 120m													
mperature Daily Max.°C	28	29	29	27	24	20	20	19	20	22	24	26	24
Daily Min.°C	19	20	19	17	16	15	14	14	14	15	16	17	16
Average Monthly °C	24	24	24	22	20	17	17	16	17	18	20	21	20
infall Monthly Total mm	1	1	1	1	5	5	8	8	8	3	3	1	45
nshine Av. Monthly Dur.	6.3	6.8	6.9	6.7	4	1.4	1.1	1	1.1	2.5	4.1	5	3.9
sbon Portugal 77m													
mperature Daily Max.°C	14	15	17	20	21	25	27	28	26	22	17	15	21
Daily Min.°C	8	8	10	12	13	15	17	17	17	14	11	9	13
Average Monthly °C	11	12	14	16	17	20	22	23	21	18	14	12	17
infall Monthly Total mm	111	76	109	54	44	16	3	4	33	62	93	103	708
nshine Av. Monthly Dur.	4.7	5.9	6	8.3	9.1	10.6	11.4	10.7	8.4	6.7	5.2	4.6	7.7
ndon (Kew) United Kingdom 5m													
mperature Daily Max.°C	6	7	10	13	17	20	22	21	19	14	10	7	14
Daily Min.°C	2	2	3	6	8	12	14	13	11	8	5	4	7
Average Monthly °C	4	5	7	9	12	16	18	17	15	11	8	5	11
infall Monthly Total mm	54	40	37	37	46	45	57	59	49	57	64	48	593
nshine Av. Monthly Dur.	1.7	2.3	3.5	5.7	6.7	7	6.6	6	5	3.3	1.9	1.4	4.3
s Angeles USA 30m													
mperature Daily Max.°C	18	18	18	19	20	22	24	24	24	23	22	19	21
Daily Min.°C	7	8	9	11	13	15	17	17	16	14	11	9	12
Average Monthly °C	12	13	14	15	17	18	21	21	20	18	16	14	17
infall Monthly Total mm	69	74	46	28	3	3	0	0	5	10	28	61	327
nshine Av. Monthly Dur.	6.9	8.2	8.9	8.8	9.5	10.3	11.7	11	10.1	8.6	8.2	7.6	9.2
saka Zambia 1154m													
mperature Daily Max.°C	26	26	26	27	25	23	23	26	29	31	29	27	27
Daily Min.°C	17	17	16	15	12	10	9	11	15	18	18	17	15
Average Monthly °C	22	22	21	21	18	17	16	19	22	25	23	22	21
infall Monthly Total mm	224	173	90	19	3	1	0	1	1	17	85	196	810
nshine Av. Monthly Dur.	5.1	5.4	6.9	8.9	9	9	9.1	9.6	9.5	9	7	5.5	7.8
anaus Brazil 45m													
mperature Daily Max.°C	31	31	31	31	31	31	32	33	34	34	33	32	32
Daily Min.°C	24	24	24	24	24	24	24	24	24	25	25	24	24
Average Monthly °C	28	28	28	27	28	28	28	29	29	29	29	28	28
infall Monthly Total mm	278	278	300	287	193	99	61	41	62	112	165	220	2096
nshine Av. Monthly Dur.	3.9	4	3.6	3.9	5.4	6.9	7.9	8.2	7.5	6.6	5.9	4.9	5.7
exico City Mexico 2309m													
mperature Daily Max.°C	21	23	26	27	26	25	23	24	23	22	21	21	24
Daily Min.°C	5	6	7	9	10	11	11	11	11	9	6	5	8
Average Monthly °C	13	15	16	18	18	18	17	17	17	16	14	13	16
infall Monthly Total mm	8	4	9	23	57	111	160	149	119	46	16	7	709
nshine Av. Monthly Dur.	7.3	8.1	8.5	8.1	7.8	7	6.2	6.4	5.6	6.3	7	7.3	7.1
ami USA 2m													
mperature Daily Max.°C	24	25	27	28	30	31	32	32	31	29	27	25	28
Daily Min.°C	14	15	16	19	21	23	24	24	24	22	18	15	20
Average Monthly °C	19	20	21	23	25	27	28	28	27	25	22	20	24
infall Monthly Total mm	51	48	58	99	163	188	170	178	241	208	71	43	1518
nshine Av. Monthly Dur.	7.7	8.3	8.7	9.4	8.9	8.5	8.7	8.4	7.1	6.5	7.5	7.1	8.1
ontreal Canada 57m													
mperature Daily Max.°C	-6	-4	2	11	18	23	26	25	20	14	5	-3	11
Daily Min.°C	-13	-11	-5	2	9	14	17	16	11	6	0	-9	3
Average Monthly °C	-9	-8	-2	6	13	19	22	20	16	10	3	-6	7
infall Monthly Total mm	87	76	86	83	81	91	98	87	96	84	89	89	1047
nshine Av. Monthly Dur.	2.8	3.4	4.5	5.2	6.7	7.7	8.2	7.7	5.6	4.3	2.4	2.2	5.1
oscow Russia 156m													
mperature Daily Max.°C	-6	-4	1	9	18	22	24	22	17	10	1	-5	9
Daily Min.°C	-14	-16	-11	-1	5	9	12	9	4	-2	-6	-12	-2
Average Monthly °C	-10	-10	-5	4	12	15	18	16	10	4	-2	-8	4
infall Monthly Total mm	31	28	33	35	52	67	74	74	58	51	36	36	575
nshine Av. Monthly Dur.	1	1.9	3.7	5.2	7.8	8.3	8.4	7.1	4.4	2.4	1	0.6	4.4
ew Delhi India 220m													
mperature Daily Max.°C	21	24	29	36	41	39	35	34	34	34	28	23	32
Daily Min.°C	6	10	14	20	26	28	27	26	24	17	11	7	18
Average Monthly °C	14	17	22	28	33	34	31	30	29	26	20	15	25
infall Monthly Total mm	25	21	13	8	13	77	178	184	123	10	2	11	665
nshine Av. Monthly Dur.	7.7	8.2	8.2	8.7	9.2	7.9	6	6.3	6.9	9.4	8.7	8.3	8

	Jan	Feb	Mar	Apr	May	June	July	Aug	Sep	Oct	Nov	Dec	Year
Perth Australia 60m													
Temperature Daily Max.°C	29	30	27	25	21	18	17	18	19	21	25	27	23
Daily Min.°C	17	18	16	14	12	10	9	9	10	11	14	16	13
Average Monthly °C	23	24	22	19	16	14	13	13	15	16	19	22	18
Rainfall Monthly Total mm	8	13	22	44	128	189	177	145	84	58	19	13	900
Sunshine Av. Monthly Dur.	10.4	9.8	8.8	7.5	5.7	4.8	5.4	6	7.2	8.1	9.6	10.4	7.8
Reykjavik Iceland 18m													
Temperature Daily Max.°C	2	3	5	6	10	13	15	14	12	8	5	4	8
Daily Min.°C	-3	-3	-1	1	4	7	9	8	6	3	0	-2	3
Average Monthly °C	0	0	2	4	7	10	12	11	9	5	3	1	5
Rainfall Monthly Total mm	89	64	62	56	42	42	50	56	67	94	78	79	779
Sunshine Av. Monthly Dur.	0.8	2	3.6	4.5	5.9	6.1	5.8	5.4	3.5	2.3	1.1	0.3	3.7
Santiago Chile 520m													
Temperature Daily Max.°C	30	29	27	24	19	15	15	17	19	22	26	29	23
Daily Min.°C	12	11	10	7	5	3	3	4	6	7	9	11	7
Average Monthly °C	21	20	18	15	12	9	9	10	12	15	17	20	15
Rainfall Monthly Total mm	3	3	5	13	64	84	76	56	31	15	8	5	363
Sunshine Av. Monthly Dur.	10.8	8.9	8.5	5.5	3.6	3.3	3.3	3.6	4.8	6.1	8.7	10.1	6.4
Shanghai China 5m													
Temperature Daily Max.°C	8	8	13	19	24	28	32	32	27	23	17	10	20
Daily Min.°C	-1	0	4	9	14	19	23	23	19	13	7	2	11
Average Monthly °C	3	4	8	14	19	23	27	27	23	18	12	6	15
Rainfall Monthly Total mm	48	59	84	94	94	180	147	142	130	71	51	36	1136
Sunshine Av. Monthly Dur.	4	3.7	4.4	4.8	5.4	4.7	6.9	7.5	5.3	5.6	4.7	4.5	5.1
Sydney Australia 40m													
Temperature Daily Max.°C	26	26	25	22	19	17	17	18	20	22	24	25	22
Daily Min.°C	18	19	17	14	11	9	8	9	11	13	16	17	14
Average Monthly °C	22	22	21	18	15	13	12	13	16	18	20	21	18
Rainfall Monthly Total mm	89	101	127	135	127	117	117	76	74	71	74	74	1182
Sunshine Av. Monthly Dur.	7.5	7	6.4	6.1	5.7	5.3	6.1	7	7.3	7.5	7.5	7.5	6.8
Tehran Iran 1191m													
Temperature Daily Max.°C	9	11	16	21	29	30	37	36	29	24	16	11	22
Daily Min.°C	-1	1	4	10	16	20	23	23	18	12	6	1	11
Average Monthly °C	4	6	10	15	22	25	30	29	23	18	11	6	17
Rainfall Monthly Total mm	37	23	36	31	14	2	1	1	1	5	29	27	207
Sunshine Av. Monthly Dur.	5.9	6.7	7.5	7.4	8.6	11.6	11.2	11	10.1	7.6	6.9	6.3	8.4
Timbuktu Mali 269m													
Temperature Daily Max.°C	31	35	38	41	43	42	38	35	38	40	37	31	37
Daily Min.°C	13	16	18	22	26	27	25	24	24	23	18	14	21
Average Monthly °C	22	26	28	31	34	34	32	30	31	31	28	23	29
Rainfall Monthly Total mm	0	0	0	1	4	20	54	93	31	3	0	0	206
Sunshine Av. Monthly Dur.	9.1	9.6	9.6	9.7	9.8	9.4	9.6	9	9.3	9.5	9.5	8.9	9.4
Tokyo Japan 5m													
Temperature Daily Max.°C	9	9	12	18	22	25	29	30	27	20	16	11	19
Daily Min.°C	-1	-1	3	4	13	17	22	23	19	13	7	1	10
Average Monthly °C	4	4	8	11	18	21	25	26	23	17	11	6	14
Rainfall Monthly Total mm	48	73	101	135	131	182	146	147	217	220	101	61	1562
Sunshine Av. Monthly Dur.	6	5.9	5.7	6	6.2	5	5.8	6.6	4.5	4.4	4.8	5.4	5.5
Tromsø Norway 100m													
Temperature Daily Max.°C	-2	-2	0	3	7	12	16	14	10	5	2	0	5
Daily Min.°C	-6	-6	-5	-2	1	6	9	8	5	1	-2	-4	0
Average Monthly °C	-4	-4	-3	0	4	9	13	11	7	3	0	-2	3
Rainfall Monthly Total mm	96	79	91	65	61	59	56	80	109	115	88	95	994
Sunshine Av. Monthly Dur.	0.1	1.6	2.9	6.1	5.7	6.9	7.9	4.8	3.5	1.7	0.3	0	3.52
Ulan Bator Mongolia 1305m													
Temperature Daily Max.°C	-19	-13	-4	7	13	21	22	21	14	6	-6	-16	4
Daily Min.°C	-32	-29	-22	-8	-2	7	11	8	2	-8	-20	-28	-11
Average Monthly °C	-26	-21	-13	-1	6	14	16	14	8	-1	-13	-22	-4
Rainfall Monthly Total mm	1	1	2	5	10	28	76	51	23	5	5	2	209
Sunshine Av. Monthly Dur.	6.4	7.8	8	7.8	8.3	8.6	8.6	8.2	7.2	6.9	6.1	5.7	7.5
Vancouver Canada 5m													
Temperature Daily Max.°C	6	7	10	14	17	20	23	22	19	14	9	7	14
Daily Min.°C	0	1	3	5	8	11	13	12	10	7	3	2	6
Average Monthly °C	3	4	6	9	13	16	18	17	14	10	6	4	10
Rainfall Monthly Total mm	214	161	151	90	69	65	39	44	83	172	198	243	1529
Sunshine Av. Monthly Dur.	1.6	3	3.8	5.9	7.5	7.4	9.5	8.2	6	3.7	2	1.4	5
Verkhoyansk Russia 137m													
Temperature Daily Max.°C	-47	-40	-20	-1	11	21	24	21	12	-8	-33	-42	-8
Daily Min.°C	-51	-48	-40	-25	-7	4	6	1	-6	-20	-39	-50	-23
Average Monthly °C	-49	-44	-30	-13	2	12	15	11	3	-14	-36	-46	-16
Rainfall Monthly Total mm	7	5	5	4	5	25	33	30	13	11	10	7	155
Sunshine Av. Monthly Dur.	0	2.6	6.9	9.6	9.7	10	9.7	7.5	4.1	2.4	0.6	0	5.4
Washington USA 22m													
Temperature Daily Max.°C	7	8	12	19	25	29	31	30	26	20	14	8	19
Daily Min.°C	-1	-1	2	8	13	18	21	20	16	10	4	-1	9
Average Monthly °C	3	3	7	13	19	24	26	25	21	15	9	4	14
Rainfall Monthly Total mm	84	68	96	85	103	88	108	120	100	78	75	75	1080
Sunshine Av. Monthly Dur.	4.4	5.7	6.7	7.4	8.2	8.8	8.6	8.2	7.5	6.5	5.3	4.5	6.8

AGRICULTURAL PRODUCTION

Staple Crops

Wheat
China 18.9% | India 12.2% | U.S.A. 11.0% | France 5.7% | Russia 5.6% | Canada 4.6%

World total (1996): 584,874,000 tonnes

Rice
China 34.0% | India 21.7% | Indonesia 9.0% | Bangladesh 4.8% | Vietnam 5.0% | Thailand 4.5% | Burma 3.5%

World total (1996): 562,259,000 tonnes

Millet
India 33.2% | Nigeria 18.3% | China 16.1% | Niger 6.4%

World total (1996): 29,563,000 tonnes

Rye
Poland 27.7% | Germany 20.0% | Russia 18.1% | Belarus 9.5% | Ukraine 5.3%

World total (1996): 23,156,000 tonnes

Maize
U.S.A. 36.4% | China 21.8% | Brazil 7.0%

World total (1996): 576,821,000 tonnes

Potatoes
China 16.0% | Russia 14.0% | Poland 8.7% | U.S.A. 7.1% | India 5.3% | Ukraine 5.7% | Germany 3.6%

World total (1996): 294,834,000 tonnes

Soya
U.S.A. 47.1% | Brazil 20.4% | China 10.7% | Argentina 9.6%

World total (1996): 130,302,000 tonnes

Cassava
Nigeria 19.2% | Brazil 15.6% | Thailand 11.1% | Congo (Zaire) 10.7% | Indonesia 9.4% | Ghana 4.2% | India 3.7% | Tanzania 3.6%

World total (1996): 162,942,000 tonnes

Animal Products

Milk
U.S.A. 15.2% | Russia 6.9% | India 6.9% | Germany 6.0% | France 5.5% | Brazil 3.9% | Ukraine 3.7%

World total (1996): 466,317,000 tonnes

Butter
India 19.0% | U.S.A. 8.9% | Germany 7.2% | France 6.7% | Russia 6.2% | Pakistan 5.5% | New Zealand 4.6%

World total (1996): 6,565,000 tonnes

Lamb and Mutton
China 15.1% | Australia 8.5% | N. Zealand 7.9% | U.K. 5.2% | Turkey 3.8% | Iran 3.6% | India 3.6% | Pakistan 3.6%

World total (1996): 7,289,000 tonnes

Beef and Veal
U.S.A. 21.7% | Brazil 8.6% | China 6.5% | Russia 5.5% | Argentina 4.6% | France 3.6%

World total (1996): 53,956,000 tonnes

Pork
China 45.1% | U.S.A. 9.7% | Germany 4.3%

World total (1996): 85,761,000 tonnes

Sugars

Sugarcane
Brazil 26.0% | India 22.2% | China 6.0% | Pakistan 5.0% | Mexico 3.6%

World total (1996): 1,192,555,000 tonnes

Sugar beet
France 11.5% | Ukraine 11.2% | Germany 9.8% | U.S.A. 8.6% | Russia 7.2% | China 5.3% | Poland 5.0% | Italy 5.0% | Turkey 4.2%

World total (1996): 255,500,000 tonnes

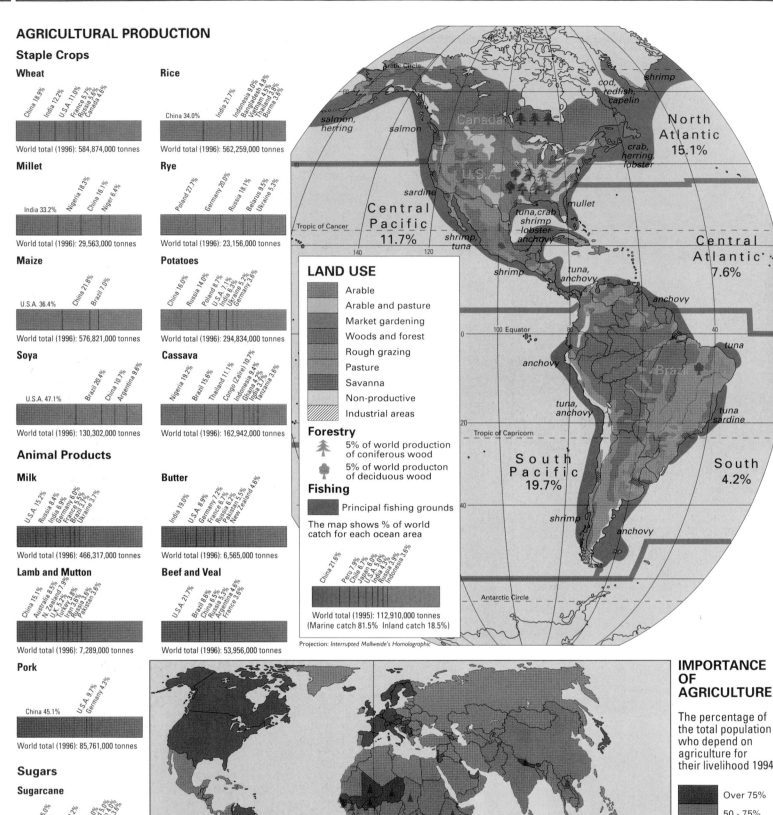

LAND USE
- Arable
- Arable and pasture
- Market gardening
- Woods and forest
- Rough grazing
- Pasture
- Savanna
- Non-productive
- Industrial areas

Forestry
🌲 5% of world production of coniferous wood
🌳 5% of world producton of deciduous wood

Fishing
⬛ Principal fishing grounds

The map shows % of world catch for each ocean area

China 21.6% | Peru 7.9% | Chile 6.7% | Japan 6.0% | U.S.A. 5.0% | India 4.3% | Russia 3.9% | Indonesia 3.6%

World total (1995): 112,910,000 tonnes
(Marine catch 81.5% Inland catch 18.5%)

Projection: *Interrupted Mollweide's Homolographic*

North Atlantic 15.1%
Central Pacific 11.7%
Central Atlantic 7.6%
South Pacific 19.7%
South 4.2%

IMPORTANCE OF AGRICULTURE

The percentage of the total population who depend on agriculture for their livelihood 1994

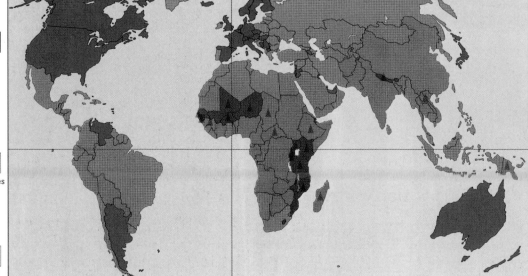

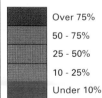

- Over 75%
- 50 - 75%
- 25 - 50%
- 10 - 25%
- Under 10%

▲ Over 75% of the total workforce employed in agriculture, forestry and fishing in 1995

Projection: *Modified Hammer Equal Area*

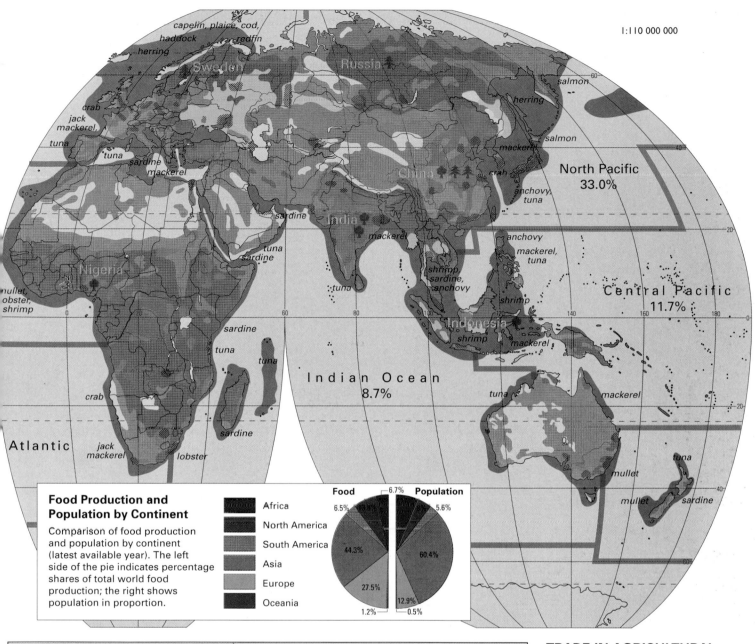

1:110 000 000

capelin, plaice, cod,
haddock   redfin
herring

Sweden

Russia

salmon

herring

North Pacific
33.0%

crab
jack
mackerel,
tuna

tuna
tuna
sardine
mackerel

China

salmon

mackerel

crab

anchovy,
tuna

sardine

India

mackerel

anchovy

mackerel,
tuna

Nigeria

tuna
sardine

shrimp

mullet,
obster,
shrimp

tuna

shrimp,
sardine,
anchovy

Central Pacific
11.7%

sardine

tuna

tuna

Indonesia

shrimp

shrimp
mackerel

Indian Ocean
8.7%

tuna

mackerel

crab

tuna

mullet

Atlantic

jack
mackerel   lobster

sardine

mullet   sardine

Food Production and Population by Continent

Comparison of food production and population by continent (latest available year). The left side of the pie indicates percentage shares of total world food production; the right shows population in proportion.

▨	Africa
▨	North America
▨	South America
▨	Asia
▨	Europe
▨	Oceania

Food   **Population**
6.7%
6.5% 13.8%   5.6%
44.3%   60.4%
27.5%
1.2%   12.9%
0.5%

TRADE IN AGRICULTURAL PRODUCTS

Balance of trade in agricultural products (food and live animals) by value (latest available year)

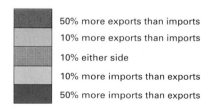

▨	50% more exports than imports
▨	10% more exports than imports
▨	10% either side
▨	10% more imports than exports
▨	50% more imports than exports

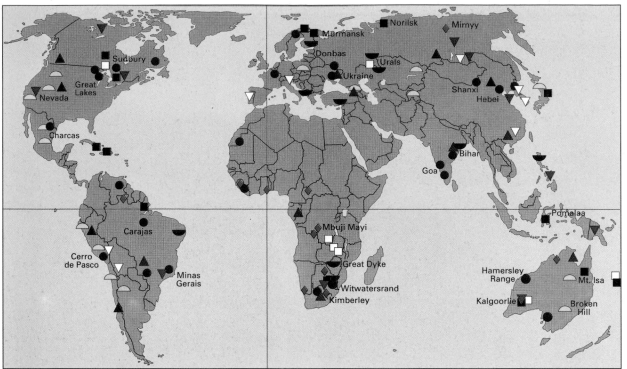

Map labels (top map): Murmansk, Norilsk, Mirnyy, Donbas, Urals, Ukraine, Sudbury, Great Lakes, Nevada, Charcas, Shanxi, Hebei, Bihar, Goa, Carajas, Cerro de Pasco, Minas Gerais, Mbuji Mayi, Great Dyke, Witwatersrand, Kimberley, Hamersley Range, Pomalaa, Mt. Isa, Kalgoorlie, Broken Hill

Precious Metals

▼ Gold
World total (1994)
2 290 tonnes

South Africa	25.3%
U.S.A.	14.2%
Australia	11.2%
Russia	6.4%
Canada	6.4%

◠ Silver
World total (1994)
13 900 tonnes

Mexico	16.8%
Peru	12.2%
U.S.A.	10.6%
Australia	7.6%
Chile	7.1%

◆ Diamonds
World total (1994)
106 000 000 carats

Australia	34.0%
Russia	18.9%
Congo (Zaïre)	16.8%
Botswana	15.6%
South Africa	8.0%

Ferrous Metals

● **Iron Ore**	■ **Nickel**	◗ **Chrome**	▲ **Manganese**	☐ **Cobalt**	▲ **Molybdenum**	▽ **Tungsten**
World total (1994)	World total (1994)	World total (1994)	World total (1994)	World total (1994)	World total (1994)	World total (1994)
995 000 000 tonnes	810 000 tonnes	9 600 000 tonnes	22 180 000 tonnes	18 500 tonnes	104 000 tonnes	25 500 tonnes
China 24.1%	Russia 22.2%	South Africa 37.4%	Ukraine 32.1%	Canada 23.4%	U.S.A. 45.0%	China 64.7%
Brazil 16.7%	Japan 13.7%	Kazakstan 21.0%	China 18.8%	Zambia 18.9%	China 16.8%	Russia 15.7%
Australia 12.9%	Canada 13.0%	India 9.5%	South Africa 14.4%	Russia 17.8%	Chile 15.4%	Portugal 3.9%
Russia 7.4%	Norway 8.4%	Turkey 8.2%	Gabon 10.9%	Australia 11.4%	Canada 9.2%	North Korea 3.5%
U.S.A. 5.9%	Australia 5.7%	Finland 6.0%	Brazil 7.7%	Congo (Zaïre) 10.8%	Russia 4.3%	Peru 3.1%

Map labels (bottom map): Bingham, Missouri, Arizona, Jamaica, Spain, Kazakstan, Yunnan, Boké, Sipalay, Malay Peninsula, Pôrto Velho, Katanga, Copperbelt, Bangka, Weipa, Mount Isa, Broken Hill

Fertilizers

■ Nitrates
World total (1993)
79 932 000 tonnes

China	20.0%
U.S.A.	17.2%
India	9.3%
Russia	7.1%
Canada	3.7%

△ Phosphates
World total (1994)
37 900 000 tonnes

U.S.A.	31.9%
China	18.5%
Morocco	15.6%
Russia	7.4%
Tunisia	4.3%

▼ Potash
World total (1994)
22 500 000 tonnes

Canada	35.7%
Germany	14.6%
Belarus	11.4%
Russia	11.0%
U.S.A.	6.2%

Non-Ferrous Metals

▦ **Copper**	▲ **Lead**	● **Bauxite**	▽ **Tin**	◆ **Zinc**	◗ **Mercury**
World total (1994)	World total (1994)	World total (1994)	World total (1994)	World total (1994)	World total (1994)
9 750 000 tonnes	5 380 000 tonnes	107 000 000 tonnes	199 000 tonnes	7 360 000 tonnes	1 760 tonnes
U.S.A. 17.5%	U.S.A. 23.4%	Australia 39.0%	China 26.6%	China 13.2%	China 28.4%
Chile 13.1%	France 8.3%	Guinea 13.5%	Malaysia 21.1%	Japan 9.7%	Algeria 27.0%
Japan 11.5%	China 7.6%	Brazil 7.6%	Indonesia 15.6%	Canada 9.4%	Spain 17.0%
Russia 6.0%	U.K. 6.4%	India 5.0%	Brazil 15.2%	Germany 4.9%	Kyrgyzstan 11.4%
Canada 5.7%	Germany 6.2%	China 3.5%	Bolivia 7.7%	U.S.A. 4.8%	Finland 5.7%

Projection: Modified Hammer Equal Area

ENERGY PRODUCTION

Primary energy production
expressed in kilograms
of coal equivalent per
person 1994

	Over 10 000 kg per person
	1 000 – 10 000 kg per person
	100 – 1 000 kg per person
	10 – 100 kg per person
	Under 10 kg per person

- ● Oil
- ▼ Natural gas
- ▲ Coal and lignite
- ◆ Uranium *(the fuel used to generate nuclear power)*

In developing countries traditional fuels are still very important. Sometimes called biomass fuels, they include wood, charcoal and dried dung. The pie graph for Nigeria at the foot of the page shows their importance.

Oil		Natural Gas		Coal (bituminous)		Coal (lignite)		Uranium		Nuclear Power		Hydro-Electric Power	
World total (1994) 3 183 500 000 tonnes		World total (1993) 2 658 000 000 tonnes of coal equivalent		World total (1993) 3 160 000 000 tonnes		World total (1993) 1 265 000 000 tonnes		World total (1993) 32 532 tonnes (metal content)		World total (1994) 820 000 000 tonnes of coal equivalent		World total (1994) 922 000 000 tonnes of coal equivalent	
audi Arabia	13.2%	Canada	28.2%	China	36.0%	U.S.A.	23.7%	Canada	28.2%	U.S.A.	31.0%	Canada	12.8%
.S.A.	12.6%	Nigeria	9.0%	U.S.A.	17.6%	Germany	17.5%	Niger	9.0%	France	16.3%	U.S.A.	12.2%
ussia	9.9%	Kazakstan	8.3%	India	7.9%	Russia	9.1%	Kazakstan	8.3%	Japan	11.8%	Former U.S.S.R.	10.4%
an	5.7%	Uzbekistan	8.0%	Russia	6.3%	China	7.4%	Uzbekistan	8.0%	Former U.S.S.R.	7.9%	Brazil	10.3%
exico	4.9%	Russia	7.4%	Australia South Africa }	5.8%	Poland	5.4%	Russia	7.4%	Germany	6.9%	China	6.9%

ENERGY CONSUMPTION

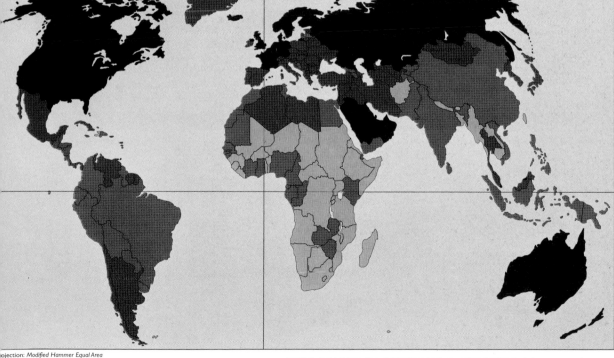

Primary energy consumption
expressed in kilograms
of coal equivalent per
person 1994

	Over 10 000 kg per person
	5 000 – 10 000 kg per person
	1 000 – 5 000 kg per person
	100 – 1 000 kg per person
	Under 100 kg per person

Energy consumption by Continent 1991

		Change 1990-91
Europe*	38.3%	*(-0.2%)*
North America	30.0%	*(+2.4%)*
Asia	25.0%	*(+1.9%)*
South America	3.0%	*(-2.9%)*
Africa	2.4%	*(-0.4%)*
Australasia	1.3%	*(no change)*
includes former U.S.S.R.		

Projection: *Modified Hammer Equal Area*

TYPE OF ENERGY CONSUMED BY SELECTED COUNTRIES 1993

- Coal & Lignite
- Oil
- Natural gas
- Hydro-electricity
- Nuclear electricity
- Traditional Fuels

NIGERIA   **CHINA**   **JAPAN**   **FRANCE**   **USA**   **NORWAY**

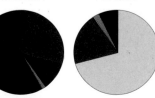

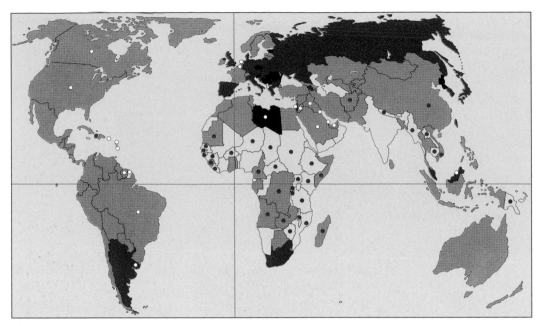

EMPLOYMENT IN INDUSTRY

Percentage of total workforce
employed in manufacturing
and mining 1995

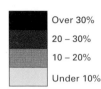

- Over 30%
- 20 – 30%
- 10 – 20%
- Under 10%

● Over two thirds of total workforce
employed in agriculture

○ Over a third of total workforce
employed in service industries
(work in offices, shops, tourism,
transport, construction and
government)

INDUSTRIAL PRODUCTION

Industrial output (mining, manufacturing,
construction, energy and water production),
top 40 nations, US $ billion (1991)

1.	U.S.A.	1,627	56	21. Saudi Arabia
2.	Japan	1,412	48	22. Indonesia
3.	Germany	614	47	23. Spain
4.	Italy	380	46	24. Argentina
5.	France	348	39	25. Poland
6.	U.K.	324	38	26. Norway
7.	Former U.S.S.R.	250	37	27. Finland
8.	Brazil	161	36	28. Thailand
9.	China	155	33	29. Turkey
10.	South Korea	127	31	30. Denmark
11.	Canada	117	23	31. Israel
12.	Australia	93	20	32. Iran
13.	Netherlands	93	19	33. Ex- Czechoslovakia
14.	Taiwan	86	17	34. Hong Kong
15.	Mexico	85	17	Portugal (1989)
16.	Sweden	70	16	36. Algeria
17.	Switzerland (1989)	61	16	Greece
18.	India	60	15	38. Iraq
19.	Austria	59	15	Philippines
	Belgium	59	15	Singapore

Graphs show the top ten producing countries for selected industrial goods.

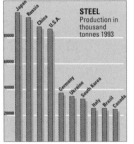

RUBBER
Natural and synthetic rubber
in thousands of tonnes 1993
World production
13 081 thousand tonnes

▬ Synthetic rubber

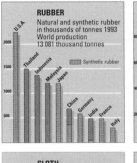

STEEL
Production in
thousand
tonnes 1993

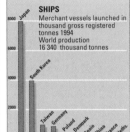

SHIPS
Merchant vessels launched in
thousand gross registered
tonnes 1994
World production
16 340 thousand tonnes

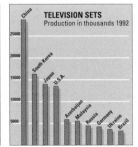

TELEVISION SETS
Production in thousands 1992

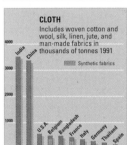

CLOTH
Includes woven cotton and
wool, silk, linen, jute, and
man-made fabrics in
thousands of tonnes 1991

▬ Synthetic fabrics

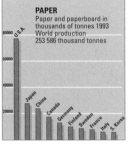

PAPER
Paper and paperboard in
thousands of tonnes 1993
World production
253 586 thousand tonnes

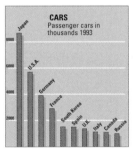

CARS
Passenger cars in
thousands 1993
World production
253 586 thousand tonnes

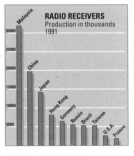

RADIO RECEIVERS
Production in thousands
1991

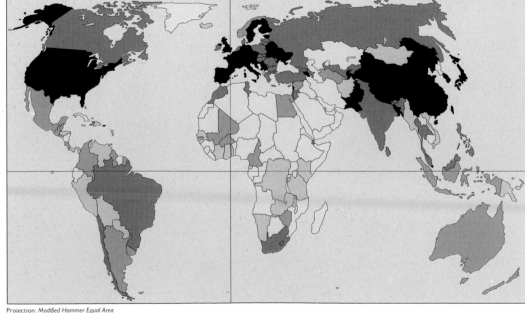

INDUSTRY AND TRADE

Manufactured goods (inc. machinery &
transport) as a percentage of total
exports (latest available year)

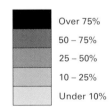

- Over 75%
- 50 – 75%
- 25 – 50%
- 10 – 25%
- Under 10%

The Far East and South-East Asia
(Japan 98.3%, Macau 97.8%,
Taiwan 92.7%, Hong Kong 93.0%,
South Korea 93.4%) are most
dominant, but many countries in
Europe (e.g. Slovenia 92.4%) are
also heavily dependent on
manufactured goods.

Projection: *Modified Hammer Equal Area*

DEPENDENCE ON TRADE

Value of exports as a percentage
of G.N.P. (Gross National Product)
1995

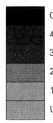

Over 50% G.N.P. from exports

40 – 50% G.N.P. from exports

30 – 40% G.N.P. from exports

20 – 30% G.N.P. from exports

10 – 20% G.N.P. from exports

Under 10% G.N.P. from exports

• Most dependent on industrial
  exports (over 75% of total exports)

• Most dependent on fuel exports
  (over 75% of total exports)

• Most dependent on metal and
  mineral exports (over 75% of total
  exports)

BALANCE OF TRADE

Value of exports in proportion to
the value of imports 1995

Exports exceed
imports by:

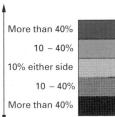

More than 40%

10 – 40%

10% either side

10 – 40%

More than 40%

Imports exceed
exports by:

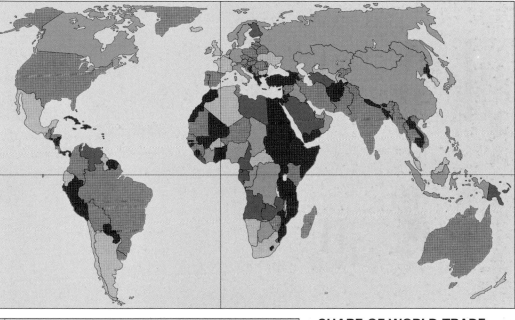

SHARE OF WORLD TRADE

Percentage share of total world
exports by value 1995

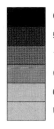

Over 10% of world trade

5 – 10% of world trade

1 – 5% of world trade

0.5 – 1% of world trade

0.1 – 0.5% of world trade

Under 0.1% of world trade

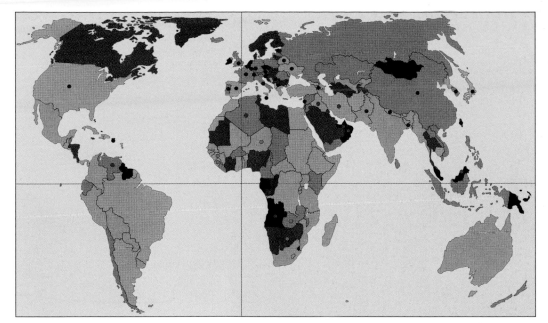

Projection: *Modified Hammer Equal Area*

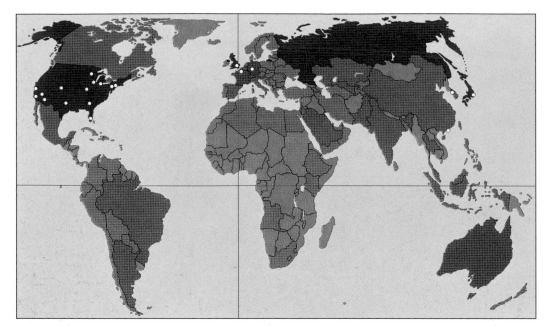

AIR TRAVEL

Passenger kilometres flown 1994

Passenger kilometres are the number of passengers (international and domestic) multiplied by the distance flown by each passenger from airport of origin.

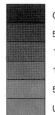

- Over 100 000 million
- 50 000 – 100 000 million
- 10 000 – 50 000 million
- 1 000 – 10 000 million
- 500 – 1 000 million
- Under 500 million

○　Major airports (handling over 25 million passengers in 1995)

World's busiest airports (total passengers)		World's busiest airports (international passengers)	
1. Chicago	(O'Hare)	1. London	(Heathrow)
2. Atlanta	(Hartsfield)	2. London	(Gatwick)
3. Dallas	(Dallas/Ft Worth)	3. Frankfurt	(International)
4. London	(Heathrow)	4. New York	(Kennedy)
5. Los Angeles	(Intern'l)	5. Paris	(De Gaulle)

TOURISM

Tourism receipts as a percentage of G.N.P. (Gross National Product) 1994

- Over 10% of G.N.P from tourism
- 5 – 10% of G.N.P. from tourism
- 2.5 – 5% of G.N.P. from tourism
- 1 – 2.5% of G.N.P. from tourism
- 0.5 – 1% of G.N.P. from tourism
- Under 0.5% of G.N.P. from tourism

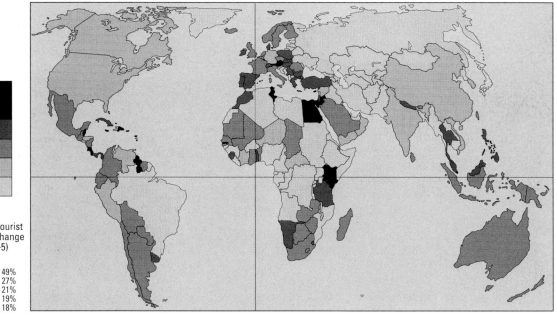

Countries spending the most on promoting tourism, millions of US $ (1996)		Fastest growing tourist destinations, % change in receipts (1994–5)	
Australia	88	South Korea	49%
Spain	79	Czech Republic	27%
U.K.	79	India	21%
France	73	Russia	19%
Singapore	54	Philippines	18%

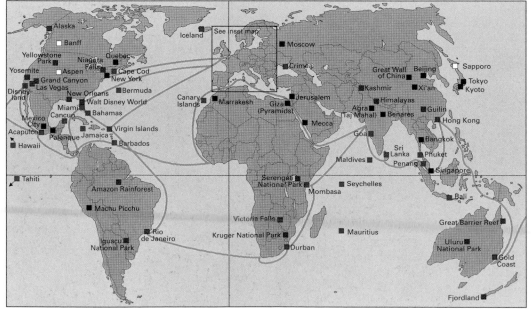

TOURIST DESTINATIONS

- ■ Cultural & historical centres
- ■ Coastal resorts
- □ Ski resorts
- ■ Centres of entertainment
- ■ Places of pilgrimage
- ■ Places of great natural beauty

—— Popular holiday cruise routes

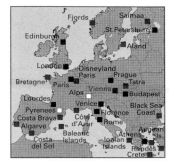

Projection: *Modified Hammer Equal Area*

CARTOGRAPHY BY PHILIP'S. COPYRIGHT GEORGE PHILIP LTD

TIME ZONES

Note: Certain of the time zones are affected by the incidence of "Summer Time" in countries where it is adopted.

Legend
- Zones using Greenwich Mean Time
- Zones slow of Greenwich Mean Time
- Half hour zones
- Zones fast of Greenwich Mean Time
- – – – International boundaries
- —— Time zone boundaries
- International date line
- Selected air routes
- 10PM   Actual Solar Time when noon at Greenwich is shown along the top of the map.
- 10   Hours slow or fast of Greenwich Mean Time
- Equatorial scale: 1:220 000 000

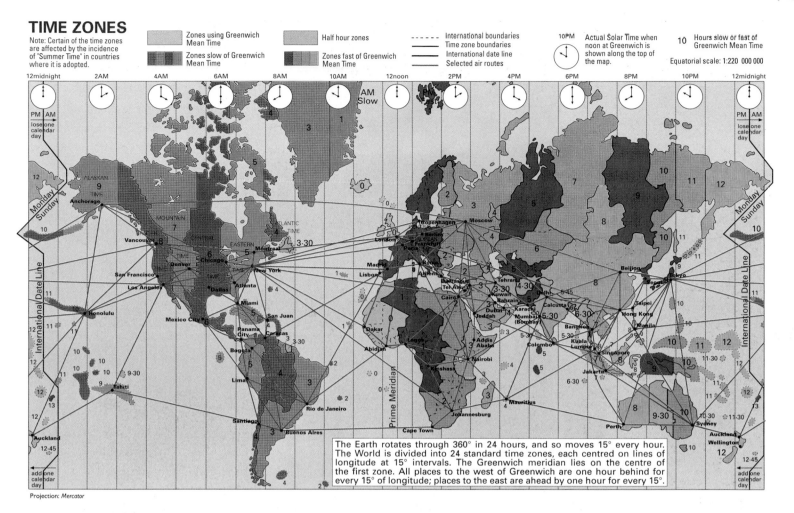

The Earth rotates through 360° in 24 hours, and so moves 15° every hour. The World is divided into 24 standard time zones, each centred on lines of longitude at 15° intervals. The Greenwich meridian lies on the centre of the first zone. All places to the west of Greenwich are one hour behind for every 15° of longitude; places to the east are ahead by one hour for every 15°.

Projection: Mercator

DISTANCE TABLE

The table shows air distances in miles and kilometres between twenty-four major cities. Known as 'Great Circle' distances, these measure the shortest routes between cities, which aircraft use where possible.

Miles (upper-right triangle)

From \ To	Bogota	Buenos Aires	Cairo	Calcutta	Caracas	Chicago	Hong Kong	Honolulu	Johannesburg	Lagos	London	Los Angeles	Mexico City	Moscow	Nairobi	New York	Paris	Rio de Janeiro	Rome	Singapore	Sydney	Tokyo	Wellington
Beijing	9263	11972	4688	2031	8947	6588	1220	5070	7276	7119	5057	6251	7742	3600	5727	6828	5106	10773	5049	2783	5561	1304	6700
Bogota		2911	6971	10223	637	2710	10480	5697	7125	5319	5262	3478	1961	6758	7672	2481	5358	2820	5831	11990	8903	8851	7527
Buenos Aires			7341	10268	3167	5599	11481	7558	5025	4919	6917	6122	4591	8374	6463	5298	6867	1214	6929	9867	7332	11410	6202
Cairo				3541	6340	6127	5064	8838	3894	2432	2180	7580	7687	1803	2197	5605	1994	6149	1325	5137	8959	5947	10268
Calcutta					9609	7978	1653	7048	5256	5727	4946	8152	9494	3438	3839	7921	4883	9366	4486	1800	5678	3195	7055
Caracas						2502	10166	6009	6847	4810	4664	3612	2228	6175	7173	2131	4738	2825	5196	11407	9534	8801	8154
Chicago							7783	4247	8689	5973	3949	1742	1694	4971	8005	711	4132	5311	4809	9369	9243	6299	8358
Hong Kong								5543	6669	7360	5980	7232	8775	4439	5453	8047	5984	11001	5769	1615	4582	1786	5857
Honolulu									11934	10133	7228	2558	3781	7036	10739	4958	7437	8290	8026	6721	5075	3854	4669
Johannesburg										2799	5637	10362	9063	5692	1818	7979	5426	4420	4811	5381	6860	8418	7308
Lagos											3118	7713	6879	3886	2366	5268	2929	3750	2510	6925	9643	8376	9973
London												5442	5552	1552	4237	3463	212	5778	889	6743	10558	5942	11691
Los Angeles													1549	6070	9659	2446	5645	6310	6331	8776	7502	5475	6719
Mexico City														6664	9207	2090	5717	4780	6365	10321	8058	7024	6897
Moscow															3942	4666	1545	7184	1477	5237	9008	4651	10283
Nairobi																7358	4029	5548	3350	4635	7552	6996	8490
New York																	3626	4832	4280	9531	9935	6741	8951
Paris																		5708	687	6671	10539	6038	11798
Rio de Janeiro																			5725	9763	8389	11551	7367
Rome																				6229	10143	6127	11523
Singapore																					3915	3306	5298
Sydney																						4861	1383
Tokyo																							5762

Kms (lower-left triangle)

From \ To	Beijing	Bogota	Buenos Aires	Cairo	Calcutta	Caracas	Chicago	Hong Kong	Honolulu	Johannesburg	Lagos	London	Los Angeles	Mexico City	Moscow	Nairobi	New York	Paris	Rio de Janeiro	Rome	Singapore	Sydney
Bogota	14908																					
Buenos Aires	19268	4685																				
Cairo	7544	11218	11814																			
Calcutta	3269	16453	16524	5699																		
Caracas	14399	1026	5096	10203	15464																	
Chicago	10603	4361	9011	9860	12839	4027																
Hong Kong	1963	16865	18478	8150	2659	16360	12526															
Honolulu	8160	9169	12164	14223	11343	9670	6836	8921														
Johannesburg	11710	11467	8088	6267	8459	11019	13984	10732	19206													
Lagos	11457	8561	7916	3915	9216	7741	9612	11845	16308	4505												
London	8138	8468	11131	3508	7961	7507	6356	9623	11632	9071	5017											
Los Angeles	10060	5596	9852	12200	13120	5812	2804	11639	4117	16676	12414	8758										
Mexico City	12460	3156	7389	12372	15280	3586	2726	14122	6085	14585	11071	8936	2493									
Moscow	5794	10877	13477	2902	5534	9938	8000	7144	11323	9161	6254	2498	9769	10724								
Nairobi	9216	12347	10402	3536	6179	11544	12883	8776	17282	2927	3807	6819	15544	14818	6344							
New York	10988	3993	8526	9020	12747	3430	1145	12950	7980	12841	8477	5572	3936	3264	7510	11842						
Paris	8217	8622	11051	3210	7858	7625	6650	9630	11968	8732	4714	342	9085	9200	2486	6485	5836					
Rio de Janeiro	17338	4539	1953	9896	15073	4546	8547	17704	13342	7113	6035	9299	10155	7693	11562	8928	7777	9187				
Rome	8126	9383	11151	2133	7219	8363	7739	9284	12916	7743	4039	1431	10188	10243	2376	5391	6888	1105	9214			
Singapore	4478	19296	15879	8267	2897	18359	15078	2599	10816	8660	11145	10852	14123	16610	8428	7460	15339	10737	15712	10025		
Sydney	8949	14327	11800	14418	9138	15343	14875	7374	8168	11040	15519	16992	12073	12969	14497	12153	15989	16962	13501	16324	6300	
Tokyo	2099	14245	18362	9571	5141	14164	10137	2874	6202	13547	13480	9562	8811	11304	10849	9718	18589	9861	5321	7823		
Wellington	10782	12113	9981	16524	11354	13122	13451	9273	7513	11761	16050	18814	10814	11100	16549	13664	14405	18987	11855	18545	8526	2226

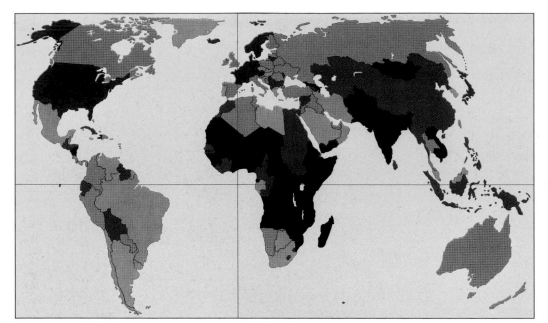

WEALTH

The value of total production in 1995 divided by the population.
(The Gross National Product per capita)

Over 400% of world average

200 – 400% of world average

100 – 200% of world average

World average wealth per person $5 714

50 – 100% of world average

25 – 50% of world average

10 – 25% of world average

Under 10% of world average

Top 5 countries		Bottom 5 countries	
Luxembourg	$41 210	Mozambique	$80
Switzerland	$40 630	Ethiopia	$100
Japan	$39 640	Congo (Zaïre)	$120
Norway	$31 250	Tanzania	$120
Denmark	$29 890	Burundi	$160
		U.K.	$18 700

CAR OWNERSHIP

Number of people per car
(latest available year)

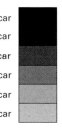

Over 1000 people per car

500 – 1000 people per car

100 – 500 people per car

25 – 100 people per car

5 – 25 people per car

Under 5 people per car

Most people per car		Most cars (millions)	
Nepal	4247	U.S.A.	143.8
Bangladesh	2618	Germany	39.1
Cambodia	2328	Japan	39.0
Somalia	1790	Italy	29.6
Ethiopia	1423	France	24.0

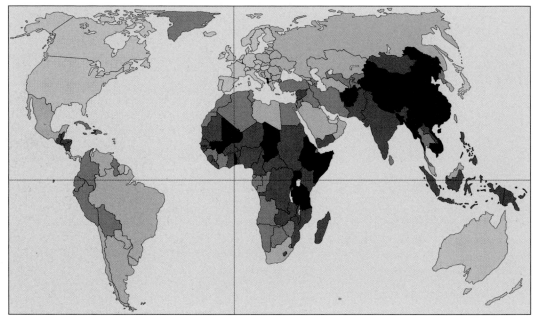

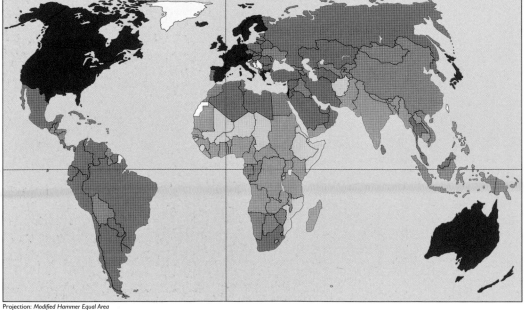

HUMAN DEVELOPMENT INDEX

The Human Development Index (H.D.I.) 1994 includes social and economic indicators and is calculated by the U.N. Development Programme as a measure of national human progress. Wealthy developed countries measure highest on the index.

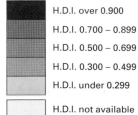

H.D.I. over 0.900

H.D.I. 0.700 – 0.899

H.D.I. 0.500 – 0.699

H.D.I. 0.300 – 0.499

H.D.I. under 0.299

H.D.I. not available

Top 5 countries		Bottom 5 countries	
Canada	0.960	Mali	0.229
France	0.946	Burkina Faso	0.221
Norway	0.943	Niger	0.206
U.S.A.	0.942	Rwanda	0.187
Iceland	0.942	Sierra Leone	0.176
		U.K.	0.931

Projection: *Modified Hammer Equal Area*

HEALTH CARE

Number of people per doctor 1993

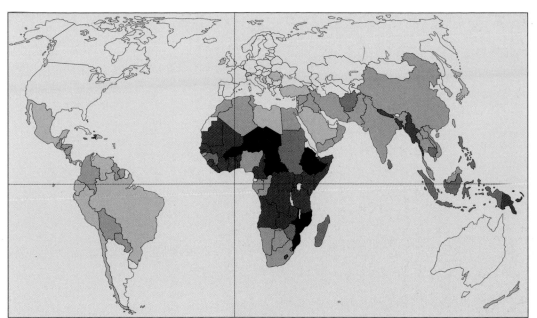

	Over 25 000 people per doctor
	10 000 – 25 000 people per doctor
	5 000 – 10 000 people per doctor
	1 000 – 5 000 people per doctor
	500 – 1 000 people per doctor
	Under 500 people per doctor

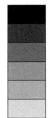

Most people per doctor 1993		Least people per doctor 1993	
Niger	53 986	Georgia	182
Malawi	44 205	Italy	207
Mozambique	36 225	Israel	220
Burkina Faso	34 804	Russia	222
Ethiopia	32 499	Ukraine	227
		U.K.	300

ILLITERACY & EDUCATION

Percentage of total population
unable to read or write 1995

Over 75% of population illiterate	
50 – 75% of population illiterate	
25 – 50% of population illiterate	
10 – 25% of population illiterate	
Under 10% of population illiterate	

• Less than 6 years compulsory
education per child

Educational expenditure per person
(latest available year)

Top five countries		Bottom five countries	
Norway	$2,820	Congo (Zaïre)	$1
Denmark	$2,450	Somalia	$2
Switzerland	$2,256	Sierra Leone	$2
Japan	$1,853	Nigeria	$3
Finland	$1,706	Haiti	$3
		U.K.	$1,009

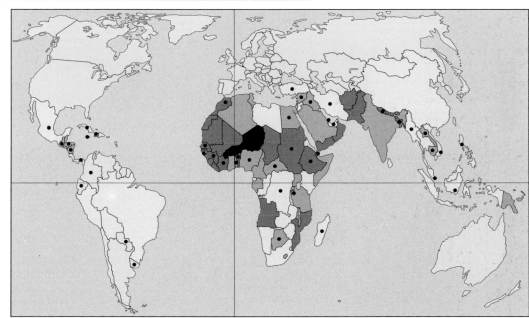

FERTILITY & EDUCATION
Fertility rates compared with female education, selected countries (1992–1995)

- Fertility rate: average number of children borne per woman
- Percentage of females aged 12 – 17 in secondary education

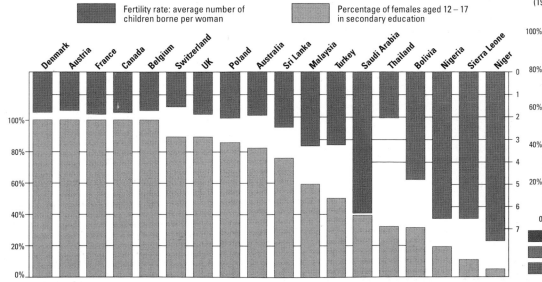

CAUSES OF DEATH
Causes of death for selected countries by percentage
(1992–1994)

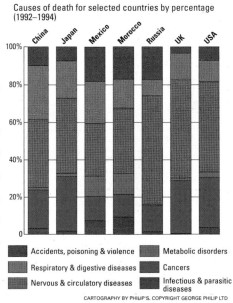

Accidents, poisoning & violence	Metabolic disorders
Respiratory & digestive diseases	Cancers
Nervous & circulatory diseases	Infectious & parasitic diseases

CARTOGRAPHY BY PHILIP'S. COPYRIGHT GEORGE PHILIP LTD

AGE DISTRIBUTION PYRAMIDS

The bars represent the percentage of the total population (males plus females) in the age group shown.

Developed countries such as the U.K. have populations evenly spread across age groups and usually a growing percentage of elderly people. Developing countries such as Kenya have the great majority of their people in the younger age groups, about to enter their most fertile years.

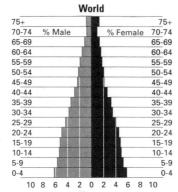

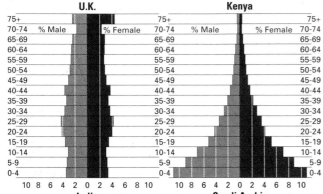

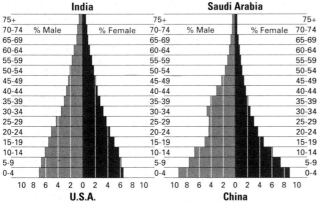

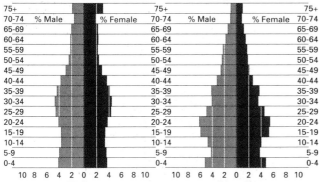

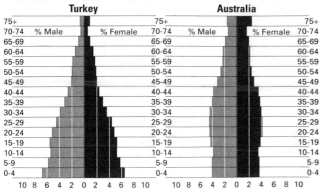

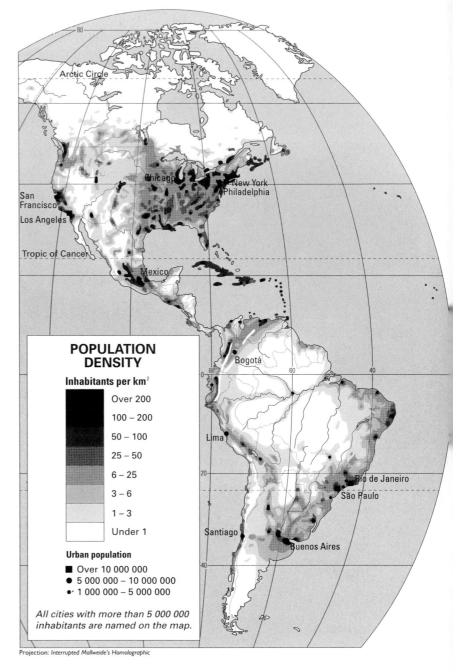

POPULATION DENSITY

Inhabitants per km²

- Over 200
- 100 – 200
- 50 – 100
- 25 – 50
- 6 – 25
- 3 – 6
- 1 – 3
- Under 1

Urban population

- ■ Over 10 000 000
- ● 5 000 000 – 10 000 000
- • 1 000 000 – 5 000 000

All cities with more than 5 000 000 inhabitants are named on the map.

Projection: Interrupted Mollweide's Homolographic

POPULATION CHANGE 1930-2020

Population totals are in millions

Figures in italics represent the percentage average annual increase for the period shown

	1930	1930-1960	1960	1960-1990	1990	1990-2020	2020
World	2013	*1.4%*	3019	*1.9%*	5292	*1.4%*	8062
Africa	155	*2.0%*	281	*2.85*	648	*2.7%*	1441
North America	135	*1.3%*	199	*1.1%*	276	*0.6%*	327
Latin America*	129	*1.8%*	218	*2.4%*	448	*1.6%*	719
Asia	1073	*1.5%*	1669	*2.1%*	3108	*1.4%*	4680
Europe	355	*0.6%*	425	*0.55*	498	*0.1%*	514
Oceania	10	*1.4%*	16	*1.75*	27	*1.1%*	37
C.I.S.†	176	*0.7%*	214	*1.0%*	288	*0.6%*	343

* South America plus Central America, Mexico, and the West Indies
† Commonwealth of Independent States, formerly the U.S.S.R.

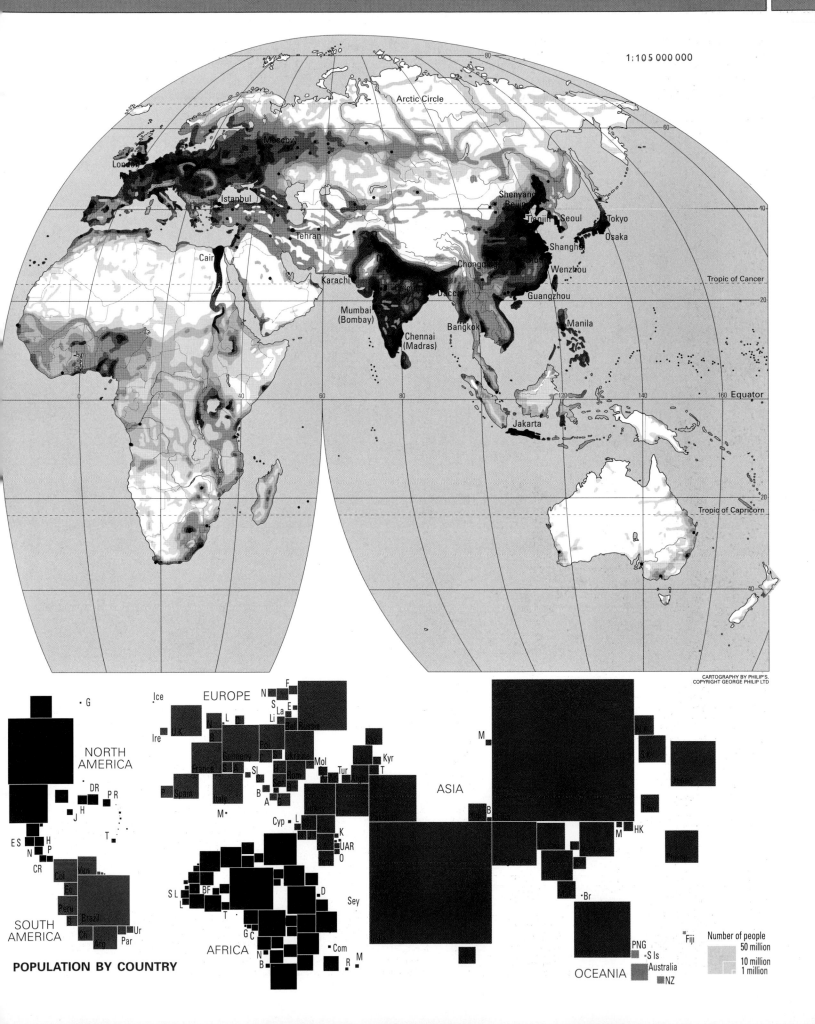

1:105 000 000

Arctic Circle

Moscow

London

Istanbul

Tehran

Cair

Karachi

Mumbai (Bombay)

Chennai (Madras)

Shenyang
Beijing
Tianjin   Seoul   Tokyo
Osaka
Shanghai
Chongqing
Wenzhou
Dacca   Guangzhou

Bangkok

Manila

Tropic of Cancer

Equator

Jakarta

Tropic of Capricorn

CARTOGRAPHY BY PHILIP'S.
COPYRIGHT GEORGE PHILIP LTD

POPULATION BY COUNTRY

EUROPE

NORTH AMERICA

SOUTH AMERICA

AFRICA

ASIA

OCEANIA

Number of people
50 million
10 million
1 million

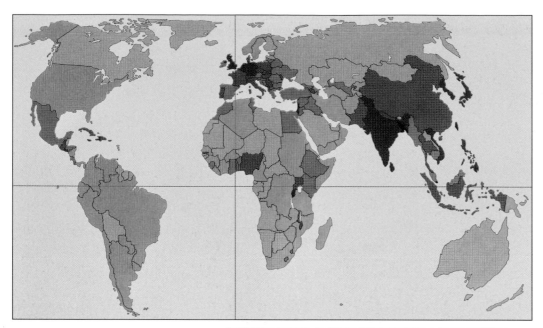

POPULATION DENSITY BY COUNTRY

Density of people per square kilometre 1997

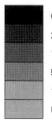

- Over 500 people per km²
- 200 – 500 people per km²
- 100 – 200 people per km²
- 50 – 100 people per km²
- 10 – 50 people per km²
- Under 10 people per km²

Top 5 countries		Bottom 5 countries	
Macau	22 111 per km²	Namibia	1.9 per km²
Monaco	20 805 per km²	French Guiana	1.5 per km²
Singapore	5 246 per km²	Mongolia	1.4 per km²
Malta	1 172 per km²	W. Sahara	0.8 per km²
Bangladesh	953 per km²	Greenland	0.2 per km²

U.K.   243 per km²

POPULATION CHANGE 1990-2000

The predicted population change for the years 1990-2000

- Over 40% population gain
- 30 – 40% population gain
- 20 – 30% population gain
- 10 – 20% population gain
- 0 – 10% population gain
- No change or population loss

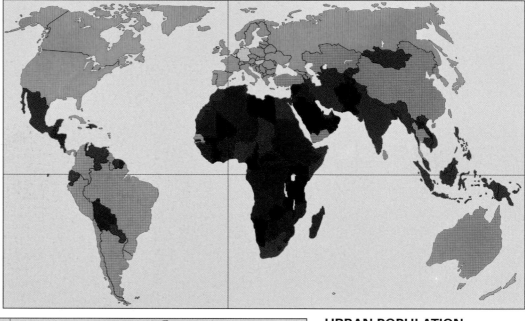

Top 5 countries		Bottom 5 countries	
Kuwait	+75.9%	Belgium	-0.1%
Namibia	+62.5%	Hungary	-0.2%
Afghanistan	+60.1%	Grenada	-2.4%
Mali	+55.5%	Germany	-3.2%
Tanzania	+54.6%	Tonga	-3.2%

U.K.   +2.0%

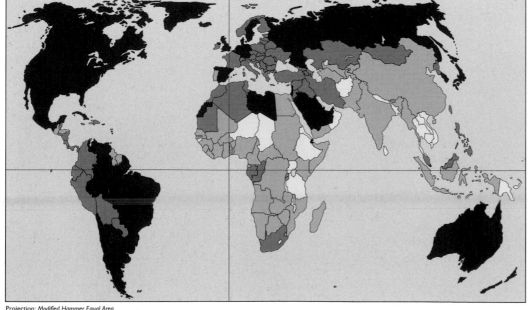

URBAN POPULATION

Percentage of total population living in towns and cities 1995

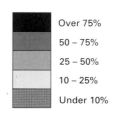

- Over 75%
- 50 – 75%
- 25 – 50%
- 10 – 25%
- Under 10%

Most urbanized		Least urbanized	
Singapore	100%	Bhutan	6%
Belgium	97%	Rwanda	6%
Kuwait	97%	Burundi	7%
Iceland	92%	Uganda	12%
Venezuela	92%	Malawi	13%

U.K.   89%

Projection: *Modified Hammer Equal Area*

CHILD MORTALITY

The number of babies who died
under the age of one
(average 1990–95)

	Over 150 deaths per 1 000 births
	100 – 150 deaths per 1 000 births
	50 – 100 deaths per 1 000 births
	20 – 50 deaths per 1 000 births
	10 – 20 deaths per 1 000 births
	Under 10 deaths per 1 000 births

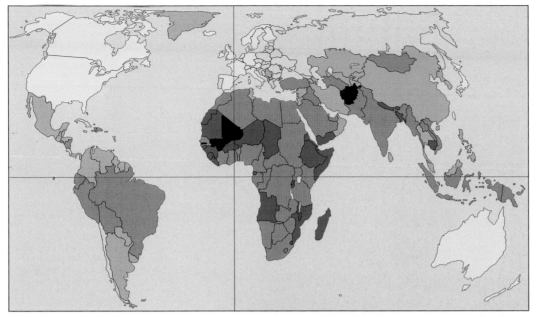

Highest child mortality		Lowest child mortality	
Afghanistan	162 deaths	Hong Kong	6 deaths
Mali	159 deaths	Denmark	6 deaths
Sierra Leone	143 deaths	Japan	5 deaths
Guinea-Bissau	140 deaths	Iceland	5 deaths
Malawi	138 deaths	Finland	5 deaths
		U.K.	8 deaths

LIFE EXPECTANCY

Average expected lifespan
of babies born in 1997

Over 75 years	
70 – 75 years	
65 – 70 years	
60 – 65 years	
55 – 60 years	
50 – 55 years	
Under 50 years	

Highest life expectancy		Lowest life expectancy	
Iceland	81 years	Tanzania	42 years
Japan	80 years	Niger	41 years
Australia	80 years	Uganda	40 years
Canada	79 years	Rwanda	39 years
Luxembourg	79 years	Malawi	35 years
		U.K.	77 years

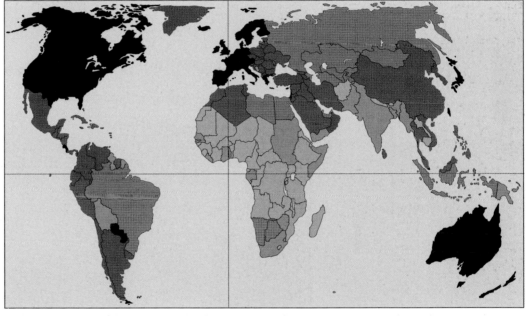

FAMILY SIZE

The average number of children a woman
can expect to bear during her lifetime 1995

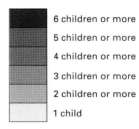

	6 children or more
	5 children or more
	4 children or more
	3 children or more
	2 children or more
	1 child

Most children per family

Yemen	7.4
Niger	7.4
Somalia	7.0
Oman	7.0
Ethiopia	7.0
U.K.	1.7

Projection: *Modified Hammer Equal Area*

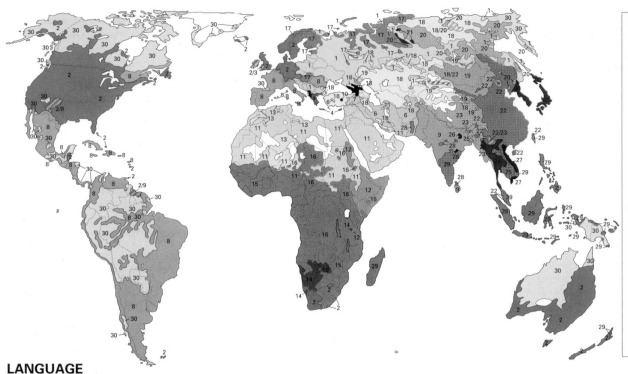

MOTHER TONGUES
Chinese 1069 million
(Mandarin 864), English
443, Hindi 352, Spanish
341, Russian 293, Arabic
197, Bengali 184,
Portuguese 173, Malay-
Indonesian 142, Japanese
125, French 121, German
118, Urdu 92, Punjabi 84,
Korean 71.

OFFICIAL LANGUAGES
English 27% of world
population, Chinese 19%,
Hindi 13.5%, Spanish 5.4%,
Russian 5.2%, French 4.2%,
Arabic 3.3%, Portuguese
3%, Malay 3%, Bengali
2.9%, Japanese 2.3%

Language can be classified
by ancestry and structure .
For example the Romance
and Germanic groups are
both derived from an Indo-
European language
believed to have been
spoken 5000 years ago.

LANGUAGE

INDO-EUROPEAN FAMILY
1 Balto-Slavic group (incl. Russian, Ukrainian)
2 Germanic group (incl. English, German)
3 Celtic group
4 Greek
5 Albanian
6 Iranian group
7 Armenian
8 Romance group (incl. Spanish, Portuguese, French, Italian)
9 Indo-Aryan group (incl. Hindi, Bengali, Urdu, Punjabi, Marathi)

CAUCASIAN FAMILY

AFRO-ASIATIC FAMILY
11 Semitic group (incl. Arabic)
12 Kushitic group
13 Berber group

14 KHOISAN FAMILY

15 NIGER-CONGO FAMILY

16 NILO-SAHARAN FAMILY

17 URALIC FAMILY

ALTAIC FAMILY
18 Turkic group
19 Mongolian group
20 Tungus-Manchu group
21 Japanese and Korean

SINO-TIBETAN FAMILY
22 Sinitic (Chinese) languages
23 Tibetic-Burmic languages

24 TAI FAMILY

AUSTRO-ASIATIC FAMILY
25 Mon-Khmer group
26 Munda group
27 Vietnamese

28 DRAVIDIAN FAMILY
(incl. Telugu, Tamil)

29 AUSTRONESIAN FAMILY
(incl. Malay-Indonesian)

30 OTHER LANGUAGES

RELIGION

- Roman Catholicism
- Orthodox and other Eastern Churches
- Protestantism
- Sunni Islam
- Shia Islam
- Buddhism
- Hinduism
- Confucianism
- Judaism
- Shintoism
- Primitive Religions

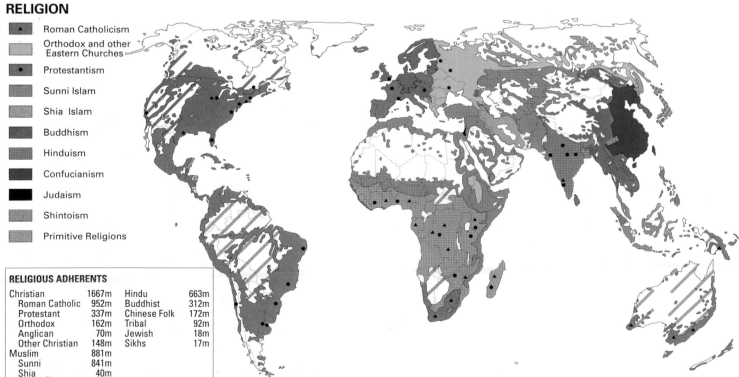

RELIGIOUS ADHERENTS

Christian	1667m	Hindu	663m
Roman Catholic	952m	Buddhist	312m
Protestant	337m	Chinese Folk	172m
Orthodox	162m	Tribal	92m
Anglican	70m	Jewish	18m
Other Christian	148m	Sikhs	17m
Muslim	881m		
Sunni	841m		
Shia	40m		

UNITED NATIONS

Created in 1945 to promote peace and co-operation and based in New York, the United Nations is the world's largest international organization, with 185 members and an annual budget of US $2.6 billion (1996–97). Each member of the General Assembly has one vote, while the permanent members of the 15-nation Security Council – USA, Russia, China, UK and France – hold a veto. The Secretariat is the UN's principal administrative arm. The 54 members of the Economic and Social Council are responsible for economic, social, cultural, educational, health and related matters. The UN has 16 specialized agencies – based in Canada, France, Switzerland and Italy, as well as the USA – which help members in fields such as education (UNESCO), agriculture (FAO), medicine (WHO) and finance (IFC). By the end of 1994, all the original 11 trust territories of The Trusteeship Council had become independent.

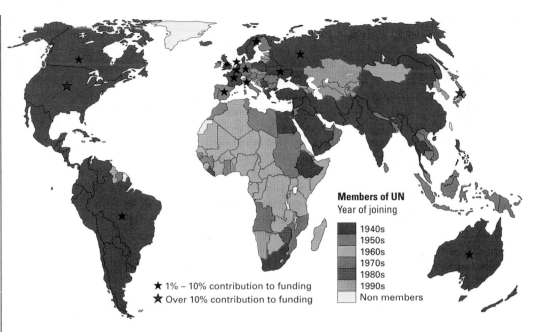

Members of UN
Year of joining

- 1940s
- 1950s
- 1960s
- 1970s
- 1980s
- 1990s
- Non members

★ 1% – 10% contribution to funding
★ Over 10% contribution to funding

The Secretariat (civil servants who run the UN)

Security Council (tries to keep the peace between countries)

Trusteeship Council (looks after Trust Territories)

Economic & Social Council (looks after UN agencies)

International Court of Justice

UN Agencies: IDA, IBRD, ILO, FAO, UNESCO, IMF, UPU, WHO, ICAO, WMO, WIPO, UNIDO, IFAD, ITU, IFC

MEMBERSHIP OF THE UN In 1945 there were 51 members; by December 1994 membership had increased to 185 following the admission of Palau. There are 7 independent states which are not members of the UN – Kiribati, Nauru, Switzerland, Taiwan, Tonga, Tuvalu and the Vatican City. All the successor states of the former USSR had joined by the end of 1992. The official languages of the UN are Chinese, English, French, Russian, Spanish and Arabic.
FUNDING The UN budget for 1996–97 was US $ 2.6 billion. Contributions are assessed by the members' ability to pay, with the maximum 25% of the total, the minimum 0.01%. Contributions for 1996 were: USA 25.0%, Japan 15.4%, Germany 9.0%, France 6.4%, UK 5.3%, Italy 5.2%, Russia 4.5%, Canada 3.1%, Spain 2.4%, Brazil 1.6%, Netherlands 1.6%, Australia 1.5%, Sweden 1.2%, Ukraine 1.1%, Belgium 1.0%.

INTERNATIONAL ORGANIZATIONS

EU European Union (evolved from the European Community in 1993). The 15 members - Austria, Belgium, Denmark, Finland, France, Germany, Greece, Ireland, Italy, Luxembourg, Netherlands, Portugal, Spain, Sweden and the UK - aim to integrate economies, co-ordinate social developments and bring about political union. These members of what is now the world's biggest market share agricultural and industrial policies and tariffs on trade. The original body, the European Coal and Steel Community (ECSC), was created in 1951 following the signing of the Treaty of Paris.
EFTA European Free Trade Association (formed in 1960). Portugal left the original 'Seven' in 1989 to join what was then the EC, followed by Austria, Finland and Sweden in 1995. Only 4 members remain: Norway, Iceland, Switzerland and Liechtenstein.
ACP African-Caribbean-Pacific (formed in 1963). Members have economic ties with the EU.
NATO North Atlantic Treaty Organization (formed in 1949). It continues after 1991 despite the winding up of the Warsaw Pact. There are 16 member nations.
OAS Organization of American States (formed in 1948). It aims to promote social and economic co-operation between developed countries of North America and developing nations of Latin America.
ASEAN Association of South-east Asian Nations (formed in 1967). Burma and Laos joined in July 1997.
OAU Organization of African Unity (formed in 1963). Its 53 members represent over 94% of Africa's population. Arabic, French, Portuguese and English are recognized as working languages.
LAIA Latin American Integration Association (1980). Its aim is to promote freer regional trade.
OECD Organization for Economic Co-operation and Development (formed in 1961). It comprises the 29 major Western free-market economies. 'G7' is its' inner group' comprising the USA, Canada, Japan, UK, Germany, Italy and France. Russia attended the G7 summit in June 1997 ('Summit of the Eight').
COMMONWEALTH The Commonwealth of Nations evolved from the British Empire; it comprises 16 Queen's realms, 32 republics and 5 indigenous monarchies, giving a total of 53.
OPEC Organization of Petroleum Exporting Countries (formed in 1960). It controls about three-quarters of the world's oil supply. Gabon left the organization in 1996.

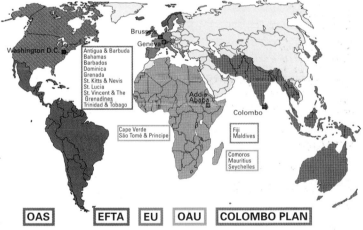

Brussels
Geneva
Washington D.C.
Addis Ababa
Colombo

Antigua & Barbuda, Bahamas, Barbados, Dominica, Grenada, St. Kitts & Nevis, St. Lucia, St. Vincent & The Grenadines, Trinidad & Tobago

Cape Verde, São Tomé & Principe

Fiji, Maldives

Comoros, Mauritius, Seychelles

| OAS | EFTA | EU | OAU | COLOMBO PLAN |

ARAB LEAGUE (formed in 1945). The League's aim is to promote economic, social, political and military co-operation. There are 21 member nations.
COLOMBO PLAN (formed in 1951). Its 26 members aim to promote economic and social development in Asia and the Pacific.

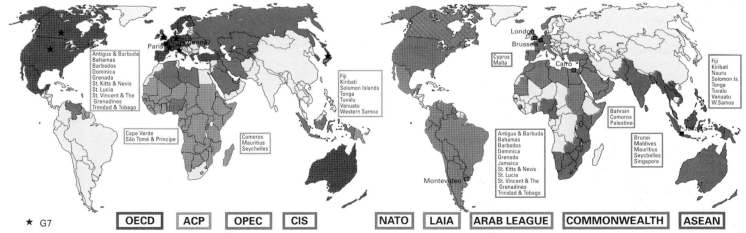

Paris, Vienna

Antigua & Barbuda, Bahamas, Barbados, Dominica, Grenada, St. Kitts & Nevis, St. Lucia, St. Vincent & The Grenadines, Trinidad & Tobago

Cape Verde, São Tomé & Principe

Comoros, Mauritius, Seychelles

Fiji, Kiribati, Solomon Islands, Tonga, Tuvalu, Vanuatu, Western Samoa

London, Brussels
Cairo
Jakarta

Cyprus, Malta

Fiji, Kiribati, Nauru, Solomon Is., Tonga, Tuvalu, Vanuatu, W.Samoa

Bahrain, Comoros, Palestine

Brunei, Maldives, Mauritius, Seychelles, Singapore

Antigua & Barbuda, Bahamas, Barbados, Dominica, Grenada, Jamaica, St. Kitts & Nevis, St. Lucia, St. Vincent & The Grenadines, Trinidad & Tobago

Montevideo

★ G7

| OECD | ACP | OPEC | CIS | | NATO | LAIA | ARAB LEAGUE | COMMONWEALTH | ASEAN |

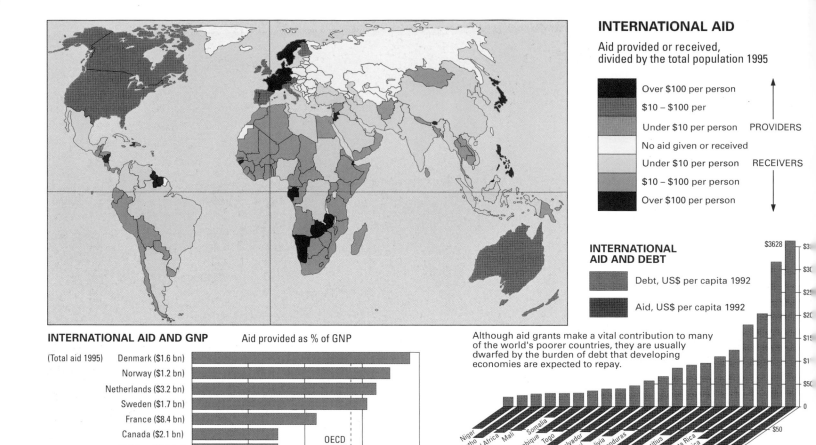

INTERNATIONAL AID

Aid provided or received,
divided by the total population 1995

Over $100 per person	
$10 – $100 per	
Under $10 per person	PROVIDERS
No aid given or received	
Under $10 per person	RECEIVERS
$10 – $100 per person	
Over $100 per person	

INTERNATIONAL AID AND DEBT

Debt, US$ per capita 1992	
Aid, US$ per capita 1992	

Although aid grants make a vital contribution to many of the world's poorer countries, they are usually dwarfed by the burden of debt that developing economies are expected to repay.

$3628

Niger, Lesotho, Central Africa, Mali, Somalia, Mozambique, Togo, Botswana, El Salvador, Senegal, Bolivia, Honduras, Zambia, Papua N. Guinea, Mauritania, Mauritius, Costa Rica, Jamaica, Jordan $247.1, Gabon, Israel $352.5

$50, $100, $150

INTERNATIONAL AID AND GNP

Aid provided as % of GNP

(Total aid 1995)
- Denmark ($1.6 bn)
- Norway ($1.2 bn)
- Netherlands ($3.2 bn)
- Sweden ($1.7 bn)
- France ($8.4 bn)
- Canada ($2.1 bn)
- Belgium ($1.0 bn)
- Australia ($1.2 bn)

OECD target 0.7%

0.25%   0.5%   0.75%   1%

INTERNATIONAL MIGRATION

Foreign born as a % of total population (latest year)

	Over 7.5%
	3 – 7.5%
	1.5 – 3%
	Under 1.5%
	No available data

Major migrations since 1945
1. 18m E. Europeans to Germany 1945 –
2. 4m Europeans to N. America 1945 –
3. 2.4m Jews to Israel 1945 –
4. 2m Irish & Commonwealth to U.K. 1945 –
5. 2m Europeans to Australia 1945
6. 2m N. Africans & S. Europeans to France 1946 –
7. 5m Chinese to Japan & Korea 1947 –
8. 2.9m Palestinian refugees 1947
9. 25m Indian & Pakistani refugees 1947–
10. 9m Mexicans to N. America 1950 –
11. 5m Korean refugees 1950 – 54
12. 4.7m C. Americans & W. Indians to N. America 1960–
13. 1.5m workers to S. Africa 1960 –
14. 2.4m S. Asian workers to the Gulf 1970 –
15. 3m workers to Nigeria & Ivory Coast 1970 –
16. 2m Bangladeshi & Pakistani refugees 1972 –
17. 1.5m Vietnamese & Cambodian refugees 1975 –
18. 6.1m Afghan refugees 1979 –
19. 2.9m Egyptian workers to Libya & the Gulf 1980 –
20. 2m workers to Argentina 1980 –
21. 1.7m Mozambique refugees 1985 –
22. 1.7m Yugoslav refugees 1992 –
23. 2.6m Rwanda - Burundi refugees 1994–

INTERNATIONAL REFUGEES

Origins of Refugees   World Total 1996: 13.6 millio

Other Europe 7.0%
North & South America 0.7%
Bosnia-Herz. 6.9%
Palestine 27.1%
Other Africa 9.1%
Eritrea 2.5%
Sierra Leone 2.5%
Somalia 3.2%
Sudan 3.2%
Liberia 5.4%
Other Asia 8.9%
Iraq 4.7%
Afghanistan 18.

Refugee Destinations 1996

Iran

Refugees in host country	
Refugees as a proportion of host country's population	

Congo (Zaïre), Yugo-slavia, Guinea, Gaza Strip, Pakistan, Jordan, Iran

2 000 0
1 500 0
1 000 0
500 00

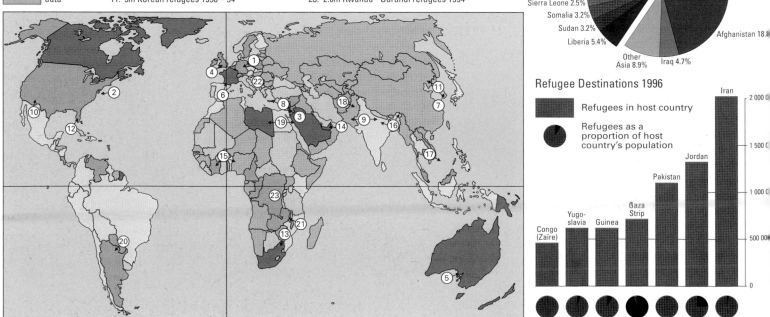

Projection: *Modified Hammer Equal Area*

HOUSING

Number of people per household
(latest available year)

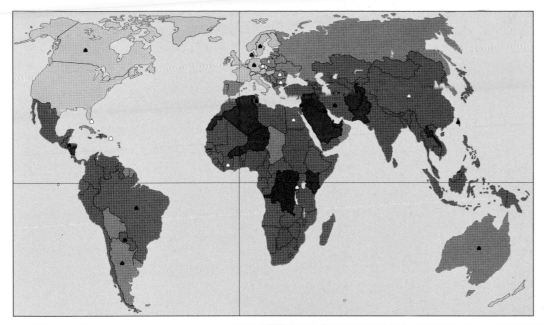

■	Over 6 people per household
■	5 – 6 people per household
■	4 – 5 people per household
■	3 – 4 people per household
■	2 – 3 people per household
■	Under 2 people per household

Expenditure on housing and energy as a
percentage of total consumer spending

▲   Over 20% spent

○   Under 5% spent

WATER SUPPLY

Percentage of total population with
access to safe drinking water
(average 1990 – 1996)

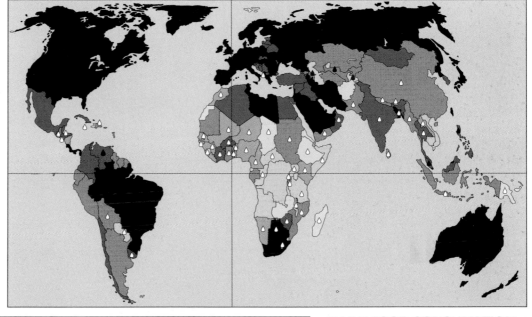

Over 90% with safe water	
75 – 90% with safe water	
60 – 75% with safe water	
45 – 60% with safe water	
30 – 45% with safe water	
Under 30% with safe water	

Least well provided countries

Afghanistan	23%	Papua New Guinea	28%
Chad	24%	Haiti	28%
Ethiopia	25%	Madagascar	29%

Average daily domestic water
consumption per person

○   Under 80 litres   ▲   Over 320 litres

*80 litres of water a day is considered
necessary for a reasonable quality of life*

DAILY FOOD CONSUMPTION

Average daily food intake
in calories per person 1992

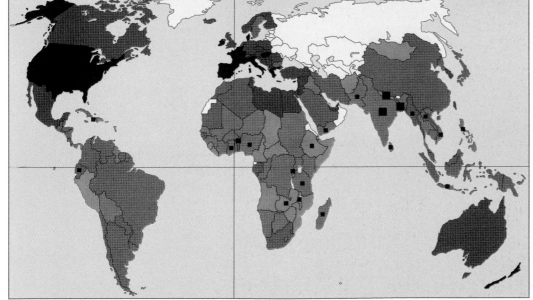

■	Over 3 500 cals. per person
■	3 000 – 3 500 cals. per person
■	2 500 – 3 000 cals. per person
■	2 000 – 2 500 cals. per person
■	Under 2 000 cals. per person
▢	No available data

Top 5 countries		Bottom 5 countries	
Ireland	3 847	Mozambique	1 680
Greece	3 815	Liberia	1 640
Cyprus	3 779	Ethiopia	1 610
U.S.A.	3 732	Afghanistan	1 523
Spain	3 708	Somalia	1 499
	U.K.	3 317	

Malnutrition in children under 5 years

■	Over 50% of children
▪	25 – 50% of children

Projection: *Modified Hammer Equal Area*

CARTOGRAPHY BY PHILIP'S. COPYRIGHT GEORGE PHILIP LTD

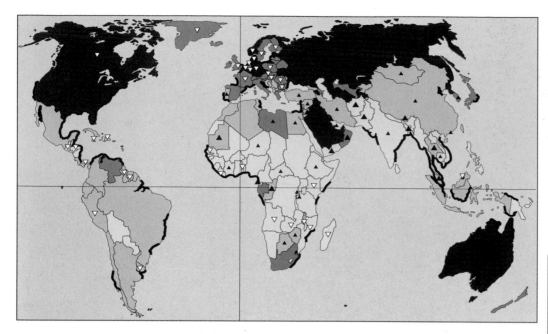

GLOBAL WARMING

Carbon dioxide emissions in tonnes per person per year (1992)

- Over 10 tonnes of CO_2
- 5 – 10 tonnes of CO_2
- 1 – 5 tonnes of CO_2
- Under 1 tonne of CO_2

Changes in CO_2 emissions 1980 – 1990

- ▲ Over 100% increase in emissions
- ▲ 50 – 100% increase in emissions
- ▽ Reduction in emissions
- ▬ Coasts in danger of flooding from rising sea levels caused by global warming

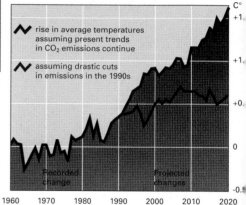

- ⟋ rise in average temperatures assuming present trends in CO_2 emissions continue
- ⟋ assuming drastic cuts in emissions in the 1990s

Recorded change   Projected changes

1960 1970 1980 1990 2000 2010 2020

5%   10%   15%   20%
U.S.A.
Former U.S.S.R.
China
Japan
Brazil
Germany
India
U.K.

Largest percentage share of total world greenhouse gas emissions 1992

Contribution to the greenhouse effect by the major heat-absorbing gases in the atmosphere

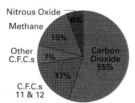

Nitrous Oxide 6%
Methane 15%
Other C.F.C.s 7%
Carbon Dioxide 55%
C.F.C.s 11 & 12 17%

THE GREENHOUSE EFFECT

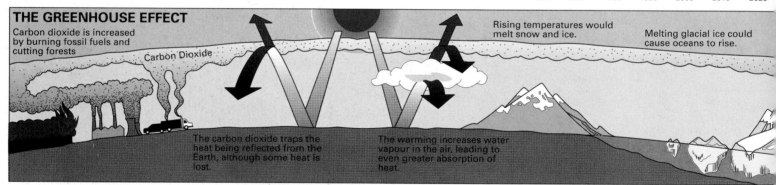

Carbon dioxide is increased by burning fossil fuels and cutting forests

Carbon Dioxide

Rising temperatures would melt snow and ice.

Melting glacial ice could cause oceans to rise.

The carbon dioxide traps the heat being reflected from the Earth, although some heat is lost.

The warming increases water vapour in the air, leading to even greater absorption of heat.

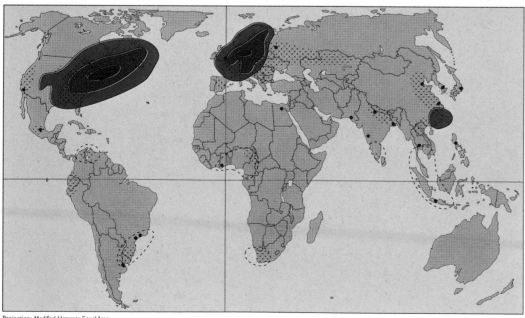

ACID RAIN

Acid rain is caused by high levels of sulphur and nitrogen in the atmosphere. They combine with water vapour and oxygen to form acids (H_2SO_4 and HNO_3) which fall as precipitation.

- Main areas of sulphur and nitrogen emissions (from the burning of fossil fuels)

- • Major cities with levels of air pollution exceeding World Health Organisation guidelines

Areas of acid deposition

(pH numbers measure acidity: normal rain is pH 5.6)

- pH less than 4.0 (most acidic)
- pH 4.0 – 4.5
- pH 4.5 – 5.0
- ⌐ ⌐ Potential problem areas

WATER POLLUTION

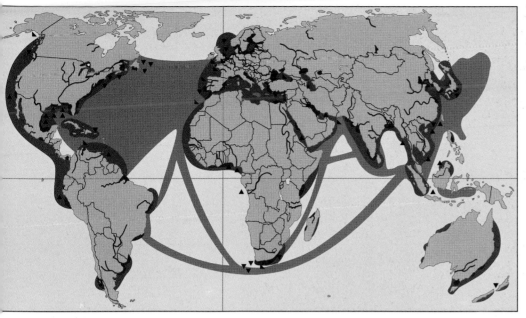

	Severely polluted sea areas and lakes
	Less polluted sea areas and lakes
	Areas of frequent oil pollution by shipping
◣	Major oil tanker spills
▲	Major oil rig blow-outs
▼	Offshore dumpsites for industrial and municipal waste
———	Severely polluted rivers and estuaries

Sources of marine oil pollution		Sources of river pollution	
Tanker operations	22%	Agriculture	64%
Municipal waste	22%	Mining	9%
Tanker accidents	13%	Land disposal	9%
River runoff	12%	Forestry	6%
Others	31%	Others	11%

DESERTIFICATION

	Existing deserts
	Areas with a high risk of desertification
	Areas with a moderate risk of desertification

DEFORESTATION IN THE TROPICS

	Former areas of rainforest
	Existing rainforest

Deforestation 1990-1995

	Extent of forest cleared annually (thousand ha)	Annual deforestation rate (%)
Brazil	2554	0.5
Indonesia	1084	1.0
Congo (Zaire)	740	0.7
Bolivia	581	1.2
Mexico	508	0.9
Venezuela	503	1.1
Malaysia	400	2.4

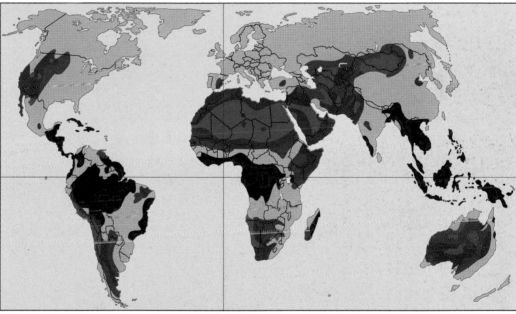

NATURAL DISASTERS

	Earthquake zones
●	Major earthquakes since 1900 (with dates)
▲	Major volcanoes (notable eruptions since 1900 with dates)
	Areas liable to flood
⇒	Paths of tropical storms
⇨	Paths of winter blizzards
	Areas liable to invasion by locusts
■	Major famines since 1900 (with dates)
⑨	Major storms and floods

1	Texas 1900
2	Central America 1966, 1974
3	West Indies 1928, 1963, 1979, 1988
4	Bangladesh 1960, 1963, 1965, 1970, 1985, 1988, 1989, 1991
5	Huang He 1887, 1931
6	Yangtze 1911, 1989, 1995
7	Hunan 1991
8	Haiphong 1881
9	Philippines 1970, 1991
10	Mississippi 1993

Projection: Modified Hammer Equal Area

CARTOGRAPHY BY PHILIP'S. COPYRIGHT GEORGE PHILIP LTD

	Population									Land and Agriculture					Energy	Trade	
	Population Total 1997	Population Density 1997	Average Annual Change 1970-80	Average Annual Change 1990-97	Birth Rate 1997	Death Rate 1997	Fertility Rate 1995	Life Expectancy Average 1997	Urban Population 1995	Land Area	Arable and Permanent Crops	Permanent grassland	Forest	Agriculture Population 1995	Consumption per capita 1994	Imports per capita 1995	Exports per capita 1995
	millions	persons per km²	%	%	births per thousand population	deaths per thousand population	children	years	%	thousand km²	% of land area	% of land area	% of land area	% of economically active pop.	tonnes of coal	US $	US $
Afghanistan	23	35	1.7	4.8	43	18	6.9	46	20	652	12	46	3	69	0.04	19	6
Albania	3.6	131	2.3	1.5	22	8	2.6	68	37	27.4	26	15	38	54	0.3	178	42
Algeria	29.3	12	3.1	2.3	28	6	3.5	69	56	2382	3	13	2	24	1.58	375	375
Angola	11.2	9	3.3	1.6	44	17	6.9	47	32	1247	3	43	18	74	0.08	198	309
Argentina	35.4	13	1.7	1.3	20	8	2.7	74	88	2737	10	52	19	11	2.15	579	603
Armenia	3.8	134	2	1.9	17	8	1.8	69	69	28.4	20	54	15	15	0.61	105	603
Australia	18.4	2	1.6	1.2	14	7	1.9	80	86	7644	6	54	19	5	7.61	3342	2942
Austria	8.2	99	0.1	1.1	11	10	1.5	77	65	82.7	18	24	39	7	4.16	8253	7166
Azerbaijan	7.7	89	1.8	1	22	9	2.3	65	56	86.1	23	52	11	30	2.6	105	86
Bahamas	0.3	28	2.1	1.5	18	6	2	73	85	10	1	0	32	5	2.97	4439	5418
Bangladesh	124	953	2.8	1	30	11	3.5	56	18	130	74	5	15	62	0.09	55	27
Barbados	0.3	616	0.4	0.6	15	8	1.8	75	46	0.43	37	5	12	6	1.58	2946	915
Belarus	10.5	51	0.7	0.3	11	13	1.4	69	69	208	31	14	34	18	3.38	297	243
Belgium	10.2	335	0.2	0.5	12	10	1.6	77	97	30.5	24	21	21	3	6.86	14702	16078
Benin	5.8	52	2.5	2.9	46	13	6	53	36	111	17	4	31	60	0.05	125	34
Bolivia	7.7	7	2.6	2.4	32	10	4.5	60	62	1084	2	24	53	45	0.49	192	149
Bosnia-Herzegovina	3.6	70	1	-2.7	6	7	1	60	41	51.2	16	24	39	10	0.36	204	12
Botswana	1.5	3	3.8	2.2	33	7	4.4	62	31	567	1	45	47	39	...	1153	1302
Brazil	159.5	19	2.4	1.4	20	9	2.4	62	78	8457	6	22	58	19	0.85	345	298
Bulgaria	8.6	77	0.4	-0.7	8	14	1.2	71	71	111	38	16	35	11	3.26	598	606
Burkina Faso	10.9	40	2.3	2.8	46	20	6.7	42	27	274	13	22	50	92	0.05	54	53
Burma	47.5	72	2.4	1.9	30	11	3.4	57	27	658	15	1	49	72	0.08	30	19
Burundi	6.3	243	1.6	0.5	42	15	6.5	49	7	25.7	46	39	13	91	0.02	39	18
Cambodia	10.5	59	-0.8	3.5	43	15	4.7	50	21	177	22	8	69	73	0.02	43	24
Cameroon	13.8	30	2.7	2.6	42	14	5.7	52	45	465	15	4	77	68	0.14	94	154
Canada	30.2	3	1.2	1.9	13	7	1.7	79	77	9221	5	3	54	3	11.21	5676	6491
Central African Rep.	3.4	5	2.3	1.8	40	18	5.1	45	39	623	3	5	75	79	0.04	54	52
Chad	6.8	5	2.1	2.5	44	17	5.9	48	22	1259	3	36	26	81	0.01	67	77
Chile	14.7	20	1.6	1.6	18	6	2.3	75	85	749	6	18	22	17	1.45	1121	1130
China	1210	130	1.8	1.2	17	7	1.9	70	29	9326	10	43	14	71	0.92	106	122
Colombia	35.9	35	2.3	1.2	21	5	2.8	73	73	1039	5	39	48	24	1	395	288
Congo	2.7	8	2.8	2.9	39	17	6	46	59	342	0	29	58	45	0.34	259	325
Congo (Zaïre)	47.2	21	2.9	4.1	48	17	6	47	29	2267	3	7	77	66	0.06	8	9
Costa Rica	3.5	69	2.8	2.2	23	4	2.8	76	50	51.1	10	46	31	22	0.87	977	811
Croatia	4.9	86	0.4	0.2	10	11	1.5	73	55	56.4	22	20	38	15	1.59	1586	969
Cuba	11.3	102	1.3	0.8	13	7	1.7	75	75	110	31	27	24	16	1.14	258	146
Cyprus	0.8	83	0.2	1.4	15	8	2.2	77	68	9.24	15	0	13	10	3.03	4986	1661
Czech Rep.	10.5	136	0.5	0.3	11	11	1.3	74	65	77	44	12	34	11	4.97	2450	2099
Denmark	5.4	126	0.4	0.3	12	10	1.8	78	86	42.4	56	7	10	4	5.15	8266	9378
Dominican Rep.	8.2	168	2.6	1.8	23	6	2.9	69	62	48.4	31	43	12	21	0.65	376	97
Ecuador	11.8	43	3	1.6	25	5	3.2	72	59	277	11	18	56	29	0.77	366	376
Egypt	63	63	2.1	2.6	28	9	3.4	62	45	995	4	0	0	33	0.66	199	58
El Salvador	6	287	2.3	1.8	27	6	3.7	69	52	20.7	35	29	5	32	0.5	504	176
Estonia	1.5	34	0.8	-1.1	12	14	1.3	68	73	43.2	27	7	48	14	4.9	1714	1240
Ethiopia	58.5	53	2.4	3.5	46	18	7	47	13	1101	11	20	13	86	0.03	19	7
Finland	5.2	17	0.4	0.6	11	11	1.8	76	63	305	9	0	76	7	7.4	5502	7744
France	58.8	107	0.6	0.7	13	9	1.7	79	74	550	35	19	27	4	5.15	4763	4941
Gabon	1.2	5	4.8	1.5	28	13	5.2	56	73	258	2	18	77	45	0.87	667	2055
Gambia, The	1.2	120	3.3	4.9	44	19	5.3	53	26	10	17	19	10	80	0.1	192	32
Georgia	5.5	78	0.8	0	14	9	1.9	68	58	69.7	16	24	33	25	0.85	39	22
Germany	82.3	236	0.1	0.5	9	11	1.2	76	87	349	34	15	31	3	5.48	5445	6227
Ghana	18.1	80	2.2	2.7	34	11	5.1	57	36	228	19	37	42	56	0.14	129	74
Greece	10.6	82	0.9	0.8	10	10	1.4	78	65	129	27	41	20	20	3.22	2056	899
Guatemala	11.3	104	2.8	2.9	33	7	4.7	66	42	108	18	24	54	51	0.29	310	203
Guinea	7.5	30	1.4	3.8	42	18	6.5	46	30	246	3	44	27	85	0.08	116	97
Guinea-Bissau	1.2	41	4.2	2.6	39	16	6	49	22	28.1	12	38	38	84	0.1	66	22
Guyana	0.8	4	0.7	-0.8	19	10	2.4	59	35	197	3	6	84	20	0.6	594	558
Haiti	7.4	269	1.7	1.8	33	15	4.4	50	32	27.6	33	18	5	66	0.04	91	16
Honduras	6.3	56	3.4	3	33	6	4.6	69	48	112	18	14	54	33	0.31	205	178
Hungary	10.2	110	0.4	-0.6	11	15	1.6	69	64	92.3	54	12	19	14	3.27	1472	1217
Iceland	0.3	3	1.1	1.2	17	6	2.1	81	92	100	0	23	1	10	6.7	6500	6678
India	980	330	2.2	2.5	25	9	3.2	60	27	2973	57	4	23	62	0.37	37	33
Indonesia	203.5	112	2.3	1.8	23	8	2.7	62	33	1812	17	7	62	53	0.47	211	234
Iran	69.5	42	3.2	3.5	33	6	4.5	68	58	1636	11	27	7	36	1.88	537	348
Iraq	22.5	51	3.6	2.5	43	6	5.4	67	73	437	12	9	4	12	1.76	278	383

Wealth							**Social Indicators**								**Aid**	
GNP 1995	GNP per capita 1995	Real GDP per capita 1995	Average Annual growth of Real GNP per capita 1985-95	GDP share Agriculture 1995	GDP share Industry 1995	GDP share services 1995	HDI Human Development Index 1994	Food Intake 1993	Population per doctor 1993	% of GNP spent on health 1990-95	% of GNP spent on education 1993-94	%o GNP spent on military 1995	Adult Illiteracy		given (*) and received per capita 1994	
million US $	US $	US $	%	%	%	%		calories per day	persons	%	%	%	Female %	Male %	US $	
5000	300	800	-6	52	32	16	...	1523	7000	...	...	9.1	85	53	10	Afghanistan
2199	670	2750	-7	56	21	23	0.655	2605	735	2.7	3	2.8	0	0	21	Albania
44609	1600	5300	-2.6	13	47	40	0.737	2897	1062	4.6	5.6	2.5	51	26	11	Algeria
4422	410	1310	-6.1	12	59	29	0.335	1839	23725	4	...	4.8	71	44	40	Angola
278431	8030	8310	1.9	6	31	63	0.884	2880	330	10.6	3.8	1.7	4	4	7	Argentina
2752	730	2260	-15.1	44	35	21	0.651	...	261	7.8	7.3	4.4	2	1	27	Armenia
337909	18720	18940	1.4	3	28	69	0.931	3179	500	8.4	6	2.5	...	...	*62	Australia
216547	26890	21250	1.9	2	34	64	0.932	3497	231	9.7	5.5	1	0	0	*82	Austria
3601	480	1460	-16.3	27	32	41	0.636	...	257	7.5	5.5	5	4	1	3	Azerbaijan
3297	11940	14710	-1	3	9	88	0.894	2624	700	...	3.9	0.6	2	1	15	Bahamas
28599	240	1380	2.1	31	18	51	0.368	2019	12884	2.4	2.3	1.8	74	51	11	Bangladesh
1745	6560	10620	-0.2	5	17	78	0.907	3207	1000	5	7.5	0.7	3	2	...	Barbados
21356	2070	4220	-5.2	13	35	52	0.806	...	236	6.4	6.1	3.3	3	1	11	Belarus
250710	24710	21660	2.2	2	31	67	0.932	3681	274	8.2	5.6	1.7	0	0	*81	Belgium
2034	370	1760	-0.4	34	12	54	0.368	2532	14216	1.7	...	1.3	74	51	53	Benin
5905	800	2540	1.7	17	30	53	0.589	2094	2348	5	5.4	2.6	24	10	96	Bolivia
11650	2600	...	1.8	...	...	...	...	...	600	...	...	...	23	3	...	Bosnia-Herzegovina
4381	3020	5580	6	5	46	49	0.673	2266	5151	1.9	8.5	7.1	40	20	64	Botswana
579787	3640	5400	-0.7	14	37	49	0.783	2824	844	7.4	1.6	1.5	17	17	2	Brazil
11225	1330	4480	-2.2	13	34	53	0.78	2831	306	4	4.5	3.3	3	1	6	Bulgaria
2417	230	780	-0.1	34	27	39	0.221	2387	34804	5.5	3.6	2.4	91	71	48	Burkina Faso
45100	1000	1050	0.4	63	9	28	0.475	2598	12528	0.9	2.4	6.2	22	11	3	Burma
984	160	630	-1.3	56	18	26	0.247	1941	17153	0.9	3.8	5.3	78	51	46	Burundi
2718	270	1084	2	51	14	35	0.348	2021	9374	7.2	...	4.7	47	20	57	Cambodia
8615	650	2110	-7	39	23	38	0.468	1981	11996	1.4	3.1	1.8	48	25	35	Cameroon
573695	19380	21130	0.4	3	30	67	0.96	3094	464	9.8	7.6	1.6	2	2	*73	Canada
1123	340	1070	-2	44	13	43	0.355	1690	25920	1.7	2.8	1.8	48	32	50	Central African Rep.
1144	180	700	0.5	44	22	34	0.288	1989	30030	1.8	2.2	2.6	65	38	38	Chad
59151	4160	9520	6.1	8	34	58	0.891	2582	942	6.5	2.9	3.8	5	5	11	Chile
744890	620	2920	8	21	48	31	0.626	2727	1063	3.8	2.6	5.7	27	10	3	China
70263	1910	6130	2.8	14	32	54	0.848	2677	1105	7.4	3.7	2	9	9	6	Colombia
1784	680	2050	-3.2	10	38	52	0.5	2296	3713	6.8	8.3	1.7	33	17	50	Congo
5313	120	490	-8.5	51	16	33	0.381	2060	15150	2.4	1	2	32	13	4	Congo (Zaïre)
8884	2610	5850	2.9	17	24	59	0.889	2883	1133	8.5	4.7	0.3	5	5	8	Costa Rica
15508	3250	3960	-20	12	25	63	0.76	...	500	10.1	...	12.6	5	1	...	Croatia
13700	1250	3000	-10	...	...	...	0.723	2833	275	7.9	6.6	2.8	5	4	6	Cuba
8510	11500	13000	4.6	6	43	51	0.907	3779	450	3.9	4.3	4.5	7	2	30	Cyprus
39990	3870	9770	-1.8	6	39	55	0.882	...	273	9.9	5.9	2.8	0	0	5	Czech Rep.
156027	29890	21230	1.5	4	29	67	0.927	3664	360	6.6	8.5	1.8	0	0	*273	Denmark
11390	1460	3870	2.1	15	22	63	0.718	2286	949	5.3	1.9	1.3	18	18	16	Dominican Rep.
15997	1390	4220	0.8	12	36	52	0.775	2583	652	5.3	3	3.4	12	8	21	Ecuador
45507	790	3820	1.1	20	21	59	0.614	3335	1316	4.9	5	4.3	61	36	35	Egypt
9057	1610	2610	2.9	14	22	64	0.592	2663	1515	5	1.6	1.8	30	27	54	El Salvador
4252	2860	4220	-4.3	8	28	64	0.776	...	253	6.5	5.8	5.3	0	0	22	Estonia
5722	100	450	-0.5	57	10	33	0.244	1610	32499	1.1	6.4	2.1	75	55	16	Ethiopia
105174	20580	17760	-0.2	6	37	57	0.94	3018	406	8.3	8.4	2	0	0	*59	Finland
1451051	24990	21030	1.5	2	27	71	0.946	3633	334	9.7	5.8	3.1	1	1	*137	France
3759	3490	3650	-1.6	9	59	32	0.562	2500	1987	0.5	3.2	1.7	47	26	138	Gabon
354	320	930	0.3	28	15	57	0.281	2360	14000	1.8	2.7	3.8	75	47	43	Gambia, The
2358	440	1470	-17	67	22	11	0.637	...	182	0.3	1.9	3.4	1	0	106	Georgia
2252343	27510	20070	1.9	1	30	69	0.924	3344	367	9.5	4.8	2	0	0	*81	Germany
6719	390	1990	1.5	46	16	38	0.468	2199	22970	3.5	3.1	1.2	47	24	38	Ghana
85885	8210	11710	1.2	21	36	43	0.923	3815	312	6.4	3	4.6	7	2	...	Greece
14255	1340	3340	0.3	25	19	56	0.572	2255	3999	2.7	1.6	1.4	51	38	21	Guatemala
3593	550	1100	1.4	24	31	45	0.271	2389	7445	0.9	2.2	1.4	78	50	62	Guinea
265	250	790	1.8	46	24	30	0.291	2556	3500	1.1	2.8	3	58	32	113	Guinea-Bissau
493	590	2420	0.8	50	35	15	0.649	2384	3000	10.4	5	1.1	2	1	...	Guyana
1777	250	910	-5.2	44	12	44	0.338	1706	10855	3.6	1.4	2.1	58	52	104	Haiti
3566	600	1900	0.2	21	33	46	0.575	2305	1266	5.6	4	1.3	27	27	75	Honduras
42129	4120	6410	-1	8	33	59	0.857	3503	306	7.3	6.7	1.4	1	1	7	Hungary
6686	24950	20460	0.3	13	29	58	0.942	3058	360	6.9	5.4	...	0	0	...	Iceland
319660	340	1400	3.1	29	29	42	0.446	2395	2459	3.5	3.8	2.5	62	35	2	India
190105	980	3800	6	17	42	41	0.668	2752	7028	1.5	1.3	1.6	22	10	7	Indonesia
328000	4800	5470	0.5	25	34	41	0.78	2860	3142	4.5	5.9	3.9	24	22	3	Iran
36200	1800	3150	...	28	20	52	0.531	2121	1659	...	5.1	14.8	55	29	16	Iraq

	Population									Land and Agriculture					Energy	Trade	
	Population Total 1997	Population Density 1997	Average Annual Change 1970-80	Average Annual Change 1990-97	Birth Rate 1997	Death Rate 1997	Fertility Rate 1995	Life Expectancy Average 1997	Urban Population 1995	Land Area	Arable and Permanent Crops	Permanent grassland	Forest	Agriculture Population 1995	Consumption per capita 1994	Imports per capita 1995	Exports per capita 1995
	millions	persons per km²	%	%	births per thousand population	deaths per thousand population	children	years	%	thousand km²	% of land area	% of land area	% of land area	% of economically active pop.	tonnes of coal	US $	US $
Ireland	3.6	53	1.4	0.5	13	9	1.9	76	58	68.9	19	45	5	13	4.31	9237	12469
Israel	5.9	286	2.7	3.6	20	6	2.4	78	91	20.6	21	7	6	3	3.26	5337	3436
Italy	57.8	196	0.5	0.2	10	10	1.2	78	67	294	38	15	23	7	3.95	3562	4038
Ivory Coast	15.1	47	4	3.4	42	17	5.3	45	46	318	12	41	34	57	0.26	231	301
Jamaica	2.6	240	1.3	0.8	22	6	2.4	75	53	10.8	20	24	17	24	1.66	1089	545
Japan	125.9	334	1.1	0.3	10	8	1.5	80	78	377	12	2	66	6	4.98	2684	3540
Jordan	5.6	63	2.4	4.9	36	4	4.8	73	72	88.9	5	9	1	15	1.01	680	325
Kazakstan	17	6	1.3	0.2	19	10	2.3	64	58	2670	13	70	4	21	5.93	40	70
Kenya	31.9	56	3.8	4.1	32	11	4.7	54	25	570	8	37	30	78	0.12	98	62
Korea, North	24.5	203	2.2	1.7	22	5	2.2	71	61	120	17	0	61	34	4.21	75	41
Korea, South	46.1	466	1.8	1.1	16	6	1.8	74	75	98.7	21	1	65	14	3.77	3013	2788
Kyrgyzstan	4.7	24	2	0.8	26	9	3.3	64	40	191	7	44	4	31	0.76	71	76
Laos	5.2	23	1.7	3.3	41	13	6.5	53	22	231	4	3	54	77	0.04	40	20
Latvia	2.5	38	0.7	-1.3	12	15	1.3	67	72	64.1	28	13	46	14	2.3	697	520
Lebanon	3.2	313	0.8	2.5	28	6	2.8	70	87	10.2	30	1	8	4	1.83	2058	197
Lesotho	2.1	69	2.3	2.7	32	14	4.6	52	23	30.4	11	66	0	39	...	520	58
Liberia	3	30	3.1	2.9	42	12	6.5	59	45	96.8	4	21	48	70	0.06	116	197
Libya	5.5	3	4.4	2.8	44	7	6.1	65	86	1760	1	8	0	6	3.34	1240	2596
Lithuania	3.7	57	0.9	-0.1	14	13	1.5	68	71	65.2	47	7	31	18	3.04	696	545
Luxembourg	0.4	163.5	0.7	1.9	13	8	1.7	79	88	2.6	...	...	...	...	12.82	20295	16090
Macedonia	2.2	86	1.6	0.9	13	9	2.2	72	60	24.9	26	25	39	17	1.9	600	500
Madagascar	15.5	27	2.7	4.8	42	14	5.8	53	27	582	5	41	40	76	0.04	36	25
Malawi	10.3	109	3.2	3.1	41	25	6.6	35	13	94.1	18	20	39	86	0.04	49	41
Malaysia	20.9	64	2.4	2.2	26	5	3.4	70	52	329	23	1	68	23	2.29	3751	3563
Mali	11	9	2.3	4.4	51	19	6.8	47	27	1220	2	25	10	84	0.02	70	42
Malta	0.4	1172	1.1	0.9	15	7	1.9	79	88	0.32	41	0	0	2	1.97	7951	5170
Mauritania	2.4	2	2.4	2.5	47	15	5.2	50	54	1025	0	38	4	49	0.61	284	223
Mauritius	1.2	569	1.6	1.1	19	7	2.2	71	44	2.03	52	3	22	12	0.7	1797	1410
Mexico	97.4	51	2.9	1.8	26	5	3	74	75	1909	13	39	26	24	2.03	508	520
Moldova	4.5	132	1.1	0.3	17	12	2	65	50	33.7	66	13	13	31	1.55	185	162
Mongolia	2.5	2	2.8	1.9	25	8	3.4	61	60	1567	1	75	9	29	1.55	158	208
Morocco	28.1	63	2.4	1.6	27	6	3.4	70	52	446	21	47	20	41	0.47	315	172
Mozambique	19.1	24	2.6	4.3	44	18	6.2	45	32	784	4	56	22	81	0.03	45	10
Namibia	1.7	2	2.5	2	37	8	5	65	34	823	1	46	15	45	...	916	881
Nepal	22.1	162	2.6	2.1	37	12	5.3	54	13	137	17	15	42	93	0.03	64	16
Netherlands	15.9	469	0.8	0.9	12	9	1.6	78	89	33.9	28	31	10	4	7.22	11419	12680
New Zealand	3.7	14	1	1.1	15	8	2.1	77	86	268	14	50	28	10	5.47	3951	3882
Nicaragua	4.6	39	3	2.5	33	6	4.1	66	63	119	10	45	26	23	0.36	212	115
Niger	9.7	8	3	3.3	54	24	7.4	41	16	1267	3	8	2	89	0.06	37	27
Nigeria	118	130	2.2	3.1	43	12	5.5	55	38	911	36	44	12	38	0.21	71	94
Norway	4.4	14	0.5	0.8	11	11	1.9	78	73	307	3	0	27	5	7.44	7563	9632
Cman	2.4	11	4.2	6.9	38	4	7	71	13	212	0	5	0	42	5.41	1994	2682
Pakistan	136	176	2.6	2.8	35	11	5.2	59	34	771	28	6	5	48	0.33	88	62
Panama	2.7	37	2.5	1.7	22	5	2.7	74	55	74.4	9	20	44	22	1.2	955	238
Papua New Guinea	4.4	10	2.5	1.8	33	10	4.8	58	16	453	1	0	93	78	0.29	357	651
Paraguay	5.2	13	3	2.8	30	4	4	74	52	397	6	55	32	35	0.38	669	196
Peru	24.5	19	2.7	1.3	24	6	3.1	70	72	1280	3	21	66	33	0.46	392	237
Philippines	73.5	247	2.6	2.4	29	7	3.7	66	52	298	31	4	46	42	0.43	403	249
Poland	38.8	127	0.9	0.1	12	10	1.6	72	64	304	48	13	29	26	3.51	753	593
Portugal	10.1	110	0.8	-0.3	11	10	1.4	76	36	92	32	11	36	14	2.13	3261	2280
Puerto Rico	3.8	432	1.7	1.4	18	8	2.1	75	77	8.86	9	26	16	3	3.07	4300	5900
Romania	22.6	98	0.9	-0.3	10	12	1.4	70	55	230	43	21	29	19	2.54	453	349
Russia	147.8	9	0.6	0	11	16	1.4	64	75	16996	8	5	45	12	6	261	427
Rwanda	7	284	3.3	-0.4	39	21	6.2	39	6	24.7	47	28	10	91	0.03	46	10
Saudi Arabia	19.1	9	5	4.4	38	5	6.2	70	79	2150	2	56	1	14	5.77	1539	2335
Senegal	8.9	46	2.9	2.8	45	11	5.7	57	42	193	12	30	39	74	0.16	156	103
Sierra Leone	4.6	64	2.1	1.5	47	18	6.5	48	35	71.6	8	31	28	67	0.05	30	6
Singapore	3.2	5246	1	2.5	16	5	1.7	79	100	0.61	2	0	5	1	9.67	41639	39553
Slovak Rep.	5.4	112	1.7	0.3	13	9	1.5	73	58	48.1	34	17	41	12	4.07	1250	1025
Slovenia	2	99	0.9	0.2	8	10	1.3	75	50	20.3	14	25	54	5	3.11	4793	4199
Somalia	9.9	16	3.8	1.9	44	13	7	56	27	627	2	69	26	74	0.05	26	5
South Africa	42.3	35	2.3	1.6	27	12	3.9	56	57	1221	11	67	7	11	2.73	718	653
Spain	39.3	79	1.1	0	10	9	1.2	79	77	499	40	21	32	9	3.01	2890	2334
Sri Lanka	18.7	289	1.7	1.2	18	6	2.3	73	22	64.6	29	7	32	47	0.16	290	212
Sudan	31	13	3	3	41	11	4.8	56	35	2376	5	46	18	68	0.06	44	21

GNP 1995	GNP per capita 1995	Real GDP per capita 1995	Average Annual growth of Real GNP per capita 1985-95	GDP share Agriculture 1995	GDP share Industry 1995	GDP share services 1995	HDI Human Development Index 1994	Food Intake	Population per doctor 1993	% of GNP spent on health 1990-95	% of GNP spent on education 1993-94	%o GNP spent on military 1995	Adult Illiteracy Female	Adult Illiteracy Male	Aid given (*) and received per capita 1994	
million US $	US $	US $	%	%	%	%		calories per day	persons	%	%	%	Female %	Male %	US $	
52765	14710	15680	5.2	9	37	54	0.929	3847	632	7.9	6.4	1.2	0	0	*35	Ireland
87875	15920	16490	2.5	3	32	65	0.913	3050	220	4.1	6	9.2	7	3	226	Israel
1088085	19020	19870	1.7	3	31	66	0.921	3561	207	8.3	5.2	1.8	4	2	*37	Italy
9548	660	1580	-4.3	31	20	49	0.368	2491	11739	3.4	...	1	70	50	87	Ivory Coast
3803	1510	3540	3.7	9	38	53	0.736	2607	6420	5.4	4.7	0.6	11	19	43	Jamaica
4963587	39640	22110	2.9	2	38	60	0.94	2903	608	7	4.7	1.1	0	0	*106	Japan
6354	1510	4060	-2.8	8	27	65	0.73	3022	554	7.9	3.8	6.7	21	7	127	Jordan
22143	1330	3010	-8.6	12	30	58	0.709	...	254	2.2	5.4	3	4	1	2	Kazakstan
7583	280	1380	0.1	29	17	54	0.463	2075	21970	1.9	6.8	2.3	30	14	42	Kenya
24000	1000	4000	-8	...	...	...	0.765	2833	370	...	...	25.2	5	5	1	Korea, North
435137	9700	11450	7.6	7	43	50	0.89	3285	951	5.4	4.5	3.4	2	2	1	Korea, South
3158	700	1800	-6.9	44	24	32	0.635	...	303	3.5	6.8	3.5	4	1	19	Kyrgyzstan
1694	350	2500	2.7	52	18	30	0.459	2259	4446	2.6	2.3	4.2	56	31	66	Laos
5708	2270	3370	-6.6	9	31	60	0.711	...	278	3.7	6.5	3.2	0	0	14	Latvia
10673	2660	4800	2.7	7	24	69	0.794	3317	537	5.3	2	5.3	10	5	48	Lebanon
1519	770	1780	1.5	10	56	34	0.457	2201	24095	3.5	4.8	5.5	38	19	57	Lesotho
2300	850	1000	1.5	...	...	...	...	1640	25000	8.2	...	4.8	78	46	23	Liberia
38000	7000	6000	1	8	48	44	0.801	3308	957	...	9.6	5.5	37	12	1	Libya
7070	1900	4120	-11.7	11	36	53	0.762	...	235	4.8	4.5	2.4	2	1	14	Lithuania
16876	41210	37930	1	1	33	66	0.899	...	460	6.3	3.1	0.9	0	0	*148	Luxembourg
1813	860	4000	-15	19	44	37	0.748	...	427	7.7	5.6	...	16	6	...	Macedonia
3178	230	640	-2	34	13	53	0.35	2135	8385	1	1.9	1.1	27	12	23	Madagascar
1623	170	750	-0.7	42	27	31	0.32	1825	44205	2.3	3.4	1.2	58	28	40	Malawi
78321	3890	9020	5.7	13	43	44	0.832	2888	2441	1.4	5.3	4.5	22	11	6	Malaysia
2410	250	550	0.6	46	17	37	0.229	2278	18376	1.3	2.1	2.4	77	61	57	Mali
4070	11000	13000	5.1	3	28	69	0.887	3486	410	12.1	5.1	1.1	4	4	...	Malta
1049	460	1540	0.5	27	30	43	0.355	2685	15772	1.5	...	1.9	74	50	99	Mauritania
3815	3380	13210	5.7	9	33	58	0.831	...	1165	2.2	3.7	0.5	21	13	21	Mauritius
304596	3320	6400	0.1	8	26	66	0.853	3146	615	5.3	5.8	0.9	13	8	4	Mexico
3996	920	1600	-8.2	50	28	22	0.612	...	250	5.1	5.5	3.7	6	1	5	Moldova
767	310	1950	-3.8	21	46	33	0.661	1899	371	4.7	5.2	2.4	23	11	88	Mongolia
29545	1110	3340	0.8	14	33	53	0.566	2984	4665	3.4	5.4	4.3	69	43	19	Morocco
1353	80	810	3.6	33	21	46	0.281	1680	36225	4.6	6.2	3.7	77	42	66	Mozambique
3098	2000	4150	2.8	14	29	57	0.57	2134	4328	7.6	8.7	2.7	26	22	125	Namibia
4391	200	1170	2.4	42	22	36	0.347	1957	13634	5	2.9	1	86	59	21	Nepal
371039	24000	19950	1.8	3	27	70	0.94	3222	399	8.8	5.5	2.2	0	0	*172	Netherlands
51655	14340	16360	0.6	7	25	68	0.937	3669	518	7.5	7.3	1.7	1	1	*31	New Zealand
1659	380	2000	-5.8	33	20	47	0.53	2293	2039	7.8	3.8	1.8	33	35	155	Nicaragua
1961	220	750	-2.1	39	18	43	0.206	2257	53986	2.2	3.1	0.9	93	79	30	Niger
28411	260	1220	1.2	43	27	30	0.393	2124	5208	2.7	1.3	2.9	53	33	2	Nigeria
136077	31250	21940	1.6	3	36	61	0.943	3244	308	7.3	9.2	2.6	0	0	*255	Norway
10578	4820	8140	0.3	3	48	49	0.718	...	1131	2.5	4.5	15.1	76	42	29	Oman
59991	460	2230	1.2	26	24	50	0.445	2315	1923	0.8	2.7	6.5	76	50	6	Pakistan
7235	2750	5980	-0.4	11	18	71	0.864	2242	562	7.5	5.2	1.3	10	9	19	Panama
4976	1160	2420	2.1	26	38	36	0.525	2613	12754	2.8	...	1.3	37	19	88	Papua New Guinea
8158	1690	3650	1.1	24	22	54	0.706	2670	1231	4.3	2.9	1.4	9	7	30	Paraguay
55019	2310	3770	-1.6	7	38	55	0.717	1882	939	4.9	1.5	1.6	17	6	18	Peru
71865	1050	2850	1.5	22	32	46	0.672	2257	8273	2.4	2.4	1.6	6	5	109	Philippines
107829	2790	5400	-0.4	6	39	55	0.834	3301	451	4.6	5.5	2.5	2	1	40	Poland
96689	9740	12670	3.7	6	40	54	0.89	3634	353	7.6	5.4	2.9	13	13	*27	Portugal
27750	7500	7000	2.1	1	42	57	...	...	350	...	...	...	10	10	...	Puerto Rico
33488	1480	4360	-4	21	49	30	0.748	3051	538	3.3	3.1	3.1	5	1	3	Romania
331948	2240	4480	-5.1	7	38	55	0.792	...	222	4.8	4.4	7.4	3	0	12	Russia
1128	180	540	-5	37	17	46	0.187	1821	24967	1.9	3.8	4.4	48	30	92	Rwanda
133540	7040	9500	-1.9	6	51	43	0.774	2735	749	2.2	6.4	10.6	50	29	1	Saudi Arabia
5070	600	1780	-1.2	20	18	62	0.326	2262	18192	1.6	4.2	1.9	77	57	82	Senegal
762	180	580	-3.4	42	27	31	0.176	1694	11000	1.6	1.4	5.7	82	55	45	Sierra Leone
79831	26730	22770	6.2	0	36	64	0.9	...	714	3.5	3.3	5.9	14	4	6	Singapore
15848	2950	3610	-2.6	6	33	61	0.873	...	287	6.3	4.9	2.8	0	0	6	Slovak Rep.
16328	8200	10400	-1	5	39	56	0.886	...	500	7.9	6.2	1.5	0	0	...	Slovenia
4625	500	1000	-2.3	65	9	26	...	1499	13300	1.5	0.4	0.9	52	39	61	Somalia
130918	3160	5030	-1	5	31	64	0.716	2695	1500	7.9	7.1	2.9	18	18	10	South Africa
532347	13580	14520	2.6	3	31	66	0.934	3708	261	7.4	4.7	1.5	6	2	*31	Spain
12616	700	3250	2.7	23	25	52	0.711	2273	6843	1.9	3.2	4.9	13	7	31	Sri Lanka
20000	750	1050	0.6	36	18	46	0.333	2202	10000	0.3	...	4.3	65	42	8	Sudan

	Population									Land and Agriculture					Energy	Trade	
	Population Total 1997	Population Density 1997	Average Annual Change 1970-80	Average Annual Change 1990-97	Birth Rate 1997	Death Rate 1997	Fertility Rate 1995	Life Expectancy Average 1997	Urban Population 1995	Land Area	Arable and Permanent Crops	Permanent grassland	Forest	Agriculture Population 1995	Consumption per capita 1994	Imports per capita 1995	Exports per capita 1995
	millions	persons per km²	%	%	births per thousand population	deaths per thousand population	children	years	%	thousand km²	% of land area	% of land area	% of land area	% of economically active pop.	tonnes of coal	US $	US $
Surinam	0.5	3	-0.6	1.5	24	6	2.6	70	52	156	0	0	96	20	2.01	1565	873
Swaziland	1	55	3	3.1	43	10	4.6	58	29	17.2	11	62	7	34	...	1090	855
Sweden	8.9	22	0.3	0.7	11	11	1.7	78	84	412	7	1	68	4	6.79	7299	9051
Switzerland	7.1	180	0.2	1	11	10	1.5	78	61	39.6	11	29	32	5	4.5	10938	11088
Syria	15.3	83	3.5	2.9	39	6	4.8	67	52	184	30	45	3	33	1.28	325	280
Taiwan	21.7	603	2	0.9	15	6	1.8	76	76	36	26	11	52	19	2.5	4868	5238
Tajikistan	6	42	3	1.8	34	8	4.2	65	32	143	6	25	4	38	0.58	93	84
Tanzania	31.2	35	3.4	2.8	41	20	5.8	42	24	884	4	40	38	83	0.04	55	23
Thailand	60.8	119	2.7	0.9	17	7	1.8	69	19	511	41	2	26	60	1.07	1236	946
Togo	4.5	82	2.6	3.4	46	10	6.4	58	31	54.4	45	4	17	62	0.08	94	51
Trinidad & Tobago	1.3	253	1.1	0.2	16	7	2.1	70	70	5.13	24	2	46	9	7.53	1329	1904
Tunisia	9.2	59	2.2	1.9	24	5	2.9	73	57	155	32	20	4	24	0.75	886	614
Turkey	63.5	83	2.3	1.1	22	5	2.7	72	65	770	36	16	26	51	1.16	579	350
Turkmenistan	4.8	10	2.7	3.9	29	9	3.8	62	47	488	3	64	9	36	3.68	250	533
Uganda	20.8	104	3	2.4	45	21	6.7	40	12	200	34	9	32	83	0.03	50	22
Ukraine	51.5	85	0.6	-0.1	12	15	1.5	67	69	604	59	13	18	18	4.39	192	187
United Kingdom	58.6	243	0.1	0.3	13	11	1.7	77	90	242	25	46	10	2	5.33	4527	4130
United States	268	28	1.1	1	15	9	2.1	76	77	9573	20	25	30	3	11.39	2929	2222
Uruguay	3.3	19	0.4	0.7	17	9	2.2	75	90	175	7	77	5	14	0.78	899	660
Uzbekistan	23.8	56	2.9	2.1	29	8	3.7	65	42	425	11	50	3	34	2.94	111	138
Venezuela	22.5	26	3.5	1.9	24	5	3.1	72	92	882	4	20	34	11	3.75	553	854
Vietnam	77.1	237	2.3	2.1	22	7	3.1	67	20	325	21	1	30	69	0.16	30	30
Yemen	16.5	31	1.9	5.6	45	9	7.4	60	34	528	3	30	4	57	0.33	165	74
Yugoslavia	10.5	103	1	0.3	14	10	1.9	72	54	102	40	21	26	20	1.22	533	452
Zambia	9.5	13	3.2	2.4	44	24	5.7	45	45	743	7	40	43	74	0.19	12	94
Zimbabwe	12.1	31	3.1	3.7	32	19	3.8	60	32	387	7	44	23	67	0.7	231	183

	Land area thousand sq km	Population 1997 thousands		Land area thousand sq km	Population 1997 thousands		Land area thousand sq km	Population 1997 thousands
American Samoa	0.2	62	French Polynesia	3.66	226	Pitcairn I.	0.05	0.05
Andorra	0.45	75	Gaza Strip	0.36	900	Qatar	11	62
Anguilla	0.1	10	Gibraltar	0.01	28	Réunion	2.5	68
Antigua & Barbuda	0.44	66	Greenland	342	57	St Kitts-Nevis	0.36	4.
Aruba	0.19	70	Grenada	0.34	99	St Helena	0.3	
Ascension I.	0.09	1.1	Guadeloupe	1.69	440	St Lucia	0.61	15
Bahrain	0.68	605	Guam	0.55	161	St Pierre & Miquelon	0.23	
Belize	22.8	228	Kiribati	0.73	85	St Vincent & the Grenadines	0.39	11
Bermuda	0.05	65	Kuwait	17.8	2050	San Marino	0.06	2
Bhutan	47	1790	Liechtenstein	0.16	32	Sâo Tomé & Principe	0.96	13
British Virgin Is.	0.15	13	Macau	0.02	450	Seychelles	0.45	7
Brunei	5.27	300	Maldives	0.3	275	Solomon Is.	28	41
Cape Verde Is.	4.03	410	Marshall Is.	0.18	60	Svalbard	63	2.
Cayman Is.	0.26	35	Martinique	1.06	405	Tokelau	0.01	
Cocos Is.	0.01	1	Mayotte	0.37	105	Tonga	0.72	10
Comoros	2.23	630	Micronesia	0.7	127	Turks & Caicos Is.	0.43	1
Cook Is.	0.23	20	Monaco	0.002	33	Tuvalu	0.03	1
Djibouti	23.2	650	Montserrat	0.1	12	United Arab Emirates	83.6	240
Dominica	0.75	78	Nauru	0.02	53	US Virgin Is.	0.34	11
Equatorial Guinea	28.1	420	Netherlands Antilles	0.8	12	Vanuatu	12.2	17
Eritrea	101	3500	New Caledonia	18.3	210	Vatican City	0.0004	
Falkland Is.	12.2	2	Niue	0.26	192	Wallis & Futuna Is.	0.2	
Faroe Is.	1.4	45	Norfolk I.	0.04	2	West Bank	5.9	149
Fiji	18.3	800	Northern Marianas	0.48	2	Western Sahara	267	28
French Guiana	88.2	155	Palau	0.49	17	Western Samoa	2.83	17

Wealth							Social Indicators								Aid	
GNP 1996	GNP per capita 1995	Real GDP per capita 1995	Average Annual growth of Real GNP per capita 1985-95	GDP share Agriculture 1995	GDP share Industry 1995	GDP share services 1995	HDI Human Development Index 1994	Food Intake	Population per doctor 1993	% of GNP spent on health 1990-95	% of GNP spent on education 1993-94	%o GNP spent on military 1995	Adult Illiteracy		given (*) and received per capita 1994	
million US $	US $	US $	%	%	%	%		calories per day	persons	%	%	%	Female %	Male %	US $	
360	880	2250	0.7	22	23	55	0.792	2547	1200	2.9	3.6	3.9	9	5	183	Surinam
1051	1170	2880	0.6	10	25	65	0.582	2706	9250	7.2	6.8	...	24	22	59	Swaziland
209720	23750	18540	-0.1	2	32	66	0.936	2972	394	7.7	8.4	2.9	0	0	*189	Sweden
286014	40630	25860	0.2	3	32	65	0.93	3379	580	9.6	5.6	1.9	0	0	*135	Switzerland
15780	1120	5320	1	18	43	39	0.755	3175	1159	2.1	4.2	6.8	44	14	25	Syria
252000	12000	13000	7	3	42	55	...	3048	800	4.3		4.8	10	3	...	Taiwan
1976	340	920	-13	27	45	28	0.58		424	6.4	9.5	6.9	3	1	5	Tajikistan
3703	120	640	0.9	58	17	25	0.357	2018	22000	2.8	5	2.7	43	21	30	Tanzania
159630	2740	7540	8.4	11	40	49	0.833	2432	4416	5.3	3.8	2.5	8	4	15	Thailand
1266	310	1130	-2.8	38	21	41	0.365	2242	11385	1.7	6.1	2.5	63	33	47	Togo
4851	3770	8610	-1.6	3	42	55	0.88	2585	1520	3.9	4.5	1.3	3	1	20	Trinidad & Tobago
16369	1820	5000	1.8	12	29	59	0.748	3330	1549	5.9	6.3	2	45	21	8	Tunisia
169452	2780	5580	2.2	16	31	53	0.772	3429	976	4.2	3.3	3.6	28	8	5	Turkey
4125	920	3500	-9.6	31	31	38	0.723	...	306	2.8	7.9	1.9	3	1	3	Turkmenistan
4668	240	1470	2.8	50	14	36	0.328	2159	22399	3.9	1.9	2.6	50	26	43	Uganda
84084	1630	2400	-9.2	18	42	40	0.689	...	227	5.4	8.2	3	3	0	5	Ukraine
1094734	18700	19260	1.4	2	32	66	0.931	3317	300	6.9	5.4	3.1	0	0	*53	United Kingdom
7100007	26980	26980	1.4	2	26	72	0.942	3732	421	14.3	5.5	3.8	5	4	*33	United States
16458	5170	6630	3.3	9	26	65	0.883	2750	500	8.5	2.5	2.6	2	3	26	Uruguay
21979	970	2370	-3.9	33	34	33	0.662	...	282	3.5	11	3.6	4	1	1	Uzbekistan
65382	3020	7900	0.5	5	38	57	0.861	2618	633	7.1	5.1	1.1	10	8	4	Venezuela
17634	240	1200	4.2	28	30	42	0.557	2250	2279	5.2	...	4.3	9	4	8	Vietnam
4044	260	850	3.1	22	27	51	0.361	2203	4498	2.6	4.6	3.9	74	47	13	Yemen
14750	1400	4000	1.8	26	36	38	...	...	232	5.1	...	...	11	2	...	Yugoslavia
3605	400	930	-1	22	40	38	0.369	1931	10917	3.3	2.6	1.9	29	14	221	Zambia
5933	540	2030	-0.6	15	36	49	0.513	1985	7384	2.1	8.3	4.2	20	10	45	Zimbabwe

any figures for Luxembourg are included in those r Belgium.

or energy, the figures for South Africa include those r Botswana, Lesotho, Swaziland and Namibia.

he sign ... means that figures are not available.

opulation Total. This is an estimate for the mid-year, 1997.

opulation Density. This is the total population ivided by the land area, both quoted in the table.

opulation Change. This shows the average nnual percentage change for the two periods, 970-80 and 1990-97.

irth and Death Rates and Life Expectancy. hese are estimates from the US Census Bureau. he Birth and Death rates are the number of those ccurrences per year, per thousand population. Life xpectancy is the number of years that a child born day can expect to live if the levels of mortality of day last throughout its life. The figure is the verage of that for men and women.

ertility Rate. This is the average number of hildren born to a woman in her lifetime.

rban Population. This is the percentage of the tal population living in urban areas. The definition urban is that of the individual nations and often cludes quite small towns.

Land Area. This is the total area of the country less the area covered by major lakes and rivers.

Arable Land and Permanent Crops. This excludes fallow land but includes temporary pasture.

Forest and Woodland. This includes natural and planted woodland and land recently cleared of timber which will be replanted.

Agricultural Population. This is the percentage of the economically active population working in agriculture. It includes those working in forestry, hunting and fishing.

Energy. All forms of energy have been expressed in an approximate equivalent of tonnes of coal per person.

Trade. The trade figures are for 1994 or 1995. In a few cases the figure is older than this but is the latest available. The total Import and Export figures have been divided by the population to give a figure in US $ per capita.

Gross National Product (GNP). This figure is an estimate of the value of a country's production and the average production per person for 1995, in US $. The GNP measures the value of goods and services produced in a country, plus the balance, positive or negative, of income from abroad, for example, from investments, interest on capital, money returned from workers abroad, etc. The Gross Domestic Product (GDP), is the GNP less the foreign balances. The adjoining three columns show the percentage contribution to the GDP made by the

agricultural, mining and manufacturing and service sectors of the economy. The average annual rate of change is for the GNP per capita in PPP $ during the period 1985-95

Real GDP per capita. Using official exchange rates to convert national currencies into US $ makes no attempt to reflect the varying domestic purchasing powers of the local currency. The UN has made these estimates of Real GDP taking into account these local purchasing values and they are called Purchasing Power Parity $.

Human Development Index. This is a calculation made by the UN Development Programme, using 1994 data and takes into account not only national income, but also life expectancy, adult literacy and the years in education. It is a measure of national human progress. The wealthy developed countries have an index approaching 1, and the figures range down to some of the poorer with an index of less than 0.1.

Food Intake. The figures are the average intake per person in calories per day. They are for 1992 and are the latest estimates that are available.

Adult Illiteracy. This is the percentage of the male and female population aged 15 and over who cannot read or write a simple sentence.

Aid. The bulk of the table is concerned with aid received but aid given is shown by an asterisk.

To convert square kilometres to square miles multiply by 0.39.

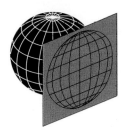

AZIMUTHAL OR ZENITHAL PROJECTIONS

MAP PROJECTIONS

A map projection is the systematic depiction of the imaginary grid of lines of latitude and longitude from a globe onto a flat surface. The grid of lines is called the graticule and it can be constructed either by graphical means or by mathematical formulae to form the basis of a map. As a globe is three dimensional it is not possible to depict its surface on a flat map without some form of distortion. Preservation of one of the basic properties listed below can only be secured at the expense of the others and the choice of projection is often a compromise solution.

Correct Area
In these projections the areas from the globe are to scale on the map. This is particularly useful in the mapping of densities and distributions. Projections with this property are termed Equal Area, Equivalent or Homolographic.

Correct Distance
In these projections the scale is correct along the meridians, or in the case of the Azimuthal Equidistant scale is true along any line drawn from the centre of the projection. They are called Equidistant.

Correct Shape
This property can only be true within small areas as it is achieved only by having a uniform scale distortion along both x and y axes of the projection. The projections are called Conformal or Orthomorphic.

Map projections can be divided into three broad categories - azimuthal, conic and cylindrical. Cartographers use different projections from these categories depending on the map scale, the size of the area to be mapped, and what they want the map to show.

These are constructed by the projection of part of the graticule from the globe onto a plane tangential to any single point on it. This plane may be tangential to the equator (equatorial case), the poles (polar case) or any other point (oblique case). Any straight line drawn from the point at which the plane touches the globe is the shortest distance from that point and is known as a great circle. In its Gnomonic construction any straight line on the map is a great circle, but there is great exaggeration towards the edges and this reduces its general uses. There are five different ways of transferring the graticule onto the plane and these are shown below. The diagrams below also show how the graticules vary, using the polar case as the example.

CONICAL PROJECTIONS

CYLINDRICAL AND OTHER WORLD PROJECTIONS

Equidistant	Equal-Area	Orthographic	Gnomonic	Stereographic (conformal)

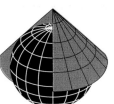

These use the projection of the graticule from the globe onto a cone which is tangential to a line of latitude (termed the standard parallel). This line is always an arc and scale is always true along it. Because of its method of construction it is used mainly for depicting the temperate latitudes around the standard parallel i.e. where there is least distortion. To reduce the distortion and include a larger range of latitudes, the projection may be constructed with the cone bisecting the surface of the globe so that there are two standard parallels each of which is true to scale. The distortion is thus spread more evenly between the two chosen parallels.

This group of projections are those which permit the whole of the Earth's surface to be depicted on one map. They are a very large group of projections and the following are only a few of them. Cylindrical projections are constructed by the projection of the graticule from the globe onto a cylinder tangential to the globe. Although cylindrical projections can depict all the main land masses, there is considerable distortion of shape and area towards the poles. One cylindrical projection, Mercator overcomes this shortcoming by possessing the unique navigational property that any straight line drawn on it is a line of constant bearing (loxodrome). It is used for maps and charts between 15° either side of the equator. Beyond this enlargement of area is a serious drawback, although it is used for navigational charts at all latitudes.

Polar Case

The polar case is the simplest to construct and the diagram on the right shows the differing effects of all five methods of construction comparing their coverage, distortion etc., using North America as the example.

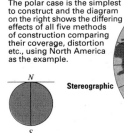

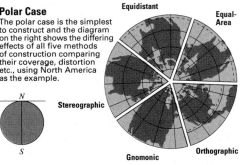

Simple Conical with one standard parallel

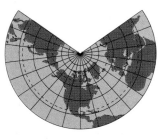

Simple Cylindrical	Cylindrical with two standard parallels

Bonne
This is a modification of the simple conic whereby the true scale along the meridians is sacrificed to enable the accurate representation of areas. However scale is true along each parallel but shapes are distorted at the edges.

Mercator

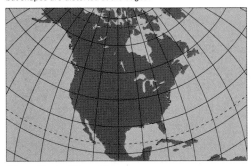

Oblique Case
The plane touches the globe at any point between the equator and poles. The oblique orthographic uses the distortion in azimuthal projections away from the centre to give a graphic depiction of the earth as seen from any desired point in space.

Albers Conical Equal Area
This projection uses two standard parallels. The selection of these relative to the land area to be mapped is very important. It is equal area and is especially useful for large land masses oriented East-West, for example the U.S.A.

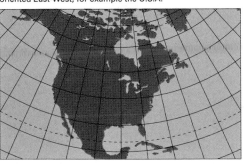

Eckert IV (pseudocylindrical equal area)

Hammer (polyconic equal area)

Equatorial Case
The example shown here is Lambert's Equivalent Azimuthal. It is the only projection which is both equal area and where bearing is true from the centre.

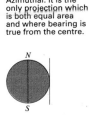

INDEX TO
WORLD MAPS

The index contains the names of all the principal places and features shown on the World Maps. Each name is followed by an additional entry in italics giving the country or region within which it is located. The alphabetical order of names composed of two or more words is governed primarily by the first word and then by the second. This is an example of the rule:

New South Wales □, *Australia*.. **34 G8**   33 0S   146 0E
New York □, *U.S.A.* **43 D10** 42 40N   76 0W
New York City, *U.S.A.* **43 E11** 40 45N   74 0W
New Zealand ■, *Oceania*............ **35 J13** 40 0S   176 0E
Newark, *U.S.A.* **43 F10** 39 42N 75 45W

Physical features composed of a proper name (Erie) and a description (Lake) are positioned alphabetically by the proper name. The description is positioned after the proper name and is usually abbreviated:

Erie, L., *N. Amer.* **42 D7** 42 15N 81 0W

Where a description forms part of a settlement or administrative name, however, it is always written in full and put in its true alphabetical position:

Mount Isa, *Australia*..................... **34 E6** 20 42S 139 26E

Names beginning with M' and Mc are indexed as if they were spelt Mac. Names beginning St. are alphabetized under Saint, but Santa and San are all spelt in full and are alphabetized accordingly. If the same placename occurs two or more times in the index and all are in the same country, each is followed by the name of the administrative subdivision in which it is located. The names are placed in the alphabetical order of the subdivision. For example:

Columbus, Ga., *U.S.A.* **41 D10** 32 30N 84 58W
Columbus, Ind., *U.S.A.* **42 F5** 39 14N 85 55W
Columbus, Ohio, *U.S.A.* **42 F6** 39 57N   83 1W

The number in bold type which follows each name in the index refers to the number of the map page where that feature or place will be found. This is usually the largest scale at which the place or feature appears.

The letter and figure which are in bold type immediately after the page number give the grid square on the map page, within which the feature is situated. The letter represents the latitude and the figure the longitude. In some cases the feature itself may fall within the specified square, while the name is outside.

For a more precise location, the geographical co-ordinates which follow the letter-figure references give the latitude and the longitude of each place. The first set of figures represent the latitude, which is the distance north or south of the Equator measured as an angle at the centre of the Earth. The Equator is latitude 0°, the North Pole is 90°N, and the South Pole 90°S.

The second set of figures represent the longitude, which is the distance east or west of the prime meridian, which runs through Greenwich, England. Longitude is also measured as an angle at the centre of the Earth and is given east or west of the prime meridian, from 0° to 180° in either direction.

The unit of measurement for latitude and longitude is the degree, which is subdivided into 60 minutes. Each index entry states the position of a place in degrees and minutes, a space being left between the degrees and the minutes. The latitude is followed by N(orth) or S(outh) and the longitude by E(ast) or W(est).

Rivers are indexed to their mouths or confluences, and carry the symbol → after their names. A solid square ■ follows the name of a country, while an open square □ refers to a first order administrative area.

ABBREVIATIONS USED IN THE INDEX

Afghan. – Afghanistan
Ala. – Alabama
Alta. – Alberta
Amer. – America(n)
Arch. – Archipelago
Ariz. – Arizona
Ark. – Arkansas
Atl. Oc. – Atlantic Ocean
B. – Baie, Bahia, Bay, Bucht, Bugt
B.C. – British Columbia
Bangla. – Bangladesh
C. – Cabo, Cap, Cape, Coast
C.A.R. – Central African Republic
C. Prov. – Cape Province
Calif. – California
Cent. – Central
Chan. – Channel
Colo. – Colorado

Conn. – Connecticut
Cord. – Cordillera
Cr. – Creek
D.C. – District of Columbia
Del. – Delaware
Domin. – Dominica
Dom. Rep. – Dominican Republic
E. – East
El Salv. – El Salvador
Eq. Guin. – Equatorial Guinea
Fla. – Florida
Falk. Is. – Falkland Is.
G. – Golfe, Golfo, Gulf
Ga. – Georgia
Guinea–Biss. – Guinea–Bissau
Hd. – Head
Hts. – Heights
I.(s). – Ile, Ilha, Insel,

Isla, Island, Isle(s)
Ill. – Illinois
Ind. – Indiana
Ind. Oc. – Indian Ocean
Ivory C. – Ivory Coast
Kans. – Kansas
Ky. – Kentucky
L. – Lac, Lacul, Lago, Lagoa, Lake, Limni, Loch, Lough
La. – Louisiana
Lux. – Luxembourg
Madag. – Madagascar
Man. – Manitoba
Mass. – Massachusetts
Md. – Maryland
Me. – Maine
Medit. S. – Mediterranean Sea
Mich. – Michigan
Minn. – Minnesota
Miss. – Mississippi

Mo. – Missouri
Mont. – Montana
Mozam.– Mozambique
Mt.(s).– Mont, Monte, Monti, Montaña, Mountain
N. – Nord, Norte, North, Northern
N.B. – New Brunswick
N.C. – North Carolina
N. Cal. – New Caledonia
N. Dak. – North Dakota
N.H. – New Hampshire
N.J. – New Jersey
N. Mex. – New Mexico
N.S. – Nova Scotia
N.S.W. – New South Wales
N.W.T. – North West Territory
N.Y. – New York
N.Z. – New Zealand

Nebr. – Nebraska
Neths. – Netherlands
Nev. – Nevada
Nfld. – Newfoundland
Nic. – Nicaragua

Okla. – Oklahoma
Ont. – Ontario
Oreg. – Oregon
P.E.I. – Prince Edward Island
Pa. – Pennsylvania
Pac. Oc. – Pacific Ocean
Papua N.G. – Papua New Guinea
Pen. – Peninsula, Peninsule
Phil. – Philippines
Pk. – Park, Peak
Plat. – Plateau
Prov. – Province,

Provincial
Pt. – Point
Pta. – Ponta, Punta
Pte. – Pointe
Qué. – Québec
Queens. – Queensland
R. – Rio, River
R.I. – Rhode Island
Ra.(s). – Range(s)
Reg. – Region
Rep. – Republic
Res. – Reserve, Reservoir
S. – San, South
Si. Arabia – Saudi Arabia
S.C. – South Carolina
S. Dak. – South Dakota
S. Leone – Sierra Leone
Sa. – Serra, Sierra
Sask. – Saskatchewan
Scot. – Scotland
Sd. – Sound

Sib. – Siberia
St. – Saint, Sankt, Sint
Str. – Strait, Stretto
Switz. – Switzerland
Tas. – Tasmania
Tenn. – Tennessee
Tex. – Texas
Trin. & Tob. – Trinidad & Tobago
U.A.E. – United Arab Emirates
U.K. – United Kingdom
U.S.A. – United States of America
Va. – Virginia
Vic. – Victoria
Vol. – Volcano
Vt. – Vermont
W. – West
W. Va. – West Virginia
Wash. – Washington
Wis. – Wisconsin

106 INDEX TO WORLD MAPS

Aachen — Banda Aceh

A

Aachen, Germany 10 C4 50 45N 6 6 E
Aalborg, Denmark 6 G9 57 2N 9 54 E
Aarau, Switz. 10 E5 47 23N 8 4 E
Aare →, Switz. 10 E5 47 33N 8 14 E
Aarhus, Denmark 6 G10 56 8N 10 11 E
Abadan, Iran 24 B3 30 22N 48 20 E
Abbeville, France 8 A4 50 6N 1 49 E
Abéché, Chad 29 F9 13 50N 20 35 E
Abeokuta, Nigeria 30 C2 7 3N 3 19 E
Aberdeen, U.K. 7 C5 57 9N 2 5W
Abidjan, Ivory C. 28 G4 5 26N 3 58W
Abitibi L., Canada 42 A8 48 40N 79 40W
Abkhazia □, Georgia 15 F7 43 12N 41 5 E
Abohar, India 23 D5 30 10N 74 10 E
Abu Dhabi, U.A.E. 24 C4 24 28N 54 22 E
Abuja, Nigeria 30 C3 9 16N 7 2 E
Acapulco, Mexico 44 D5 16 51N 99 56W
Accomac, U.S.A. 43 G10 37 43N 75 40W
Accra, Ghana 30 C1 5 35N 0 6W
Acklins I., Bahamas 45 C10 22 30N 74 0W
Aconcagua, Argentina 47 F3 32 39S 70 0W
Acre □, Brazil 46 C2 9 1S 71 0W
Adamawa Highlands, Cameroon 29 G7 7 20N 12 20 E
Adana, Turkey 15 G6 37 0N 35 16 E
Adapazarı, Turkey 15 F5 40 48N 30 25 E
Addis Ababa, Ethiopia 29 G12 9 2N 38 42 E
Adelaide, Australia 34 G6 34 52S 138 30 E
Adelaide, S. Africa 31 C4 32 42S 26 20 E
Aden, Yemen 24 D3 12 45N 45 0 E
Aden, G. of, Asia 24 D3 12 30N 47 30 E
Adirondack Mts., U.S.A. 43 D10 44 0N 74 0W
Admiralty Is., Papua N. G. 36 H6 2 0S 147 0 E
Ado-Ekiti, Nigeria 30 C3 7 38N 5 12 E
Adoni, India 25 D6 15 33N 77 18 E
Adour →, France 8 E3 43 32N 1 32W
Adrar, Algeria 28 C4 27 51N 0 11W
Adrian, U.S.A. 42 E5 41 54N 84 2W
Adriatic Sea, Medit. S. 12 C6 43 0N 16 0 E
Ægean Sea, Medit. S. 13 E11 38 30N 25 0 E
Afghanistan ■, Asia 24 B5 33 0N 65 0 E
'Afif, Si. Arabia 24 C3 23 53N 42 56 E
Agadès, Niger 30 A3 16 58N 7 59 E
Agadir, Morocco 28 B3 30 28N 9 55W
Agartala, India 23 H13 23 50N 91 23 E
Agen, France 8 D4 44 12N 0 38 E
Agra, India 23 F6 27 17N 77 58 E
Agrigento, Italy 12 F5 37 19N 13 34 E
Aguascalientes, Mexico 44 C4 21 53N 102 12W
Agulhas, C., S. Africa 31 C3 34 52S 20 0 E
Ahmadabad, India 23 H4 23 0N 72 40 E
Ahmadnagar, India 25 D6 19 7N 74 46 E
Ahmadpur, Pakistan 23 E3 29 12N 71 10 E
Ahvaz, Iran 24 B3 31 20N 48 40 E
Ahvenanmaa Is., Finland 6 F11 60 15N 20 0 E
Aïr, Niger 28 E6 18 30N 8 0 E
Aisne →, France 8 B5 49 26N 2 50 E
Aix-en-Provence, France 8 E6 43 32N 5 27 E
Aix-les-Bains, France 8 D6 45 41N 5 53 E
Ajaccio, France 8 F8 41 55N 8 40 E
Ajanta Ra., India 23 J5 20 28N 75 50 E
Ajaria □, Georgia 15 F7 41 30N 42 0 E
Ajmer, India 23 F5 26 28N 74 37 E
Akashi, Japan 19 B4 34 45N 134 58 E
Akita, Japan 19 A7 39 45N 140 7 E
Akola, India 23 J6 20 42N 77 2 E
Akranes, Iceland 6 B2 64 19N 22 5W
Akron, U.S.A. 42 E7 41 5N 81 31W
Aktyubinsk, Kazakstan 15 D10 50 17N 57 10 E
Akure, Nigeria 30 C3 7 15N 5 5 E
Akureyri, Iceland 6 B4 65 40N 18 6W
Al Ḥudaydah, Yemen 24 D3 14 50N 43 0 E
Al Hufūf, Si. Arabia 24 C3 25 25N 49 45 E
Al Jawf, Si. Arabia 24 C2 29 55N 39 40 E
Al Kut, Iraq 24 B3 32 30N 46 0 E
Al Qatif, Si. Arabia 24 C3 26 35N 50 0 E
Al 'Ula, Si. Arabia 24 C2 26 35N 38 0 E
Alabama □, U.S.A. 41 D9 33 0N 87 0W
Aland Is. = Ahvenanmaa Is., Finland 6 F11 60 15N 20 0 E
Alaska □, U.S.A. 38 B5 64 0N 154 0W
Alaska, G. of, Pac. Oc. 38 C5 58 0N 145 0W
Alaska Peninsula, U.S.A. 38 C4 56 0N 159 0W
Alaska Range, U.S.A. 38 B4 62 50N 151 0W
Alba-Iulia, Romania 11 E12 46 8N 23 39 E
Albacete, Spain 9 C5 39 0N 1 50W
Albania ■, Europe 13 D9 41 0N 20 0 E
Albany, Australia 34 H2 35 1S 117 58 E
Albany, Ga., U.S.A. 41 D10 31 35N 84 10W
Albany, N.Y., U.S.A. 43 D11 42 39N 73 45W
Albany →, Canada 39 C11 52 17N 81 31W
Albert L., Africa 32 D6 1 30N 31 0 E
Alberta □, Canada 38 C8 54 40N 115 0W
Albertville, France 8 D7 45 40N 6 22 E
Albi, France 8 E5 43 56N 2 9 E
Albion, U.S.A. 42 D5 42 15N 84 45W
Albuquerque, U.S.A. 40 C5 35 5N 106 39W
Albury, Australia 34 H8 36 3S 146 56 E
Alcalá de Henares, Spain 9 B4 40 28N 3 22W
Aldabra Is., Seychelles 27 G8 9 22S 46 28 E
Aldan →, Russia 18 C14 63 28N 129 35 E
Aleksandrovsk-Sakhalinskiy, Russia 18 D16 50 50N 142 20 E
Alençon, France 8 B4 48 27N 0 4 E
Alès, France 8 D6 44 9N 4 5 E
Alessándria, Italy 12 B3 44 54N 8 37 E
Ålesund, Norway 6 F9 62 28N 6 12 E
Aleutian Is., Pac. Oc. 36 B10 52 0N 175 0W
Alexander Arch., U.S.A. 38 C6 56 0N 136 0W
Alexandria, Egypt 29 B10 31 13N 29 58 E
Alexandria, La., U.S.A. 41 D8 31 18N 92 27W
Alexandria, Va., U.S.A. 42 F9 38 48N 77 3W
Algarve, Portugal 9 D1 36 58N 8 20W
Algeciras, Spain 9 D3 36 9N 5 28W
Algeria ■, Africa 28 C5 28 30N 2 0 E
Algiers, Algeria 28 A5 36 42N 3 8 E
Alicante, Spain 9 C5 38 23N 0 30W
Alice Springs, Australia 34 E5 23 40S 133 50 E
Aligarh, India 23 F7 27 55N 78 10 E
Alipur Duar, India 23 F12 26 30N 89 35 E
Aliquippa, U.S.A. 42 E7 40 37N 80 15W
Aliwal North, S. Africa 31 C4 30 45S 26 45 E
Alkmaar, Neths. 10 B3 52 37N 4 45 E
Allahabad, India 23 G8 25 25N 81 58 E
Allegan, U.S.A. 42 D5 42 32N 85 51W
Allegheny →, U.S.A. 42 E8 40 27N 80 1W
Allegheny Plateau, U.S.A. 42 G7 38 0N 80 0W
Allentown, U.S.A. 43 E10 40 37N 75 29W
Alleppey, India 25 E6 9 30N 76 28 E
Allier →, France 8 C5 46 57N 3 4 E
Alma, U.S.A. 42 D5 43 23N 84 39W
Almaty, Kazakstan 18 E9 43 15N 76 57 E
Almelo, Neths. 10 B4 52 22N 6 42 E
Almería, Spain 9 D4 36 52N 2 27W
Alor, Indonesia 22 D4 8 15S 124 30 E
Alpena, U.S.A. 42 C6 45 4N 83 27W
Alps, Europe 10 E5 46 30N 9 30 E
Alsace, France 8 B7 48 15N 7 25 E
Altai, Mongolia 20 B4 46 40N 92 45 E
Altay, China 20 B3 47 48N 88 10 E
Altoona, U.S.A. 42 E8 40 31N 78 24W
Altun Shan, China 20 C3 38 30N 88 0 E
Alwar, India 23 F6 27 38N 76 34 E
Amadjuak L., Canada 39 B12 65 0N 71 8W
Amagasaki, Japan 19 B4 34 42N 135 20 E
Amarillo, U.S.A. 40 C6 35 13N 101 50W
Amazon →, S. Amer. 46 C4 0 5S 50 0W
Ambala, India 23 D6 30 23N 76 56 E
Ambikapur, India 23 H9 23 15N 83 15 E
Ambon, Indonesia 22 D4 3 35S 128 20 E
American Samoa □, Pac. Oc. 35 C17 14 20S 170 40W
Amiens, France 8 B5 49 54N 2 16 E
Amman, Jordan 24 B2 31 57N 35 52 E
Amos, Canada 42 A8 48 35N 78 5W
Amravati, India 23 J6 20 55N 77 45 E
Amreli, India 23 J3 21 35N 71 17 E
Amritsar, India 23 D5 31 35N 74 57 E
Amroha, India 23 E7 28 53N 78 30 E
Amsterdam, Neths. 10 B3 52 23N 4 54 E
Amsterdam, U.S.A. 43 D10 42 56N 74 11W
Amudarya →, Uzbekistan 18 E7 43 58N 59 34 E
Amundsen Gulf, Canada 38 A7 71 0N 124 0W
Amundsen Sea, Antarctica 48 E1 72 0S 115 0W
Amur →, Russia 18 D16 52 56N 141 10 E
An Najaf, Iraq 24 B3 32 3N 44 15 E
An Nasiriyah, Iraq 24 B3 31 0N 46 15 E
An Nhon, Vietnam 22 B2 13 55N 109 7 E
Anadyr, Russia 18 C19 64 35N 177 20 E
Anadyr, G. of, Russia 18 C20 64 0N 180 0 E
Anaheim, U.S.A. 40 D3 33 50N 117 55W
Anambas Is., Indonesia 22 C2 3 20N 106 30 E
Anantnag, India 23 C5 33 45N 75 10 E
Anar, Iran 24 B4 30 55N 55 13 E
Anatolia, Turkey 15 G5 39 0N 30 0 E
Anchorage, U.S.A. 38 B5 61 13N 149 54W
Ancona, Italy 12 C5 43 38N 13 30 E
Anda, China 21 B7 46 24N 125 19 E
Andalucía □, Spain 9 D3 37 35N 5 0W
Andaman Is., Ind. Oc. 25 D8 12 30N 92 30 E
Anderson, U.S.A. 42 E5 40 10N 85 41W
Andes, S. Amer. 46 E3 20 0S 68 0W
Andhra Pradesh □, India 25 D6 18 0N 79 0 E
Andorra ■, Europe 9 A6 42 30N 1 30 E
Andreanof Is., U.S.A. 38 C2 52 0N 178 0W
Ándria, Italy 12 D7 41 13N 16 17 E
Andros I., Bahamas 45 C9 24 30N 78 0W
Angara →, Russia 18 D11 58 5N 94 20 E
Ånge, Sweden 6 F11 62 31N 15 35 E
Angel Falls, Venezuela 46 B3 5 57N 62 30W
Angerman →, Sweden 6 F11 62 40N 18 0 E
Angers, France 8 C3 47 30N 0 35W
Anglesey, U.K. 7 E4 53 17N 4 20W
Angola ■, Africa 33 G3 12 0S 18 0 E
Angoulême, France 8 D4 45 39N 0 10 E
Angoumois, France 8 D3 45 50N 0 25 E
Anguilla ■, W. Indies 44 J18 18 14N 63 5W
Anhui □, China 21 C6 32 0N 117 0 E
Anjou, France 8 C3 47 20N 0 15W
Ankara, Turkey 15 G5 39 57N 32 54 E
Ann, C., U.S.A. 43 D12 42 38N 70 35W
Ann Arbor, U.S.A. 42 D6 42 17N 83 45W
Annaba, Algeria 28 A6 36 50N 7 46 E
Annapolis, U.S.A. 42 F9 38 59N 76 30W
Annecy, France 8 D7 45 55N 6 8 E
Annobón, Atl. Oc. 27 G4 1 25S 5 36 E
Anshun, China 20 D5 26 18N 105 57 E
Antalya, Turkey 15 G5 36 52N 30 45 E
Antananarivo, Madag. 33 H9 18 55S 47 31 E
Antarctic Pen., Antarctica 48 D4 67 0S 60 0W
Antibes, France 8 E7 43 34N 7 6 E
Anticosti I., Canada 43 A16 49 30N 63 0W
Antigua & Barbuda ■, W. Indies 44 K20 17 20N 61 48W
Antofagasta, Chile 47 E2 23 50S 70 30W
Antsiranana, Madag. 33 G9 12 25S 49 20 E
Antwerp, Belgium 10 C3 51 13N 4 25 E
Anyang, China 21 C6 36 5N 114 21 E
Aomori, Japan 19 F12 40 45N 140 45 E
Aparri, Phil. 22 B4 18 22N 121 38 E
Apeldoorn, Neths. 10 B3 52 13N 5 57 E
Apennines, Italy 12 B4 44 0N 10 0 E
Apia, W. Samoa 35 C16 13 50S 171 50W
Appalachian Mts., U.S.A. 42 G7 38 0N 80 0W
Appleton, U.S.A. 42 C3 44 16N 88 25W
Aqmola, Kazakstan 18 D9 51 10N 71 30 E
Ar Ramadi, Iraq 24 B3 33 25N 43 20 E
Arabian Desert, Egypt 29 C11 27 30N 32 30 E
Arabian Gulf = Gulf, The, Asia 24 C4 27 0N 50 0 E
Arabian Sea, Ind. Oc. 24 D5 16 0N 65 0 E
Aracaju, Brazil 46 D6 10 55S 37 4W
Arad, Romania 11 E11 46 10N 21 20 E
Arafura Sea, E. Indies 22 D5 9 0S 135 0 E
Aragón □, Spain 9 B5 41 25N 0 40W
Araguaia →, Brazil 46 C5 5 21S 48 41W
Arak, Iran 24 B3 34 0N 49 40 E
Arakan Yoma, Burma 25 C8 20 0N 94 40 E
Aral, Kazakstan 18 E8 46 41N 61 45 E
Aral Sea , Asia 18 E8 44 30N 60 0 E
Arcachon, France 8 D3 44 40N 1 10W
Arctic Ocean, Arctic 48 B17 78 0N 160 0W
Arctic Red River, Canada 38 B6 67 15N 134 0W
Ardabil, Iran 24 B3 38 15N 48 18 E
Ardennes, Belgium 10 D3 49 50N 5 5 E
Arendal, Norway 6 G9 58 28N 8 46 E
Arequipa, Peru 46 D2 16 20S 71 30W
Argentan, France 8 B3 48 45N 0 1W
Argentina ■, S. Amer. 47 F3 35 0S 66 0W
Arima, Trin. & Tob. 44 S20 10 38N 61 17W
Arizona □, U.S.A. 40 D4 34 0N 112 0W
Arkansas □, U.S.A. 41 D8 35 0N 92 30W
Arkansas →, U.S.A. 41 D8 33 47N 91 4W
Arkhangelsk, Russia 14 B7 64 38N 40 36 E
Arles, France 8 E6 43 41N 4 40 E
Arlington, U.S.A. 42 F9 38 53N 77 7W
Arlon, Belgium 10 D3 49 42N 5 49 E
Armenia ■, Asia 15 F7 40 20N 45 0 E
Arnhem, Neths. 10 C3 51 58N 5 55 E
Arnhem Land, Australia 34 C5 13 10S 134 30 E
Arnprior, Canada 42 C9 45 26N 76 21W
Arrah, India 23 G10 25 35N 84 32 E
Arran, U.K. 7 D4 55 34N 5 12W
Arras, France 8 A5 50 17N 2 46 E
Artois, France 8 A5 50 20N 2 30 E
Aru Is., Indonesia 22 D5 6 0S 134 30 E
Arunachal Pradesh □, India 25 C8 28 0N 95 0 E
Arusha, Tanzania 32 E7 3 20S 36 40 E
Arviat, Canada 38 B10 61 10N 94 15W
Asab, Namibia 31 B2 25 30S 18 0 E
Asahigawa, Japan 19 F12 43 46N 142 22 E
Asansol, India 23 H11 23 40N 87 1 E
Asbestos, Canada 43 C12 45 47N 71 58W
Asbury Park, U.S.A. 43 E10 40 13N 74 1W
Ascension I., Atl. Oc. 27 G2 8 0S 14 15W
Ashkhabad, Turkmenistan 18 F7 38 0N 57 50 E
Ashland, Ky., U.S.A. 42 F6 38 28N 82 38W
Ashland, Ohio, U.S.A. 42 E6 40 52N 82 19W
Ashtabula, U.S.A. 42 E7 41 52N 80 47W
Asifabad, India 23 K7 19 20N 79 24 E
Asir □, Si. Arabia 24 D3 18 40N 42 30 E
Asmara, Eritrea 29 E12 15 19N 38 55 E
Assam □, India 23 F13 26 0N 93 0 E
Assen, Neths. 10 B4 53 0N 6 35 E
Assisi, Italy 12 C5 43 4N 12 37 E
Asti, Italy 12 B3 44 54N 8 12 E
Astrakhan, Russia 15 E8 46 25N 48 5 E
Asturias □, Spain 9 A3 43 15N 6 0W
Asunción, Paraguay 47 E4 25 10S 57 30W
Aswân, Egypt 29 D11 24 4N 32 57 E
Atacama Desert, Chile 47 E3 24 0S 69 20W
Atbara, Sudan 29 E11 17 42N 33 59 E
Atbara →, Sudan 29 E11 17 40N 33 56 E
Athabasca →, Canada 38 C8 58 40N 110 50W
Athabasca, L., Canada 38 C9 59 15N 109 15W
Athens, Greece 13 F10 37 58N 23 46 E
Athens, U.S.A. 42 F6 39 20N 82 6W
Atikokan, Canada 42 A2 48 45N 91 37W
Atlanta, U.S.A. 41 D10 33 45N 84 23W
Atlantic City, U.S.A. 43 F10 39 21N 74 27W
Atlantic Ocean 2 E9 0 0 20 0W
Atyraū, Kazakstan 18 E7 47 5N 52 0 E
Au Sable →, U.S.A. 42 C6 44 25N 83 20W
Aube →, France 8 B5 48 34N 3 43 E
Auburn, Ind., U.S.A. 42 E5 41 22N 85 4W
Auburn, N.Y., U.S.A. 42 D9 42 56N 76 34W
Aubusson, France 8 D5 45 57N 2 11 E
Auch, France 8 E4 43 39N 0 36 E
Auckland, N.Z. 35 H13 36 52S 174 46 E
Aude →, France 8 E5 43 13N 3 14 E
Augrabies Falls, S. Africa 31 B3 28 35S 20 20 E
Augsburg, Germany 10 D6 48 25N 10 52 E
Augusta, Ga., U.S.A. 41 D10 33 28N 81 58W
Augusta, Maine, U.S.A. 43 C13 44 19N 69 47W
Aunis, France 8 C3 46 5N 0 50W
Aurangabad, Bihar, India 23 G10 24 45N 84 18 E
Aurangabad, Maharashtra, India 23 K5 19 50N 75 23 E
Aurillac, France 8 D5 44 55N 2 26 E
Aurora, U.S.A. 42 E3 41 45N 88 19W
Austin, U.S.A. 40 D7 30 17N 97 45W
Australia ■, Oceania 34 E5 23 0S 135 0 E
Australian Alps, Australia 34 H8 36 30S 148 30 E
Australian Capital Territory □, Australia 34 H8 35 30S 149 0 E
Austria ■, Europe 10 E8 47 0N 14 0 E
Autun, France 8 C6 46 58N 4 17 E
Auvergne, France 8 D5 45 20N 3 15 E
Auxerre, France 8 C5 47 48N 3 32 E
Avallon, France 8 C5 47 30N 3 53 E
Avellino, Italy 12 D6 40 54N 14 47 E
Avignon, France 8 E6 43 57N 4 50 E
Ávila, Spain 9 B3 40 39N 4 43W
Avranches, France 8 B3 48 40N 1 20W
Axiós →, Greece 13 D10 40 57N 22 35 E
Ayers Rock, Australia 34 F5 25 23S 131 5 E
Ayr, U.K. 7 D4 55 28N 4 38W
Azamgarh, India 23 F9 26 5N 83 13 E
Azerbaijan ■, Asia 15 F8 40 20N 48 0 E
Azores, Atl. Oc. 2 C8 38 44N 29 0W
Azov, Sea of, Europe 15 E6 46 0N 36 30 E
Azuero Pen., Panama 45 F8 7 30N 80 30W

B

Babol, Iran 24 B4 36 40N 52 50 E
Babuyan Chan., Phil. 22 B4 18 40N 121 30 E
Bacău, Romania 11 E14 46 35N 26 55 E
Bacolod, Phil. 22 B4 10 40N 122 57 E
Bad Axe, U.S.A. 42 D6 43 48N 83 0W
Badajoz, Spain 9 C2 38 50N 6 59W
Badalona, Spain 9 B7 41 26N 2 15 E
Baden-Württemberg □, Germany 10 D5 48 20N 8 40 E
Baffin I., Canada 39 B12 68 0N 75 0W
Baghdad, Iraq 24 B3 33 20N 44 30 E
Baguio, Phil. 22 B4 16 26N 120 34 E
Bahamas ■, N. Amer. 45 C10 24 0N 75 0W
Baharampur, India 23 G12 24 2N 88 27 E
Bahawalpur, Pakistan 23 E3 29 24N 71 40 E
Bahía = Salvador, Brazil 46 D6 13 0S 38 30W
Bahía □, Brazil 46 D5 12 0S 42 0W
Bahía Blanca, Argentina 47 F3 38 35S 62 13W
Bahraich, India 23 F8 27 38N 81 37 E
Bahrain ■, Asia 24 C4 26 0N 50 35 E
Baia Mare, Romania 11 E12 47 40N 23 35 E
Baie-St-Paul, Canada 43 B12 47 28N 70 32W
Baikal, L., Russia 18 D12 53 0N 108 0 E
Baja California, Mexico 44 B2 31 10N 115 12W
Bakersfield, U.S.A. 40 C3 35 23N 119 1W
Bakhtaran, Iran 24 B3 34 23N 47 0 E
Baku, Azerbaijan 15 F8 40 29N 49 56 E
Balabac Str., E. Indies 22 C3 7 53N 117 5 E
Balaghat, India 23 J8 21 49N 80 12 E
Balaton, Hungary 11 E9 46 50N 17 40 E
Balboa, Panama 44 H14 8 57N 79 34W
Baldwin, U.S.A. 42 D5 43 54N 85 51W
Balearic Is., Spain 9 C7 39 30N 3 0 E
Baleshwar, India 23 J11 21 35N 87 3 E
Bali, Indonesia 22 D3 8 20S 115 0 E
Balikeşir, Turkey 13 E12 39 35N 27 58 E
Balikpapan, Indonesia 22 D3 1 10S 116 55 E
Balkan Mts., Bulgaria 13 C10 43 15N 23 0 E
Balkhash, L., Kazakstan 18 E9 46 0N 74 50 E
Ballarat, Australia 34 H7 37 33S 143 50 E
Balqash, Kazakstan 18 E9 46 50N 74 50 E
Balrampur, India 23 F9 27 30N 82 20 E
Balsas →, Mexico 44 D4 17 55N 102 10W
Baltic Sea, Europe 6 G11 57 0N 19 0 E
Baltimore, U.S.A. 42 F9 39 17N 76 37W
Bam, Iran 24 C4 29 7N 58 14 E
Bamako, Mali 28 F3 12 34N 7 55W
Bamberg, Germany 10 D6 49 54N 10 54 E
Bamenda, Cameroon 30 C4 5 57N 10 11 E
Bancroft, Canada 42 C9 45 3N 77 51W
Banda, India 23 G8 25 30N 80 26 E
Banda Aceh, Indonesia 22 C1 5 35N 95 20 E

Place names on the yellow-coded large scale map section are to be found in the index at the end of that section

Banda Is.   **Brussels**

Place names on the yellow-coded large scale map section are to be found in the index at the end of that section.

Bryan, *U.S.A.* 42 E5 41 28N 84 33W
Bryansk, *Russia* 14 D5 53 13N 34 25 E
Bucaramanga, *Colombia* 46 B2 7 0N 73 0W
Bucharest, *Romania* 11 F14 44 27N 26 10 E
Buckhannon, *U.S.A.* 42 F7 39 0N 80 8W
Buckingham, *Canada* 43 C10 45 37N 75 24W
Bucyrus, *U.S.A.* 42 E6 40 48N 82 59W
Budapest, *Hungary* 11 E10 47 29N 19 5 E
Buena Vista, *U.S.A.* 42 G8 37 44N 79 21W
Buenos Aires, *Argentina* 47 F4 34 30S 58 20W
Buffalo, *U.S.A.* 42 D8 42 53N 78 53W
Bug →, *Poland* 11 B11 52 31N 21 5 E
Buh →, *Ukraine* 15 E5 46 59N 31 58 E
Bujumbura, *Burundi* 32 E5 3 16S 29 18 E
Bukavu, *Congo (Zaïre)* 32 E5 2 20S 28 52 E
Bukittinggi, *Indonesia* 22 D2 0 20S 100 20 E
Bulandshahr, *India* 23 E6 28 28N 77 51 E
Bulawayo, *Zimbabwe* 33 J5 20 7S 28 32 E
Bulgaria ■, *Europe* 13 C11 42 35N 25 30 E
Bunbury, *Australia* 34 G2 33 20S 115 35 E
Bundaberg, *Australia* 34 E9 24 54S 152 22 E
Bundi, *India* 23 G5 25 30N 75 35 E
Buraydah, *Si. Arabia* 24 C3 26 20N 44 8 E
Burgas, *Bulgaria* 13 C12 42 33N 27 29 E
Burgersdorp, *S. Africa* 31 C4 31 0S 26 20 E
Burgos, *Spain* 9 A4 42 21N 3 41W
Burgundy = Bourgogne, *France* 8 C6 47 0N 4 50 E
Burkina Faso ■, *Africa* 30 B1 12 0N 1 0W
Burlington, *Vt., U.S.A.* 43 C11 44 29N 73 12W
Burlington, *Wis., U.S.A.* 42 D3 42 41N 88 17W
Burlyu-Tyube, *Kazakstan* 18 E9 46 30N 79 10 E
Burma ■, *Asia* 25 C8 21 0N 96 30 E
Burnie, *Australia* 34 J8 41 4S 145 56 E
Bursa, *Turkey* 13 D13 40 15N 29 5 E
Buru, *Indonesia* 22 D4 3 30S 126 30 E
Burundi ■, *Africa* 32 E5 3 15S 30 0 E
Bushehr, *Iran* 24 C4 28 55N 50 55 E
Butler, *U.S.A.* 42 E8 40 52N 79 54W
Buton, *Indonesia* 22 D4 5 0S 122 45 E
Butterworth, *Malaysia* 22 C2 5 24N 100 23 E
Butuan, *Phil.* 22 C4 8 57N 125 33 E
Buzău, *Romania* 11 F14 45 10N 26 50 E
Bydgoszcz, *Poland* 11 B9 53 10N 18 0 E
Byelorussia = Belarus ■, *Europe* 11 B14 53 30N 27 0 E
Bytom, *Poland* 11 C10 50 25N 18 54 E

C

Cabinda □, *Angola* 32 F2 5 0S 12 30 E
Cabonga, Réservoir, *Canada* 42 B9 47 20N 76 40W
Čačak, *Serbia, Yug.* 13 C9 43 54N 20 20 E
Cáceres, *Spain* 9 C2 39 26N 6 23W
Cadillac, *U.S.A.* 42 C5 44 15N 85 24W
Cádiz, *Spain* 9 D2 36 30N 6 20W
Caen, *France* 8 B3 49 10N 0 22W
Cagayan de Oro, *Phil.* 22 C4 8 30N 124 40 E
Cágliari, *Italy* 12 E3 39 13N 9 7 E
Cahors, *France* 8 D4 44 27N 1 27 E
Caicos Is., *W. Indies* 45 C10 21 40N 71 40W
Cairns, *Australia* 34 D8 16 57S 145 45 E
Cairo, *Egypt* 29 B11 30 1N 31 14 E
Calabar, *Nigeria* 30 D3 4 57N 8 20 E
Calábria □, *Italy* 12 E7 39 0N 16 30 E
Calais, *France* 8 A4 50 57N 1 56 E
Calais, *U.S.A.* 43 C14 45 11N 67 17W
Calamian Group, *Phil.* 22 B3 11 50N 119 55 E
Calapan, *Phil.* 22 B4 13 25N 121 7 E
Calcutta, *India* 23 H12 22 36N 88 24 E
Caledon, *S. Africa* 31 C2 34 14S 19 26 E
Caledon →, *S. Africa* 31 C4 30 31S 26 5 E
Calgary, *Canada* 38 C8 51 0N 114 10W
Cali, *Colombia* 46 B2 3 25N 76 35W
Calicut, *India* 25 D6 11 15N 75 43 E
California □, *U.S.A.* 40 C2 37 30N 119 30W
California, G. of, *Mexico* 44 B2 27 0N 111 0W
Calitzdorp, *S. Africa* 31 C3 33 33S 21 42 E
Callao, *Peru* 46 D2 12 0S 77 0W
Caltanissetta, *Italy* 12 F6 37 29N 14 4 E
Calvi, *France* 8 E8 42 34N 8 45 E
Calvinia, *S. Africa* 31 C2 31 28S 19 45 E
Camagüey, *Cuba* 45 C9 21 20N 78 0W
Camargue, *France* 8 E6 43 34N 4 34 E
Cambay, G. of, *India* 23 J4 20 45N 72 30 E
Cambodia ■, *Asia* 22 B2 12 15N 105 0 E
Cambrai, *France* 8 A5 50 11N 3 14 E
Cambrian Mts., *U.K.* 7 E5 52 3N 3 57W
Cambridge, *U.K.* 7 E7 52 12N 0 8 E
Cambridge, *Mass., U.S.A.* 43 D12 42 22N 71 6W
Cambridge, *Md., U.S.A.* 43 F9 38 34N 76 5W
Cambridge, *Ohio, U.S.A.* 42 E7 40 2N 81 35W
Cambridge Bay = Ikaluktutiak, *Canada* 38 B9 69 10N 105 0W
Camden, *U.S.A.* 43 F10 39 56N 75 7W
Cameroon ■, *Africa* 30 C4 6 0N 12 30 E
Cameroun, Mt., *Cameroon* 30 D3 4 13N 9 10 E
Campánia □, *Italy* 12 D6 41 0N 14 30 E
Campbellsville, *U.S.A.* 42 G5 37 21N 85 20W
Campbellton, *Canada* 43 B14 47 57N 66 43W
Campeche, *Mexico* 44 D6 19 50N 90 32W
Campeche, G. of, *Mexico* 44 D6 19 30N 93 0W
Campina Grande, *Brazil* 46 C6 7 20S 35 47W
Campinas, *Brazil* 47 E5 22 50S 47 0W
Campo Grande, *Brazil* 46 E4 20 25S 54 40W
Campos, *Brazil* 46 E5 21 50S 41 20W
Camrose, *Canada* 38 C8 53 0N 112 50W
Can Tho, *Vietnam* 22 B2 10 2N 105 46 E
Canada ■, *N. Amer.* 38 C10 60 0N 100 0W
Canadian Shield, *Canada* 39 C10 53 0N 75 0W
Canandaigua, *U.S.A.* 42 D9 42 54N 77 17W
Canary Is., *Atl. Oc.* 28 C1 28 30N 16 0W
Canaveral, C., *U.S.A.* 41 E10 28 27N 80 32W
Canberra, *Australia* 34 H8 35 15S 149 8 E
Cannes, *France* 8 E7 43 32N 7 1 E
Canso, *Canada* 43 C17 45 20N 61 0W
Cantabria □, *Spain* 9 A4 43 10N 4 0W
Cantabrian Mts., *Spain* 9 A3 43 0N 5 10W
Canterbury, *U.K.* 7 F7 51 16N 1 6 E
Canton, *N.Y., U.S.A.* 43 C10 44 36N 75 10W
Canton, *Ohio, U.S.A.* 42 E7 40 48N 81 23W
Cap-Chat, *Canada* 43 A14 49 6N 66 40W
Cap-de-la-Madeleine, *Canada* 43 B11 46 22N 72 31W
Cape Breton I., *Canada* 43 B17 46 0N 60 30W
Cape Charles, *U.S.A.* 43 G10 37 16N 76 1W
Cape Coast, *Ghana* 30 C1 5 5N 1 15W
Cape May, *U.S.A.* 43 F10 38 56N 74 56W
Cape Town, *S. Africa* 31 C2 33 55S 18 22 E
Cape Verde Is. ■, *Atl. Oc.* 27 E1 17 10N 25 20W
Cape York Peninsula, *Australia* 34 C7 12 0S 142 30 E
Capreol, *Canada* 42 B7 46 43N 80 56W
Capri, *Italy* 12 D6 40 33N 14 14 E
Caracas, *Venezuela* 46 A3 10 30N 66 55W
Carbondale, *U.S.A.* 43 E10 41 35N 75 30W
Carcassonne, *France* 8 E5 43 13N 2 20 E
Cardiff, *U.K.* 7 F5 51 29N 3 10W
Caribbean Sea, *W. Indies* 45 E10 15 0N 75 0W
Caribou, *U.S.A.* 43 B13 46 52N 68 1W
Carleton Place, *Canada* 43 C9 45 8N 76 9W
Carletonville, *S. Africa* 31 B4 26 23S 27 22 E
Carlisle, *U.S.A.* 42 E9 40 12N 77 12W
Carmaux, *France* 8 D5 44 3N 2 10 E
Carmi, *U.S.A.* 42 F3 38 5N 88 10W
Carnarvon, *Australia* 34 E1 24 51S 113 42 E
Carnarvon, *S. Africa* 31 C3 30 56S 22 8 E
Carnegie, L., *Australia* 34 F3 26 5S 122 30 E
Caro, *U.S.A.* 42 D6 43 29N 83 24W
Carolina, *S. Africa* 31 B5 26 5S 30 6 E
Caroline Is., *Pac. Oc.* 36 G6 8 0N 150 0 E
Carpathians, *Europe* 11 D11 49 30N 21 0 E
Carpentaria, G. of, *Australia* 34 C6 14 0S 139 0 E
Carpentras, *France* 8 D6 44 3N 5 2 E
Cartagena, *Colombia* 46 A2 10 25N 75 33W
Cartagena, *Spain* 9 D5 37 38N 0 59W
Casablanca, *Morocco* 28 B3 33 36N 7 36W
Cascade Ra., *U.S.A.* 40 A2 47 0N 121 30W
Casper, *U.S.A.* 40 B5 42 51N 106 19W
Caspian Sea, *Eurasia* 15 F9 43 0N 50 0 E
Cass City, *U.S.A.* 42 D6 43 36N 83 11W
Castellón de la Plana, *Spain* 9 C5 39 58N 0 3W
Castelsarrasin, *France* 8 E4 44 2N 1 7 E
Castilla La Mancha □, *Spain* 9 C4 39 30N 3 30W
Castilla y Leon □, *Spain* 9 B3 42 0N 5 0W
Castres, *France* 8 E5 43 37N 2 13 E
Castries, *St. Lucia* 44 N21 14 2N 60 58W
Cataluña □, *Spain* 9 B6 41 40N 1 15 E
Catanduanes, *Phil.* 22 B4 13 50N 124 20 E
Catánia, *Italy* 12 F6 37 30N 15 6 E
Catanzaro, *Italy* 12 E7 38 54N 16 35 E
Catskill, *U.S.A.* 43 D11 42 14N 73 52W
Catskill Mts., *U.S.A.* 43 D10 42 10N 74 25W
Caucasus Mountains, *Eurasia* 15 F7 42 50N 44 0 E
Caxias do Sul, *Brazil* 47 E4 29 10S 51 10W
Cayenne, *Fr. Guiana* 46 B4 5 5N 52 18W
Cayuga L., *U.S.A.* 42 D9 42 41N 76 41W
Cedar Rapids, *U.S.A.* 41 B8 41 59N 91 40W
Cegléd, *Hungary* 11 E10 47 11N 19 47 E
Celebes Sea, *Indonesia* 22 C4 3 0N 123 0 E
Celina, *U.S.A.* 42 E5 40 33N 84 35W
Central African Rep. ■, *Africa* 32 C4 7 0N 20 0 E
Central Makran Range, *Pakistan* 24 C5 26 30N 64 15 E
Cephalonia = Kefallinia, *Greece* 13 E9 38 20N 20 30 E
Ceram, *Indonesia* 22 D4 3 10S 129 0 E
Ceram Sea, *Indonesia* 22 D4 2 30S 128 30 E
Ceres, *S. Africa* 31 C2 33 21S 19 18 E
Cerignola, *Italy* 12 D6 41 17N 15 53 E
České Budějovice, *Czech Rep.* 10 D8 48 55N 14 25 E
Ceuta, *N. Afr.* 9 E3 35 52N 5 18W
Cévennes, *France* 8 D5 44 10N 3 50 E
Chad ■, *Africa* 29 E8 15 0N 17 15 E
Chakradharpur, *India* 23 H10 22 45N 85 40 E
Chaleur B., *Canada* 43 B15 47 55N 65 30W
Chalisgaon, *India* 23 J5 20 30N 75 10 E
Chalon-sur-Saône, *France* 8 C6 46 48N 4 50 E
Châlons-en-Champagne, *France* 8 B6 48 58N 4 20 E
Chamba, *India* 23 C6 32 35N 76 10 E
Chambal →, *India* 23 F7 26 29N 79 15 E
Chambersburg, *U.S.A.* 42 F9 39 56N 77 40W
Chambéry, *France* 8 D6 45 34N 5 55 E
Champagne, *France* 8 B6 48 40N 4 20 E
Champaign, *U.S.A.* 42 E3 40 7N 88 15W
Champlain, L., *U.S.A.* 43 C11 44 40N 73 20W
Chandigarh, *India* 23 D6 30 43N 76 47 E
Chandpur, *Bangla.* 23 H13 23 8N 90 45 E
Changchun, *China* 21 B7 43 57N 125 17 E
Changde, *China* 21 D6 29 4N 111 35 E
Changsha, *China* 21 D6 28 12N 113 0 E
Changzhou, *China* 21 C6 31 47N 119 58 E
Chanthaburi, *Thailand* 22 B2 12 38N 102 12 E
Chapleau, *Canada* 42 B6 47 50N 83 24W
Chapra, *India* 23 G10 25 48N 84 44 E
Chardzhou, *Turkmenistan* 18 F8 39 6N 63 34 E
Chārīkār, *Afghan.* 23 B2 35 0N 69 10 E
Charleroi, *Belgium* 10 C3 50 24N 4 27 E
Charles, C., *U.S.A.* 43 G10 37 7N 75 58W
Charleston, *Ill., U.S.A.* 42 F3 39 30N 88 10W
Charleston, *S.C., U.S.A.* 41 D11 32 46N 79 56W
Charleston, *W. Va., U.S.A.* 42 F7 38 21N 81 38W
Charleville, *Australia* 34 F8 26 24S 146 15 E
Charleville-Mézières, *France* 8 B6 49 44N 4 40 E
Charlevoix, *U.S.A.* 42 C5 45 19N 85 16W
Charlotte, *Mich., U.S.A.* 42 D5 42 34N 84 50W
Charlotte, *N.C., U.S.A.* 41 C10 35 13N 80 51W
Charlottesville, *U.S.A.* 42 F8 38 2N 78 30W
Charlottetown, *Canada* 43 B16 46 14N 63 8W
Charolles, *France* 8 C6 46 27N 4 16 E
Charters Towers, *Australia* 34 E8 20 5S 146 13 E
Chartres, *France* 8 B4 48 29N 1 30 E
Châteaubriant, *France* 8 C3 47 43N 1 23W
Châteaulin, *France* 8 B1 48 11N 4 8W
Châteauroux, *France* 8 C4 46 50N 1 40 E
Châtellerault, *France* 8 C4 46 50N 0 30 E
Chatham, *N.B., Canada* 43 B15 47 2N 65 28W
Chatham, *Ont., Canada* 42 D6 42 24N 82 11W
Chattanooga, *U.S.A.* 41 C9 35 3N 85 19W
Chaumont, *France* 8 B6 48 7N 5 8 E
Cheb, *Czech Rep.* 10 C7 50 9N 12 28 E
Cheboksary, *Russia* 14 C8 56 8N 47 12 E
Cheboygan, *U.S.A.* 42 C5 45 39N 84 29W
Chechenia □, *Russia* 15 F8 43 30N 45 29 E
Chedabucto B., *Canada* 43 C17 45 25N 61 8W
Chełm, *Poland* 11 C12 51 8N 23 30 E
Chelyabinsk, *Russia* 18 D8 55 10N 61 24 E
Chelyuskin, C., *Russia* 18 B12 77 30N 103 0 E
Chemnitz, *Germany* 10 C7 50 51N 12 54 E
Chenab →, *Pakistan* 23 D3 30 23N 71 2 E
Chengdu, *China* 20 C5 30 38N 104 2 E
Chennai, *India* 25 D7 13 8N 80 19 E
Cher →, *France* 8 C4 47 21N 0 29 E
Cherbourg, *France* 8 B3 49 39N 1 40W
Cheremkhovo, *Russia* 18 D12 53 8N 103 1 E
Cherepovets, *Russia* 14 C6 59 5N 37 55 E
Cherkassy, *Ukraine* 15 E5 49 27N 32 4 E
Chernigov, *Ukraine* 14 D5 51 28N 31 20 E
Chernobyl, *Ukraine* 11 C16 51 20N 30 15 E
Chernovtsy, *Ukraine* 11 D13 48 15N 25 52 E
Cherski Ra., *Russia* 18 C16 65 0N 143 0 E
Chesapeake B., *U.S.A.* 42 F9 38 0N 76 10W
Chester, *U.S.A.* 43 F10 39 51N 75 22W
Chesterfield Inlet = Igluligaarjuk, *Canada* 38 B10 63 30N 90 45W
Chesuncook L., *U.S.A.* 43 B13 46 0N 69 21W
Chhatarpur, *India* 23 G7 24 55N 79 35 E
Chiai, *Taiwan* 21 D7 23 29N 120 25 E
Chiba, *Japan* 19 B7 35 30N 140 7 E
Chibougamau, *Canada* 43 A10 49 56N 74 24W
Chibougamau L., *Canada* 43 A10 49 50N 74 20W
Chicago, *U.S.A.* 42 E4 41 53N 87 38W
Chiclayo, *Peru* 46 C2 6 42S 79 50W
Chicopee, *U.S.A.* 43 D11 42 9N 72 37W
Chicoutimi, *Canada* 43 A12 48 28N 71 5W
Chidley, C., *Canada* 39 B13 60 23N 64 26W
Chieti, *Italy* 12 C6 42 21N 14 10 E
Chihli, G. of, *China* 21 C6 39 0N 119 0 E
Chihuahua, *Mexico* 44 B3 28 40N 106 3W
Chile ■, *S. Amer.* 47 F2 35 0S 72 0W
Chilka L., *India* 23 K10 19 40N 85 25 E
Chillán, *Chile* 47 F2 36 40S 72 10W
Chillicothe, *U.S.A.* 42 F6 39 20N 82 59W
Chilpancingo, *Mexico* 44 D5 17 30N 99 30W
Chilton, *U.S.A.* 42 C3 44 2N 88 10W
Chilung, *Taiwan* 21 D7 25 3N 121 45 E
Chimborazo, *Ecuador* 46 C2 1 29S 78 55W
Chimbote, *Peru* 46 C2 9 0S 78 35W
Chimkent, *Kazakstan* 18 E8 42 18N 69 36 E
China ■, *Asia* 21 C6 30 0N 110 0 E
Chindwin →, *Burma* 25 C8 21 26N 95 15 E
Chingola, *Zambia* 33 G5 12 31S 27 53 E
Chinon, *France* 8 C4 47 10N 0 15 E
Chíos, *Greece* 13 E12 38 27N 26 9 E
Chipata, *Zambia* 33 G6 13 38S 32 28 E
Chipman, *Canada* 43 B15 46 6N 65 53W
Chita, *Russia* 18 D13 52 0N 113 35 E
Chitral, *Pakistan* 23 B3 35 50N 71 56 E
Chittagong, *Bangla.* 23 H13 22 19N 91 48 E
Cholet, *France* 8 C3 47 4N 0 52W
Chŏngjin, *N. Korea* 21 B7 41 47N 129 50 E
Chongqing, *China* 20 D5 29 35N 106 25 E
Chorzów, *Poland* 11 C10 50 18N 18 57 E
Choybalsan, *Mongolia* 21 B6 48 4N 114 30 E
Christchurch, *N.Z.* 35 J13 43 33S 172 47 E
Christiana, *S. Africa* 31 B4 27 52S 25 8 E
Chukot Ra., *Russia* 18 C19 68 0N 175 0 E
Chumphon, *Thailand* 22 B1 10 35N 99 14 E
Chur, *Switz.* 10 E5 46 52N 9 32 E
Churchill →, *Man., Canada* 38 C10 58 47N 94 12W
Churchill →, *Nfld., Canada* 39 C13 53 19N 60 10W
Churu, *India* 23 E5 28 20N 74 50 E
Chushal, *India* 23 C7 33 40N 78 40 E
Chuvashia □, *Russia* 14 C8 55 30N 47 0 E
Cicero, *U.S.A.* 42 E4 41 48N 87 48W
Ciechanów, *Poland* 11 B11 52 52N 20 38 E
Ciénaga, *Colombia* 46 A2 11 1N 74 15W
Cienfuegos, *Cuba* 45 C8 22 10N 80 30W
Cincinnati, *U.S.A.* 42 F5 39 6N 84 31W
Cinto, Mte., *France* 8 E8 42 24N 8 54 E
Circleville, *U.S.A.* 42 F6 39 36N 82 57W
Cirebon, *Indonesia* 22 D2 6 45S 108 32 E
Citlaltépetl, *Mexico* 44 D5 19 0N 97 20W
Ciudad Bolívar, *Venezuela* 46 B3 8 5N 63 36W
Ciudad Guayana, *Venezuela* 46 B3 8 0N 62 30W
Ciudad Juárez, *Mexico* 44 A3 31 40N 106 28W
Ciudad Madero, *Mexico* 44 C5 22 19N 97 50W
Ciudad Obregón, *Mexico* 44 B3 27 28N 109 59W
Ciudad Real, *Spain* 9 C4 38 59N 3 55W
Ciudad Victoria, *Mexico* 44 C5 23 41N 99 9W
Clanwilliam, *S. Africa* 31 C2 32 11S 18 52 E
Claremont, *U.S.A.* 43 D11 43 23N 72 20W
Clarksburg, *U.S.A.* 42 F7 39 17N 80 30W
Clarksville, *U.S.A.* 41 C9 36 32N 87 21W
Clearfield, *U.S.A.* 42 E8 41 2N 78 27W
Clermont-Ferrand, *France* 8 D5 45 46N 3 4 E
Cleveland, *U.S.A.* 42 E7 41 30N 81 42W
Clifton Forge, *U.S.A.* 42 G8 37 49N 79 50W
Cluj-Napoca, *Romania* 11 E12 46 47N 23 38 E
Clyde →, *U.K.* 7 D4 55 55N 4 30W
Coast Mts., *Canada* 38 C7 55 0N 129 20W
Coast Ranges, *U.S.A.* 40 B2 39 0N 123 0W
Coaticook, *Canada* 43 C12 45 10N 71 46W
Coatzacoalcos, *Mexico* 44 D6 18 7N 94 25W
Cobourg, *Canada* 42 D8 43 58N 78 10W
Cochabamba, *Bolivia* 46 D3 17 26S 66 10W
Cochin, *India* 25 E6 9 59N 76 22 E
Cochrane, *Canada* 42 A7 49 0N 81 0W
Cockburn I., *Canada* 42 C6 45 55N 83 22W
Cod, C., *U.S.A.* 41 B13 42 5N 70 10W
Cognac, *France* 8 D3 45 41N 0 20W
Coimbatore, *India* 25 D6 11 2N 76 59 E
Coimbra, *Portugal* 9 B1 40 15N 8 27W
Colebrook, *U.S.A.* 43 C12 44 54N 71 30W
Colesberg, *S. Africa* 31 C4 30 45S 25 5 E
Colima, *Mexico* 44 D4 19 14N 103 43W
Collingwood, *Canada* 42 C7 44 29N 80 13W
Colmar, *France* 8 B7 48 5N 7 20 E
Cologne, *Germany* 10 C4 50 56N 6 57 E
Colombia ■, *S. Amer.* 46 B2 3 45N 73 0W
Colombo, *Sri Lanka* 25 E6 6 56N 79 58 E
Colón, *Panama* 44 H14 9 20N 79 54W
Colonial Heights, *U.S.A.* 42 G9 37 15N 77 25W
Colorado □, *U.S.A.* 40 C5 39 30N 105 30W
Colorado →, *N. Amer.* 40 D4 31 45N 114 40W
Colorado →, *U.S.A.* 41 E7 28 36N 95 59W
Colorado Plateau, *U.S.A.* 40 C4 37 0N 111 0W
Colorado Springs, *U.S.A.* 40 C6 38 50N 104 49W
Columbia, *U.S.A.* 41 D10 34 0N 81 2W
Columbia →, *U.S.A.* 40 A2 46 15N 124 5W
Columbia, District of □, *U.S.A.* 42 F9 38 55N 77 0W
Columbus, *Ga., U.S.A.* 41 D10 32 28N 84 59W
Columbus, *Ind., U.S.A.* 42 F5 39 13N 85 55W
Columbus, *Ohio, U.S.A.* 42 F6 39 58N 83 0W
Comilla, *Bangla.* 23 H13 23 28N 91 10 E
Communism Pk., *Tajikistan* 18 F9 39 0N 72 2 E
Como, *Italy* 12 B3 45 47N 9 5 E
Como, L. di, *Italy* 12 B3 46 0N 9 11 E

Place names on the yellow-coded large scale map section are to be found in the index at the end of that section

Comodoro Rivadavia

Eskilstuna

Place names on the yellow-coded large scale map section are to be found in the index at the end of that section

Groot Vis · **James B.**

112 INDEX TO WORLD MAPS

Jamestown — Kushtia

Jamestown, Ky., U.S.A. 42 G5 36 59N 85 4W
Jamestown, N.Y., U.S.A. 42 D8 42 6N 79 14W
Jammu, India 23 C5 32 43N 74 54 E
Jammu & Kashmir □, India 23 B6 34 25N 77 0 E
Jamnagar, India 23 H3 22 30N 70 6 E
Jamshedpur, India 23 H11 22 44N 86 12 E
Jaora, India 23 H5 23 40N 75 10 E
Japan ■, Asia 19 G11 36 0N 136 0 E
Japan, Sea of, Asia 19 G11 40 0N 135 0 E
Japurá →, Brazil 46 C3 3 8S 65 46W
Jask, Iran 24 C4 25 38N 57 45 E
Jaunpur, India 23 G9 25 46N 82 44 E
Java, Indonesia 22 D3 7 0S 110 0 E
Java Sea, Indonesia 22 D2 4 35S 107 15 E
Jedda, Si. Arabia 24 C2 21 29N 39 10 E
Jeffersonville, U.S.A. 42 F5 38 17N 85 44W
Jelenia Góra, Poland 10 C8 50 50N 15 45 E
Jena, Germany 10 C6 50 54N 11 35 E
Jerez de la Frontera, Spain 9 D2 36 41N 6 7W
Jersey City, U.S.A. 43 E10 40 44N 74 4W
Jerusalem, Israel 24 B2 31 47N 35 10 E
Jessore, Bangla. 23 H12 23 10N 89 10 E
Jhang Maghiana, Pakistan 23 D4 31 15N 72 22 E
Jhansi, India 23 G7 25 30N 78 36 E
Jhelum, Pakistan 23 C4 33 0N 73 45 E
Jhelum →, Pakistan 23 D4 31 20N 72 10 E
Jiamusi, China 21 B8 46 40N 130 26 E
Jian, China 21 D6 27 6N 114 59 E
Jiangsu □, China 21 C7 33 0N 120 0 E
Jiangxi □, China 21 D6 27 30N 116 0 E
Jihlava →, Czech Rep. 11 D9 48 55N 16 36 E
Jilin, China 21 B7 43 44N 126 30 E
Jilin □, China 21 B7 44 0N 127 0 E
Jima, Ethiopia 29 G12 7 40N 36 47 E
Jinan, China 21 C6 36 38N 117 1 E
Jinja, Uganda 32 D6 0 25N 33 12 E
Jinzhou, China 21 B7 41 5N 121 3 E
Jixi, China 21 B8 45 20N 130 50 E
João Pessoa, Brazil 46 C6 7 10S 34 52W
Jodhpur, India 23 F4 26 23N 73 8 E
Johannesburg, S. Africa 31 B4 26 10S 28 2 E
Johnson City, U.S.A. 43 D10 42 7N 75 58W
Johnstown, U.S.A. 42 E8 40 20N 78 55W
Johor Baharu, Malaysia 22 C2 1 28N 103 46 E
Joliet, U.S.A. 42 E3 41 32N 88 5W
Joliette, Canada 43 B11 46 3N 73 24W
Jolo, Phil. 22 C4 6 0N 121 0 E
Jönköping, Sweden 6 G10 57 45N 14 10 E
Jonquière, Canada 43 A12 48 27N 71 14W
Jordan ■, Asia 24 B2 31 0N 36 0 E
Jos, Nigeria 30 C3 9 53N 8 51 E
Juan de Fuca Str., Canada 40 A2 48 15N 124 0W
Juiz de Fora, Brazil 46 E5 21 43S 43 19W
Jullundur, India 23 D5 31 20N 75 40 E
Junagadh, India 23 J3 21 30N 70 30 E
Juneau, U.S.A. 38 C6 58 18N 134 25W
Junggar Pendi, China 20 B3 44 30N 86 0 E
Jupiter →, Canada 43 A16 49 29N 63 37W
Jura, Europe 8 C7 46 40N 6 5 E
Jutland, Denmark 6 G9 56 25N 9 30 E
Jyväskylä, Finland 6 F13 62 14N 25 50 E

K

K2, Pakistan 23 B6 35 58N 76 32 E
Kabardino Balkaria □, Russia 15 F7 43 30N 43 30 E
Kābul, Afghan. 23 B2 34 28N 69 11 E
Kabwe, Zambia 33 G5 14 30S 28 29 E
Kachin □, Burma 25 C8 26 0N 97 30 E
Kaduna, Nigeria 30 B3 10 30N 7 21 E
Kaesong, N. Korea 21 C7 37 58N 126 35 E
Kagoshima, Japan 19 D2 31 35N 130 33 E
Kai Is., Indonesia 22 D5 5 55S 132 45 E
Kaifeng, China 21 C6 34 48N 114 21 E
Kaiserslautern, Germany 10 D4 49 26N 7 45 E
Kaitaia, N.Z. 35 H13 35 8S 173 17 E
Kajaani, Finland 6 F13 64 17N 27 46 E
Kakinada, India 25 D7 16 57N 82 11 E
Kalaallit Nunaat = Greenland □, N. Amer. 48 C4 66 0N 45 0W
Kalahari, Africa 31 A3 24 0S 21 30 E
Kalamazoo, U.S.A. 42 D5 42 17N 85 35W
Kalamazoo →, U.S.A. 42 D4 42 40N 86 10W
Kalemie, Congo (Zaïre) 32 F5 5 55S 29 9 E
Kalgoorlie-Boulder, Australia 34 G3 30 40S 121 22 E
Kalimantan, Indonesia 22 D3 0 0 114 0 E
Kaliningrad, Russia 14 D3 54 42N 20 32 E
Kalisz, Poland 11 C10 51 45N 18 8 E
Kalkaska, U.S.A. 42 C5 44 44N 85 11W
Kalmar, Sweden 6 G11 56 40N 16 20 E
Kalmykia □, Russia 15 E8 46 5N 46 1 E
Kaluga, Russia 14 D6 54 35N 36 10 E
Kama →, Russia 14 C9 55 45N 52 0 E
Kamchatka, Russia 18 D18 57 0N 160 0 E
Kamina, Congo (Zaïre) 32 F5 8 45S 25 0 E
Kamloops, Canada 38 C7 50 40N 120 20W
Kampala, Uganda 32 D6 0 20N 32 30 E
Kampuchea = Cambodia ■, Asia 22 B2 12 15N 105 0 E
Kamyanets-Podilskyy, Ukraine 11 D14 48 45N 26 40 E
Kananga, Congo (Zaïre) 32 F4 5 55S 22 18 E
Kanawha →, U.S.A. 42 F6 38 50N 82 9W
Kanazawa, Japan 19 A5 36 30N 136 38 E
Kanchenjunga, Nepal 23 F12 27 50N 88 10 E
Kanchipuram, India 25 D6 12 52N 79 45 E
Kandy, Sri Lanka 25 E7 7 18N 80 43 E
Kane, U.S.A. 42 E8 41 40N 78 49W
Kangean Is., Indonesia 22 D3 6 55S 115 23 E
Kanin Pen., Russia 14 A8 68 0N 45 0 E
Kankakee, U.S.A. 42 E4 41 7N 87 52W
Kankakee →, U.S.A. 42 E3 41 23N 88 15W
Kankan, Guinea 28 F3 10 23N 9 15W
Kano, Nigeria 30 B3 12 2N 8 30 E
Kanpur, India 23 F8 26 28N 80 20 E
Kansas □, U.S.A. 40 C7 38 30N 99 0W
Kansas City, Kans., U.S.A. 41 C8 39 7N 94 38W
Kansas City, Mo., U.S.A. 41 C8 39 6N 94 35W
Kanye, Botswana 31 A4 24 55S 25 28 E
Kaohsiung, Taiwan 21 D7 22 35N 120 16 E
Kaolack, Senegal 28 F1 14 5N 16 8W
Kaposvár, Hungary 11 E9 46 25N 17 47 E
Kapuas →, Indonesia 22 D2 0 25S 109 20 E
Kapuas Hulu Ra., Malaysia 22 C3 1 30N 113 30 E
Kapuskasing, Canada 42 A6 49 25N 82 30W
Kara Bogaz Gol, Turkmenistan 15 F9 41 0N 53 30 E
Kara Kum, Turkmenistan 18 F8 39 30N 60 0 E
Kara Sea, Russia 18 B8 75 0N 70 0 E
Karachi, Pakistan 23 G1 24 53N 67 0 E
Karaganda, Kazakstan 18 E9 49 50N 73 10 E
Karakoram Ra., Pakistan 23 B6 35 30N 77 0 E
Karasburg, Namibia 31 B2 28 0S 18 44 E
Karbala, Iraq 24 B3 32 36N 44 3 E
Karelia □, Russia 14 A5 65 30N 32 30 E
Karimata Is., Indonesia 22 D2 1 25S 109 0 E
Karimunjawa Is., Indonesia 22 D3 5 50S 110 30 E
Karlskrona, Sweden 6 G11 56 10N 15 35 E
Karlsruhe, Germany 10 D5 49 0N 8 23 E
Karlstad, Sweden 6 G10 59 23N 13 30 E
Karnal, India 23 E6 29 42N 77 2 E
Karnataka □, India 25 D6 13 15N 77 0 E
Kärnten □, Austria 10 E8 46 52N 13 30 E
Karsakpay, Kazakstan 18 E8 47 55N 66 40 E
Kasai →, Congo (Zaïre) 32 E3 3 30S 16 10 E
Kashan, Iran 24 B4 34 5N 51 30 E
Kashi, China 20 C2 39 30N 76 2 E
Kassalâ, Sudan 29 E12 15 30N 36 0 E
Kassel, Germany 10 C5 51 18N 9 26 E
Kasur, Pakistan 23 D5 31 5N 74 25 E
Katha, Burma 25 C8 24 10N 96 30 E
Katihar, India 23 G11 25 34N 87 36 E
Katmandu, Nepal 23 F10 27 45N 85 20 E
Katowice, Poland 11 C10 50 17N 19 5 E
Katsina, Nigeria 30 B3 13 0N 7 32 E
Kattegat, Denmark 6 G10 57 0N 11 20 E
Kauai, U.S.A. 40 H15 22 3N 159 30W
Kaukauna, U.S.A. 42 C3 44 17N 88 17W
Kaunas, Lithuania 14 D3 54 54N 23 54 E
Kavála, Greece 13 D11 40 57N 24 28 E
Kawagoe, Japan 19 B6 35 55N 139 29 E
Kawardha, India 23 J8 22 0N 81 17 E
Kawasaki, Japan 19 B6 35 35N 139 42 E
Kayes, Mali 28 F2 14 25N 11 30W
Kayseri, Turkey 15 G6 38 45N 35 30 E
Kazakstan ■, Asia 18 E9 50 0N 70 0 E
Kazan, Russia 14 C8 55 50N 49 10 E
Kazerun, Iran 24 C4 29 38N 51 40 E
Kebnekaise, Sweden 6 E11 67 53N 18 33 E
Kecskemét, Hungary 11 E10 46 57N 19 42 E
Kediri, Indonesia 22 D3 7 51S 112 1 E
Keene, U.S.A. 43 D11 42 56N 72 17W
Keetmanshoop, Namibia 31 B2 26 35S 18 8 E
Kefallinía, Greece 13 E9 38 20N 20 30 E
Keflavík, Iceland 6 B2 64 2N 22 35W
Kelang, Malaysia 22 C2 3 2N 101 26 E
Kelowna, Canada 38 D8 49 50N 119 25W
Kemerovo, Russia 18 D10 55 20N 86 5 E
Kemi, Finland 6 E12 65 44N 24 34 E
Kemi →, Finland 6 E12 65 47N 24 32 E
Kendari, Indonesia 22 D4 3 50S 122 30 E
Kenhardt, S. Africa 31 B3 29 19S 21 12 E
Kenitra, Morocco 28 B3 34 15N 6 40W
Kenosha, U.S.A. 42 D4 42 35N 87 49W
Kent, U.S.A. 42 E7 41 9N 81 22W
Kenton, U.S.A. 42 E6 40 39N 83 37W
Kentucky □, U.S.A. 42 G5 37 0N 84 0W
Kentucky →, U.S.A. 42 F5 38 41N 85 11W
Kentville, Canada 43 C15 45 6N 64 29W
Kenya ■, Africa 32 D7 1 0N 38 0 E
Kenya, Mt., Kenya 32 E7 0 10S 37 18 E
Kerala □, India 25 D6 11 0N 76 15 E
Kerch, Ukraine 15 E6 45 20N 36 20 E
Kerinci, Indonesia 22 D2 1 40S 101 15 E
Kermadec Trench, Pac. Oc. 35 G15 30 30S 176 0W
Kerman, Iran 24 B4 30 15N 57 1 E
Kestell, S. Africa 31 B4 28 17S 28 42 E
Ketchikan, U.S.A. 38 C6 55 21N 131 39W
Kewaunee, U.S.A. 42 C4 44 27N 87 31W
Keweenaw B., U.S.A. 42 B3 47 0N 88 15W
Keweenaw Pen., U.S.A. 42 B3 47 30N 88 0W
Keweenaw Pt., U.S.A. 42 B4 47 25N 87 43W
Key West, U.S.A. 41 F10 24 33N 81 48W
Keyser, U.S.A. 42 F8 39 26N 78 59W
Khabarovsk, Russia 18 E15 48 30N 135 5 E
Khairpur, Pakistan 23 F2 27 32N 68 49 E
Khamas Country, Botswana 31 A4 21 45S 26 30 E
Khandwa, India 23 J6 21 49N 76 22 E
Khanewal, Pakistan 23 D3 30 20N 71 55 E
Khaniá, Greece 13 G11 35 30N 24 4 E
Kharagpur, India 23 H11 22 20N 87 25 E
Khargon, India 23 J5 21 45N 75 40 E
Kharkov, Ukraine 15 E6 49 58N 36 20 E
Khartoum, Sudan 29 E11 15 31N 32 35 E
Khaskovo, Bulgaria 13 D11 41 56N 25 30 E
Khatanga, Russia 18 B12 72 0N 102 20 E
Kherson, Ukraine 15 E5 46 35N 32 35 E
Khmelnitskiy, Ukraine 11 D14 49 23N 27 0 E
Khorixas, Namibia 31 A1 20 16S 14 59 E
Khorramshahr, Iran 24 B3 30 29N 48 15 E
Khouribga, Morocco 28 B3 32 58N 6 57W
Khulna, Bangla. 23 H12 22 45N 89 34 E
Khulna □, Bangla. 23 H12 22 25N 89 35 E
Khumago, Botswana 31 A3 20 26S 24 32 E
Khushab, Pakistan 23 C4 32 20N 72 20 E
Khuzdar, Pakistan 23 F1 27 52N 66 30 E
Kicking Horse Pass, Canada 38 C8 51 28N 116 16W
Kiel, Germany 10 A6 54 19N 10 8 E
Kiel Canal = Nord-Ostsee-Kanal →, Germany 10 A5 54 12N 9 32 E
Kielce, Poland 11 C11 50 52N 20 42 E
Kieler Bucht, Germany 10 A6 54 35N 10 25 E
Kiev, Ukraine 11 C16 50 30N 30 28 E
Kigali, Rwanda 32 E6 1 59S 30 4 E
Kigoma-Ujiji, Tanzania 32 E5 4 55S 29 36 E
Kikwit, Congo (Zaïre) 32 E3 5 0S 18 45 E
Kilimanjaro, Tanzania 32 E7 3 7S 37 20 E
Kimberley, S. Africa 31 B3 28 43S 24 46 E
Kimberley Plateau, Australia 34 D4 16 20S 127 0 E
Kincardine, Canada 42 C7 44 10N 81 40W
Kindu, Congo (Zaïre) 32 E5 2 55S 25 50 E
King William's Town, S. Africa 31 C4 32 51S 27 22 E
Kingston, Canada 42 C9 44 14N 76 30W
Kingston, Jamaica 44 K17 18 0N 76 50W
Kingston, N.Y., U.S.A. 43 E10 41 56N 73 59W
Kingston, Pa., U.S.A. 43 E10 41 16N 75 54W
Kingston upon Hull, U.K. 7 E6 53 45N 0 21W
Kingstown, St. Vincent 44 P20 13 10N 61 10W
Kinshasa, Congo (Zaïre) 32 E3 4 20S 15 15 E
Kirensk, Russia 18 D12 57 50N 107 55 E
Kirgiz Steppe, Eurasia 15 D10 50 0N 55 0 E
Kiribati ■, Pac. Oc. 36 H10 5 0S 180 0 E
Kirkenes, Norway 6 E14 69 40N 30 5 E
Kirkland Lake, Canada 42 A7 48 9N 80 2W
Kirkuk, Iraq 24 B3 35 30N 44 21 E
Kirkwood, S. Africa 31 C4 33 22S 25 15 E
Kirov, Russia 14 C8 58 35N 49 40 E
Kirovograd, Ukraine 15 E5 48 35N 32 20 E
Kirthar Range, Pakistan 23 F1 27 0N 67 0 E
Kiruna, Sweden 6 E12 67 52N 20 15 E
Kisangani, Congo (Zaïre) 32 D5 0 35N 25 15 E
Kishanganj, India 23 F12 26 3N 88 14 E
Kishinev, Moldova 11 E15 47 0N 28 50 E
Kisumu, Kenya 32 E6 0 3S 34 45 E
Kitakyūshū, Japan 19 C2 33 50N 130 50 E
Kitchener, Canada 42 D7 43 27N 80 29W
Kíthira, Greece 13 F10 36 8N 23 0 E
Kitimat, Canada 38 C7 54 3N 128 38W
Kittanning, U.S.A. 42 E8 40 49N 79 31W
Kitwe, Zambia 33 G5 12 54S 28 13 E
Kivu, L., Congo (Zaïre) 32 E5 1 48S 29 0 E
Kladno, Czech Rep. 10 C8 50 10N 14 7 E
Klagenfurt, Austria 10 E8 46 38N 14 20 E
Klar →, Sweden 6 G10 59 23N 13 32 E
Klawer, S. Africa 31 C2 31 44S 18 36 E
Klerksdorp, S. Africa 31 B4 26 53S 26 38 E
Klipplaat, S. Africa 31 C3 33 1S 24 22 E
Klondike, Canada 38 B6 64 0N 139 26W
Klyuchevsk Vol., Russia 18 D18 55 50N 160 30 E
Knossós, Greece 13 G11 35 16N 25 10 E
Knoxville, U.S.A. 41 C10 35 58N 83 55W
Knysna, S. Africa 31 C3 34 2S 23 2 E
Kōbe, Japan 19 B4 34 45N 135 10 E
Koblenz, Germany 10 C4 50 21N 7 36 E
Kobroor, Indonesia 22 D5 6 10S 134 30 E
Koch Bihar, India 23 F12 26 22N 89 29 E
Kodiak I., U.S.A. 38 C4 57 30N 152 45W
Koffiefontein, S. Africa 31 B4 29 30S 25 0 E
Koforidua, Ghana 30 C1 6 3N 0 17W
Koh-i-Bābā, Afghan. 23 B1 34 30N 67 0 E
Kohat, Pakistan 23 C3 33 40N 71 29 E
Kokchetav, Kazakstan 18 D8 53 20N 69 25 E
Kokomo, U.S.A. 42 E4 40 29N 86 8W
Kokstad, S. Africa 31 C4 30 32S 29 29 E
Kola Pen., Russia 14 A6 67 30N 38 0 E
Kolar, India 25 D6 13 12N 78 15 E
Kolguyev I., Russia 14 A8 69 20N 48 30 E
Kolhapur, India 25 D6 16 43N 74 15 E
Kolomna, Russia 14 C6 55 8N 38 45 E
Kolwezi, Congo (Zaïre) 32 G5 10 40S 25 25 E
Kolyma →, Russia 18 C18 69 30N 161 0 E
Kolyma Ra., Russia 18 C17 63 0N 157 0 E
Komandorskiye Is., Russia 18 D18 55 0N 167 0 E
Komatipoort, S. Africa 31 B5 25 25S 31 55 E
Komi □, Russia 14 B10 64 0N 55 0 E
Kompong Cham, Cambodia 22 B2 12 0N 105 30 E
Kompong Chhnang, Cambodia 22 B2 12 20N 104 35 E
Kompong Som, Cambodia 22 B2 10 38N 103 30 E
Komsomolets I., Russia 18 A11 80 30N 95 0 E
Komsomolsk, Russia 18 D15 50 30N 137 0 E
Konin, Poland 11 B10 52 12N 18 15 E
Konya, Turkey 15 G5 37 52N 32 35 E
Korce, Albania 13 D9 40 37N 20 50 E
Korea, North ■, Asia 21 C7 40 0N 127 0 E
Korea, South ■, Asia 21 C7 36 0N 128 0 E
Korea Strait, Asia 21 C7 34 0N 129 30 E
Kōriyama, Japan 19 A7 37 24N 140 23 E
Korla, China 20 B3 41 45N 86 4 E
Körös →, Hungary 11 E11 46 43N 20 12 E
Kortrijk, Belgium 10 C2 50 50N 3 17 E
Kos, Greece 13 F12 36 50N 27 15 E
Košice, Slovak Rep. 11 D11 48 42N 21 15 E
Kosovo □, Serbia, Yug. 13 C9 42 30N 21 0 E
Kosti, Sudan 29 F11 13 8N 32 43 E
Kostroma, Russia 14 C7 57 50N 40 58 E
Koszalin, Poland 10 A9 54 11N 16 8 E
Kota, India 23 G5 25 14N 75 49 E
Kota Baharu, Malaysia 22 C2 6 7N 102 14 E
Kota Kinabalu, Malaysia 22 C3 6 0N 116 4 E
Kotka, Finland 6 F13 60 28N 26 58 E
Kotri, Pakistan 23 G2 25 22N 68 22 E
Kotuy →, Russia 18 B12 71 54N 102 6 E
Kounradskiy, Kazakstan 18 E9 46 59N 75 0 E
Kra, Isthmus of, Thailand 22 B1 10 15N 99 30 E
Kragujevac, Serbia, Yug. 13 B9 44 2N 20 56 E
Krajina, Bos.-H. 12 B7 44 45N 16 35 E
Kraków, Poland 11 C10 50 4N 19 57 E
Krasnodar, Russia 15 E6 45 5N 39 0 E
Krasnoturinsk, Russia 14 C11 59 46N 60 12 E
Krasnovodsk, Turkmenistan 15 F9 40 5N 53 5 E
Krasnoyarsk, Russia 18 D11 56 8N 93 0 E
Kratie, Cambodia 22 B2 12 32N 106 10 E
Krefeld, Germany 10 C4 51 20N 6 33 E
Kremenchug, Ukraine 15 E5 49 5N 33 25 E
Krishna →, India 25 D7 15 57N 80 59 E
Krishnanagar, India 23 H12 23 24N 88 33 E
Kristiansand, Norway 6 G9 58 8N 8 1 E
Kristiansund, Norway 6 F9 63 7N 7 45 E
Krivoy Rog, Ukraine 15 E5 47 51N 33 20 E
Kroonstad, S. Africa 31 B4 27 43S 27 19 E
Krosno, Poland 11 D11 49 42N 21 46 E
Kruger Nat. Park, S. Africa 31 A5 23 30S 31 40 E
Krugersdorp, S. Africa 31 B4 26 5S 27 46 E
Kruisfontein, S. Africa 31 C3 33 59S 24 43 E
Kruševac, Serbia, Yug. 13 C9 43 35N 21 28 E
Kuala Lumpur, Malaysia 22 C2 3 9N 101 41 E
Kuala Terengganu, Malaysia 22 C2 5 20N 103 8 E
Kualakapuas, Indonesia 22 D3 2 55S 114 20 E
Kucing, Malaysia 22 C3 1 33N 110 25 E
Kudat, Malaysia 22 C3 6 55N 116 55 E
Kugluktuk, Canada 38 B8 67 50N 115 5W
Kumanovo, Macedonia 13 C9 42 9N 21 42 E
Kumasi, Ghana 30 C1 6 41N 1 38W
Kumayri = Gyumri, Armenia 15 F7 40 47N 43 50 E
Kumbakonam, India 25 D6 10 58N 79 25 E
Kunlun Shan, Asia 20 C3 36 0N 86 30 E
Kunming, China 20 D5 25 1N 102 41 E
Kuopio, Finland 6 F13 62 53N 27 35 E
Kupang, Indonesia 22 E4 10 19S 123 39 E
Kür →, Azerbaijan 15 G8 39 29N 49 15 E
Kurashiki, Japan 19 B3 34 40N 133 50 E
Kurdistan, Asia 24 B3 37 20N 43 30 E
Kure, Japan 19 B3 34 14N 132 32 E
Kurgan, Russia 18 D8 55 26N 65 18 E
Kuril Is., Russia 18 E17 45 0N 150 0 E
Kurnool, India 25 D6 15 45N 78 0 E
Kursk, Russia 14 D6 51 42N 36 11 E
Kuruman, S. Africa 31 B3 27 28S 23 28 E
Kuruman →, S. Africa 31 B3 26 56S 20 39 E
Kurume, Japan 19 C2 33 15N 130 30 E
Kushiro, Japan 19 F12 43 0N 144 25 E
Kushtia, Bangla. 23 H12 23 55N 89 5 E

Place names on the yellow-coded large scale map section are to be found in the index at the end of that section

INDEX TO WORLD MAPS

113

Kütahya **Mandal**

Kütahya, *Turkey* 15 G5 39 30N 30 2 E
Kutaisi, *Georgia* 15 F7 42 19N 42 40 E
Kutch, Gulf of, *India* 23 H2 22 50N 69 15 E
Kutch, Rann of, *India* 23 G2 24 0N 70 0 E
Kuwait, *Kuwait* 24 C3 29 30N 48 0 E
Kuwait ■, *Asia* 24 C3 29 30N 47 30 E
Kuybyshev = Samara, *Russia* 14 D9 53 8N 50 6 E
KwaMashu, *S. Africa* 31 B5 29 45S 30 58 E
Kwangju, *S. Korea* 21 C7 35 9N 126 54 E
Kyōto, *Japan* 19 B4 35 0N 135 45 E
Kyrgyzstan ■, *Asia* 18 E9 42 0N 75 0 E
Kyūshū, *Japan* 19 C2 33 0N 131 0 E
Kyzyl Kum, *Uzbekistan* 18 E8 42 30N 65 0 E
Kzyl-Orda, *Kazakstan* 18 E8 44 48N 65 28 E

L

La Chorrera, *Panama* 44 H14 8 50N 79 50W
La Coruña, *Spain* 9 A1 43 20N 8 25W
La Mancha, *Spain* 9 C4 39 10N 2 54W
La Paz, *Bolivia* 46 D3 16 20S 68 10W
La Perouse Str., *Asia* 36 C6 45 40N 142 0 E
La Plata, *Argentina* 47 F4 35 0S 57 55W
La Porte, *U.S.A.* 42 E4 41 36N 86 43W
La Rioja □, *Spain* 9 A4 42 20N 2 20W
La Roche-sur-Yon, *France* 8 C3 46 40N 1 25W
La Rochelle, *France* 8 C3 46 10N 1 9W
La Sarre, *Canada* 42 A8 48 45N 79 15W
La Spézia, *Italy* 12 B3 44 7N 9 50 E
La Tuque, *Canada* 43 B11 47 30N 72 50W
Labé, *Guinea* 28 F2 11 24N 12 16W
Labrador □, *Canada* 39 C13 53 20N 61 0W
Labuk B., *Malaysia* 22 C3 6 10N 117 50 E
Lac-Mégantic, *Canada* 43 C12 45 35N 70 53W
Laccadive Is. = Lakshadweep Is., *Ind. Oc.* 25 D6 10 0N 72 30 E
Lachine, *Canada* 43 C11 45 30N 73 40W
Laconia, *U.S.A.* 43 D12 43 32N 71 28W
Ladakh Ra., *India* 23 B6 34 0N 78 0 E
Ladoga, L., *Russia* 14 B5 61 15N 30 30 E
Ladybrand, *S. Africa* 31 B4 29 9S 27 29 E
Ladysmith, *S. Africa* 31 B4 28 32S 29 46 E
Lae, *Papua N. G.* 34 B8 6 40S 147 2 E
Lafayette, *Ind., U.S.A.* 42 E4 40 25N 86 54W
Lafayette, *La., U.S.A.* 41 D8 30 14N 92 1W
Lagos, *Nigeria* 30 C2 6 25N 3 27 E
Lagos, *Portugal* 9 D1 37 5N 8 41W
Lahn →, *Germany* 10 C4 50 19N 7 37 E
Lahore, *Pakistan* 23 D5 31 32N 74 22 E
Lahti, *Finland* 6 F13 60 58N 25 40 E
Laingsburg, *S. Africa* 31 C3 33 9S 20 52 E
Lake Charles, *U.S.A.* 41 D8 30 14N 93 13W
Lakewood, *U.S.A.* 42 E7 41 29N 81 48W
Lakshadweep Is., *Ind. Oc.* 25 D6 10 0N 72 30 E
Lamon Bay, *Phil.* 22 B4 14 30N 122 20 E
Lancaster, *N.H., U.S.A.* 43 C12 44 29N 71 34W
Lancaster, *Pa., U.S.A.* 42 E9 40 2N 76 19W
Lancaster Sd., *Canada* 39 A11 74 13N 84 0W
Landes, *France* 8 D3 44 0N 1 0W
Land's End, *U.K.* 7 F4 50 4N 5 44W
Langres, *France* 8 C6 47 52N 5 20 E
Langres, Plateau de, *France* 8 C6 47 45N 5 3 E
Languedoc, *France* 8 E5 43 58N 3 55 E
Lannion, *France* 8 B2 48 46N 3 29W
L'Annonciation, *Canada* 43 B10 46 25N 74 55W
L'Anse, *U.S.A.* 42 B3 46 45N 88 27W
Lansing, *U.S.A.* 42 D5 42 44N 84 33W
Lanzhou, *China* 20 C5 36 1N 103 52 E
Laoag, *Phil.* 22 B4 18 7N 120 34 E
Laon, *France* 8 B5 49 33N 3 35 E
Laos ■, *Asia* 22 B2 17 45N 105 0 E
Lapeer, *U.S.A.* 42 D6 43 3N 83 19W
Lapland, *Europe* 6 E12 68 7N 24 0 E
Laptev Sea, *Russia* 18 B14 76 0N 125 0 E
Laredo, *U.S.A.* 40 E7 27 30N 99 30W
Lárisa, *Greece* 13 E10 39 36N 22 27 E
Larvik, *Norway* 6 G10 59 4N 10 0 E
Las Palmas, *Canary Is.* 28 C1 28 7N 15 26W
Las Vegas, *U.S.A.* 40 C3 36 10N 115 9W
Lashio, *Burma* 25 C8 22 56N 97 45 E
Latakia, *Syria* 24 B2 35 30N 35 45 E
Latina, *Italy* 12 D5 41 28N 12 52 E
Latvia ■, *Europe* 14 C3 56 50N 24 0 E
Launceston, *Australia* 34 J8 41 24S 147 8 E
Laurentian Plateau, *Canada* 39 C13 52 0N 70 0W
Lausanne, *Switz.* 10 E4 46 32N 6 38 E
Laut, *Indonesia* 22 C2 4 45N 108 0 E
Lauzon, *Canada* 43 B12 46 48N 71 10W
Laval, *France* 8 B3 48 4N 0 48W
Lawrence, *U.S.A.* 43 D12 42 43N 71 10W
Layla, *Si. Arabia* 24 C3 22 10N 46 40 E
Lazio □, *Italy* 12 C5 42 10N 12 30 E
Le Creusot, *France* 8 C6 46 48N 4 24 E
Le Havre, *France* 8 B4 49 30N 0 5 E
Le Mans, *France* 8 C4 48 0N 0 10 E
Le Puy-en-Velay, *France* 8 D5 45 3N 3 52 E
Leamington, *Canada* 42 D6 42 3N 82 36W
Lebanon, *Ind., U.S.A.* 42 E4 40 3N 86 28W
Lebanon, *Ky., U.S.A.* 42 G5 37 34N 85 15W
Lebanon, *Pa., U.S.A.* 42 E9 40 20N 76 26W
Lebanon ■, *Asia* 24 B2 34 0N 36 0 E
Lecce, *Italy* 13 D8 40 23N 18 11 E
Leduc, *Canada* 38 C8 53 15N 113 30W
Leeds, *U.K.* 7 E6 53 48N 1 33W
Leeuwarden, *Neths.* 10 B3 53 15N 5 48 E
Leeuwin, C., *Australia* 34 G2 34 20S 115 9 E
Leeward Is., *Atl. Oc.* 44 L18 16 30N 63 30W
Leganés, *Spain* 9 B4 40 19N 3 45W
Legnica, *Poland* 10 C9 51 12N 16 10 E
Leh, *India* 23 B6 34 9N 77 35 E
Lehututu, *Botswana* 31 A3 23 54S 21 55 E
Leicester, *U.K.* 7 E6 52 38N 1 8W
Leiden, *Neths.* 10 B3 52 9N 4 30 E
Leine →, *Germany* 10 B5 52 43N 9 36 E
Leipzig, *Germany* 10 C7 51 18N 12 22 E
Léman, L., *Europe* 10 E4 46 26N 6 30 E
Lena →, *Russia* 18 B14 72 52N 126 40 E
Leningrad = St. Petersburg, *Russia* 14 C5 59 55N 30 20 E
Leninsk-Kuznetskiy, *Russia* 18 D10 54 44N 86 10 E
Lens, *France* 8 A5 50 26N 2 50 E
Leominster, *U.S.A.* 43 D12 42 32N 71 46W
León, *Mexico* 44 C4 21 7N 101 40W
León, *Spain* 9 A3 42 38N 5 34W
Lérida, *Spain* 9 B6 41 37N 0 39 E
Les Sables-d'Olonne, *France* 8 C3 46 30N 1 45W
Leskovac, *Serbia, Yug.* 13 C9 43 0N 21 58 E
Lesotho ■, *Africa* 31 B4 29 40S 28 0 E
Lésvos, *Greece* 13 E12 39 10N 26 20 E
Leszno, *Poland* 11 C9 51 50N 16 30 E
Lethbridge, *Canada* 38 D8 49 45N 112 45W
Leti Is., *Indonesia* 22 D4 8 10S 128 0 E
Letiahau →, *Botswana* 31 A3 21 16S 24 0 E
Leuven, *Belgium* 10 C3 50 52N 4 42 E
Lévis, *Canada* 43 B12 46 48N 71 9W
Levkás, *Greece* 13 E9 38 40N 20 43 E
Lewiston, *U.S.A.* 43 C12 44 6N 70 13W
Lewistown, *U.S.A.* 42 E9 40 36N 77 34W
Lexington, *U.S.A.* 42 F5 38 3N 84 30W
Lexington Park, *U.S.A.* 42 F9 38 16N 76 27W
Leyte, *Phil.* 22 B4 11 0N 125 0 E
Lhasa, *China* 20 D4 29 25N 90 58 E
Liaoning □, *China* 21 B7 41 40N 122 30 E
Liaoyang, *China* 21 B7 41 15N 122 58 E
Liaoyuan, *China* 21 B7 42 58N 125 2 E
Liberec, *Czech Rep.* 10 C8 50 47N 15 7 E
Liberia ■, *W. Afr.* 28 G3 6 30N 9 30W
Libourne, *France* 8 D3 44 55N 0 14W
Libreville, *Gabon* 32 D1 0 25N 9 26 E
Libya ■, *N. Afr.* 29 C8 27 0N 17 0 E
Libyan Desert, *Africa* 29 C9 25 0N 25 0 E
Lichinga, *Mozam.* 33 G7 13 13S 35 11 E
Lichtenburg, *S. Africa* 31 B4 26 8S 26 8 E
Liechtenstein ■, *Europe* 10 E5 47 8N 9 35 E
Liège, *Belgium* 10 C3 50 38N 5 35 E
Liepāja, *Latvia* 14 C3 56 30N 21 0 E
Liguria □, *Italy* 12 B3 44 30N 8 50 E
Ligurian Sea, *Medit. S.* 12 C3 43 20N 9 0 E
Likasi, *Congo (Zaïre)* 32 G5 10 55S 26 48 E
Lille, *France* 8 A5 50 38N 3 3 E
Lillehammer, *Norway* 6 F10 61 8N 10 30 E
Lilongwe, *Malawi* 33 G6 14 0S 33 48 E
Lim Fjord, *Denmark* 6 G9 56 55N 9 0 E
Lima, *Peru* 46 D2 12 0S 77 0W
Lima, *U.S.A.* 42 E5 40 44N 84 6W
Limerick, *Ireland* 7 E2 52 40N 8 37W
Límnos, *Greece* 13 E11 39 50N 25 5 E
Limoges, *France* 8 D4 45 50N 1 15 E
Limousin, *France* 8 D4 45 30N 1 30 E
Limoux, *France* 8 E5 43 4N 2 12 E
Limpopo →, *Africa* 33 K6 25 5S 33 30 E
Linares, *Spain* 9 C4 38 10N 3 40W
Lincoln, *Maine, U.S.A.* 43 C13 45 22N 68 30W
Lincoln, *Nebr., U.S.A.* 41 B7 40 49N 96 41W
Lincoln Sea, *Arctic* 48 A4 84 0N 55 0W
Lindsay, *Canada* 42 C8 44 22N 78 43W
Lingga Arch., *Indonesia* 22 D2 0 10S 104 30 E
Linhai, *China* 21 D7 28 50N 121 8 E
Linköping, *Sweden* 6 G11 58 28N 15 36 E
Linton, *U.S.A.* 42 F4 39 2N 87 10W
Linxia, *China* 20 C5 35 36N 103 10 E
Linz, *Austria* 10 D8 48 18N 14 18 E
Lion, G. du, *France* 8 E6 43 10N 4 0 E
Lipetsk, *Russia* 14 D6 52 37N 39 35 E
Lippe →, *Germany* 10 C4 51 39N 6 36 E
Lisbon, *Portugal* 9 C1 38 42N 9 10W
Lisieux, *France* 8 B4 49 10N 0 12 E
Lismore, *Australia* 34 F9 28 44S 153 21 E
Listowel, *Canada* 42 D7 43 44N 80 58W
Lithuania ■, *Europe* 14 C3 55 30N 24 0 E
Little Current, *Canada* 42 C7 45 55N 82 0W
Little Karoo, *S. Africa* 31 C3 33 45S 21 0 E
Little Laut Is., *Indonesia* 22 D3 4 45S 115 40 E
Little Rock, *U.S.A.* 41 D8 34 45N 92 17W
Liuzhou, *China* 21 D5 24 22N 109 22 E
Liverpool, *U.K.* 7 E5 53 25N 3 0W
Livingstone, *Zambia* 33 H5 17 46S 25 52 E
Livonia, *U.S.A.* 42 D6 42 23N 83 23W
Livorno, *Italy* 12 C4 43 33N 10 19 E
Ljubljana, *Slovenia* 10 E8 46 4N 14 33 E
Ljusnan →, *Sweden* 6 F11 61 12N 17 8 E
Llanos, *S. Amer.* 46 B2 5 0N 71 35W
Lloret de Mar, *Spain* 9 B7 41 41N 2 53 E
Lobatse, *Botswana* 31 B4 25 12S 25 40 E
Lobito, *Angola* 33 G2 12 18S 13 35 E
Loches, *France* 8 C4 47 7N 1 0 E
Lock Haven, *U.S.A.* 42 E9 41 8N 77 28W
Łódź, *Poland* 11 C10 51 45N 19 27 E
Lofoten, *Norway* 6 E10 68 30N 14 0 E
Logan, *Ohio, U.S.A.* 42 F6 39 32N 82 25W
Logan, *W. Va., U.S.A.* 42 G7 37 51N 81 59W
Logan, Mt., *Canada* 38 B5 60 31N 140 22W
Logansport, *U.S.A.* 42 E4 40 45N 86 22W
Logroño, *Spain* 9 A4 42 28N 2 27W
Lohardaga, *India* 23 H10 23 27N 84 45 E
Loir →, *France* 8 C3 47 33N 0 32W
Loire →, *France* 8 C2 47 16N 2 10W
Lombárdia □, *Italy* 12 B3 45 40N 9 30 E
Lomblen, *Indonesia* 22 D4 8 30S 123 32 E
Lombok, *Indonesia* 22 D3 8 45S 116 30 E
Lomé, *Togo* 30 C2 6 9N 1 20 E
Lomond, L., *U.K.* 7 C4 56 8N 4 38W
Łomza, *Poland* 11 B12 53 10N 22 2 E
London, *Canada* 42 D7 42 59N 81 15W
London, *U.K.* 7 F6 51 30N 0 3W
Londrina, *Brazil* 47 E4 23 18S 51 10W
Long Beach, *U.S.A.* 40 D3 33 47N 118 11W
Long Branch, *U.S.A.* 43 E11 40 18N 74 0W
Long I., *Bahamas* 45 C9 23 20N 75 10W
Long I., *U.S.A.* 43 E11 40 45N 73 30W
Long Xuyen, *Vietnam* 22 B2 10 19N 105 28 E
Longlac, *Canada* 42 A4 49 45N 86 25W
Lons-le-Saunier, *France* 8 C6 46 40N 5 31 E
Lop Nor, *China* 20 B4 40 20N 90 10 E
Lorain, *U.S.A.* 42 E6 41 28N 82 11W
Loralai, *Pakistan* 23 D2 30 20N 68 41 E
Lorca, *Spain* 9 D5 37 41N 1 42W
Lorient, *France* 8 C2 47 45N 3 23W
Lorraine, *France* 8 B7 48 53N 6 0 E
Los Angeles, *Chile* 47 F2 37 28S 72 23W
Los Angeles, *U.S.A.* 40 D3 34 4N 118 15W
Los Mochis, *Mexico* 44 B3 25 45N 108 57W
Lot →, *France* 8 D4 44 18N 0 20 E
Louis Trichardt, *S. Africa* 31 A4 23 1S 29 43 E
Louisa, *U.S.A.* 42 F6 38 7N 82 36W
Louiseville, *Canada* 43 B11 46 20N 72 56W
Louisiana □, *U.S.A.* 41 D8 30 50N 92 0W
Louisville, *U.S.A.* 42 F5 38 15N 85 46W
Lourdes, *France* 8 E3 43 6N 0 3W
Lowell, *U.S.A.* 43 D12 42 38N 71 19W
Lower Tunguska →, *Russia* 18 C10 65 48N 88 4 E
Lowville, *U.S.A.* 43 D10 43 47N 75 29W
Luanda, *Angola* 32 F2 8 50S 13 15 E
Luanshya, *Zambia* 33 G5 13 3S 28 28 E
Lubbock, *U.S.A.* 40 D6 33 35N 101 51W
Lübeck, *Germany* 10 B6 53 52N 10 40 E
Lublin, *Poland* 11 C12 51 12N 22 38 E
Lubumbashi, *Congo (Zaïre)* 33 G5 11 40S 27 28 E
Lucknow, *India* 23 F8 26 50N 81 0 E
Lüda = Dalian, *China* 21 C7 38 50N 121 40 E
Lüderitz, *Namibia* 31 B2 26 41S 15 8 E
Ludhiana, *India* 23 D5 30 57N 75 56 E
Ludington, *U.S.A.* 42 D4 43 57N 86 27W
Ludwigshafen, *Germany* 10 D5 49 29N 8 26 E
Lugano, *Switz.* 10 E5 46 0N 8 57 E
Lugansk, *Ukraine* 15 E6 48 38N 39 15 E
Lugo, *Spain* 9 A2 43 2N 7 35W
Lule →, *Sweden* 6 E12 65 35N 22 10 E
Luleå, *Sweden* 6 E12 65 35N 22 10 E
Lüneburger Heide, *Germany* 10 B6 53 10N 10 12 E
Lunéville, *France* 8 B7 48 36N 6 30 E
Luni →, *India* 23 G3 24 41N 71 14 E
Luoyang, *China* 21 C6 34 40N 112 26 E
Luray, *U.S.A.* 42 F8 38 40N 78 28W
Lusaka, *Zambia* 33 H5 15 28S 28 16 E
Lutsk, *Ukraine* 11 C13 50 50N 25 15 E
Luxembourg, *Lux.* 10 D4 49 37N 6 9 E
Luxembourg ■, *Europe* 10 D4 49 45N 6 0 E
Luzern, *Switz.* 10 E5 47 3N 8 18 E
Luzhou, *China* 20 D5 28 52N 105 20 E
Luzon, *Phil.* 22 B4 16 0N 121 0 E
Lvov, *Ukraine* 11 D13 49 50N 24 0 E
Lyakhov Is., *Russia* 18 B16 73 40N 141 0 E
Lydenburg, *S. Africa* 31 B5 25 10S 30 29 E
Lynchburg, *U.S.A.* 42 G8 37 25N 79 9W
Lynn Lake, *Canada* 38 C9 56 51N 101 3W
Lyonnais, *France* 8 D6 45 45N 4 15 E
Lyons, *France* 8 D6 45 46N 4 50 E

M

Ma'an, *Jordan* 24 B2 30 12N 35 44 E
Maas →, *Neths.* 10 C3 51 45N 4 32 E
Maastricht, *Neths.* 10 C3 50 50N 5 40 E
Macapá, *Brazil* 46 B4 0 5N 51 4W
Macau ■, *China* 21 D6 22 16N 113 35 E
M'Clintock Chan., *Canada* 38 A9 72 0N 102 0W
Macdonnell Ras., *Australia* 34 E5 23 40S 133 0 E
Macedonia □, *Greece* 13 D10 40 39N 22 0 E
Macedonia ■, *Europe* 13 D9 41 53N 21 40 E
Maceió, *Brazil* 46 C6 9 40S 35 41W
Mach, *Pakistan* 23 E1 29 50N 67 20 E
Machakos, *Kenya* 32 E7 1 30S 37 15 E
Machias, *U.S.A.* 43 C14 44 43N 67 28W
Machilipatnam, *India* 25 D7 16 12N 81 8 E
Mackay, *Australia* 34 E8 21 8S 149 11 E
Mackay, L., *Australia* 34 E4 22 30S 129 0 E
McKeesport, *U.S.A.* 42 E8 40 21N 79 52W
Mackenzie →, *Canada* 38 B6 69 10N 134 20W
Mackenzie Mts., *Canada* 38 B6 64 0N 130 0W
Mackinaw City, *U.S.A.* 42 C5 45 47N 84 44W
McKinley, Mt., *U.S.A.* 38 B4 63 4N 151 0W
McKinley Sea, *Arctic* 48 A6 82 0N 0 0 E
Maclear, *S. Africa* 31 C4 31 2S 28 23 E
Mâcon, *France* 8 C6 46 19N 4 50 E
Macon, *U.S.A.* 41 D10 32 51N 83 38W
Macquarie Is., *Pac. Oc.* 36 N7 54 36S 158 55 E
Madadeni, *S. Africa* 31 B5 27 43S 30 3 E
Madagascar ■, *Africa* 33 J9 20 0S 47 0 E
Madaripur, *Bangla.* 23 H13 23 19N 90 15 E
Madeira, *Atl. Oc.* 28 B1 32 50N 17 0W
Madeira →, *Brazil* 46 C4 3 22S 58 45W
Madhya Pradesh □, *India* 23 H7 21 50N 78 0 E
Madison, *Ind., U.S.A.* 42 F5 38 44N 85 23W
Madison, *Wis., U.S.A.* 41 B9 43 4N 89 24W
Madisonville, *U.S.A.* 42 G4 37 20N 87 30W
Madiun, *Indonesia* 22 D3 7 38S 111 32 E
Madras = Chennai, *India* 25 D7 13 8N 80 19 E
Madrid, *Spain* 9 B4 40 25N 3 45W
Madurai, *India* 25 E6 9 55N 78 10 E
Mafeking, *S. Africa* 31 B4 25 50S 25 38 E
Mafeteng, *Lesotho* 31 B4 29 51S 27 15 E
Magadan, *Russia* 18 D17 59 38N 150 50 E
Magdalen Is., *Canada* 43 B17 47 30N 61 40W
Magdalena →, *Colombia* 46 A2 11 6N 74 51W
Magdeburg, *Germany* 10 B6 52 7N 11 38 E
Magelang, *Indonesia* 22 D3 7 29S 110 13 E
Magellan's Str., *Chile* 47 H2 52 30S 75 0W
Maggiore, L., *Italy* 12 B3 45 57N 8 39 E
Magnetic Pole (North), *Canada* 48 B1 77 58N 102 8W
Magnetic Pole (South), *Antarctica* 48 D13 64 8S 138 8 E
Magnitogorsk, *Russia* 14 D10 53 27N 59 4 E
Magog, *Canada* 43 C11 45 18N 72 9W
Mahakam →, *Indonesia* 22 D3 0 35S 117 17 E
Mahalapye, *Botswana* 31 A4 23 1S 26 51 E
Mahanadi →, *India* 23 J11 20 20N 86 25 E
Maharashtra □, *India* 23 J5 20 30N 75 30 E
Mahesana, *India* 23 H4 23 39N 72 26 E
Maiduguri, *Nigeria* 29 F7 12 0N 13 20 E
Maijdi, *Bangla.* 23 H13 22 48N 91 10 E
Maikala Ra., *India* 23 J8 22 0N 81 0 E
Maimana, *Afghan.* 24 B5 35 53N 64 38 E
Main →, *Germany* 10 C5 50 0N 8 18 E
Maine, *France* 8 C3 47 55N 0 25W
Maine □, *U.S.A.* 43 C13 45 20N 69 0W
Mainz, *Germany* 10 C5 50 1N 8 14 E
Majorca = Mallorca, *Spain* 9 C7 39 30N 3 0 E
Makasar, Str. of, *Indonesia* 22 D3 1 0S 118 20 E
Makgadikgadi Salt Pans, *Botswana* 31 A4 20 40S 25 45 E
Makhachkala, *Russia* 15 F8 43 0N 47 30 E
Makiyivka, *Ukraine* 15 E6 48 0N 38 0 E
Makkah, *Si. Arabia* 24 C2 21 30N 39 54 E
Makunda, *Botswana* 31 A3 22 30S 20 7 E
Malabar Coast, *India* 25 D6 11 0N 75 0 E
Malacca, Str. of, *Indonesia* 22 C2 3 0N 101 0 E
Málaga, *Spain* 9 D3 36 43N 4 23W
Malang, *Indonesia* 22 D3 7 59S 112 45 E
Malanje, *Angola* 32 F3 9 36S 16 17 E
Mälaren, *Sweden* 6 G11 59 30N 17 10 E
Malatya, *Turkey* 15 G6 38 25N 38 20 E
Malawi ■, *Africa* 33 G6 11 55S 34 0 E
Malaysia ■, *Asia* 22 C3 5 0N 110 0 E
Maldives ■, *Ind. Oc.* 25 E6 5 0N 73 0 E
Malegaon, *India* 23 J5 20 30N 74 38 E
Mali ■, *Africa* 28 E4 17 0N 3 0W
Mallorca, *Spain* 9 C7 39 30N 3 0 E
Malmö, *Sweden* 6 G10 55 36N 12 59 E
Malone, *U.S.A.* 43 C10 44 51N 74 18W
Malta ■, *Europe* 12 G6 35 50N 14 30 E
Malvinas, Is. = Falkland Is. □, *Atl. Oc.* 47 H4 51 30S 59 0W
Man, I. of, *U.K.* 7 D4 54 15N 4 30W
Manado, *Indonesia* 22 C4 1 29N 124 51 E
Managua, *Nic.* 44 E7 12 6N 86 20W
Manama, *Bahrain* 24 C4 26 10N 50 30 E
Manaus, *Brazil* 46 C4 3 0S 60 0W
Mancelona, *U.S.A.* 42 C5 44 54N 85 4W
Manchester, *U.K.* 7 E5 53 29N 2 12W
Manchester, *U.S.A.* 43 D12 42 59N 71 28W
Manchuria, *China* 21 B7 42 0N 125 0 E
Mandal, *Norway* 6 G9 58 2N 7 25 E

Place names on the yellow-coded large scale map section are to be found in the index at the end of that section

Place names on the yellow-coded large scale map section are to be found in the index at the end of that section

Nagoya
Oskarshamn

Place names on the yellow-coded large scale map section are to be found in the index at the end of that section.

Oslo

Queensland

Place names on the yellow-coded large scale map section are to be found in the index at the end of that section

T

Tabas, *Iran* **24 B4** 33 35N 56 55 E
Tablas, *Phil.* **22 B4** 12 25N 122 2 E
Table Mt., *S. Africa* **31 C2** 34 0S 18 22 E
Tabora, *Tanzania* **32 F6** 5 2S 32 50 E
Tabriz, *Iran* **24 B3** 38 7N 46 20 E
Tacloban, *Phil.* **22 B4** 11 15N 124 58 E
Tacna, *Peru* **46 D2** 18 0S 70 20W
Tacoma, *U.S.A.* **40 A2** 47 14N 122 26W
Tacuarembó, *Uruguay* **47 F4** 31 45S 56 0W
Tadzhikistan = Tajikistan ■, *Asia* **18 F8** 38 30N 70 0 E
Taegu, *S. Korea* **21 C7** 35 50N 128 37 E
Taejon, *S. Korea* **21 C7** 36 20N 127 28 E
Taganrog, *Russia* **15 E6** 47 12N 38 50 E
Tagus ~►, *Europe* **9 C1** 38 40N 9 24W
Tahiti, *Pac. Oc.* **37 J13** 17 37S 149 27W
Taibei, *Taiwan* **21 D7** 25 4N 121 29 E
Taichung, *Taiwan* **21 D7** 24 12N 120 35 E
Taimyr Peninsula, *Russia* **18 B11** 75 0N 100 0 E
Tainan, *Taiwan* **21 D7** 23 17N 120 18 E
Taiping, *Malaysia* **22 C2** 4 51N 100 44 E
Taiwan ■, *Asia* **21 D7** 23 30N 121 0 E
Taiyuan, *China* **21 C6** 37 52N 112 33 E
Ta'izz, *Yemen* **24 D3** 13 35N 44 2 E
Tajikistan ■, *Asia* **18 F8** 38 30N 70 0 E
Tak, *Thailand* **22 B1** 16 52N 99 8 E
Takamatsu, *Japan* **19 B4** 34 20N 134 5 E
Takaoka, *Japan* **19 A5** 36 47N 137 0 E
Takasaki, *Japan* **19 A6** 36 20N 139 0 E
Takla Makan, *China* **20 C3** 38 0N 83 0 E
Talaud Is., *Indonesia* **22 C4** 4 30N 127 10 E
Talca, *Chile* **47 F2** 35 28S 71 40W
Talcahuano, *Chile* **47 F2** 36 40S 73 10W
Tallahassee, *U.S.A.* **41 D10** 30 27N 84 17W
Tallinn, *Estonia* **14 C3** 59 22N 24 48 E
Tamale, *Ghana* **30 C1** 9 22N 0 50W
Tambov, *Russia* **14 D7** 52 45N 41 28 E
Tamil Nadu □, *India* **25 D6** 11 0N 77 0 E
Tamo Abu Ra., *Malaysia* **22 C3** 3 10N 115 5 E
Tampa, *U.S.A.* **41 E10** 27 57N 82 27W
Tampere, *Finland* **6 F12** 61 30N 23 50 E
Tampico, *Mexico* **44 C5** 22 20N 97 50W
Tamworth, *Australia* **34 G9** 31 7S 150 58 E
Tana ~►, *Norway* **6 D13** 70 30N 28 14 E
Tana, L., *Ethiopia* **29 F12** 13 5N 37 30 E
Tanami Desert, *Australia* **34 D5** 18 50S 132 0 E
Tananarive = Antananarivo, *Madag.* **33 H9** 18 55S 47 31 E
Tando Adam, *Pakistan* **23 G2** 25 45N 68 40 E
Tanga, *Tanzania* **32 F7** 5 5S 39 2 E
Tanganyika, L., *Africa* **32 F6** 6 40S 30 0 E
Tangier, *Morocco* **28 A3** 35 50N 5 49W
Tangshan, *China* **21 C6** 39 38N 118 10 E
Tanimbar Is., *Indonesia* **22 D5** 7 30S 131 30 E
Tanjungbalai, *Indonesia* **22 C1** 2 55N 99 44 E
Tanzania ■, *Africa* **32 F6** 6 0S 34 0 E
Tapajós ~►, *Brazil* **46 C4** 2 24S 54 41W
Tapi ~►, *India* **23 J4** 21 8N 72 41 E
Tappahannock, *U.S.A.* **42 G9** 37 56N 76 52W
Tarābulus, *Lebanon* **24 B2** 34 31N 35 50 E
Tarābulus, *Libya* **29 B7** 32 49N 13 7 E
Tarakan, *Indonesia* **22 C3** 3 20N 117 35 E
Táranto, *Italy* **12 D7** 40 28N 17 14 E
Táranto, G. di, *Italy* **12 D7** 40 8N 17 20 E
Tarbagatai Ra., *Kazakstan* **18 E10** 48 0N 83 0 E
Tarbes, *France* **8 E4** 43 15N 0 3 E
Tarim Basin, *China* **20 B3** 40 0N 84 0 E
Tarkastad, *S. Africa* **31 C4** 32 0S 26 16 E
Tarn ~►, *France* **8 E4** 44 5N 1 6 E
Tarnów, *Poland* **11 C11** 50 3N 21 0 E
Tarragona, *Spain* **9 B6** 41 5N 1 17 E
Tarrasa, *Spain* **9 B7** 41 34N 2 1 E
Tashkent, *Uzbekistan* **18 E8** 41 20N 69 10 E
Tasman Sea, *Pac. Oc.* **36 L8** 36 0S 160 0 E
Tasmania □, *Australia* **34 J8** 42 0S 146 30 E
Tatarsk, *Russia* **18 D9** 55 14N 76 0 E
Tatarstan □, *Russia* **14 C9** 55 30N 51 30 E
Tatra, *Slovak Rep.* **11 D11** 49 20N 20 0 E
Tatta, *Pakistan* **23 G1** 24 42N 67 55 E
Tauern, *Austria* **10 E7** 47 15N 12 40 E
Taung, *S. Africa* **31 B3** 27 33S 24 47 E
Taunton, *U.S.A.* **43 E12** 41 54N 71 6W
Taunus, *Germany* **10 C5** 50 13N 8 34 E
Taurus Mts., *Turkey* **15 G5** 37 0N 32 30 E
Tawas City, *U.S.A.* **42 C6** 44 16N 83 31W
Tawau, *Malaysia* **22 C3** 4 20N 117 55 E
Tbilisi, *Georgia* **15 F7** 41 43N 44 50 E
Tchad, L., *Chad* **29 F7** 13 30N 14 30 E
Tebingtinggi, *Indonesia* **22 C1** 3 20N 99 9 E
Tegal, *Indonesia* **22 D2** 6 52S 109 8 E
Tegucigalpa, *Honduras* **44 E7** 14 5N 87 14W
Tehran, *Iran* **24 B4** 35 44N 51 30 E
Tehuantepec, Gulf of, *Mexico* **44 D5** 15 50N 95 12W
Tehuantepec, Isthmus of, *Mexico* **44 D6** 17 0N 94 30W
Tel Aviv-Jaffa, *Israel* **24 B2** 32 4N 34 48 E
Tell City, *U.S.A.* **42 G4** 37 57N 86 46W
Telukbutun, *Indonesia* **22 C2** 4 13N 108 12 E
Tema, *Ghana* **30 C2** 5 41N 0 0 E
Temba, *S. Africa* **31 B4** 25 20S 28 17 E
Témiscaming, *Canada* **42 B8** 46 44N 79 5W
Tenerife, *Canary Is.* **28 C1** 28 15N 16 35W
Tennessee □, *U.S.A.* **41 C9** 36 0N 86 30W
Tennessee ~►, *U.S.A.* **41 C9** 37 4N 88 34W
Tepic, *Mexico* **44 C4** 21 30N 104 54W
Téramo, *Italy* **12 C5** 42 39N 13 42 E
Teresina, *Brazil* **46 C5** 5 9S 42 45W
Ternate, *Indonesia* **22 C4** 0 45N 127 25 E
Terni, *Italy* **12 C5** 42 34N 12 37 E
Ternopol, *Ukraine* **11 D13** 49 30N 25 40 E
Terre Haute, *U.S.A.* **42 F4** 39 28N 87 25W
Teruel, *Spain* **9 B5** 40 22N 1 8W
Tetouan, *Morocco* **28 A3** 35 35N 5 21W
Tetovo, *Macedonia* **13 C9** 42 1N 21 2 E
Teutoburger Wald, *Germany* **10 B5** 52 5N 8 22 E
Texas □, *U.S.A.* **40 D7** 31 40N 98 30W
Texel, *Neths.* **10 B3** 53 5N 4 50 E
Tezpur, *India* **23 F14** 26 40N 92 45 E
Thabana Ntlenyana, *Lesotho* **31 B4** 29 30S 29 16 E
Thabazimbi, *S. Africa* **31 A4** 24 40S 27 21 E
Thailand ■, *Asia* **22 B2** 16 0N 102 0 E
Thailand, G. of, *Asia* **22 B2** 11 30N 101 0 E
Thal, *Pakistan* **23 C3** 33 28N 70 33 E
Thal Desert, *Pakistan* **23 D3** 31 10N 71 30 E
Thames ~►, *Canada* **42 D6** 42 20N 82 25W
Thames ~►, *U.K.* **7 F7** 51 29N 0 34 E
Thane, *India* **23 K4** 19 12N 72 59 E
Thar Desert, *India* **23 E4** 28 0N 72 0 E
The Hague, *Neths.* **10 B3** 52 7N 4 17 E
The Pas, *Canada* **38 C9** 53 45N 101 15W
Thessalon, *Canada* **42 B6** 46 20N 83 30W
Thessaloniki, *Greece* **13 D10** 40 38N 22 58 E
Thessaloniki, Gulf of, *Greece* **13 D10** 40 15N 22 45 E
Thetford Mines, *Canada* **43 B12** 46 8N 71 18W
Thiers, *France* **8 D5** 45 52N 3 33 E
Thiès, *Senegal* **28 F1** 14 50N 16 51W
Thimphu, *Bhutan* **23 F12** 27 31N 89 45 E
Thionville, *France* **8 B7** 49 20N 6 10 E
Thunder B., *U.S.A.* **42 C6** 45 0N 83 20W
Thunder Bay, *Canada* **42 A3** 48 20N 89 15W
Thüringer Wald, *Germany* **10 C6** 50 35N 11 0 E
Tian Shan, *China* **20 B3** 43 0N 84 0 E
Tianjin, *China* **21 C6** 39 8N 117 10 E
Tianshui, *China* **20 C5** 34 32N 105 40 E
Tiber ~►, *Italy* **12 D5** 41 44N 12 14 E
Tibesti, *Chad* **29 D8** 21 0N 17 30 E
Tibet □, *China* **20 C3** 32 0N 88 0 E
Ticino ~►, *Italy* **12 B3** 45 9N 9 14 E
Ticonderoga, *U.S.A.* **43 D11** 43 51N 73 26W
Tierra del Fuego, *Argentina* **47 H3** 54 0S 69 0W
Tiffin, *U.S.A.* **42 E6** 41 7N 83 11W
Tignish, *Canada* **43 B15** 46 58N 64 2W
Tigris ~►, *Asia* **24 B3** 31 0N 47 25 E
Tijuana, *Mexico* **44 A1** 32 30N 117 10W
Tiksi, *Russia* **18 B14** 71 40N 128 45 E
Tilburg, *Neths.* **10 C3** 51 31N 5 6 E
Timaru, *N.Z.* **35 J13** 44 23S 171 14 E
Timişoara, *Romania* **11 F11** 45 43N 21 15 E
Timmins, *Canada* **42 A7** 48 28N 81 25W
Timor, *Indonesia* **22 D4** 9 0S 125 0 E
Tinaca Pt., *Phil.* **22 C4** 5 30N 125 25 E
Tirana, *Albania* **13 D8** 41 18N 19 49 E
Tiraspol, *Moldova* **11 E15** 46 55N 29 35 E
Tîrgovişte, *Romania* **11 F13** 44 55N 25 27 E
Tîrgu-Jiu, *Romania* **11 F12** 45 5N 23 19 E
Tîrgu Mureş, *Romania* **11 E13** 46 31N 24 38 E
Tirich Mir, *Pakistan* **23 A3** 36 15N 71 55 E
Tirol □, *Austria* **10 E6** 47 3N 10 43 E
Tiruchchirappalli, *India* **25 D6** 10 45N 78 45 E
Tirunelveli, *India* **25 E6** 8 45N 77 45 E
Tisa ~►, *Serbia, Yug.* **13 B9** 45 15N 20 17 E
Titicaca, L., *S. Amer.* **46 D3** 15 30S 69 30W
Titusville, *U.S.A.* **42 E8** 41 38N 79 41W
Tizi-Ouzou, *Algeria* **28 A5** 36 42N 4 3 E
Toamasina, *Madag.* **33 H9** 18 10S 49 25 E
Toba Kakar, *Pakistan* **23 D2** 31 30N 69 0 E
Tobago, *W. Indies* **44 R21** 11 10N 60 30W
Tobermory, *Canada* **42 C7** 45 12N 81 40W
Tocantins ~►, *Brazil* **46 C5** 1 45S 49 10W
Togliatti, *Russia* **14 D8** 53 32N 49 24 E
Togo ■, *W. Afr.* **30 C2** 8 30N 1 35 E
Tokelau Is., *Pac. Oc.* **35 B16** 9 0S 171 45W
Tōkyō, *Japan* **19 B6** 35 45N 139 45 E
Toledo, *Spain* **9 C3** 39 50N 4 2W
Toledo, *U.S.A.* **42 E6** 41 39N 83 33W
Toliara, *Madag.* **33 J8** 23 21S 43 40 E
Toluca, *Mexico* **44 D5** 19 20N 99 40W
Tomaszów Mazowiecki, *Poland* **11 C10** 51 30N 19 57 E
Tombouctou, *Mali* **30 A1** 16 50N 3 0W
Tomini, G. of, *Indonesia* **22 D4** 0 10S 122 0 E
Tomsk, *Russia* **18 D10** 56 30N 85 5 E
Tonga ■, *Pac. Oc.* **35 D16** 19 50S 174 30W
Tonga Trench, *Pac. Oc.* **35 E16** 18 0S 173 0W
Tongaat, *S. Africa* **31 B5** 29 33S 31 9 E
Tongking, G. of, *Asia* **20 E5** 20 0N 108 0 E
Tonk, *India* **23 F5** 26 6N 75 54 E
Tonlé Sap, *Cambodia* **22 B2** 13 0N 104 0 E
Toowoomba, *Australia* **34 F9** 27 32S 151 56 E
Topeka, *U.S.A.* **41 C7** 39 3N 95 40W
Torne ~►, *Sweden* **6 E12** 65 50N 24 12 E
Torne, L., *Sweden* **6 E11** 68 24N 19 15 E
Tornio, *Finland* **6 E12** 65 50N 24 12 E
Toronto, *Canada* **42 D8** 43 39N 79 20W
Torre del Greco, *Italy* **12 D6** 40 47N 14 22 E
Torreón, *Mexico* **44 B4** 25 33N 103 26W
Tortosa, *Spain* **9 B6** 40 49N 0 31 E
Toruń, *Poland* **11 B10** 53 2N 18 39 E
Toscana □, *Italy* **12 C4** 43 25N 11 0 E
Toteng, *Botswana* **31 A3** 20 22S 22 58 E
Toul, *France* **8 B6** 48 40N 5 53 E
Toulon, *France* **8 E6** 43 10N 5 55 E
Toulouse, *France* **8 E4** 43 37N 1 27 E
Touraine, *France* **8 C4** 47 20N 0 30 E
Tournai, *Belgium* **10 C2** 50 35N 3 25 E
Tournon, *France* **8 D6** 45 4N 4 50 E
Tours, *France* **8 C4** 47 22N 0 40 E
Touwsrivier, *S. Africa* **31 C3** 33 20S 20 2 E
Towanda, *U.S.A.* **42 E9** 41 46N 76 27W
Townsville, *Australia* **34 D8** 19 15S 146 45 E
Towson, *U.S.A.* **42 F9** 39 24N 76 36W
Toyama, *Japan* **19 A5** 36 40N 137 15 E
Toyohashi, *Japan* **19 B5** 34 45N 137 25 E
Trabzon, *Turkey* **15 F6** 41 0N 39 45 E
Trafalgar, C., *Spain* **9 D2** 36 10N 6 2W
Trail, *Canada* **38 D8** 49 5N 117 40W
Trang, *Thailand* **22 C1** 7 33N 99 38 E
Trangan, *Indonesia* **22 D5** 6 40S 134 20 E
Transantarctic Mts., *Antarctica* **48 F16** 85 0S 170 0W
Transylvania, *Romania* **11 E12** 45 19N 25 0 E
Transylvanian Alps, *Romania* **11 F13** 45 30N 25 0 E
Trápani, *Italy* **12 E5** 38 1N 12 29 E
Traverse City, *U.S.A.* **42 C5** 44 46N 85 38W
Trento, *Italy* **12 A4** 46 4N 11 8 E
Trenton, *Canada* **42 C9** 44 10N 77 34W
Trenton, *U.S.A.* **43 E10** 40 14N 74 46W
Trier, *Germany* **10 D4** 49 45N 6 38 E
Trieste, *Italy* **12 B5** 45 40N 13 46 E
Trincomalee, *Sri Lanka* **25 E7** 8 38N 81 15 E
Trinidad & Tobago ■, *W. Indies* **44 S20** 10 30N 61 20W
Tripura □, *India* **23 H13** 24 0N 92 0 E
Trivandrum, *India* **25 E6** 8 41N 77 0 E
Trnava, *Slovak Rep.* **11 D9** 48 23N 17 35 E
Trois-Rivières, *Canada* **43 B11** 46 25N 72 34W
Trollhättan, *Sweden* **6 G10** 58 17N 12 20 E
Trondheim, *Norway* **6 F10** 63 36N 10 25 E
Trondheim Fjord, *Norway* **6 F10** 63 35N 10 30 E
Troy, *N.Y., U.S.A.* **43 D11** 42 44N 73 41W
Troy, *Ohio, U.S.A.* **42 E5** 40 2N 84 12W
Troyes, *France* **8 B6** 48 19N 4 3 E
Trujillo, *Peru* **46 C2** 8 6S 79 0W
Truk, *Pac. Oc.* **36 G7** 7 25N 151 46 E
Truro, *Canada* **43 C16** 45 21N 63 14W
Tsau, *Botswana* **31 A3** 20 8S 22 22 E
Tshabong, *Botswana* **31 B3** 26 2S 22 29 E
Tshane, *Botswana* **31 A3** 24 5S 21 54 E
Tshwane, *Botswana* **31 A3** 22 24S 22 1 E
Tsimlyansk Res., *Russia* **15 E7** 48 0N 43 0 E
Tsu, *Japan* **19 B5** 34 45N 136 25 E
Tsumis, *Namibia* **31 A2** 23 39S 17 29 E
Tuamotu Arch., *Pac. Oc.* **37 J13** 17 0S 144 0W
Tubuai Is., *Pac. Oc.* **37 K12** 25 0S 150 0W
Tucson, *U.S.A.* **40 D4** 32 13N 110 58W
Tugela ~►, *S. Africa* **31 B5** 29 14S 31 30 E
Tula, *Russia* **14 D6** 54 13N 37 38 E
Tulcea, *Romania* **11 F15** 45 13N 28 46 E
Tulle, *France* **8 D4** 45 16N 1 46 E
Tulsa, *U.S.A.* **41 C7** 36 10N 95 55W
Tunis, *Tunisia* **28 A7** 36 50N 10 11 E
Tunisia ■, *Africa* **28 B6** 33 30N 9 10 E
Tunja, *Colombia* **46 B2** 5 33N 73 25W
Tura, *India* **23 G13** 25 30N 90 16 E
Turabah, *Si. Arabia* **24 C3** 28 20N 43 15 E
Turin, *Italy* **12 B2** 45 3N 7 40 E
Turkana, L., *Africa* **32 D7** 3 30N 36 5 E
Turkey ■, *Eurasia* **15 G6** 39 0N 36 0 E
Turkmenistan ■, *Asia* **18 F7** 39 0N 59 0 E
Turks & Caicos Is. □, *W. Indies* **45 C10** 21 20N 71 20W
Turku, *Finland* **6 F12** 60 30N 22 19 E
Tuscany = Toscana □, *Italy* **12 C4** 43 25N 11 0 E
Tuticorin, *India* **25 E6** 8 50N 78 12 E
Tuvalu ■, *Pac. Oc.* **35 B14** 8 0S 178 0 E
Tuxtla Gutiérrez, *Mexico* **44 D6** 16 50N 93 10W
Tuz Gölü, *Turkey* **15 G5** 38 42N 33 18 E
Tuzla, *Bos.-H.* **13 B8** 44 34N 18 41 E
Tver, *Russia* **14 C6** 56 55N 35 55 E
Two Rivers, *U.S.A.* **42 C4** 44 9N 87 34W
Tychy, *Poland* **11 C10** 50 9N 18 59 E
Tyrol = Tirol □, *Austria* **10 E6** 47 3N 10 43 E
Tyrrhenian Sea, *Medit. S.* **12 E5** 40 0N 12 30 E
Tyumen, *Russia* **18 D8** 57 11N 65 29 E
Tzaneen, *S. Africa* **31 A5** 23 47S 30 9 E

U

U.S.A. = United States of America ■, *N. Amer.* **40 C7** 37 0N 96 0W
Ubangi = Oubangi ~►, *Congo (Zaïre)* **32 E3** 0 30S 17 50 E
Ube, *Japan* **19 C2** 33 56N 131 15 E
Uberaba, *Brazil* **46 D5** 19 50S 47 55W
Uberlândia, *Brazil* **46 D5** 19 0S 48 20W
Ucayali ~►, *Peru* **46 C2** 4 30S 73 30W
Udaipur, *India* **23 G4** 24 36N 73 44 E
Udaipur Garhi, *Nepal* **23 F11** 27 0N 86 35 E
Údine, *Italy* **12 A5** 46 3N 13 14 E
Udmurtia □, *Russia* **14 C9** 57 30N 52 30 E
Udon Thani, *Thailand* **22 B2** 17 29N 102 46 E
Ufa, *Russia* **14 D10** 54 45N 55 55 E
Uganda ■, *Africa* **32 D6** 2 0N 32 0 E
Uitenhage, *S. Africa* **31 C4** 33 40S 25 28 E
Ujjain, *India* **23 H5** 23 9N 75 43 E
Ujung Pandang, *Indonesia* **22 D3** 5 10S 119 20 E
Ukraine ■, *Europe* **15 E5** 49 0N 32 0 E
Ulan Bator, *Mongolia* **20 B5** 47 55N 106 53 E
Ulan Ude, *Russia* **18 D12** 51 45N 107 40 E
Ulhasnagar, *India* **23 K4** 19 15N 73 10 E
Ulm, *Germany* **10 D5** 48 23N 9 58 E
Ulyasutay, *Mongolia* **20 B4** 47 56N 97 28 E
Ume ~►, *Sweden* **6 F12** 63 45N 20 20 E
Umeå, *Sweden* **6 F12** 63 45N 20 20 E
Umtata, *S. Africa* **31 C4** 31 36S 28 49 E
Umzimvubu = Port St. Johns, *S. Africa* **31 C4** 31 38S 29 33 E
Umzinto, *S. Africa* **31 C5** 30 15S 30 45 E
Ungava B., *Canada* **39 C13** 59 30N 67 30W
Ungava Pen., *Canada* **39 C12** 60 0N 74 0W
Uniontown, *U.S.A.* **42 F8** 39 54N 79 44W
United Arab Emirates ■, *Asia* **24 C4** 23 50N 54 0 E
United Kingdom ■, *Europe* **7 E6** 53 0N 2 0W
United States of America ■, *N. Amer.* **40 C7** 37 0N 96 0W
Upington, *S. Africa* **31 B3** 28 25S 21 15 E
Uppsala, *Sweden* **6 G11** 59 53N 17 38 E
Ural ~►, *Kazakstan* **15 E9** 47 0N 51 48 E
Ural Mts., *Eurasia* **14 C10** 60 0N 59 0 E
Uralsk, *Kazakstan* **14 D9** 51 20N 51 20 E
Uranium City, *Canada* **38 C9** 59 34N 108 37W
Urbana, *Ill., U.S.A.* **42 E3** 40 7N 88 12W
Urbana, *Ohio, U.S.A.* **42 E6** 40 7N 83 45W
Urmia, L., *Iran* **24 B3** 37 50N 45 30 E
Uruguay ■, *S. Amer.* **47 F4** 32 30S 56 30W
Uruguay ~►, *S. Amer.* **47 F4** 34 12S 58 18W
Ürümqi, *China* **20 B3** 43 45N 87 45 E
Usakos, *Namibia* **31 A2** 21 54S 15 31 E
Ushant, *France* **8 B1** 48 28N 5 6W
Ust Urt Plateau, *Asia* **18 E7** 44 0N 55 0 E
Ústí nad Labem, *Czech Rep.* **10 C8** 50 41N 14 3 E
Utah □, *U.S.A.* **40 C4** 39 20N 111 30W
Utica, *U.S.A.* **43 D10** 43 6N 75 14W
Utrecht, *Neths.* **10 B3** 52 5N 5 8 E
Utsunomiya, *Japan* **19 A6** 36 30N 139 50 E
Uttar Pradesh □, *India* **23 F8** 27 0N 80 0 E
Uttaradit, *Thailand* **22 B2** 17 36N 100 5 E
Uusikaupunki, *Finland* **6 F12** 60 47N 21 25 E
Uzbekistan ■, *Asia* **18 E8** 41 30N 65 0 E
Uzhhorod, *Ukraine* **11 D12** 48 36N 22 18 E

V

Vaal ~►, *S. Africa* **31 B3** 29 4S 23 38 E
Vaal Dam, *S. Africa* **31 B4** 27 0S 28 14 E
Vaasa, *Finland* **6 F12** 63 6N 21 38 E
Vadodara, *India* **23 H4** 22 20N 73 10 E
Vadsø, *Norway* **6 D13** 70 3N 29 50 E
Vaduz, *Liech.* **10 E5** 47 8N 9 31 E
Váh ~►, *Slovak Rep.* **11 D9** 47 43N 18 7 E
Val d'Or, *Canada* **42 A9** 48 7N 77 47W
Valahia, *Romania* **11 F13** 44 35N 25 0 E
Valdés, Pen., *Argentina* **47 E3** 42 30S 63 45W
Valdez, *U.S.A.* **38 B5** 61 7N 146 16W
Valdivia, *Chile* **47 F2** 39 50S 73 14W
Valence, *France* **8 D6** 44 57N 4 54 E
Valencia, *Spain* **9 C5** 39 27N 0 23W
Valencia, *Venezuela* **46 A3** 10 11N 68 0W
Valenciennes, *France* **8 A5** 50 20N 3 34 E
Valladolid, *Spain* **9 B3** 41 38N 4 43W
Valletta, *Malta* **12 G6** 35 54N 14 31 E
Valparaíso, *Chile* **47 F2** 33 2S 71 40W
Van, L., *Turkey* **15 G7** 38 30N 43 0 E
Van Buren, *U.S.A.* **43 B13** 47 10N 67 58W
Van Wert, *U.S.A.* **42 E5** 40 52N 84 35W
Vancouver, *Canada* **38 D7** 49 15N 123 10W
Vancouver I., *Canada* **38 D7** 49 50N 126 0W
Vanderbijlpark, *S. Africa* **31 B4** 26 42S 27 54 E
Vanderkloof Dam, *S. Africa* **31 C3** 30 4S 24 40 E
Vänern, *Sweden* **6 G10** 58 47N 13 30 E

Place names on the yellow-coded large scale map section are to be found in the index at the end of that section

Vanino   **Zwolle**

Place names on the yellow-coded large scale map section are to be found in the index at the end of that section